Ancient Complexities

ANCIENT COMPLEXITIES

NEW PERSPECTIVES
IN PRECOLUMBIAN
NORTH AMERICA

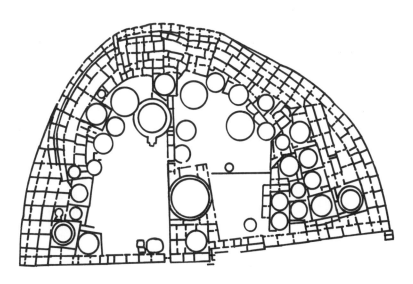

Edited by
Susan M. Alt

THE UNIVERSITY OF UTAH PRESS
Salt Lake City

Foundations of Archaeological Inquiry
James M. Skibo, series editor

 The Defiance House Man colophon is a registered trademark
of the University of Utah Press. It is based upon a four-foot-tall,
Ancient Puebloan pictograph (late PIII) near Glen Canyon, Utah.

14 13 12 11 10   1 2 3 4 5

Library of Congress Cataloging-in-Publication Data

Ancient complexities : new perspectives in Precolumbian North America /
edited by Susan M. Alt.
    p. cm. — (Foundations of archaeological inquiry)
  Includes bibliographical references and index.
  ISBN 978-1-60781-026-1 (cloth : alk. paper) 1. Social archaeology—
North America. 2. Indians of North America—Antiquities. 3. Indians
of North America—Social life and customs. 4. North America—
Antiquities. I. Alt, Susan M., 1959–
  E77.9.A49 2010
  970.01'1—dc22   2010023989

Cover drawing of Pueblo Bonito from *The Chaco Handbook: An Encyclopedic Guide*
(Vivian and Hilpert 2002, Figure 73). Courtesy of R. Gwinn Vivian.

Printed and bound by Sheridan Books, Inc., Ann Arbor, Michigan.

Contents

Contents

Figures

Tables

Considering Complexity

Confounding Categories with Practices

Susan M. Alt

Simplifications that reduce a complex reality to whatever it is that fits into a simple scheme tend to "forget" about the complex, which may mean that the latter is surprising and disturbing when it reappears later.
(LAW AND MOL 2002:3)

The intent of this book is to reconsider the ways that we, as archaeologists, evaluate complexity in some North American precolumbian societies. We are concerned with how past people in North America organized their societies, interacted with one another, and expressed their understandings of the world and the cosmos in ways that were multifaceted and, yes, complex. We begin with an underlying concern that the methods and theories that once served archaeologists so well are no longer facilitating our attempts to understand the past but are, in fact, hindering those efforts. Of particular concern is how we understand complexity, or how we fail to understand complexity, especially within a paradigm that labels all North American precolumbian people not complex at the outset. To sidestep these issues we try a different tactic in this book: we ask not "How complex were people?" (a categorical question), but follow a suggestion made by Nelson (1995) and instead ask "How were people complex?" Our answers to this question are interrogations of what complexity means in multiple dimensions.

I want to emphasize that the purpose of this book is not simply to criticize categories and categorical terminology. Rather, we wish to demonstrate different ways of viewing complexity by presenting case studies and approaches to un-

derstanding complexities in the past that will of themselves point to the problems inherent in categorical studies at the same time as they suggest new solutions.

What Is Complexity?

Complexity has been a matter of increasing concern as the modern world is perceived as ever more complex and chaotic. Numerous institutes and organizations dedicate themselves to understanding complex systems, or complex adaptive systems (for example, the Santa Fe Institute, the New England Complex Systems Institute, University of Michigan Center for the Study of Complex Systems, and the Institute for Complexity Sciences).

But what exactly is complexity? Fine wines are called complex, but so too are biological systems, physics, and economics. *Complex*, in these different realms, has shades of variable meanings (Finkenthal 2008). What the definitions share is ambiguity (Cilliers 1998), and thus the definitions of complexity offered by physicists, mathematicians, economists, and even complexity theorists seem just as subjective as those used by archaeologists.

Complex is used as a description, but one without absolute boundaries or clearly defined characteristics (Gell-Mann 1995; Helbing 2008). However, Gell-Mann (1995) writes that measures of complexity are varied, context dependent, and subjective. Bonner, a biologist, defines complexity as the number of types of cells in an organism (Bonner 1988). Taylor, an environmental scientist, defines complexity as a composite of the number of interconnections as well as the heterogeneity and variability influencing the situation (Taylor 2005:224). As expressed by Kauffman (1993), "complex phenomena are those that reside between simplicity and randomness, and the edge of chaos" (in Sawyer 2005:3). For many theorists, complexity describes a dynamic system that is more than the sum of its parts (Gell-Mann 1995; Helbing 2008; Kwa 2002; Sawyer 2005; Taylor 2005; Urry 2003).

Complexity theorists see the world as made up of systems, and systems that are complex have such characteristics as being open, dynamic, self-organizing, and importantly, nonlinear. A key concern in complex adaptive systems approaches is "emergence," which refers to the collective properties of phenomena that somehow transcend the properties of their particular parts. Complexity theory (related to and at times equated with chaos theory) seeks to combine the physical and social, to blur the lines of social science and physics, history and mathematics, order and disorder (Lansing 2003; Sawyer 2005; Urry 2003).

Complexity theory has been utilized in anthropology and archaeology (for example, Bentley and Maschner 2000; Gumerman and Gell-Mann 1994; Kohler and Gumerman 2000; Lansing 2003) but has not made much of an impact on the greater discipline (Lansing 2003). In part this is likely related to an earlier rejection of overtly systemic approaches in anthropology (Ingold 2000; Miller 2005; Pauketat 2001). But although complex systems approaches may offer advantages in certain kinds of macroscale analyses (Urry 2003) and can provide thought-provoking concepts such as that of "emergence," they suffer from the deficits of other kinds of systems studies and an overreliance on modeling (for specific critiques, see Horgan 1995 or Helmreich 1998, 1999). Complex systems approaches do not in fact help us evaluate the microscale day-to-day workings of particular societies (where complexity of the sort we are interested in is engendered).

Utilizing complexity theory is a different project and on a very different scale than that of understanding the historical particulars of a given society and the generation of complex interactions on the microscale. It is a project that to see the whole ignores the particular idiosyncratic capabilities of people to the detriment of creating a more comprehensive and detailed portrait of that society. In complex systems theories, as with the categorical, we risk losing the historical particulars of individual societies in generalizations. While complexity theorists acknowledge the effects of individual agents on the whole, their focus is on the emergent properties that arise from combinations of particular actions, on a systemic level. If, as complex adaptive systems theorists state, any number of variables can affect the whole and create unexpected results, it still seems we must examine the particular details of any society to truly understand it.

Ancient Complexity

As archaeologists, when we talk about the complexity of human societies, we more commonly mean that we wish to understand how societies came to be differentiated, stratified, institutionalized, and multilayered. We begin with an idea that some societies are complex and others are not. The search for complexity originated in early evolutionary musings and was in fact modeled after biological evolution (see, for example, Flannery 1972; Service 1962). Just as living single cells became more complex life-forms through a process whereby ever more cells joined together to become a single unit but with differentiated and specialized parts, so too did human social and political life become more complex as people joined together in more layered and differentiated societies.

It is important to keep in mind that as a discipline we began explorations of complexity with the assumption that modern Western society was the top of an evolutionary ladder and that other societies had failed to quite achieve the same level of accomplishment. Therefore, other types of political and social organization were not just different but were not as complex. Early evolutionary theorists supposed that these societies were living examples of the steps on the way to becoming more like us, thus more complex (Morgan 1877;

for example, Service 1962; Tylor 1871). Although evolutionary determinism has been discarded, the underpinnings of modern paradigms follow from this history (Spencer 1990). In fact, the way we operationalize definitions of complexity still reference this early thinking (Chapman 2003; Lekson 2007; Pauketat 2007).

Few have gone back and asked whether other societies were in fact complex but in alternative ways (not like us). The assumption has remained ideologically and terminologically that Western society is complex, thus setting the standard for what is complex elsewhere. While the door has been opened in a few cases to allow that other civilizations may have been complex (see discussions on orientalism; for example, Said 1978), the unspoken, or perhaps unevaluated, ideal remains that complex tends to mean complex like us, not complex in realms such as ritual, religion, or kinship relationships.

What we intend in this book is to disentangle complexities in ancient North America, particularly by focusing on the ways in which complexities are not always what we have been led to believe. The chapters in this volume illustrate the substantially increased knowledge of precolumbian North America gained in recent years, as well as the difficulties researchers have had in working with their data given current categorical limitations. We open this discussion because we are all, in some way, frustrated with traditional, reductionist representations of complexity. We present chapters that we hope offer insights and approaches that move toward improving our understanding of North American societies by embracing complexity in its many forms and dimensions. We do not all agree in the particulars or find the same solutions concerning how best to define and understand complexity. But then our purpose is to compare approaches, share our knowledge, and encourage better ways of communicating and understanding: to open a dialogue that is not just a critique of prior approaches, and to offer examples of how complexity might otherwise be considered. And interestingly enough, by being open to different kinds of complexities, the authors of this book begin to redefine the dimensionality of complexity, even where conventional wisdom says there should be simplicity.

We need to think about how we evaluate complexity because we know more about North American prehistory than we ever have. A growing database is creating a widening chasm between our evidence and the tools we use to organize, compare, and understand archaeological information. Because these tools are failing us, it has become ever more difficult to talk to each other about complexity and the societies we study. In North America I believe we have hit a wall. There are times an entire discipline hits a wall, and paradigmatic changes are necessary for progress (Kuhn 1962). Archaeology has had those moments before, and I think we are at a turning point again. Only this time we have outgrown our need to rely on categorical statements. I will explain.

There seem to be never-ending disagreements over complexity in places like Chaco Canyon and Cahokia, and these same kinds of disagreements are now becoming more common for earlier time periods as well (see, for example, Anderson 1997; Cobb 2003; Lekson 2005; Neitzel 1999; Pauketat 2007; Sassaman 2004). Investigations at places such as Archaic shell mounds in the Deep South or Far West are demonstrating ways people were complex in societies that have previously been defined, paradoxically, as lacking complexity (Sassaman 2004, 2005). We cannot agree on what should be labeled a state, chiefdom, or tribe because the categories just do not accommodate the data we have so carefully accumulated. The inability of categorical models to help explain all our data is only going to be exacerbated as we continue to accumulate more information. We already know the societies we study are more diverse and complex in ways not accounted for by such models. I therefore suggest that the traditional models for complexity are not only inappropriate; they are causing us to waste time in categorical arguments rather than helping us craft better histories.

Categorical models bind us with words like tribe, chiefdom, and state. These words come with very particular associations, possibilities, and constraints such that if we believe we are investigating one sort of society, we will not look for the attributes of another. Complexity is too often reduced to a trait list even in the most recent statements on the subject, where they stand for social and political organizations (for example, Christie and Sarro 2006; Flannery 1998). For instance, palaces, royal burials, and four-tiered settlement hierarchies are still considered necessary and sufficient indicators of states, and big mounds are still equated with great power (Christie and Sarro 2006; Flannery 1998; Gibson and Carr 2004). The studies presented in this book transcend this kind of thinking.

What archaeologists mean to measure by looking for things like palaces, royal burials, or settlement hierarchies are a limited range of organizational factors and ideologies that a priori we label complex. But there are multiple ways to be complex, and we know that archaeology can do much better than look for simple markers thought to stand for larger processes. Recently, Sassaman (2004) defined complexity as the interconnectedness of multiple parts of society and made a case for considering complexity as relational rather than in typological terms. Likewise, Chapman (2003) has suggested that too often complexity means "like us." As he reminds us, the concept of complexity has been tied to evolution and directionality, as well as technology and progress. Those qualities are still evoked when we say "complex." Thus we say "complex," but we really mean state-like, and by that, a state "like us." However, complexity can occur in many dimensions and in many different ways. People can be complex, and not be state-like, or "like us." As Crumley (1995), Yoffee (2005), and others have suggested, heterarchies can be more complex than hierarchies, rituals can be expressions of complex ruling ideologies, and monumentality can be the materialization of complex social relationships. The state, Yoffee (2005) has pointed out, can be a simplification, a reduction of parts and interconnections. And if Yoffee is correct, the term "complex society" is not just a categorical designation but also a contradiction.

Thus, I suggest that in reconsidering complexity, we cease identifying complex societies. Instead, we should seek the particular histories and details of a society in a way that adheres more closely to Nelson's (1995) proposal that we ask "How were people complex?" rather than "How complex were they?" I think this was good advice in 1995 and an actionable plan today. I advocate measuring complexity historically through a mul-

tiscalar analysis of fine-grained sequences, object biographies, and genealogies of practices arrayed in enmeshed relational webs (Dobres and Robb 2005; Ingold 2007; Johnson 2006; Meskell 2004). What should take precedence are the real histories, the complexities of enactment and social experience. Complexity should not be negated or assumed based on constructed categories.

What is it that people actually did through discrete actions, during particular events, and within variously scaled spaces, and how were these actions, events, or spaces contingent on persons, practices, or landscapes? Complexity is not a series of traits, nor is it simply a set of relationships at a single point in time. Complexity is practiced. It is continuously produced and reproduced in a society or a region through the day-to-day actions, and interactions, of all participants. Archaeologically, we can, and do, find the details of those practices all the time.

The next step is to begin to write more thorough histories of the people we study. In a sense, the studies in this book demonstrate the need for rethinking all kinds of complexity as historicized complexity. We have the details of past lives, and we can now better identify and explore the many dimensions and contingencies of such complexities. And those details rarely, if ever, fit the carefully constructed categories.

Case Studies

This book demonstrates the potential for understanding complexity in a multifaceted way, for writing histories based on data rather than on categorical assumptions, and for appreciating how some North American societies were complex in ways that were not like us.

The chapters in this volume demonstrate that complexity can be located in ritual, interpersonal relations, and the relationships engendered by monumental constructions. The authors present new ways to view how interactions and symbolic acts occur and what they can tell us about complex political and social interactions. Complexity is discovered in the interactions of heterarchical societies, in mobile farmers, and in kinship. In North America it seems that ritual was often an arena for complex practices, the playing out of kinship, politics, and economics through metaphors of rites and ceremony.

Asa Randall and Kenneth Sassaman present a case study of early hunter-gatherer societies that built shell mounds and "engaged in practices and reproduced institutions not anticipated by evolutionary models." They locate complexity, "the process of social becoming," and complex relationships in the memorial intentions of monuments such as Archaic shell mounds built by people who are in evolutionary typological terms described as "tribal," and thus not complex. Tristram R. Kidder describes research on another case of Archaic period hunter-gatherer complexity, this one from Poverty Point. Kidder considers the importance of a historical approach as he examines the "rich and complex worldview" materialized in the construction of an earthen monument, as well as the roles this monumentality played in the integration of diverse groups.

Woodland farmers in eastern North America, the Southeast, and the Midwest are societies typically considered "simple," yet Elizabeth Chilton, Meghan Howey, and Thomas Pluckhahn find unexpectedly complex practices that do not fit current models. Chilton examines the relationships between agriculture sedentism, social hierarchy, and complexity in the Late Woodland peoples of New England. Using a case study from Late Woodland northern Michigan, Howey questions the relegation of kinship to the biological and to the not-complex despite the ways that social actors "can readily construct, negotiate, and deploy media of relations beyond biological kinship."

Using a case study of Kolomoki and the Middle Woodland period, Pluckhahn reconsiders the role of ethnographic analogy to consider past complexities, and he argues for complexity without hierarchy based in ritual networks. Also working in the Middle Woodland, but with a Hopewell case study, Bretton Giles employs the concepts of baroque and romantic complexity (in the sense of Kwa 2002) to understand complex interactions of persons, the material, and the immaterial. Giles explores how "Hopewell communities enacted a dynamic sacrificial economy in which persons, objects, and spaces served as containers that were transformed to open up spaces for renewal."

Jon Marcoux and Gregory Wilson focus on ritual interactions in Mississippian societies through a study of Moundville and the applica-

tion of actor-network theory, a "view that the social consists of performed networks of human and nonhuman 'actors.'" Marcoux and Wilson follow Latour (2005) and Law (1992), viewing social structure as a verb rather than a noun in order to track what it is that people did and to tease out the meanings and transformations in those actions. As for myself, also working in the Mississippian period, I examine the microscale details of events at a Cahokian administrative center to understand the tensions within polity integration and the politicization of religion. Complexity here is found in the interactions of divergent people as they come together, reinvent themselves, and inadvertently create a new kind of society.

In the Southwest, arguments over complexity find compatible but different suggestions for resolution by Jill Neitzel and Stephen Lekson. Both consider complexity in greater regional and superregional terms, questioning how interactions can generate greater complexity. Neitzel considers why complexity is a regional phenomenon, updating Renfrew's peer polity model (Renfrew 1986) and using case studies from the Hohokam and the Chacoans. Lekson asks us to consider the case for secondary states, questioning why it is that Native North American societies are not considered states.

Severin Fowles takes a different approach and considers simplicity. He examines ideals of counterculture and the determined maintenance of simplicity in the hippie community of New Buffalo and comparatively in southwestern societies. Fowles offers a provocative way to consider tensions between complexity and simplicity, and asks us to think about simplicity as not less than, but in opposition to, the state.

We end with comments from scholars whose work on complexity helped prompt this book, Robert Chapman and Norman Yoffee. These chapters offer us commentary on complexity from archaeologists working outside North American archaeological traditions, trained to think about complexity in other regions of the world. These points of view are critical in helping us, mired as we are in North American archaeological traditions, see past our deeply embedded ideologies.

Our aim in this book is to inspire thought and discussion about how complexity manifests in North American societies. We hope we succeed in providing more representative histories for North American people than those of the past.

Acknowledgments

I thank the University of Utah Press, particularly Jim Skibo and Rebecca Rauch, as well as Kim Vivier, for assistance with all phases of this book. Their work made this an easier process and a better book. Great thanks are also due an anonymous reviewer and David Anderson, who provided detailed and thoughtful comments. Thanks also to the School of American Research and James Brooks, for providing a haven for writing and the compilation of this volume. And thanks to Norm Yoffee, Bob Chapman, Tim Pauketat, and those others who have long asked us to reconsider complexity. Greatest thanks go to the contributors to this volume, who did the hard work and made it easy to keep inspired and see this project through.

References

Anderson, D. G.
1997   The Role of Cahokia in the Evolution of Southeastern Mississippian Society. In *Cahokia: Domination and Ideology in the Mississippian World*, edited by T. R. Pauketat and T. E. Emerson, pp. 248–268. University of Nebraska Press, Lincoln.

Bentley, R. A., and H. Maschner (editors)
2000   *Complex Systems and Archaeology*. University of Utah Press, Salt Lake City.

Bonner, J. T.
1988   *The Evolution of Complexity by Means of Natural Selection*. Princeton University Press, Princeton.

Chapman, R.
2003   *Archaeologies of Complexity*. Routledge, London.

Christie, J. J., and P. J. Sarro (editors)
2006   *Palaces and Power in the Americas*. University of Texas Press, Austin.

Cilliers, P.
1998   *Complexity and Postmodernism*. Routledge, London.

Cobb, C. R.
2003   Mississippian Chiefdoms: How Complex? *Annual Review of Anthropology* 32(1):63–84.

Crumley, C. L.
1995   Heterarchy and the Analysis of Complex Societies. In *Heterarchy and the Analysis of Complex Societies*, edited by R. Ehrenreich, C. L. Crumley, and J. Levy, pp. 1–6. Archaeological Papers of the American Anthropological Association, Vol. 6. American Anthropological Association, Washington, D.C.

Dobres, M.-A., and J. E. Robb
2005   Doing Agency: Introductory Remarks on Methodology. *Journal of Archaeological Method and Theory* 13(3):159–166.

Finkenthal, M.
2008   *Complexity, Multi-Disciplinarity and Beyond*. Peter Lang, New York.

Flannery, K. V.
1972   The Cultural Evolution of Chiefdoms. *Annual Review of Ecology and Systematics* 3:399–426.

1998   The Ground Plans of Archaic States. In *Archaic States*, edited by G. M. Feinman and J. Marcus, pp. 15–58. School of American Research Press, Santa Fe.

Gell-Mann, M.
1995   What Is Complexity? *Complexity* 1:16–19.

Gibson, J. L., and P. J. Carr (editors)
2004   *Signs of Power: The Rise of Cultural Complexity in the Southeast*. University of Alabama Press, Tuscaloosa.

Gumerman, G., and M. Gell-Mann (editors)
1994   *Understanding Complexity in the Prehistoric Southwest*. Addison-Wesley, Reading, Massachusetts.

Helbing, D.
2008   *Managing Complexity: Insights, Concepts, Applications*. Springer, Berlin.

Helmreich, S.
1998   *Silicon Second Nature: Culturing Artificial Life in a Digital World*. University of California Press, Berkeley.

1999   Digitizing "Development": Balinese Water Temples, Complexity and the Politics of Simulation. *Critique of Anthropology* 19(3):249–265.

Horgan, J.
1995   From Complexity to Perplexity. *Scientific American* 272(6):104–110.

Ingold, T.
2000   *The Perception of the Environment: Essays on Livelihood, Dwelling and Skill*. Routledge, London.

2007   Earth, Sky, Wind and Weather. *Journal of the Royal Anthropological Institute*, NS:19–38.

Johnson, M. H.
2006   On the Nature of Theoretical Archaeology and Archaeological Theory. *Archaeological Dialogues* 13(2):117–132.

Kauffman, S.
1993   Principles of Adaptation in Complex Systems. In *Lectures in the Sciences of Complexity*, edited by E. Stein, pp. 619–712. Addison-Wesley, Reading, Massachusetts.

Kohler, T., and G. Gumerman (editors)
2000   *Dynamics in Human and Primate Societies: Agent-Based Modeling of Social and Spatial Processes*. Oxford University Press, New York.

Kuhn, T. S.
1962   *The Structure of Scientific Revolutions*. University of Chicago Press, Chicago.

Kwa, C.
2002   Romantic and Baroque Conceptions of Complex Wholes in the Sciences. In *Complexities: Social Studies of Knowledge Practices*, edited by J. Law and A. M. Mol. Duke University Press, Durham, North Carolina.

Lansing, S. J.
2003   Complex Adaptive Systems. *Annual Review of Anthropology* 32:183–204.

Latour, B.
2005   *Reassembling the Social: An Introduction to Actor-Network Theory*. Oxford University Press, Oxford.

Law, J.
1992   Notes on the Theory of the Actor Network: Ordering, Strategy and Heterogeneity. Centre for Science Studies, Lancaster University. Electronic document, http://www.comp.lancs.as.uk/sociology/papers/Law-Notes-on-ANT.pdf.

Law, J., and A. Mol
2002   *Complexities: Social Studies of Knowledge Practices*. Duke University Press, Durham, North Carolina.

Lekson, S. H.
2005   Chaco and Paquime: Complexity, History, Landscape. In *North American Archaeology*, edited by T. R. Pauketat and D. D. Loren, pp. 235–273. Blackwell, Oxford.
2007   *The Archaeology of Chaco Canyon*. University of Utah Press, Salt Lake City.

Meskell, L. M.
2004   *Object Worlds in Ancient Egypt: Material Biographies Past and Present*. Berg, London.

Miller, D. (editor)
2005   *Materiality (Politics, History and Culture)*. Duke University Press, Durham, North Carolina.

Morgan, L. H.
1877   *Ancient Society*. Holt, New York.

Neitzel, J. E. E.
1999   *Great Towns and Regional Polities: In the Prehistoric American Southwest and Southeast*. Amerind Foundation and University of New Mexico Press, Albuquerque.

Nelson, B. A.
1995   Complexity, Hierarchy and Scale: A Controlled Comparison between Chaco Canyon, New Mexico, and La Quemada, Zacatecas. *American Antiquity* 60:597–618.

Pauketat, T. R.
2001   Practice and History in Archaeology: An Emerging Paradigm. *Anthropological Theory* 1:73–98.
2007   *Chiefdoms and Other Archaeological Delusions*. AltaMira Press, Walnut Canyon, California.

Renfrew, C.
1986   Introduction. In *Peer Polity Interaction and Socio-Political Change*, edited by C. Renfrew and J. F. Cherry, pp. 1–18. Cambridge University Press, Cambridge.

Said, E. W.
1978   *Orientalism*. Pantheon Books, New York.

Sassaman, K.
2004   Complex Hunter-Gatherers in Evolution and History: A North American Perspective. *Journal of Archaeological Research* 12(3):227–280.
2005   Poverty Point as Structure, Event, Process. *Journal of Archaeological Method and Theory* 12(4):335–365.

Sawyer, K. R.
2005   *Social Emergence: Societies as Complex Systems*. Cambridge University Press, Cambridge.

Service, E. R.
1962   *Primitive Social Organization*. Random House, New York.

Spencer, C. S.
1990   On the Tempo and Mode of State Formation: Neoevolutionism Reconsidered. *Journal of Anthropological Archaeology* 9:1–30.

Taylor, P. J.
2005   *Unruly Complexity: Ecology, Interpretation, Engagement*. University of Chicago Press, Chicago.

Tylor, E. B.
1871   *Primitive Culture*. John Murray, London.

Urry, J.
2003   *Global Complexity*. Polity Press, Cambridge.

Yoffee, N.
2005   *Myths of the Archaic State: Evolution of the Earliest Cities, States and Civilization*. Cambridge University Press, Cambridge.

2

(E)mergent Complexities during the Archaic Period in Northeast Florida

Asa R. Randall and Kenneth E. Sassaman

It has been axiomatic that monumental construction is incompatible with hunting and gathering. Mounds and other monuments are ostensibly representative of labor coordination, territoriality, and attendant power structures (Dunham 1999; Gibson and Carr 2004; Shennan 1983; Trigger 1990). As often massive constructions or accumulations of material, they are conspicuous evidence of modification of the environment (Denevan 1992:377). Monumental places also exist as materialized declarations of historicities and assertions of cosmology (Barrett 1999; Bradley 1998; Tilley 1994). Such impressions stand in opposition to the abundance of ethnographically documented hunter-gatherer societies that did not engage in monumental construction; were characterized by low population densities, egalitarian social relations, and settlement impermanence (Kelly 1995:15; Lee and Daly 1999); and for whom cosmologies and commemorative events were presumed inconsequential to ongoing social reproduction (Fogelson 1989; Küchler 1993). For archaeologists, monuments remain emblematic of a fundamental evolutionary shift away from foraging toward food production, sedentism, higher population densities, and inevitable social hierarchies (Feinman 1995; Sherratt 1990). In this view, only societies that have met such preconditions for social complexity would have the labor, naturalized authority, and worldview to construct monuments. Likewise, any massive edifices erected by hunter-gatherer communities must represent fundamentally different processes

(e.g., Hamilton 1999; Milner and Jefferies 1998; J. Saunders 2004).

Some Consequences of De Facto Simplicity

The reproduction of the monumental axiom, along with the embedded concepts of social evolution and complexity, has guided and, as we argue herein, hindered examination of the significance of mounds constructed during the Archaic period in the southeastern United States (see also Kidder, this volume). In this chapter we are primarily concerned with shell mounds of Archaic age (ca. 7300–4000 cal BP) in northeast Florida, situated throughout the wetlands and terraces of the St. Johns River (Figure 2.1). Some are truly imposing, extending over many acres with summits reaching 10 m in height, while others are subtle, low lying, and scattered across the landscape. In conventional thought, the long-term use of shell mounds by foraging societies, coupled with their deceivingly mundane composition (i.e., shellfish), is regarded as testament to enduring aquatic adaptations established seven millennia ago during the Archaic period and continued until European contact (Goggin 1952:67; Milanich 1994:256; Miller 1998). Archaic period depositional events are treated as the continued disposal of subsistence refuse, preferentially but unreflexively heaped in certain places on the banks of the river. In the words of one regional synthesizer, "there are changes apparent in the archaeological record of the Late Archaic period.... But

8

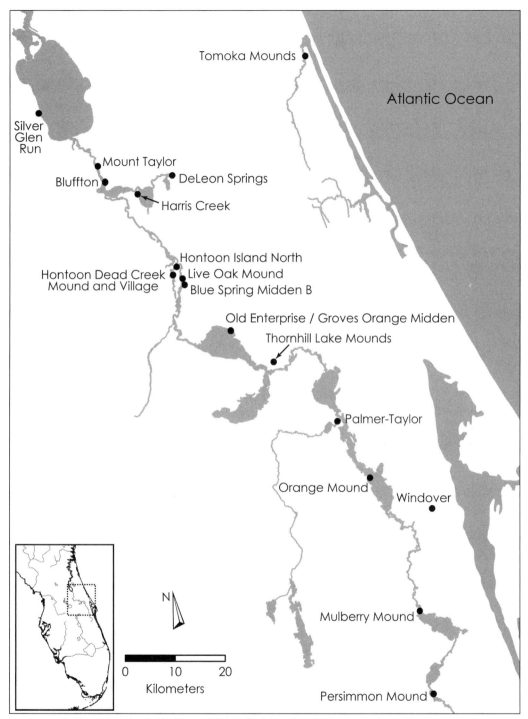

FIGURE 2.1. Shell-bearing sites in the Upper/Middle St. Johns River Valley in northeast Florida.

these changes are related to demography rather than changes in basic lifeways" (Milanich 1994: 86). Undeniably, intensive forager economies and seasonal population movements predicated on the collection of aquatic resources persisted throughout the Archaic (Quitmyer 2001; Russo et al. 1992). Moreover, we currently lack any evidence for widespread population replacements or obvious structural changes in social organization. Taken at face value, Archaic mounds reflect long-standing and undifferentiated social categories reproduced through the seemingly unending performance of habitual subsistence practices.

A more critical examination of prior excavations and recent research suggests that shell mounds represent anything but de facto refuse, and that the practices apparent now as accumulated shell at mounds register anything but unreflexive disposal patterns. Data emerging from new excavations and a reconsideration of past work indicate that Archaic inhabitants of the St. Johns actively constructed monumental mounds early and often. What is more, practices at mounds were not unchanging. Numerous transformations in the scale, temporality, and location of monumental acts over ensuing millennia indicate that mounds were renewed, modified, and avoided as an ongoing component of social reproduction. After locales were established as places to dwell, communal mortuary mounds were constructed on some of them (Aten 1999). Subsequently, these monuments were covered with mounded shell, which included materials mined from prior places (Randall and Sassaman 2005a). At the same time, new mortuary mounds were constructed on preexisting middens elsewhere (Endonino 2009; Piatek 1994). These early mound-building events contrast starkly with the succeeding ceramic Archaic Orange period (ca. 4700 and 4000 cal BP), known best for the emergence of pottery production in the region. Mound-top activities appear limited to a few places, yet settlements were emplaced adjacent to dormant mounds (Sassaman 2003a). Although not a focus of this chapter, a final transformation is evident after the Archaic, when mound-top mortuary practices resumed during the long-lived St. Johns period (Randall and Sassaman 2005a). Interwoven with alterations in monumental acts are the reorganization of area populations and ever-widening networks of exchange that brought individuals, knowledge, and objects with diverse histories into local frames of reference (Sassaman 2004).

Alternative Complexities

The St. Johns shell mounds and the communities that participated in their construction present marked contradictions to established axioms and categories. They join an ever-accumulating list of chronologically early hunter-gatherer societies that engaged in practices and reproduced institutions not anticipated by evolutionary models. What are we to make of these apparently precocious societies? Lacking appropriate frameworks, we are left searching for avenues to understand the significance of mound building within Archaic social life and how it may have affected the long-term histories of regional inhabitants. One possibility would be simply to downstream accepted monumental significance and test whether presumed-to-be attendant dimensions of social hierarchy (large populations, economic inequalities, permanent leadership, etc.) are materially manifested among Archaic communities. Pluckhahn (this volume) illustrates well the potentially erroneous conclusions that can arise from this practice. Yet such a tactic approximates recent attempts to evaluate archaeologically identified hunter-gatherer societies characterized by relative settlement permanence, constructed facilities, and social ranking. Inspiration is typically drawn from those few historically documented groups that defy traditional forager definitions, such as the Northwest Coastal communities and the ethnohistoric Calusa of southwest Florida (Marquardt 1985, 1988; Renouf 1984). In archaeological contexts, such "non-egalitarian" yet "nonstratified" socialities have been routinely conceptualized as emergently complex, transegalitarian, and even affluent (Arnold 1995; Hayden 1994; Price and Brown 1985; Sasaki 1981). Complexity is reduced to the degree to which enduring economic inequalities can arise under the context of varying resource abundance, with social trajectories preordained by ecology or technological innovation (Arnold 1995; Hayden 1994, 1995; Keen 2006). Prestige-based power structures have also been advanced as tenuous yet transformative alternatives to social complexification (Clark and Blake 1994; Hayden 1995). In this light, Archaic monuments along the St. Johns and elsewhere throughout the southeastern United States may be significant for the social relations, and potential hierarchies, they represent (Russo 2004; Sassaman and Heckenberger 2004). The demonstrated intensive shellfishing economies could be readily interpreted as a more than adequate foundation for large populations, while mounds could simply represent materialized contestations and politics regarding territorial rights to resources between any number of social categories (individuals, lineages, or communities).

Despite the Western logic surrounding an economic model of intensification, we can ask whether conceptualizing complexity among hunter-gatherers along purely economic lines obscures significant social processes. As discussed by Flanagan (1989), egalitarian social relations presumed to be original to the human condition, and ubiquitous among most ethnographically documented small-scale hunter-gatherer societies, are also present within states. Such relations are perhaps better understood as ideologies of autonomy or as traditions of resistance (Sassaman 2001), and have more to do with the historical relationships and contestations between communities than with a natural condition characteristic of early societies. Moreover, there is ample evidence that the essentialization of hunter-gatherers to economics (complex or otherwise) surreptitiously recapitulates orthodox evolutionary schema and typologies. Barnard (1999, 2004) and Pluciennik (2004) have documented how the social category of hunter-gatherer, which describes a mode of subsistence, is the product of an eighteenth-century preoccupation with systems of land tenure. Foragers, apparently lacking land ownership, provided a useful antithesis for thought experiments regarding contemporary economic patterns. A century later hunter-gatherers emerged as both a spatial and temporal "other" for evolutionary thought, and they arguably remain the pro forma baseline for anthropological inquiry by providing an original simplicity or egalitarian foundation from which complexity could arise. Current models invoking emergently complex social relations, then,

solve the apparent contradiction between hunting and gathering and other dimensions such as monumental construction by emplacing such communities on an evolutionarily liminal pathway. Prior simplicities are presumed as a standard against which complexities can be tested (e.g., White 2004). Barring ecological catastrophes or truncation through contact with technologically advanced others, early complex foragers are significant principally because they provided the foundation for later developments. Simplicity is thus preserved for the sake of complexity.

Viewed through the lens of economics and stepwise social change, early monuments and the communities that were constructed through them fade back into anthropological curios, intriguing yet inconsequential. However, monuments are increasingly recognized not as essentialized objects but as processes in which peoples with distinct social and cosmological histories were integrated through shared yet likely contested ritual commemorative practices (Adler and Wilshusen 1990; Barrett 1999; Bernardini 2004; Bradley 1998; Pauketat and Alt 2003; Van Dyke 2003). That is, monuments are not emblematic of a particular mode of subsistence, degree of social ranking, or stage of social differentiation. Instead, they are the process of social becoming that we describe as societies (Barrett 1999); or as Pauketat (2000, 2001) asserts, monumental acts are one of many dimensions of ongoing tradition making. From this perspective, monuments are but one (particularly obvious) materialized way through which communities were constructed. The many complexities that arise through monumentality are embedded in difference recognition and negotiations that are arguably central to all peoples at all times.

In this chapter we expand on this line of thought and consider how the ongoing politics of monument construction were a process in which multiple histories were made meaningful. In particular, we emphasize how the long-term life histories of monuments (sensu Holtorf 1998; Pauketat and Alt 2005) provide key avenues into understanding the process of social memory construction among Archaic communities. Central to our argument is that past Archaic communities were not composed of undifferentiated subsistence practitioners. We consider how on-going monumental acts structured and were structured by the generation of social memory as a selective process by which agents actively re-signify, reference, or discard past practices and materialities as a means of negotiating contemporary social concerns (Bradley 2002:12; Connerton 1989; Shils 1981:45; Van Dyke and Alcock 2003:3). As framed by tradition, selective memories provide the medium for ongoing culture making. There are, however, potentially diverse and dissonant reasons for referencing the past. As the basis for social reproduction, then, monuments, narratives, landscapes, heirlooms, ceremonial performances, or habitual practices all afford dominant discursive and experiential versions of history that structure potential action (Barrett 1999; Bourdieu 1977; Mills 2004).

Despite intentions of agents to create enduring histories that authenticate their own identities and naturalize social differences, the contexts in which traditions are enacted are inherently dynamic (Bradley 2003; Edmonds 1999:134; Giles, this volume; Marcoux and Wilson, this volume; Pauketat and Alt 2003; Rumsey 1994). Throughout the lifetime of an individual, differentiated biographies and networks of relationships can accumulate. In such cases, the potential discordance between practice and structure can be subverted in commemorative ceremonies that reproduce shared ancestral pasts (Morphy 1995), or through institutionalized and politicized "forgetting" as a means of relinquishing change to history (Küchler 1993). Selected memories are equally effective during moments of radical social change, such as culture contact or political upheaval. In such cases the conspicuous manipulation of the past is likely as histories are asserted and negotiated across diverse social fields (Sahlins 1985; Shils 1981). Expected is the rapid reconfiguration or invention of tradition by which agents can assert a timeless ancestry, real or imagined (Hobsbawm 1983; Pauketat and Alt 2003). Equally effective are iconoclastic practices in which particular traces and perspectives on the past are obliterated or avoided (Bradley 2002; Forty 1999). The complexity for archaeologists, and no doubt agents of the past, is to discern the commemorative strategies embedded in the performance of past practices

and the referencing of prior materialities selectively drawn from tradition.

At the Center of Difference

New traditions involving the collection and deposition of shellfish emerged some 7,000 years ago throughout the St. Johns River basin during the preceramic Archaic Mount Taylor period (ca. 7300–4700 cal BP). Events attending the appearance of these practices have been largely obscured by rising water levels that inundated early places, as well as the output of later inhabitation, which has encased them under meters of deposits. We do know that the earliest denizens of the region lived in an environment fundamentally different from that experienced today. In contrast to ubiquitous surface waters, northeast Florida before the Middle Holocene was considerably drier (Watts et al. 1996). Settlement centered on permanent sources of water, such as springs and ponds (Dunbar and Waller 1983). We currently do not have detailed reconstructions of either the establishment of wetlands or the early distribution of shellfish beds, although those species of importance were available nearly a millennium before their exploitation by Mount Taylor peoples (Adams 1976). The appearance of shellfishing is thus roughly coeval with the onset of a near-modern hydrologic regime, which arguably provided abundant and sustainable wetland resources that would have been a draw for regional populations. Despite the apparent ecological impetus for regional settlement, a consideration of the community histories, coresident populations, and incipient mound-construction events suggests that these new traditions were themselves embedded in extant commemorative strategies. In this sense, the importance of the St. Johns was that it provided a spatial domain for the creation and negotiation of diverse memories and ancestries in place.

Creating Places
in a Diverse Neighborhood

Data on early settlement are restricted to now-inundated middens, the bases of shell mounds, and deposits adjacent to mounds. Inundated components have been identified at most shell mounds in the region (Wheeler et al. 2000). The most

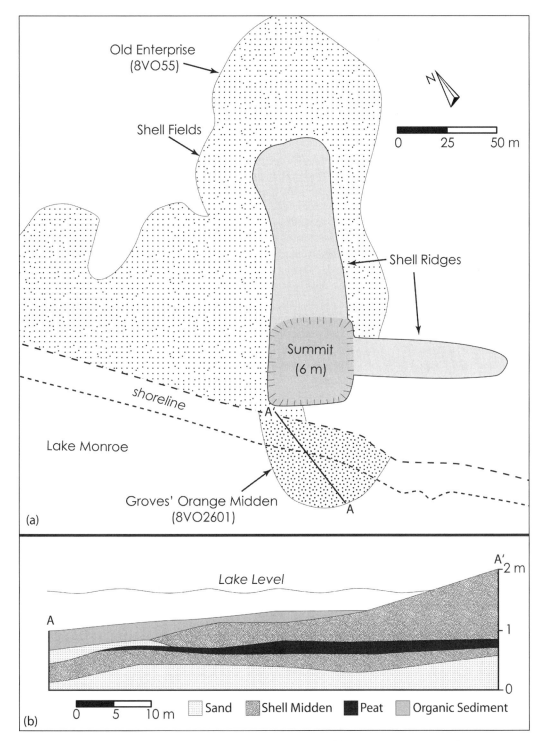

FIGURE 2.2. Old Enterprise Complex on Lake Monroe: (a) Plan view of the terrestrial (8VO55) and wet site (8VO2601) components, redrawn from Wheeler et al. (2000:Fig. 12); (b) cross section of Groves' Orange Midden saturated deposits, redrawn from McGee and Wheeler (1994:Fig. 9).

intensively studied of these is Groves' Orange Midden, the underwater segment of the much more expansive and multicomponent Old Enterprise complex (Figure 2.2a). Recent research has focused on the saturated component, which extends from the base of the primary mound some 50 m into Lake Monroe (McGee and Wheeler 1994; Figure 2.2b). Beginning nearly 7,000 years ago, inhabitants deposited shell midden materials along a now-extinct stream channel, eventually filling it in. Over successive millennia, materials were consistently laid down at the margin of the lake or within the associated low-lying marsh. The excavators have argued that because of the high level of organic preservation within the deposits, the materials were deposited underwater. Although surface water levels fluctuated, at times likely obscuring middens for several centuries and resulting in the development of peat deposits, deposition preferentially moved landward, creating a midden that increases in thickness toward the terrestrial edge. Analysis of cultural materials from these early deposits demonstrates that deposition was largely domestic in character (Wheeler and McGee 1994).

The Hontoon Dead Creek Mound and Village complex provides data on both subaqueous and terrestrial deposition (Figure 2.3). In its shape, a crescentric ridge, the mound at this complex is consistent with other preceramic mounds identified in the valley (Randall and Sassaman 2005b). Unlike Old Enterprise, the site is situated some 300 m from moving water. Cores extracted at the base of the mound, and extending into the swamp, identified saturated midden deposits beneath a meter of organic sediment extending some 30 m out from the base and abruptly ending in what is presumed to be a relict stream channel. This midden was similarly composed of shell and diverse fauna and flora, and dates to around 6900 cal BP. We do not know when deposition first occurred underneath the mound. At the nearby and similarly configured preceramic Archaic Live Oak Mound, near-basal deposits were dated to ca. 7200 cal BP (Sassaman 2003a).

At the Hontoon Dead Creek complex, inhabitants also deposited shell on the higher, landward edge of the terrace south of the mound. This portion of the site is referred to as the Hontoon Dead Creek Village and is characterized by

spatially discrete shell heaps evident in Figure 2.3 as elevated topography, typically 50 cm high and upward of 20 m long (Randall 2007). Those two closest to the mound date between 7300 and 6300 cal BP, coeval with the inundated midden and bracket mound construction, while the southernmost heap in Figure 2.3 dates to the later Orange period. The heap closest to the mound is composed of concreted midden and ash, apparently an area reserved for the discrete disposal and potential burning of shell. To the south is a linear ridge, which in cross section is composed of alternating lenses of crushed and whole shell. Whether such lenses were created by trampling or postabandonment processes can be debated. Regardless of the ultimate cause, the sequence and structure are indicative of serial occupations and may represent the floors of residential structures. When taken together, the ash deposits and the ridge heap indicate that materials were not haphazardly strewn throughout the habitation area. In fact, the patterns of midden emplacement implicate intentional attempts at maintaining and renewing the spatial organization of the settlement. Such patterns appear to represent a community organized in a linear array along the water (Randall 2007).

The routinized creation of settlements belies considerable diversity in the life histories of inhabitants and communities. Juxtaposed to the local composition of shell middens, most nonperishable material culture was derived from nonlocal sources. Notably, lithic raw materials and shell tools provide evidence for travels to and contacts with communities throughout much of central Florida. The St. Johns basin is devoid of stone suitable for the production of lithic tools. As a consequence, all lithic raw material was transported into the region from sources at least 100 km to the east. Sourcing studies of Florida's chert and silicified coral have identified no fewer than 16 quarry clusters throughout the state, from the panhandle to southwest Florida (Austin and Estabrook 2000; Endonino 2007; Upchurch et al. 1982). Likewise, examination of lithic materials incorporated within the St. Johns shell mounds indicates that a number of quarries within peninsular Florida are represented in Mount Taylor assemblages. In some cases, the majority of materials appear to be derived from the interior

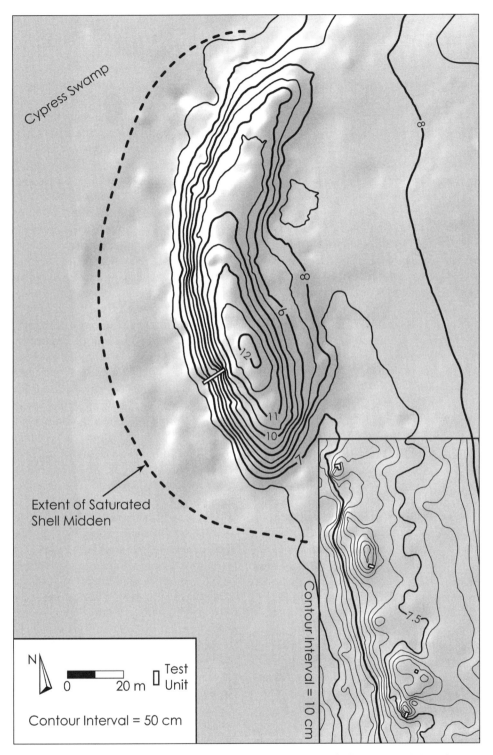

FIGURE 2.3. Plan view of the Hontoon Dead Creek Mound (8VO214) and Village (8VO215) Complex. The higher-resolution contour intervals highlight the village component.

highlands, to the west of the St. Johns basin. However, a minority of the examples are also derived from the west-central and southwest quarries (Austin and Estabrook 2000; Endonino 2007). In either case, such raw materials are found outside the source region in quantities and forms suggestive of direct procurement. Settlements within the source areas included large residential sites and smaller encampments, indicative of multiseasonal regional occupations, in addition to large quarries (Milanich 1994:79). In contrast, marine shell was likely obtained from coastal sources either 40 km to the east along the Atlantic Coast or farther afield to the west and southwest. Objects manufactured from marine shell have a wide range of functional forms, including axes, adzes, and gouges. Marine shell vessels have also been recovered from Mount Taylor assemblages and are frequently sooted from use. However, most appear to be associated with woodworking. Unfortunately, we know nothing of the structure of early coastal inhabitation, as coastal sites predating 5500 years ago have been inundated by sea-level rise.

Negotiating Diverse Ancestries

The available data on settlement and mobility suggest that the early preceramic Archaic communities along the St. Johns were composed of inhabitants with different, and potentially dissonant, social histories who were drawn together for portions of the year in structured settlements along the St. Johns. It is in this milieu of diversity that the first mortuary monuments along the St. Johns were constructed. Shortly after being established as places to dwell, certain places of prior settlement were converted into communal mortuary mounds. In one sense, the removal of components of the landscape from daily practice appears a radical departure from tradition as highly visible commemorative ceremonies at mound sites replaced routine tasks. A consideration of the social context and structure of these emergent commemorative strategies indicates that these seemingly new ways of manufacturing memories were extensions of prior routine tasks coupled with long-standing perspectives on ancestry. Such places emerged as contexts for recognizing and subverting divergent histories among coresident inhabitants.

The details of this emergent practice are known to us best from the Harris Creek shellmound and mortuary complex on Tick Island. Before its destruction via shell mining, it was a complex of ridges, mounds, and middens covering five acres. Modern salvage excavations were restricted to the basal deposits of the presumed Archaic crescentric ridge. At the time it was documented, most stratigraphic information was derived from a relict profile and areas exposed by shell mining, the results of which have been detailed by Aten (1999). The foundation of the mortuary (Layer 1) was saturated and not excavated but was approximately 1 m thick and composed of low-lying heterogeneous midden deposits. After a period of indeterminate abandonment, inhabitants returned and emplaced shell in a dark brown soil matrix, as well as shell lacking organic matter or sediment, hereafter referred to as "clean shell." These materials comprise Layer 2, which in plan view is a 1-m-high ridge, some 15 m wide and 30 m long (Figure 2.4). Aten (1999) suggests that these materials were emplaced to accentuate a preexisting ridge in this location. In both structure and shape, Layer 2 is similar to the low-lying ridge identified at the Hontoon Dead Creek Village site. It is unknown what the temporal relationship of this event was to either earlier habitation or later monumentality, but these actions do not appear to be associated directly with mortuary activities.

After this transformative event, the Layer 2 surface was used as a foundation for the construction of two successive mortuaries, in which more than 140 individuals were interred (Figure 2.4). Tightly clustered radiocarbon dates on human bone suggest that this mortuary was relatively short-lived, perhaps on the order of two centuries before and after at least 7000 cal BP (Tucker 2009). Burials were restricted to the northern and eastern aspects of these zones. Because of the recent extensive shell mining, it is unknown whether burials were present along the western edge, but anecdotal evidence indicates that many burials were present in the core of the mound. The lower mortuary (A) corresponds with Layer 3 and lies unconformably on Layer 2. This zone is characterized by allochthonous white sand deposits interspersed with clean shell and dark soil. The geologic origin of this sediment is currently

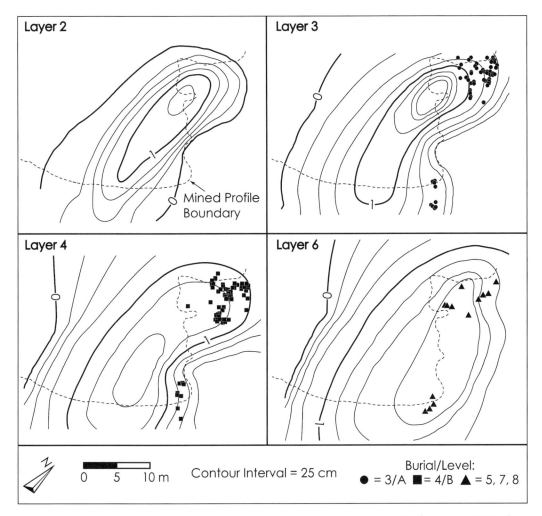

FIGURE 2.4. Sequence of mound construction stages and burial plans at the Harris Creek mortuary (8VO24), redrawn from Aten (1999:Fig. 11). Location of burials reflects those identified during salvage excavations and is not a discrete distribution.

unknown. Tightly flexed single and multiple interments were placed into piles of sand less than a meter high and several meters wide, or alternatively, pits were excavated into the basal Layer 2 midden into which burials and white sand were placed. Eventually, this mortuary covered the entire basal mound. A series of superimposed post holes located near the burial area may represent the repeated erection of a structure, possibly a charnel house. A lens of charcoal-impregnated sand adjacent to the structure was also identified. Taken together, these suggest that the deceased were processed at the mortuary for some time prior to their inhumation. Above this layer was Mortuary B. Practices continued to emphasize

the original structure of the mound but did not appear to include white sand as a burial medium. Instead, the burial matrix and mound fill was composed of shell and vertebrate faunal remains.

At the scale of individual burials, there is considerable diversity in the matrices and objects included. Some individuals were placed in pits and then covered in sand, while others were placed on the mound surface and covered with sand or shell. However, interments were structured along temporal axes that suggest that distinctions in the performance of burial rituals were made based on origins. As discussed by Aten (1999), burials were of two types. The majority (60 percent) were vertical and tightly flexed, suggesting that the bodies were processed for an extended period of time prior to inhumation. In contrast, another 38 percent were loosely flexed, suggesting that the bodies were emplaced within the mound soon after death. Recent stable isotope analysis by Tucker (2009) of individual burials provides key details on the relationship between the mode of interment and the origins of the interred individuals. Using oxygen and carbon isotope ratios, he was able to demonstrate that the differences in interment strategies do not represent differential access to foodstuffs. Instead, different modes of interment are closely associated with either local or nonlocal points of origin. So-called delayed or flexed burials are typically associated with individuals who spent their childhood years in the vicinity of the mound, while immediate or "primary" burials are associated with individuals who spent their childhood years away from the St. Johns to the south, as far as Lake Okeechobee or the Atlantic Coast. The implication is that the timing of burials, and by extension, the co-presencing of living individuals, was central to the ordering, juxtaposition, and subversion of regional differences. Delayed burials would have provided the opportunity for multiple gatherings, likely drawing in kin and allied groups from throughout the basin, possibly in the context of the recently deceased. Far from reflecting territoriality or community isolation, the creation of above-ground dedicated mortuary spaces provided integrative arenas.

Harris Creek remains the only well-documented and radiocarbon-dated example of this mortuary practice. However, Endonino (2003) and Wheeler et al. (2000) have argued that similar sequences were exposed by C. B. Moore in his late-nineteenth-century exploits. For example, in a profile at Orange mound, Moore (1999:103) observed human bones in a brown sand and shell matrix. This stratum was superimposed over a 1.5-m sequence of whole and crushed shell and overlain by 50 cm of white sand. Endonino has identified many other likely candidates for early mortuary mounds, including Persimmon, Mulberry, Palmer-Taylor, DeLeon Springs, and Mount Taylor. The similarity in composition and structure among these sites suggests that mortuary mound construction may have been synchronous throughout the basin.

These new ways of making places were themselves transformations of long-standing traditions. Even before inhabitants of the St. Johns collected shellfish, the region was deeply imbued with ancestral presence. Ponds and springs served as the locus of interment. Mortuary ponds have been identified at sites widely distributed throughout Florida. The majority of these pond burials date to the Middle Holocene, ca. 7600–6000 cal BP, and are located in the western and southern portions of the state (Doran 2002a). A notable exception, however, is the Windover site, located in the upper reaches of the St. Johns basin. Between 9000 and 7900 cal BP at least 168 individuals were interred in peat deposits along the margins of this pond (Doran 2002b). Analysis of the burial patterns indicates that a prescribed treatment was typically followed (Dickel 2002). The deceased were interred rapidly after death, likely on the order of a day or two. They were wrapped in textiles and buried in shallow depressions excavated in the underlying peat and sand. Frequently, wood was piled on top of the burial below the water level. Stakes were placed upright near the bodies, although it is unclear if these would have been visible above the surface of the water.

The transition from mortuary ponds to burial mounds appears coeval with the inundation of the valley, which may have obscured many prior settlements and required the restructuring of regional populations. As demonstrated at Harris Creek, Archaic inhabitants referenced the materiality of past living not only in the emplacement of the mortuary atop a likely domestic midden, but by re-creating its overall form, a low-lying ridge. The interment of the dead involved arguably small-scale depositional acts, the media of which were materials such as sand and shell collected from elsewhere. The presence of both secondary and primary burials, in addition to a possible mortuary structure, indicates that the preparation of the dead was an extended performance, which stands in contrast to prior mortuary programs in which the deceased were rapidly interred after death. This shifting temporality in the timing of interment, as well as the widespread distribution of these mortuaries, suggests that commemorative performances at burial mounds incorporated individuals from throughout the valley, creating collective memories across diverse social fields. The emerging picture is one of alterity, in which coastal and interior populations were variously drawn together for only a portion of the year and in which differences in ancestry and worldviews were obscured through shared traditions of settlement layout.

Complexities, Simplified

Writing about the early establishment of states, Yoffee (2005:91–92) notes that perhaps the most fundamental shift in the organization of politics and ritual was the reduction or simplification of numerous identities and histories through centralized laws and commemorative practices. While there is no evidence for kings, chiefs, or other like social categories along the St. Johns, there is evidence for increasing simplification in commemorative strategies after 5,500 years ago, when the socialities reproduced through mortuary ritual at mound centers appear to have collapsed. The ensuing millennium is characterized by several, likely interrelated, regional processes indicative, we think, of differentiation among residential groups with extra-regional alliances. In what is best described as a revolution in the structure and organization of ritual at both the local and regional scales, prior mortuaries and associated domestic compounds were capped with mounded shell that effectively removed all traces of prior practices. Such transformations were operationalized through new commemorative strategies that, while drawn from tradition and referencing presumed shared pasts, present a simplification of increasingly diverse social biographies.

Obscuring Histories

The mortuary program at Harris Creek was succeeded by routinized deposition of organically enriched shell deposits to increase the height and breadth of the mound summit (Aten 1999). Toward the end of the sequence, inhabitants actually excavated a portion of the mound, furthering its height by placing these older materials on top (Figure 2.2, Layer 6). Such events characterize the latter half of preceramic Archaic mound-building practices along the St. Johns. Both mortuaries and prior domestic compounds were transformed into platform mounds through successive con-

struction episodes, whereas new mounds were constructed for individuals or subsets of society. While diverse in composition and content, mounding events obscured traces of past practices and created platforms for monumental renewal through commemorative ceremonies. These new ways of experiencing mounds suggest that the relationships, histories, and worldviews that commemorative performances in past places afforded became increasingly dissonant with emerging social realities. In part, the details of these traditions align closely with iconoclasm (Forty 1999), as these actions appear to have removed traces of past practice and severed direct historical links between the living and the dead. What appears in place are new nonmortuary traditions that referenced a more generalized or mythical past. This may be akin to the physical separation of "mythical" and "historical" pasts (Gosden and Lock 1998; Rumsey 1994).

One pervasive theme of this era was the eradication of the traces of prior places through large-scale depositional events. These have been documented by our own excavations at the Hontoon Island North site (Randall and Sassaman 2005b) (Figure 2.5). Before being mined during the early twentieth century for shell, the site was composed of at least two ridges of shell, the largest some 300 m long (Wyman 1875). Shell-mining practices afforded the opportunity to explore basal deposits that are normally covered by later deposition. Excavations in the basal components revealed the presence of drastically different stratigraphic profiles distributed across the site. To the east, excavations revealed a stratigraphically homogeneous but compositionally diverse assemblage of shellfish, vertebrate fauna, tool fragments, ash, and copious quantities of paleofeces. This is indicative, we think, of a secondary refuse area. In the central portion of the site, excavations revealed a highly structured sequence of alternating lenses of crushed and whole shellfish of different species, in addition to occasional features. This sequence appears to represent renewed floor surfaces. Finally, we uncovered disarticulated human remains in a highly organic matrix, similar to that discussed by Aten (1999) for the upper Harris Creek mortuary. While these provide only snapshots of what is likely a much more complicated spatial arrangement,

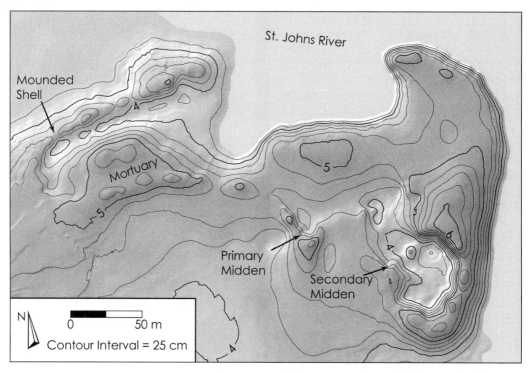

FIGURE 2.5. Differentiated spaces at Hontoon Island North (8VO202). The irregular topography is the result of shell mining.

they suggest that there was once a highly structured settlement composed of a secondary midden, a primary habitation space, and a dedicated mortuary. However, massive lenses of shell in the western portion of the site indicate that the prior diversity in practices in place were abandoned, replaced by a tradition of capping and obscuring. Such deposits were over a meter thick and composed entirely of thick lenses of homogeneous shell, largely lacking vertebrate fauna or material culture that would indicate that the deposits were refuse. While identified as whole deposits only in the west, disconformities that were witnessed in the eastern aspect of the mound seem to reflect the same practice.

The extant mound at the south end of Hontoon Island, Hontoon Dead Creek Mound, offers a window into the larger stratigraphic sequence of these transformations (Figure 2.6). That the construction of this mound was an interpretation of the past is evidenced by the presence of submerged shell deposits extending into the adjacent swamp. The terrestrial portion of the mound, which appears to have been constructed after in-

undation was under way, is entirely conformant to the preexisting shell midden. Yet while the mound may have been situated to reference or juxtapose the past, details of mound-building events revealed in a 9-m-long trench suggest that its specific significance was largely erased (Randall and Sassaman 2005b). The initial deposits were relatively localized and involved small-scale events. Although we cannot be certain that these were mortuary events (we did not dig into the core of the mound), we suspect they were, given its morphological similarity to Harris Creek. The initial mound stage of whole shell was later expanded laterally with an apron of crushed shell that included large, concreted midden clasts, apparently mined from the existing midden. As shell layers were added to cap the initial feature, an increasingly enlarged summit platform formed, implying that these places were intentionally modified to accommodate more people. Profiles show that these were large-scale events, and the limited amount of vertebrate fauna and artifacts supports the inference that these modifications were episodic and not simply the grad-

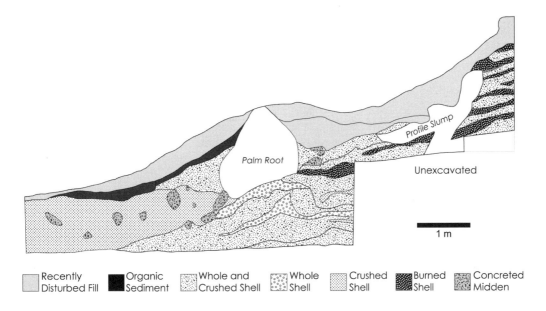

Recently Disturbed Fill · Organic Sediment · Whole and Crushed Shell · Whole Shell · Crushed Shell · Burned Shell · Concreted Midden

FIGURE 2.6. Construction stages at the Hontoon Dead Creek Mound (8VO214).

ual accumulation of everyday refuse. Moreover, the presence of allochthonous concreted midden clasts indicates that the preexisting midden, as well as fresh shell, was mined for construction material to enlarge the base.

After its transformation into a platform mound, the expanded base allowed for a more routine renewal of the surface, as indicated by the highly repetitive deposition of crushed, burned, and whole shell in the upper levels of the mound. Although these depositional practices at first appear to be a drastic contrast to the earlier mortuary components, they have analogues in the renewal of house floors as seen near the base of Hontoon Island North, and recent dating shows that the renewals occurred in rapid sequence following the capping of the mound. The presence of large, potentially thermal features near the summit, like those recovered at Harris Creek, may attest to more intensive but short-term moments of food preparation and consumption, but these moments were not intensive enough (or of long enough duration) for thick organic middens to form. We observed similar sequences of staged capping at Live Oak Mound across the east river channel that fronts Hontoon Island (Sassaman 2003a), and Wyman (1875) frequently made mention of them at sites throughout the basin. Like prior mortuary mounds, such sequences appear to be widespread.

Expanded Identities

Because we lack detailed chronologies, it is difficult to assess what specific events may have precipitated iconoclastic practices at mound sites. However, concomitant with the transformation of mounds from mortuaries to platforms is evidence for ever-widening exchange alliances that would eventually range from the Atlantic Coast, to the lower Coastal Plain, and into the interior Southeast (Figure 2.7). For example, exchange with groups in southeastern Florida is documented by the presence of marine shell celts made of the queen conch, *Strombus gigas* (Wheeler et al. 2000). These items appear only after initial capping events were under way at mortuary mounds such as at Harris Creek (Aten 1999) and likely postdate 6000 cal BP. The celts occur most frequently within general midden contexts, suggesting that they were used and deposited in the course of routine tasks.

Other classes of objects appear to be restricted to mounds, however. Tomoka, Bluffton, and Thornhill Lake all contain nonlocal bannerstones either in caches or directly associated with burials. These items provide a link to people of

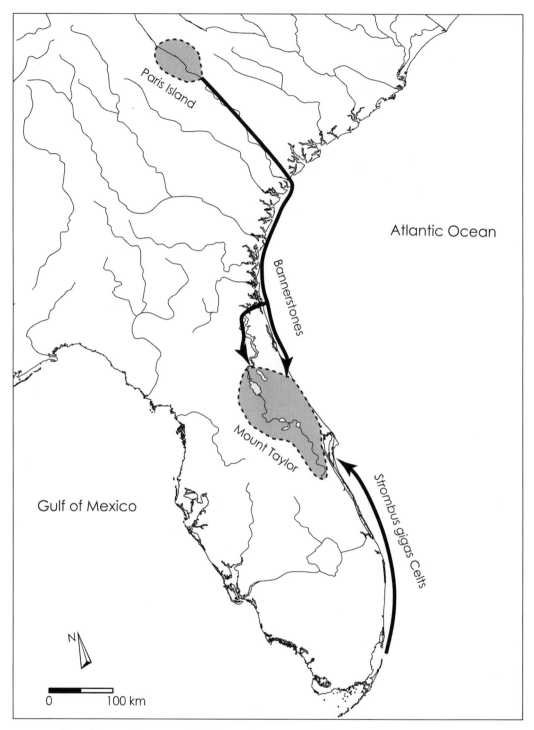

FIGURE 2.7. Map of the southeastern United States showing origins of bannerstones and Strombus gigas shell celts that were incorporated into Mount Taylor period mounds.

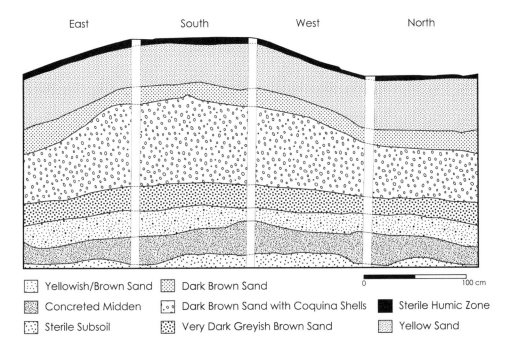

FIGURE 2.8. Composite profile of Unit B at Tomoka Mound (8VO81), redrawn from Piatek (1994:Fig. 5).

the Paris Island phase of the Middle Savannah River Valley (Georgia and South Carolina), dating roughly 5200–4700 cal BP (Sassaman and Randall 2007). Within the Savannah River Valley, bannerstones were being exchanged, possibly for shell beads, with communities in the lower Coastal Plain (Sassaman 2004). In these contexts bannerstones do not appear to have been heavily involved in mortuary ceremonialism. In Florida, however, bannerstones are almost entirely restricted to mortuary contexts. At least one burial at Thornhill Lake was interred with a series of bannerstones, as well as numerous shell beads and beads of red jasper (Moore 1999). More frequently, bannerstones occur as caches such as at Tomoka Mounds (Douglass 1882) or Coontie Island (a nonmound site) (Clausen 1964). This suggests that both the memory and biographies of these exchanges were incorporated into local histories through their deposition within mounds. For example, at Tomoka Mounds at least one cache of bannerstones was recovered in what was determined to be a large pit (Douglass 1882). Recent excavations at the site have demonstrated that like earlier mounds, Tomoka was built on an earlier midden, dated to ca. 5500 cal BP (Piatek

1994). The midden itself predates the production of bannerstones in the source region by centuries, indicating that the mound was constructed considerably later. On the buried midden are thick lenses of sand or sand and shell, which arguably represent materials mined from preexisting middens (Figure 2.8). Some fragments of human bone within the matrix indicate that the mound was constructed in part as a burial mound. In either case, just like the biographies of individuals, bannerstones—and their link with distinct and distant cultures outside the region—were interpreted through the lens of local monumentality.

These networks likely resulted in the emergence of differentiated biographies locally (sensu Gosden and Marshall 1999) which appear to have enabled or necessitated yet another re-creation of the past as new mounds were constructed. While these have the shape and structure of earlier mound-building traditions, which occurred as a process, they were constructed as an event. The best example of this practice is evident at the Bluffton site. Stratigraphic excavations at the midden-mound portion of the site demonstrated that it was predominantly Archaic in age, spanning the Mount Taylor and Orange periods

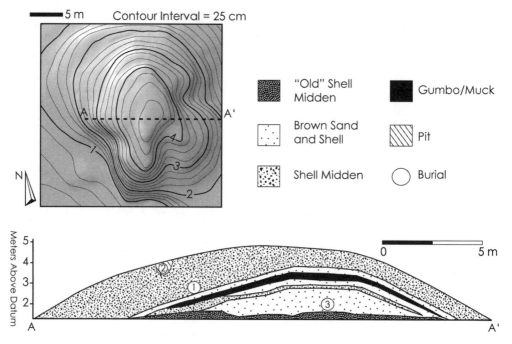

FIGURE 2.9. Plan and cross-section views of the Bluffton Burial Mound (8VO23), redrawn from Sears (1960: Fig. 1.2).

(Bullen 1955). The composition of this aspect of the site suggests that it was likely a village compound. To the rear and landward side of these larger shell sites are small mounds of sand and shell, in which Wyman (1875:37) encountered human interments. Successive stratigraphic excavations in one of the mounds have demonstrated that at least one of them was initially built before the emergence of pottery (Moore 1999:166–170; Sears 1960).

The burial mound for which we have the most information at Bluffton was described as an oval some 35 m in maximum width and 3.5 m high (Figure 2.9). The base of the mound, with which later deposits are entirely conformant, is composed exclusively of an older shell deposit. While Sears (1960:57) describes this basal component as nearly flat or undulating, Moore's early excavations encountered a small mounded ridge some 1.5 m high near the center of the mound. This earlier midden deposit was burned, and then a single individual, in this case a male, was placed on top of the basal midden and covered with an organic material. Emplaced above this burial was a striking sequence that essentially recapitulates earlier mound structures. Brown sand mixed with

concreted midden fragments were placed in basket loads above the burial. On top of this sand deposit was placed a lens of "dirty" shell midden containing Mount Taylor shell tools and other debris, likely derived from a midden somewhere. After another layer of sand was deposited, it was covered with a 6-inch thick layer of black organic sediment, variously referred to as "gumbo" or "muck," that may be derived from a nearby slough. This was covered with more sand and then upward of 2 m of mined-midden materials, within which basket loading was evident. It is unknown from where these materials were mined. The structure is strikingly similar to other mortuary mounds, but unlike those that occurred as a long-term process, mounding sequences like Bluffton re-created history as a single event. It is likely that the sequence of mound construction was itself a narrative, much like that proposed by Kidder (this volume) for the construction of Mound A at Poverty Point.

A New World Order

Mounds clearly remained prominent components in the ongoing daily and ritual lives of inhabitants throughout the Mount Taylor period, as they were routinely maintained, referenced, and manipulated. Yet beginning some 4,800 years ago, practices at most mounds ceased despite evidence for continued inhabitation locally. This abandonment of mounds is coeval with the emergence of fiber-tempered pottery production, which appears to have been facilitated by the alliances that delivered bannerstones to Florida (Sassaman 2004). Fiber-tempered pottery first appears along the lower reaches of the Savannah River some 5,200 years ago, about the same time as bannerstones from the upper Savannah found their way to Florida. The earliest dates for fiber-tempered pottery in northeast Florida, locally referred to as Orange ware, cluster at 4800 cal BP. Until recently, fiber-tempered pottery in Florida was modeled as a local innovation that underwent changes in technology and style over a 1,500-year span. New radiocarbon dates and petrographic analysis, however, show that variations in technology and decoration presumed to be temporal were actually synchronic (Cordell 2004; Sassaman 2003b). In other words, most of the pottery innovations in Florida appeared instantaneously some 4,800 years ago. But although these variations no longer hold the temporal relevance once thought, they embody a marked degree of spatial and contextual differentiation.

Assemblages of Orange Plain pottery in the Middle St. Johns are widespread but largely restricted to deposits away from mounds. Our excavations at the Blue Spring Midden B village site revealed a relatively continuous sequence of occupation spanning the appearance of Orange pottery (Sassaman 2003a). In its overall structure, this site consisted of discrete houses arranged in an arcuate pattern, forming a compound that also included associated secondary refuse. In fact, it shares many similarities with the preceramic Archaic basal components at Hontoon Island North. Despite the apparent continuity, the onset of pottery use coincides with the apparent abandonment of an adjacent Mount Taylor mound, or at least the avoidance of mound-top activities involving the deposition of plain fiber-tempered pottery. A similar juxtaposition between Orange period domestic space and preceramic mounds is evidenced at the Hontoon Dead Creek Village site (Randall 2007). As we have previously discussed, this site consists of a series of small nodes of shell

that were deposited in a time-transgressive manner down the terrace and away from the mound. The first two shell nodes, in proximity to the mound, appear to be largely preceramic, while successive nodes to the south date to either the Orange or later St. Johns periods. Orange pottery testifies to habitation in this area, merely tens of meters from the mound, yet sherds were apparently never deposited on the mound (Figure 2.3). The spatial division between old shell mounds and assemblages of plain fiber-tempered pottery is reproduced at a number of other localities in the region, such as at the Bluffton site (Bullen 1955).

In contrast to the widespread occurrence of plain vessels, assemblages dominated by thick, decorated, and sooted Orange Incised vessels appear to be restricted to four large mound sites. This inference is based primarily on descriptions by Wyman and Moore. From north to south these include the mouth of Silver Glen Run, Tick Island, Enterprise, and Orange Mound (Figure 2.1). These sites are spaced at relatively regular intervals, some 30–40 km apart, and in their distribution encapsulate the northern and southern extent of preexisting Mount Taylor shell mounds. Although these assemblages were emplaced on prior shell mounds, it is unclear the extent to which they are shell mound construction or mortuary ceremony. For example, Moore (1999) demonstrated that Orange vessels were isolated to a 1-m-thick sequence of shell and earth superimposed on the earlier Mount Taylor mortuary. Much later, during the latter half of the ensuing St. Johns period, after roughly 1200 cal BP, many mounds became not only locations of activities resulting in the consumption and deposition of large numbers of vessels but also sites for the emplacement once again of the dead (Randall and Sassaman 2005a). The widespread mortuary sand mound tradition of this later time period was expressed in both novel forms and, arguably, revitalization movements of past practice, especially in cases where conical mounds were added to the ends of ancient shell ridges.

Although there is no evidence for major changes in subsistence and settlement in the Middle St. Johns for over 6,000 years, there were numerous transformations in the ways in which mounds were experienced by the constituent populations. In contrast to preceding Mount Taylor traditions of incorporating both local and regional biographies in monumental places, Orange communities reconfigured and actively erased memories of an ever-present ancestral past. Unlike previous practices in which the past was literally erased, most mounds were avoided. The extent to which this represents benevolent neglect out of respect (Barrett 1994) or fear and avoidance (Whitley 2002) is unknown. This pattern of avoidance likely reflects the introduction of not only new ideas (i.e., pottery production) but also new personnel into the region. A similar separation between domestic places and monuments has been identified on the coast, where Orange Incised is frequently found at monumental shell rings (R. Saunders 2004). In contrast with the coast, however, inhabitants of the St. Johns do not presently appear to have been involved in widespread mound construction. The likely division between individuals who could claim ancestry to coastal populations and those who had ties to a local past appears to have been largely reconfigured through a reinterpretation of the materiality of past places. That is, multiethnic households and communities created an entirely new social history by selectively referencing the past. Although in part modeled on coastal traditions of commemorative practices, evidenced by the segregation of domestic and ritual spaces, new histories were interpreted through past mortuary places.

Merging Complexities

As both Küchler (1999) and Bradley (2003) remind us, we must always question the memorial intentions of monuments, as well as be aware of the potentially diverse and discordant memories that could be negotiated in places through time. This is nowhere more apparent than in the Middle St. Johns Valley, where memories and the materiality of the past were selectively referenced, mined, or ignored through monumental acts. Beneath the commonplace composition and veneer of continuity that these places evoke lie complex transformations in practice and structure that were the unintended consequence of repeatedly inhabiting places, as well as the deliberate actions of agents creating new social memories from the

raw materials of tradition. The emergence of basinwide mortuary mound construction some 5,500 years ago appears to have been an attempt at homogenization of the biographies of communities with distinct social histories. Throughout the subsequent millennia, both mortuaries and past living spaces were largely obscured through routine, transformative practices. These seem largely coeval with ever-widening social horizons, which may have necessitated the reconstitution of shared local histories at the same time as the incorporation of new contacts and alliances. Throughout the preceramic Archaic, despite the diversity in traditional practices in place and shifting scales of social integration, mounds remained active components in daily and ritual life. This highly sedimented landscape was reconfigured as personnel with diverse ancestries were incorporated into local communities during Orange times. New social memories were negotiated through the recombination of both local and regional pasts. Monumental traditions enabled the creation of shared and diverse social memories in times of both social transformation and reproduction.

Writing over a century ago, Jeffries Wyman (1875:11) commented that anyone seeing the St. Johns shell mounds for the first time "might well be excused for doubting that such immense quantities of small shells could have been brought together by human labor." While Wyman accurately recognized mounds as anthropogenic, questions of agency still surround their origins and histories. Decontextualized and repositioned along a complexity continuum, shell mounds and the practices with which they were reproduced rapidly fade as epiphenomena. However, a consideration of the social contexts of their construction indicates that these places, whether they were early settlements, dedicated mortuaries, or ritual platforms, structured and were structured by the complexities of ongoing, and nondirectional, emergent diversity. In this frame of reference the density and distribution of Archaic monuments along the St. Johns is not a reflection of abundant aquatic resources. Instead, the St. Johns was relationally ranked as the center of the world by virtue of the diverse social relationships and cosmologies that could be asserted in place.

References

Adams, W. D.

1976   *Geologic History of Crescent Lake, Florida.* Master's thesis, Department of Geology, University of Florida.

Adler, M. A., and R. H. Wilshusen

1990   Large-Scale Integrative Facilities in Tribal Societies: Cross-Cultural and Southwestern US Examples. *World Archaeology* 22(2):133–146.

Arnold, J. E.

1995   Transportation Innovation and Social Complexity among Maritime Hunter-Gatherer Societies. *American Anthropologist* 37(4):733–747.

Aten, L. E.

1999   Middle Archaic Ceremonialism at Tick Island, Florida: Ripley P. Bullen's 1961 Excavations at the Harris Creek Site. *Florida Anthropologist* 52(3):131–200.

Austin, R. J., and R. W. Estabrook

2000   Chert Distribution and Exploitation in Peninsular Florida. *Florida Anthropologist* 53(2–3):116–130.

Barnard, A.

1999   Images of Hunters and Gatherers in European Social Thought. In *The Cambridge Encyclopedia of Hunters and Gatherers*, edited by R. B. Lee and R. Daly, pp. 375–383. Cambridge University Press, Cambridge.

2004   Hunting-and-Gathering Society: An Eighteenth-Century Scottish Invention. In *Hunter-Gatherers in History, Archaeology, and Anthropology*, edited by A. Barnard, pp. 31–13. Berg, New York.

Barrett, J. C.

1994   *Fragments from Antiquity: An Archaeology of Social Life in Britain, 2900–1200 BC.* Blackwell, Oxford.

1999   The Mythical Landscapes of the British Iron Age. In *Archaeologies of Landscape: Contemporary Perspectives*, edited by W. Ashmore and A. B. Knapp, pp. 253–265. Blackwell, Malden, Massachusetts.

Bernardini, W.

2004   Hopewell Geometric Earthworks: A Case Study in the Referential and Experiential Meaning of Monuments. *Journal of Anthropological Archaeology* 23:331–356.

Bourdieu, Pierre

1977   *Outline of a Theory of Practice.* Cambridge University Press, Cambridge.

Bradley, R.

1998   *The Significance of Monuments.* Routledge, London.

2002   *The Past in Prehistoric Societies.* Routledge, New York.

2003   The Translation of Time. In *Archaeologies of Memory*, edited by R. M. Van Dyke and S. E. Alcock, pp. 221–227. Blackwell, Malden, Massachusetts.

Bullen, R. P.

1955   Stratigraphic Tests at Bluffton, Volusia County, Florida. *Florida Anthropologist* 8(1):1–16.

Clark, J. E., and M. Blake

1994   The Power of Prestige: Competitive Generosity and the Emergence of Ranked Societies in Lowland Mesoamerica. In *Factional Competition and Political Development in the New World*, edited by E. M. Brumfiel and J. W. Fox, pp. 17–30. Cambridge University Press, Cambridge.

Clausen, C. J.

1964   The A-356 Site and the Florida Archaic. Master's thesis, University of Florida, Gainesville.

Connerton, P.

1989   *How Societies Remember.* Cambridge University Press, Cambridge.

Cordell, A. S.

2004   Paste Variability and Possible Manufacturing Origins of Late Archaic Fiber-Tempered Pottery from Selected Sites in Peninsular Florida. In *Early Pottery: Technology, Function, Style and Interaction in the Lower Southeast*, edited by R. Saunders and C. T. Hays, pp. 63–104. University of Alabama Press, Tuscaloosa.

Denevan, W. M.

1992   The Pristine Myth: The Landscape of the Americas in 1492. *Annals of the Association of American Geographers* 82(3):369–385.

Dickel, D. N.

2002   Analysis of Mortuary Patterns. In *Windover: Multidisciplinary Investigations of an Early Archaic Florida Cemetery*, edited by G. H. Doran, pp. 73–96. University Press of Florida, Gainesville.

Doran, G. H.

2002a   Introduction to Wet Sites and Windover (8BR246) Investigations. In *Windover: Multidisciplinary Investigations of an Early Archaic Florida Cemetery*, edited by G. H. Doran, pp. 1–38. University Press of Florida, Gainesville.

2002b   The Windover Radiocarbon Chronology. In *Windover: Multidisciplinary Investigations of an Early Archaic Florida Cemetery*, edited by G. H. Doran, pp. 59–72. University Press of Florida, Gainesville.

Douglass, A. E.
1882   A Find of Ceremonial Axes in a Florida
        Mound. *American Antiquarian and Oriental
        Journal* 4:100–109.
Dunbar, J. S., and B. Waller
1983   A Distribution Analysis of the Clovis/Suwan-
        nee Paleo-Indian Sites of Florida: A Geo-
        graphic Approach. *Florida Anthropologist*
        36(1):18–30.
Dunham, G. H.
1999   Marking Territory, Making Territory: Burial
        Mounds in Interior Virginia. In *Material
        Symbols: Culture and Economy in Prehistory*,
        edited by J. E. Robb. Center for Archaeologi-
        cal Investigations, Southern Illinois Univer-
        sity, Carbondale.
Edmonds, M. R.
1999   *Ancestral Geographies of the Neolithic: Land-
        scape, Monuments and Memory*. Routledge,
        New York.
Endonino, J. C.
2003   Pre-Ceramic Archaic Burial Mounds along
        the St. Johns River, Florida. Paper presented
        at the 59th Annual Southeastern Archaeo-
        logical Conference, Charlotte, North Caro-
        lina.
2007   A Reevaluation of the Gainesville, Ocala, and
        Lake Panasoffkee Quarry Clusters. *Florida
        Anthropologist* 60(2–3):77–96.
2009   The Thornhill Lake Archaeological Research
        Project: 2005–2008. *Florida Anthropologist*
        61:149–165.
Feinman, G. M.
1995   The Emergence of Inequality: A Focus on
        Strategies and Processes. In *Foundations of
        Social Inequality*, edited by T. D. Price and
        G. M. Feinman, pp. 255–279. Plenum Press,
        New York.
Flanagan, J. G.
1989   Hierarchy in Simple "Egalitarian" Societies.
        Annual Review of Anthropology 18:245–266.
Fogelson, R. D.
1989   The Ethnohistory of Events and Nonevents.
        Ethnohistory 36:133–147.
Forty, A.
1999   Introduction. In *The Art of Forgetting*, edited
        by A. Forty and S. Küchler, pp. 1–18. Berg,
        New York.
Gibson, J. L., and P. J. Carr
2004   Big Mounds, Big Rings, Big Power. In *Signs of
        Power: The Rise of Cultural Complexity in the
        Southeast*, edited by J. L. Gibson and P. J. Carr,
        pp. 1–9. University of Alabama Press, Tusca-
        loosa.

Goggin, J. M.
1952   *Space and Time Perspectives in Northern
        St. Johns Archaeology, Florida*. University
        Press of Florida, Gainesville.
Gosden, C., and G. Lock
1998   Prehistoric Histories. *World Archaeology*
        30(1):2–12.
Gosden, C., and Y. Marshall
1999   The Cultural Biography of Objects. *World
        Archaeology* 31(2):169–178.
Hamilton, F. E.
1999   Southeastern Archaic Mounds: Examples
        of Elaboration in a Temporally Fluctuat-
        ing Environment? *Journal of Anthropological
        Archaeology* 18:344–355.
Hayden, B.
1994   Competition, Labor, and Complex Hunter-
        Gatherers. In *Key Issues in Hunter-Gatherer
        Research*, edited by E. S. Burch, Jr., and L. J.
        Ellanna, pp. 223–239. Berg, Oxford.
1995   Pathways to Power: Principles for Creat-
        ing Socioeconomic Inequalities. In *Founda-
        tions of Social Inequality*, edited by T. D. Price
        and G. M. Feinman, pp. 15–86. Plenum Press,
        New York.
Hobsbawm, E. J.
1983   Introduction: Inventing Tradition. In
        The Invention of Tradition, edited by E. J.
        Hobsbawm and T. O. Ranger, pp. 1–14. Cam-
        bridge University Press, New York.
Holtorf, C.
1998   The Life-Histories of Megaliths in
        Mecklenburg-Vorpommern (Germany).
        World Archaeology 30(1):23–38.
Keen, I.
2006   Constraints on the Development of Enduring
        Inequalities in Late Holocene Australia. *Cur-
        rent Anthropology* 47(1):7–38.
Kelly, R. L.
1995   *The Foraging Spectrum*. Smithsonian Institu-
        tion Press, Washington, D.C.
Küchler, S.
1993   Landscape as Memory: The Mapping of Pro-
        cess and Its Representation in a Melanesian
        Society. In *Landscape: Politics and Perspec-
        tives*, edited by B. Bender, pp. 85–106. Berg,
        Oxford.
1999   The Place of Memory. In *The Art of For-
        getting*, edited by A. Forty and S. Küchler,
        pp. 53–72. Berg, New York.
Lee, R. B., and R. Daly
1999   Introduction: Foragers and Others. In *The
        Cambridge Encyclopedia of Hunters and
        Gatherers*, edited by R. Lee and R. Daly,

pp. 1–19. Cambridge University Press, Cambridge.

Marquardt, W.

1985   Complexity and Scale in the Study of Fisher-Gatherer-Hunters: An Example from the Eastern United States. In *Prehistoric Hunter-Gatherers: The Emergence of Cultural Complexity*, edited by T. D. Price and J. A. Brown, pp. 59–98. Academic Press, Orlando, Florida.

1988   Politics and Production among the Calusa of South Florida. In *Hunters and Gatherers, Volume 1: History, Evolution, and Social Change*, edited by T. Ingold, D. Riches, and J. Woodburn, pp. 161–188. Berg, Washington, D.C.

McGee, R. M., and R. J. Wheeler

1994   Stratigraphic Excavations at Groves' Orange Midden, Lake Monroe, Volusia County, Florida: Methodology and Results. *Florida Anthropologist* 47(4):333–349.

Milanich, J. T.

1994   *Archaeology of Precolumbian Florida*. University Press of Florida, Gainesville.

Miller, J. J.

1998   *An Environmental History of Northeast Florida*. University Press of Florida, Gainesville.

Mills B. J.

2004   The Establishment and Defeat of Hierarchy: Inalienable Possessions and the History of Collective Prestige Structures in the Pueblo Southwest. *American Anthropologist* 106:238–251.

Milner, G. R., and R. W. Jefferies

1998   The Read Archaic Shell Midden in Kentucky. *Southeastern Archaeology* 17(2):119–132.

Moore, C. B.

1999   *The East Florida Expeditions of Clarence Bloomfield Moore*. Classics in Southeastern Archaeology. University of Alabama Press, Tuscaloosa.

Morphy, H.

1995   Landscape and the Reproduction of the Ancestral Past. In *The Anthropology of Landscape: Perspectives on Place and Space*, edited by E. Hirsch and M. O'Hanlon, pp. 184–209. Clarendon Press, Oxford.

Pauketat, T. R.

2000   The Tragedy of the Commoners. In *Agency in Archaeology*, edited by M.-A. Dobres and J. E. Robb, pp. 113–129. Routledge, London.

2001   A New Tradition in Archaeology. In *The Archaeology of Traditions: Agency and History before and after Columbus*, edited by T. R. Pauketat, pp. 1–16. University Press of Florida, Gainesville.

Pauketat, T. R., and S. M. Alt

2003   Mounds, Memory, and Contested Mississippian History. In *Archaeologies of Memory*, edited by R. M. Van Dyke, pp. 151–179. Blackwell, Malden, Massachusetts.

2005   Agency in a Postmold? Physicality and the Archaeology of Culture-Making. *Journal of Archaeological Method and Theory* 12(3):213–236.

Piatek, B. J.

1994   The Tomoka Mound Complex in Northeast Florida. *Southeastern Archaeology* 13(2):109–118.

Pluciennik, M.

2004   The Meaning of "Hunter-Gatherers" and Modes of Subsistence: A Comparative Historical Perspective. In *Hunter-Gatherers in History, Archaeology, and Anthropology*, edited by A. Barnard, pp. 17–29. Berg, New York.

Price, T. D., and J. A. Brown

1985   Aspects of Hunter-Gatherer Complexity. In *Prehistoric Hunter-Gatherers: The Emergence of Cultural Complexity*, edited by T. D. Price and J. A. Brown, pp. 3–20. Academic Press, Orlando, Florida.

Quitmyer, I. R.

2001   Zooarchaeological Analyses. In *Phase III Mitigative Excavations at Lake Monroe Outlet Midden (8VO53), Volusia County, Florida*, pp. 1–25. Report submitted to U.S. Department of Transportation, Federal Highway Administration, and Florida Department of Transportation, District Five, by Archaeological Consultants, Inc., and Janus Research.

Randall, A. R.

2007   *St. Johns Archaeological Field School 2005: Hontoon Island State Park*. Technical Report No. 7. Laboratory of Southeastern Archaeology, Department of Anthropology, University of Florida, Gainesville.

Randall, A. R., and K. E. Sassaman

2005a   (Re)Placing Archaic History. Paper presented at the 70th Annual Meeting of the Society for American Archaeology, March 30–April 3, Salt Lake City.

2005b   *St. Johns Archaeological Field School 2003–2004: Hontoon Island State Park*. Technical Report No. 6. Laboratory of Southeastern Archaeology, Department of Anthropology, University of Florida, Gainesville.

Renouf, M. A. P.

1984   Northern Coastal Hunter-Fishers: An Archaeological Model. *World Archaeology* 16(1):18–27.

Rumsey, A.
1994 The Dreaming, Human Agency and Inscriptive Practice. *Oceania* 65(2):116–130.
Russo, M.
2004 Measuring Shell Rings for Social Inequality. In *Signs of Power: The Rise of Cultural Complexity in the Southeast*, edited by J. L. Gibson and P. J. Carr, pp. 26–70. University of Alabama Press, Tuscaloosa.
Russo, M., B. Purdy, L. A. Newsom, and R. M. McGee
1992 A Reinterpretation of Late Archaic Adaptations in Central-East Florida: Grove's Orange Midden (8Vo2601). *Southeastern Archaeology* 11(2):95–108.
Sahlins, M.
1985 *Islands of History*. University of Chicago Press, Chicago.
Sasaki, K.
1981 Keynote Address: From Affluent Foraging to Agriculture in Japan. In *Affluent Foragers: Pacific Coasts East and West*, edited by S. Koyama and D. H. Thomas, pp. 13–15. Senri Ethnological Studies No. 9. National Museum of Ethnology, Osaka, Japan.
Sassaman, K. E.
2001 Hunter-Gatherers and Traditions of Resistance. In *The Archaeology of Traditions: Agency and History Before and After Columbus*, edited by T. R. Pauketat, pp. 218–236. University Press of Florida, Gainesville.
2003a *St. Johns Archaeological Field School, 2000–2001: Blue Spring and Hontoon Island State Parks*. Technical Report No. 4. Laboratory of Southeastern Archaeology, Department of Anthropology, University of Florida, Gainesville.
2003b New AMS Dates on Orange Fiber-Tempered Pottery from the Middle St. Johns Valley and Their Implications for Culture History in Northeast Florida. *Florida Anthropologist* 56(1):5–14.
2004 Common Origins and Divergent Histories in the Early Pottery Traditions of the American Southeast. In *Early Pottery: Technology, Function, Style and Interaction in the Lower Southeast*, edited by R. Saunders and C. T. Hays, pp. 23–39. University of Alabama Press, Tuscaloosa.
Sassaman, K. E., and M. J. Heckenberger
2004 Crossing the Symbolic Rubicon in the Southeast. In *Signs of Power: The Rise of Cultural Complexity in the Southeast*, edited by J. L. Gibson and P. J. Carr, pp. 214–233. University of Alabama Press, Tuscaloosa.

Sassaman, K. E., and A. R. Randall
2007 The Cultural History of Bannerstones in the Savannah River Valley. *Southeastern Archaeology* 26(2):196–211.
Saunders, J.
2004 Are We Fixing to Make the Same Mistake Again? In *Signs of Power: The Rise of Cultural Complexity in the Southeast*, edited by C. C. Gibson and P. J. Carr, pp. 146–161. University of Alabama Press, Tuscaloosa.
Saunders, R.
2004 Spatial Variation in Orange Culture Pottery: Interaction and Function. In *Early Pottery: Technology, Function, Style and Interaction in the Lower Southeast*, edited by R. Saunders and C. T. Hays, pp. 40–62. University of Alabama Press, Tuscaloosa.
Sears, W. H.
1960 The Bluffton Burial Mound. *Florida Anthropologist* 13(2–3):55–60.
Shennan, S.
1983 Monuments: An Example of Archaeologists' Approach to the Massively Material. *RAIN* 59:9–11.
Sherratt, A.
1990 The Genesis of Megaliths: Monumentality, Ethnicity and Social Complexity in Neolithic North-West Europe. *World Archaeology* 22(2):147–167.
Shils, E.
1981 *Tradition*. University of Chicago Press, Chicago.
Tilley, C.
1994 *A Phenomenology of Landscape: Places, Paths and Monuments*. Berg, Oxford.
Trigger, B. G.
1990 Monumental Architecture: A Thermodynamic Explanation of Symbolic Behavior. *World Archaeology* 22(2):119–132.
Tucker, B. D.
2009 Piercing the Seasonal Round: Isotopic Investigations of Archaic Period Subsistence and Settlement in the St. Johns River Drainage, Florida. Unpublished Ph.D. dissertation, Department of Anthropology, University of Florida, Gainesville.
Upchurch, S. B., R. N. Strom, and M. G. Nuckels
1982 *Methods of Chert Provenance: Determination of Florida Cherts*. Report prepared for the Florida Division of Archives, History, and Records Management, Bureau of Historic Sites and Properties, Tallahassee.
Van Dyke, R. M.
2003 Memory and the Construction of Chacoan

Society. In *Archaeologies of Memory*, edited by R. M. Van Dyke and S. E. Alcock, pp. 180–200. Blackwell, Malden, Massachusetts.

Van Dyke, R. M., and S. E. Alcock

2003   Archaeologies of Memory: An Introduction. In *Archaeologies of Memory*, edited by R. M. Van Dyke and S. E. Alcock, pp. 1–14. Blackwell, Malden, Massachusetts.

Watts, W. A., E. C. Grimm, and T. C. Hussey

1996   Mid-Holocene Forest History of Florida and the Coastal Plain of Georgia and South Carolina. In *Archaeology of the Mid-Holocene Southeast*, edited by K. E. Sassaman and D. G. Anderson, pp. 28–38. University Press of Florida, Gainesville.

Wheeler, R. J., and R. M. McGee

1994   Technology of Mount Taylor Occupation, Groves Orange Midden (8VO2601), Volusia County, Florida. *Florida Anthropologist* 47: 350–379.

Wheeler, R. J., C. L. Newman, and R. M. McGee

2000   A New Look at the Mount Taylor and Bluff-ton Sites, Volusia County, with an Outline of the Mount Taylor Culture. *Florida Anthropologist* 53(2–3):133–157.

White, N. M.

2004   Late Archaic Fisher-Foragers in the Apalachicola-Lower Chattahoochee Valley, Northwest Florida-South Georgia/Alabama. In *Signs of Power: The Rise of Cultural Complexity in the Southeast*, edited by J. L. Gibson and P. J. Carr, pp. 10–25. University of Alabama Press, Tuscaloosa.

Whitley, J.

2002   Too Many Ancestors. *Antiquity* 76(291):119–126.

Wyman, J.

1875   *Fresh-Water Shell Mounds of the St. John's River, Florida*. Peabody Academy of Science, Salem, Massachusetts.

Yoffee, N.

2005   *Myths of the Archaic State: Evolution of the Earliest Cities, States and Civilizations*. Cambridge University Press, Cambridge.

3

Hunter-Gatherer Ritual and Complexity

New Evidence from Poverty Point, Louisiana

Tristram R. Kidder

In recent years, archaeologists have explored notions of hunter-gatherer complexity, which has largely been defined to include those groups that practice the appropriate hunter-gatherer subsistence behavior but demonstrate evidence of economic and political differentiation not seen among ethnographically studied exemplars. As archaeological groups are studied in detail, complexity is emerging at every turn. In North America, complex hunter-gatherers are everywhere—from the Aleutians to south Florida and from the southern California coast to the Maritime Provinces of Canada. Complex hunter-gatherers exist at all times, too. They can be found among the earliest Clovis and Clovis-related occupants of the continent up to historic times, as witnessed by the iconic Calusa and the various Northwest Coast societies. Of course, the validity of these claims turns entirely on the definition(s) of complexity. A restricted reading of what constitutes complexity is likely to exclude most of the hunter-gatherer groups in North America and would restrict the populations to a limited number of places and times.

There have been in recent years a number of definitions of complexity, and more specifically, definitions of hunter-gatherer complexity (Arnold 1993, 1996a, 1996b, ed. 1996, 2000a, 2000b, 2001; Hayden 1994, 1995, 1996; Kim and Grier 2006; Price 1981, 2003; Price and Feinman 1995). Befitting how anthropologists tend to classify hunting and gathering as a form of economic adaptation, discussions of complexity emphasize definitions that privilege the political economy of these societies. Complex hunter-gatherer social groups are generally seen to embody inequalities in political, social, or economic organization. Different authors have stressed certain aspects to the exclusion of others, but the fundamental criteria have been some form of disparity in access to economic or political resources (Ames 2004; Grier 2006; Ingold 1988; Kim and Grier 2006; Koyama and Uchiyama 2006; Sahlins 1968; Shnirelman 1992).

Hunter-Gatherer Complexity

Archaeological fascination with hunter-gatherer complexity is a relatively new phenomenon. In the last forty years the major theoretical thrusts in the study of hunter-gatherer peoples have emphasized cultural and behavioral ecology, which has placed the relationship of these peoples with their environment at the forefront of considerations of behavior (Bettinger 1987, 1991; Binford 2001; Kelly 1995; Winterhalder 2001). These studies have focused on the commonalities of human societies, with hunter/fisher/foragers as the archetype. In recent years, however, there has been an increasing interest in understanding the particular historical trajectories of human societies. In hunter-gatherer archaeology, this has been manifested by the rise of the study of hunter-gatherer complexity. In these instances, archaeologists have been exploring the variability of human societies. Indeed, embedded in the definition of social complexity is the notion not only that groups with more parts and more interacting parts are complex, but more to the point, that the interaction of people and social groups can give rise to novel human social, political, and economic formations. As noted by Corning (2001), "complexity per se is one of the less interesting properties of complex phenomena. The differences, and the unique combined properties (synergies) that arise in each case, are vastly more important than the commonalities." Thus, among hunter-gatherer studies, the notion of studying the universal is giving way to trying to understand the particular. This concept in no way means a rejection of the universal characteristics that underlie human behavior; instead, it directs our attention to the questions that arise from the fact that despite the basic requirements of human biology, and despite common physical, climatic, and resource opportunities and challenges, human societies past and present are incredibly variable and are not only different from one another but also change through time (e.g., Kelly 1995:33–35).

Current research on hunters and gatherers in North America is, in part, a reaction to generations of work that saw non-food-producing societies as relatively unchanged and timeless. In the eastern United States, this form of thinking was best exemplified by Caldwell (1958), who characterized Archaic hunter-gatherer societies as simple and emphasized their slow, gradual accumulation of adaptive characteristics that, in time, allowed them to make the jump to food production. Caldwell was expressing a neo-evolutionary perspective that was then, and is still, widely held. Jennings (1964) did much the same for the Desert West with his Desert Archaic concept. As noted by Winters (1968:191), Archaic hunter-gatherers were treated as "though they were idiots savants capable only of changing styles of artifacts, producing an occasional nicely ground piece of stone, continuously foraging for a precarious and uncertain subsistence, and in general doing little beyond surviving as noble and unspoiled primitives." In most instances, the driving force of social evolution was imputed to physical changes in climate and their attendant effects on natural and geological parameters. In some historical instances, hunter-gatherers were affected by proximity to more advanced food-producing

neighbors, who by virtue of a superior subsistence technology (and the cultural baggage that went with it) in time dominated or transformed the hunter-gatherers into food producers or, by proximity, lent to them some of the characteristics needed to achieve social or political inequality and thus complexity (Price 1995, 2002, 2003).

While there is considerable debate about criteria for defining complexity and thus which groups merit inclusion among the ranks of complex hunter-gatherers, one thing is certain. Among those who study hunters and gatherers, no matter how complex they may or may not be, the archaeological record of North America and elsewhere shows conclusively that these types of societies were highly variable in almost every aspect of their social, political, and economic organization (Panter-Brick et al. 2001; Rowley-Conwy 2001; Sassaman 2004). Scholarship has thus turned from explorations of cultural evolution to historically informed analyses of variance in economic, social, and political dimensions of hunter-gatherer behavior.

However nuanced our analysis of hunter-gatherer complexity, the emphasis on complexity as an aspect of political economy limits the dimensions of investigation and leads to a situation in which, for example, social, symbolic, and ritual aspects are frequently ignored or neglected, especially in the study of the archaeological record (Barnard 2004:6; Jordan 2008). Complexity, however defined, is multidimensional and scalar (O'Shea and Barker 1996), and limiting our study to only one or even several of the many possible axes of variability is problematic (Chapman 1996, 2003). In fact, if we reframe our analysis to encompass neglected social, symbolic, or ritual facets of people who are identified as hunter-gatherers, we challenge the basic configuration of these so-called complex groups as exceptional social units.

If we investigate myth or ritual behavior, for example, we find there is an exceptionally rich and complex worldview embodied among people who derive their subsistence exclusively from hunting, fishing, and foraging (Berndt 1994; Guenther 1999; Lourandos 1988). What, then, is the utility of hunter-gatherer as typological category? As with many anthropological issues once seen as immutable and natural (e.g., race), the concept of hunter-gatherer appears to have increasingly less utility as an exclusive social type (Burch 1994). While only recently seen as a unique characteristic of a limited number of societies in North America and elsewhere, complexity among hunter-gatherers is not exceptional if we reframe the question of what constitutes complexity. To illustrate how we can reevaluate hunter-gatherer complexity, I turn to an analysis of what might be one of the most obvious cases of prehispanic hunter-gatherer complexity, the so-called Poverty Point culture.

The archaeology of social complexity has more often been about what makes complexity—is it institutionalized control of labor, or social inequality, or is it in fact derived from contacts with more advanced societies?—than it is about what complexity makes. In the southeastern United States, the archaeology of social complexity has been invigorated by the discovery of Archaic period hunter-fisher-foragers who constructed architecturally complicated if not complex mounds and monuments involving considerable labor effort and planning to execute (Ames 1999; Gibson 2000; Gibson and Carr 2004; Randall and Sassaman, this volume; Russo 1994, 1996, 2004; Russo and Heide 2001; Sassaman 2004; Saunders and Allen 1994; Saunders et al. 2005; Saunders et al. 1997; Saunders 1994). Because of their antiquity, these sites, mostly located in the Lower Mississippi Valley or in coastal Florida, are pristine examples of the development of hunter-gatherer social complexity. These sites and the societies that constructed them, however, do not easily fall into standard categories of political and/or economic organization wherein inequality is manifest through obvious institutional means such as political ranking. In fact, although these early mound builders seem complex by many definitions—most clearly as manifested in different forms of architecture and what it is presumed to entail (Clark 2004; Widmer 2004)—it is not clear these people ever developed social, political, or economic processes that differ in any way from those of contemporary groups that did not build mounds and monuments (Saunders 2004). There is, however, a widespread sense that the investment in monumental architecture at this time marks a departure from the contemporary norm and certainly from the theoretical expectation of what hunter-gatherers do (or don't do, i.e., make large mounds) (Ames 1999). Thus, complexity among these Archaic societies is taken more or less as a given even though it does not conform to some of the definitions posited for ethnographically identified, generalized hunter-gatherers.

Poverty Point

In the Lower Mississippi Valley especially (Figure 3.1), these early mound sites and mound-building cultures are seen as the antecedents to later Archaic complexity, most notably evident at the Poverty Point site and in the so-called Poverty Point culture. Dating from ca. 3600 to 3000 cal BP, Poverty Point culture is generally acknowledged to be the pinnacle of cultural elaboration for the Archaic period (Gibson 2000; Webb 1982). The people who lived at the Poverty Point site engaged in heretofore unprecedented levels of mound construction and interregional exchange. The Poverty Point site consists of a 3-km^2 complex of more than 765,000 m^3 of mounded earth in six nested, elliptical half-rings, two massive mounds thought by some to be bird-shaped effigies, two conical mounds, and one flat-topped mound (Ford and Webb 1956; Gibson 2000; Kidder 2002; Kidder et al. 2004; Ortmann 2007) (Figure 3.2). The site rests on the eastern edge of Macon Ridge, an ancient braided stream terrace standing roughly 5 m above the Mississippi floodplain to the east. Other settlements of Poverty Point affiliation were distributed across a nearly 2,000-km^2 area of the Lower Mississippi Valley and adjacent upland terraces, with more distant communities throughout the Southeast and midcontinent participating through exchange with core groups (see Byrd 1991). These populations practiced a subsistence system based solely on hunting, fishing, and foraging, with some emphasis on fishing (Fritz and Kidder 1993; Gibson 2000; Jackson 1989, 1991a; Ward 1998). Limited evidence indicates that site occupations spanned all four seasons (Jackson 1986, 1989), and some communities were largely sedentary (Gibson 2006). Although neither long-distance exchange nor mound construction can be considered innovations of Poverty Point culture, the scale of both activities eclipsed anything that came before.

Poverty Point is an unusual site for many reasons, including its remarkable size relative to

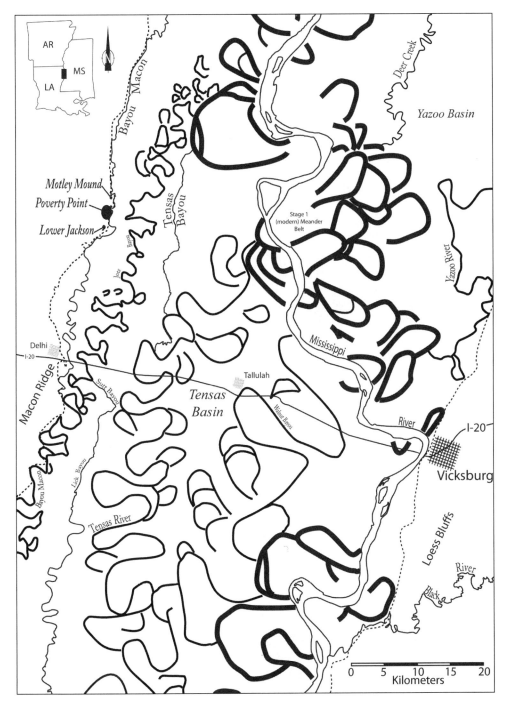

FIGURE 3.1. Map of the Upper Tensas Basin, northeast Louisiana and southeast Arkansas, showing the location of Poverty Point, Motley Mound, and Lower Jackson.

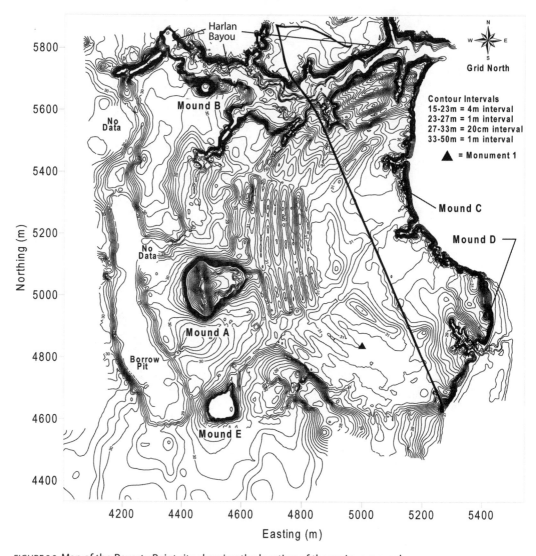

FIGURE 3.2. Map of the Poverty Point site showing the location of the various mounds.

contemporary communities, and its monumental architecture, which is extravagant in the context of North America at any time. However, because archaeologists historically characterize hunter-gatherer societies as having relatively simple social systems that cannot or do not support large, sedentary populations, the development of the site and its monumental architecture has been assumed by some to result from a long period of slow, incremental growth by successive, relatively small populations occupying the site either for brief intervals or during part of a seasonal round (Crothers 2004; Jackson 1991b; Willey 1957). The implication of such a set of assumptions is that the social and political organization of the people living at the site need never have risen above a rudimentary egalitarian level such as that found among generalized hunter-gatherers known from the historic and ethnographic record.

Recent work at Poverty Point challenges this notion of slow, incremental growth and provides evidence to argue the majority of the earthworks may have been constructed over a shorter period of time, perhaps a span of no more than one or two generations. If such a schedule were kept, the size and monumentality of the earthen architecture at Poverty Point would imply the existence of a substantial labor force and a corresponding social structure capable of mobilizing, organizing, and directing the labor force or forces that built these earthworks. One of the most debated aspects of the earthworks at Poverty Point is their implications for population size and sociopolitical complexity. An earth-moving project of this magnitude and sophistication, no matter how protracted over time, required a relatively large pool of labor and a sociopolitical system capable of formally orchestrating monument building while ensuring day-to-day subsistence needs.

Ford and Webb (1956:128; see also Gibson 1973: 127–139) asserted that Poverty Point was home to thousands of people, whose houses were distributed along each of the six nested ridges. However, evidence for an advanced level of sociopolitical organization, much less a large resident population, has not been convincingly demonstrated (on the latter issue, however, see Gibson 2006). Repeated efforts to locate domestic architectural evidence have failed (Connolly 2002). On the other hand, Jackson (1986, 1989, 1991a) argues that Poverty Point could not have sustained a large, sedentary population because it would have rapidly depleted available wild resources, and evidence of such depletion has not been witnessed in small settlements near the Poverty Point sites. He suggests instead that Poverty Point developed as the locus of large-scale trade fairs that integrated widely scattered populations from a large geographic area and provided a physical location for the exchange of goods, mates, and most important, information (Jackson 1991b). Information, he argues, was a prized commodity that was used to minimize risk in an environment of uncertain productivity, uncertainty that resulted from the inability of hunter-gatherers to control the biological basis of subsistence production. Monumental architecture was a physical manifestation of the periodic aggregation of ethnically and socially diverse people and served as a means to integrate populations from distant lands through communal work on a common monument (Crothers 2004; Jackson 1991b).

The implication of the various models (implicit and explicit) for mound building at Poverty Point is that the mounds and earthworks at the site were built over a prolonged period of time

and were erected incrementally, possibly on a seasonal basis. Moreover, with the discovery of earlier mound-building cultures in the region, the necessity of explaining Poverty Point diminished because it was no longer unique but rather it supposedly represented the culmination of a very long evolutionary development of hunter-gatherer complexity (Gibson 1994). These two notions, however, were based on assumptions about the archaeology of the Poverty Point site that have never been fully tested. In fact, recent work confirms two critical flaws in these assumptions. First, there is a nearly thousand-year hiatus between the construction of the latest Middle Archaic mounds and the first Poverty Point earthwork, and second, recent work on Mound A at Poverty Point indicates that this massive edifice was constructed in a remarkably brief period of time. In the rest of this chapter, I focus on these findings and use the data to discuss the new history of Poverty Point and its implications for the archaeology of social complexity.

Although the Poverty Point site area has been occupied from Paleoindian times (Webb et al. 1963), the occupation we identify with the Poverty Point material culture at Poverty Point itself appears relatively suddenly about 3600 years cal BP (Connolly 2006; Kidder 2006). Although it was once assumed to represent a continuous outgrowth of earlier Middle Archaic mound building, we now know that the last of the Middle Archaic mounds were erected ca. 4800 cal BP, making a nearly 1,200-year hiatus in mound construction between Middle and Terminal Late Archaic times. Furthermore, there are no sites in the nearly 2,000-km^2 catchment of Poverty Point that are confidently dated to the interval ca. 4800–3800 cal BP. This apparent occupation hiatus is unlikely the effect of localized geological processes such as river avulsion or erosion (Kidder et al. 2008); there simply are very few occupations dated to this time throughout the Mississippi River Valley from Memphis south to Baton Rouge.

The earliest occupations affiliated with the material culture we identify with Poverty Point are stratigraphically associated with what some call the "old humus" layer, or the pre-ridge occupation, which is found beneath the ridges and across much of the terrain fronting the edge of

Macon Ridge. The limited radiocarbon dates for this stratigraphic unit suggest that it formed rapidly, with contemporary dates found across the breadth of the site. Nothing in the extant material culture associated with this stratigraphic unit indicates that it is distinct from what would follow. Moreover, all the material criteria that define the Poverty Point culture are present at this point. There is no antecedent or developmental material culture assemblage (Gibson 2007), although there are fluctuations within specific artifact categories through time.

An intriguing aspect of this earliest Poverty Point assemblage is that it encompasses a bewildering array of morphologically dissimilar projectile point styles. In some instances, there appears to be spatial differentiation of projectile point types (e.g., Motley points are most common in the north sector of the site) as well as other artifact classes (Connolly 2000; Gibson 1973; Webb 1970; Webb et al. 1963), but these styles are not stratigraphically sequential. Throughout the Archaic of the American Southeast a dominant trend through time is the stratigraphic/temporal isolation of distinct morphological styles of projectile points. This trend is often masked by stratigraphic mixing, but in high-resolution stratigraphic contexts it has been duplicated throughout the region and over a long period of time (Chapman 1981; Coe 1964; Morse and Morse 1983:101–103; Schambach 1998:34, 109–116). The implication is that at any one time a local/regional group produces one specific form or a limited range of morphologically related variation that makes it distinctive. The diversity of point styles at Poverty Point is one reason Jackson (1991b) proposes the trade-fair model, suggesting that this variability in morphology is the product of episodic visits by people of different ethnic and/or geographic backgrounds. In contrast, Gibson (2006) argues Poverty Point was the product of a sedentary society's inhabiting of the site on a yearly or nearly year-round basis; however, he has not accounted for the stylistic diversity of point types.

Data on the origins of Poverty Point's occupation are still unclear, but one hypothesis to account for the stylistic diversity is that the site was initially founded and occupied by people of diverse social, ethnic, linguistic, and/or geographically distinct origins (however, cf. Gibson 2007; Sassaman 2004, 2005). The explanation for the founding of the site arguably lies in an as yet unknown but historically distinctive factor or factors that drew together multiple populations from a regionally widespread area. The stratigraphic, radiocarbon, and material culture stylistic evidence suggests that this colonization was abrupt and rapid. At present we cannot identify an obvious exogamous process (e.g., climate, warfare, changes in local hydrology) that can be cited to explain how Poverty Point rose to prominence relative to contemporary sites.

The initial occupation of the site corresponds with only limited earth-moving activities, and the extant radiocarbon data suggest the site was occupied for 100–300 years before much of the monumental architecture was constructed. The first mound building that can be dated took place at Mound B, where a flat-topped earthwork was begun as early as ca. 3600 cal BP, which is coincident with the initial occupation of the site. This mound was added to in a series of at least three more flat-topped mound stages before being terminated by the addition of a conical cap that entombed the existing construction (Ford and Webb 1956; Kidder et al. 2004; Ortmann 2007). The chronology of the termination of the mound is unclear, but it seems to coincide with the onset of ridge construction. One factor often noted about the placement of Mound B is that it is aligned on a direct N–S axis in line with the Lower Jackson Mound, a Middle Archaic tumulus 5 km to the south (Clark 2004; Gibson 1986, 1987, 1999, 2000; Saunders et al. 2001). This axis also incorporates Mounds A and E. Mound A was constructed after Mound B, but Mound E may be contemporary with Mound B. Limited excavation of Mound E failed to provide sufficient materials for dating, but the construction history is an almost exact duplicate of that of Mound B, except E was never terminated by a conical cap (Kidder et al. 2004; Ortmann 2007). The incorporation of Lower Jackson Mound into the developing Poverty Point landscape was not likely an accident and suggests that from the early occupation of the site onward the inhabitants were consciously harking back to the traditions of their past as a way of legitimizing the founding of the community.

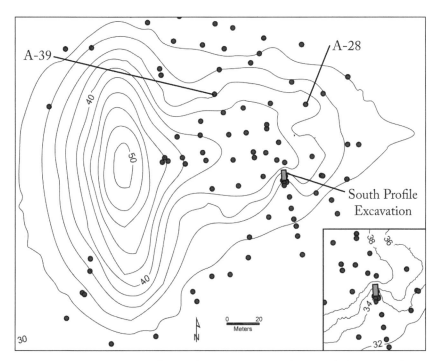

FIGURE 3.3. Topographic map of Mound A at Poverty Point showing the locations of cores and the excavation unit on the south side of the platform. The inset shows details of cores in the South Profile excavation unit.

Archaeology of Mound A at Poverty Point

The central monument that dominates the Poverty Point landscape is Mound A (Figures 3.2, 3.3). This mound is located on the western edge of the site, just to the west of the outermost ridge and roughly equidistant from Mounds B and E (Kidder 2002). Mound A is the second-largest earthen mound in the United States, with an estimated volume of 238,500 m³ of fill. In profile the mound consists of a steep conical portion on the west, rising 22 m above the ground surface and sloping down to a nearly level, 10-m-tall platform. In plan view the mound is very roughly T-shaped. The western arms of the T, comprising the conical part of the mound, have a rough N–S length of 210 m; the length of the mound E–W from cone to the end of the platform is roughly the same distance. Given the size of the mound and its centrality in the settlement, surprisingly little work has been done on Mound A; it is generally thought the mound represents an effigy of a bird flying west, but beyond that assertion there has been little attempt to explain or understand

the mound itself or to place it in the context of the site and its history. To better understand the construction history of this massive earthwork and to explore its place in Poverty Point's settlement history, we excavated a 10-m-deep profile into the south side of the mound's platform; in addition, we removed 89 cores from across the mound and its adjacent slopes using a Giddings Soil Coring Rig. This work has produced a consistent stratigraphic sequence that allows us to understand the preconstruction landscape and the construction history of Mound A (Kidder et al. 2009).

The ground surface on which the mound would be built was originally a natural wet depression, or swale. Similar water-filled features can be seen today on Macon Ridge, and depending on depth they hold water for much of the year but periodically dry out in very dry times. The premound depression was 1–2 m deep. The depression is entirely isomorphic with the mound. This premound surface is composed of very dark brown/black clay-rich silt. Like modern swales, the one beneath Mound A was originally thickly

FIGURE 3.4. Photographs of the contact between the premound sediment and the overlying Stage I and Stage II mound deposits in the South Profile excavation. (A) The contact between the submound (Ab horizon) and the Stage I sediments (light-colored deposit above the dark Ab), showing the exceptionally sharp boundary between these deposits. The box shows the area illustrated in B. (B) Detail showing a close-up of the contact between the submound dark sediment and the overlying mound stages. (C) "Flame structures," or ribbons of darker sediment (on right of image marked by arrow), from the submound extruded into the Stage I layer when the Stage II deposit was rapidly emplaced over these strata.

vegetated. We found abundant uncarbonized roots in the premound sediments, and micromorphological samples show the presence of intact root systems in their original orientation extending downward from the surface of these deposits. The sediments beneath Mound A contained abundant fired earth, burned and unburned organic matter, natural concretions, and numerous rounded, small pebble- to sand-sized quartz and unidentified mineral grains we interpret as bird or turtle gastroliths. Despite screening for microartifacts, we found no chipped stone nor did we recover fired clay pieces or other artifacts that are ubiquitous in cultural deposits elsewhere on the site. One radiocarbon date from the premound dark sediment indicates that charcoal (possibly natural but of unknown origin) was deposited as early as ca. 3950 cal BP. Three other radiocar-

bon dates, all from short-lived plant parts, one of which came from a piece of uncarbonized root, indicate that the depression was abruptly covered by mound deposits ca. 3036 cal BP (Kidder et al. 2009:104–115).

The process of mound building began with clearing the swale. Abundant charcoal and fired earth suggests that the process involved burning the vegetation. The initial construction of the mound was the deposition of a 5–25-cm-thick layer of gray to grayish-white fine silt (labeled Stage I). This first construction stage was deposited rapidly and covers the entire premound swale. The contact between the premound sediments and the Stage I deposits is remarkably sharp, and there is no evidence of animal or plant disturbance from the Stage I deposits into the underlying Ab horizon (Figures 3.4 and 3.5). This silt

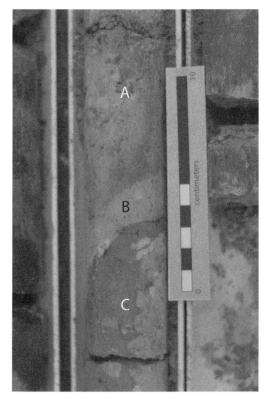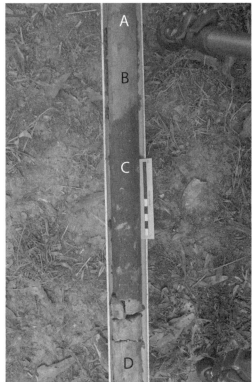

FIGURE 3.5. The stratigraphic sequence in Mound A as demonstrated in core A-28 (*left*) and core A-39, showing the variegated Stage II mound (A), light-colored Stage I (B), and the dark submound (Ab horizon) (C). In core A-39 the natural Eb horizon (D) beneath the buried Ab is visible at the bottom of the core. The top of the cores is to the top of the image. For core location, see Figure 3.3.

is unusual because such light-colored silts are not common on the surface of Macon Ridge; they are found only in certain soil associations at depths in excess of 75 cm below the surface (Allen 1990; Allen and Touchet 1990; Weems et al. 1977). Thus, procuring very pure deposits of these silts in a quantity sufficient to cover the entire premound depression required a great deal of labor and is reasonably inferred to be a very deliberate act. The Stage I silt level was in turn very rapidly covered by multicolored (predominantly orange, tan, red, and yellow-hued sediments) nearly pure silts that comprised the Stage II mound fill.

Once started, the Stage II mound construction proceeded at a remarkably rapid pace. The western, conical portion of the mound was initiated first. Sediments used to build this mound came from nearby borrow areas and are highly weathered, suggesting that they were stripped from near the surface. The eastern platform was

built after the conical portion had been erected. Sediments used to construct this portion of the mound were less weathered and probably came from deeper parts of borrow areas or from different borrow areas than the materials used to make the cone. Borrow areas have been located to the north and west of the mound at distances ranging from 50 m to more than 500 m.

Mound fill accumulated so rapidly that we cannot detect evidence of construction hiatuses or pauses of sufficient duration to promote the formation of either organically enriched A-horizons or erosion wash on sloping construction surfaces. Despite analysis at the macro- and microscopic levels, there is no evidence to indicate the mound construction surfaces were exposed to rainfall or were open long enough for insects, animals, or plants to disturb the soil. No hearths, features, living surfaces, or other evidence of mound use or function have been detected. The fill used to construct the mound was remarkably free of cultural debris. Despite systematic sampling of mound fill sediments, only eight macro-artifacts of certain cultural origin were recovered (Kidder et al. 2009:Table 5).

After its completion, Mound A was never used by the inhabitants for any obvious function with a material signal. Excavations by Ford in 1954, and again by Haag in the early 1970s, failed to yield evidence of any structures, postholes, pits, or other features on the summit of the platform (Ford 1954, 1955a, 1955b, 1969; Ford and Webb 1956; Haag 1990; Kidder et al. 2009:17–27). Earlier work by Moore (1913) on the summit of the cone likewise resulted in negative evidence for use. Examination of the mound's slopes and the fields immediately around the mound has produced no evidence of activities on or around the mounds. Thus, the mound neither supported perishable architecture nor contained any stages, floors, occupation surfaces, or features. If the summit of the cone or the platform was ever used for any activities, the occupants of the site fastidiously cleaned up after themselves.

Reading the Record of Mound A

Mound A is only one of five earthen mounds at Poverty Point. In addition to the mounds, the earthen architecture at Poverty Point included the construction of six semicircular ridges, each estimated to be between 20 and 40 m wide and standing 1.5–3 m tall. The ridges have a cumulative estimated length of 18–21 km. Depending on how one calculates the volume of fill, the total amount of earth moved at Poverty Point is estimated to be 665,163–764,555 m³. When we consider that this effort was accomplished solely by manual human labor by a populace engaged in a hunting and gathering subsistence economy, it is a remarkable achievement. However, if as has been claimed by some, these constructions are the end product of a nearly thousand-year-long effort, the actual per-person labor investment diminishes considerably. Furthermore, if these labor efforts were accomplished over the length of the Late Archaic occupation at Poverty Point, it suggests that no great political, social, or economic achievement or institution was necessary.

However, Mound A at Poverty Point was built in a single construction over a very short period of time. Two types of data support our conclusion of rapid mound construction. First, the Stage I silt horizon found on top of the premound deposit was emplaced rapidly over the entire submound depression immediately after the vegetation was burned, and it was then buried so quickly that there was no time for plants to grow or insects to burrow into or through it. The mound (Stage II) was then erected over this and was done so swiftly that the underlying submound sediments were squeezed upward by the weight of the mound fill and extruded in places through the Stage I layer. This process suggests that the mound fill was loaded remarkably quickly across the entire extent of the mound while the submound sediments were still wet and plastic. Second, the complete lack of any signs of weathering indicates there was no cessation in construction once the building was begun. We are especially struck by the complete absence within the mound of any indications of exposure to water, such as wash episodes, erosion deposits, or, at the microscopic level, even raindrop splash signatures (Kidder et al. 2009:92–97, 115–116).

The absence of weathering and most especially the absence of erosion provide compelling evidence Mound A was built rapidly. Northeast Louisiana has an average monthly rainfall of 11.35 cm; summer and fall are the driest seasons with 9.75 cm of rain per month for the June–November period (Thompson et al. 1983). Over 120 years of climate records for northeast Louisiana document only two years during which no rain fell for an entire month. Even so, in October, the driest month, there are on average 5.3 days with precipitation greater than 3 mm. Evaluation of the regional climate records indicates that the probability that a rain-free period will last longer than 25 days is £0.01 percent; there is zero percent probability that there will be no rain for a period longer than two months (Helfert 1978:Table XIX; Thompson et al. 1983:Tables 8, 13). Thus, it is hard to believe that the reason we did not pick up evidence of erosion, slope wash, or water sorting on multiple sloping surfaces is because there was a prolonged drought. Although these data are only for the historic instrument record, they indicate that it is highly unlikely for there to be a rain-free period in northeast Louisiana for more than a month. Because the loess-derived silt used to

42

construct the platform of Mound A is highly susceptible to erosion and mobilization during even the briefest rain event (Weems et al. 1977), it is unlikely that weathering is being masked by the construction materials or methods. We conclude that Mound A was built in a period no more than 90 days, and we cannot falsify a hypothesis that it was built in an even shorter time span. Gibson (2000:79–110) also has mustered evidence to suggest the ridges were built rapidly, perhaps in a period of two or fewer generations.

Lost amid the interest in early (Middle and Late Archaic) mound building in the lower Mississippi Valley and its implications for labor effort, social structure, and complexity has been the question of why these structures were built and what they were built for (but see Anderson 2002, 2004; Gibson 1994:177–179). With one doubtful exception (Monte Sano), there is no evidence that they were erected as burial tumuli. In no instance is there evidence that these mounds served as platforms for perishable structures; the majority appear to have been erected rapidly and contain few if any features or inclusions. In fact, the available evidence indicates that these mounds were constructed to entomb something—at the Middle Archaic Frenchmen's Bend and Monte Sano sites, it was a structure or structures, and the same appears to be true for Poverty Point's Mound C (Ortmann 2007:148–181), while at Mound A, it was a wetland. In fact, in the absence of evidence for uses of the mound surfaces, attempts to explain these mounds and their function ultimately turn on their ritual role as a way of materializing rapidly emerging or coalescing corporate group identity.

Mound building in eastern North America is usually studied as a means to explore the function of the completed edifice. Mounds are generally seen as serving two distinct (but occasionally complementary) roles. The first is as a container for the dead. The classic expression of this function is in the Middle Woodland, when burial in (usually) conical or dome-shaped mounds was common. Mounds were erected to house the dead and to serve as a memorial to those contained within. An extension of this function is the notion that mounds as places for the dead further serve to demarcate space and to act as a marker for group (or subgroup) claims to territo-

rial identity (Buikstra and Charles 1999; Charles and Buikstra 1983; Charles et al. 1986). A second function, understood both from archaeological data and from ethnohistoric accounts of contact-period Mississippian societies, is as a platform for perishable architecture, usually the homes of elites or religious structures of some sort (Knight 1986, 2006). In both instances, the mound itself was of importance because it served as the foundation for or container of the social function being expressed. Knight (1986:678–679), however, specifically acknowledges that constructing the mound itself is the important symbolic act, one that draws on the community or some subset of the community (e.g., clan, kin units) to act as a group and thus serves to express corporate unity.

The question of mound function may be misplaced if by function we mean the end product and its use as a complete, unitary form. As noted by Richards, our perception of mounds "reflects our perspective on architecture so we tend to think about monuments, as we do other buildings, by privileging their built form" (2004:73). Mound construction may be a means to an end—as in Middle Woodland burial mounds or Mississippian platforms—but there is no reason to think that Mound A at Poverty Point was erected only to serve a purpose in its final form. Indeed, the evidence suggests the opposite. Instead, given the structured pattern of sediments used in the building of Mound A, its location over a wetland, and its history of remarkably rapid construction, it seems reasonable to think that the mound can be understood as a ritual feature whose significance lies in its building. Specifically, we can hypothesize that the construction of Mound A was the recapitulation of creation as recorded in historic mythology (see also Gibson 2000:109).

Historic Indians of the Southeast emphasize two creation myths (Bushnell 1910; Grantham 2002; Lankford 1987; Swanton 1907, 1917, 1929, 1931). Most common is the emergence myth, in which humans were created within the earth from clay by a spirit and emerged from a precreated formlessness to populate the earth. In Choctaw mythology the place of emergence was a mound (specifically identified with a mound site known as Nanih Waiya in Mississippi) that served as a conduit for different people, including the Choctaw, to emerge (Blitz 1993; Carleton

1996). Another myth was that of the Earth Diver (Hall 1997:17–23). In this myth, animals who populated the formless, watery chaos of precreation agree that one of their members must seek something on which creation may rest. A member is elected (most commonly Crawfish, at least in the tales of the Southeast), and after a mighty struggle it succeeds in capturing a speck of dirt from beneath the water. This speck of dirt expands to be the earth and while wet and still plastic is given shape by the beating of the wings of a bird (usually Eagle). These two mythic forms are generally separate but in some cases seem to have overlaps within specific groups such as the Choctaw and the Chitimacha (which likely reflects their tangled postcontact histories). In the emergence myth the symbolism of humans being created of the earth and their emergence from the earth demonstrates the latent force immanent in the earth as a repository of all creation. In Choctaw myth and history this latency is given physical form as the mound known as Nanih Waiya. Furthermore, the historic tribes recognized this myth as an explanation for specific corporate claims to territory and as a means to "legitimate descent-based principles of corporate group formation" (Blitz 1993:34).

Mound A at Poverty Point can be read as the story of creation. The wet depression beneath the mound, readily seen as a dark, formless void on the landscape, was rapidly buried beneath the initial mound stage of gray to white nearly pure silt. This silt entombs the low depression—quite literally—and seals off the watery darkness of chaotic precreation from the created world of light and form. The color symbolism of the dark premound sediment and the light-colored Stage I deposit is in keeping with historically recorded ideas about the colors of creation and their linkages to chaos (dark) and order (light) (Cobb and Drake 2008; DeBoer 2005). Above this was built, in remarkably rapid fashion, an original version of Nanih Waiya, the "Mother Mound" (Carleton 1996). The rapid construction of this edifice required remarkable effort and the cooperation of every able-bodied person at Poverty Point and many of those living in nearby and surrounding communities. The effort of construction was the embodiment of the creation of a new community that through the building of Mound A celebrated and commemorated its novel society. We hypoth-esize that the function of Mound A was to bind together a diverse community and to symbolize, through the ritual theater of its creation and its recapitulation of the mythic story of emergence, a new social order. Through this and other practices, the diverse genesis of the original founders of Poverty Point was erased and a new identity was forged.

Mound Building and Hunter-Gatherer Complexity

Mounds in the Southeast (and monumental architecture elsewhere) are often seen as expressing the consolidation and legitimization of power and authority by some segment of the population that controls access to resources (Pauketat 2000: 117; Trigger 1990). However, ethnographic evidence suggests monumental architecture need not be the product of centralized political authority (Hoskins 1986; Tuzin 2001). At Poverty Point there is no evidence of any developed institutional social ranking based on wealth, materiality, or kinship. In its archaeological manifestation it was a classic egalitarian society. In this vein, Gibson (2004) argues that the construction of the earthworks at Poverty Point derives from freely given labor and an ethos of cooperative sharing. In this assertion he appears to reflect the widespread notion that hunter-gatherers practice a common ethos of egalitarian sharing.

Egalitarian, however, does not mean material equality or political agreement. In fact, as noted by Tuzin (2001:126–128), egalitarianism is "typically a rather savage doctrine.... Competition, not harmony, is the hallmark of egalitarian systems." Societies everywhere manifest inequality in access to resources, political power, and ritual prestige, among many possible factors (Flanagan 1989). Egalitarian social systems are different in part because inequalities in social structure are masked by rules and ideologies that ostensibly prohibit the accumulation and perpetuation of social, political, and economic imbalances through heredity and hierarchy. Egalitarian societies exhibit mechanical solidarity wherein there is minimal differentiation in occupational and social structure. The minimal social unit is, in theory, functionally independent and self-sufficient. This independence is illusory, however, because no human society is truly autonomous.

The most common form of interdependency is manifest in marital exchanges and rules governing such interactions. However, beyond marital exchange, many if not most societies practice other forms of like-for-like exchanges, the logic of which is to produce interdependency either for its own sake or for the collateral benefits that derive (or are perceived to derive) from such a contrived interaction.

Archaeologists studying hunter-gatherer societies have seen these exchanges in the context of information flow with a practical rationale of reducing uncertainty in a risk-prone world. However, it is critical to recognize that these exchanges are initially motivated and derived by social and/or symbolic factors regardless of the material baggage that comes with them. The labor needed to build Mound A may well have been one of these like-for-like exchanges. This labor and effort, undergirded by mythic structure and given tangible form by ritual practices in the building of the mound, was needed to create a unified society from dissimilar social groups that came from different geographic localities and likely brought to the initial founding of Poverty Point a diversity of symbolic and ritual practices inimical to the existence of a stable functioning and unified society.

Conclusion

The rapid construction of Mound A, not to mention the building of the other mounds and monuments at Poverty Point, reminds us that complexity per se is not always the interesting thing. Here I argue Mound A is a ritual marker and explicitly materialized expression of the creation of a new community. To the extent this is true, we can see in the outcome of this practice a novel social formation. We might term this a self-organizing phenomenon. Mound A implies a level of ritual complexity that rivals anything seen in what are traditionally considered to be far more advanced societies. Even if there is no evidence of

social, political, or economic inequality at Poverty Point (all of which were likely bound up in the process of the construction of this mound but are not readily visible in the archaeological record), the building of this monument tells us that understanding complexity requires a more expansive view of the term and its implications. Intrinsically, all human societies are complex—because they have many parts and many interacting parts but also because the interaction of the parts leads to novel self-organizing behaviors. The issue is not whether hunter-gatherers are complex, but in what way they are complex and how, if at all, this complexity differs from the properties found in any other society (see also Nelson 1995:599).

The history of the Poverty Point site suggests that its population developed rapidly by integrating (or assimilating?) diverse groups from a wide area of the Lower Mississippi Valley and adjacent regions. Typically, external processes, such as climate change or warfare, are cited to explain these transformations. However, we do not necessarily need to invoke only exogamous processes. Corporate groups emerge with the coincidence of residential permanence, delayed consumption, and exchange (Anderson 2002, 2004). Poverty Point witnessed all three. There is no evidence that the subsistence pursuits of Poverty Point's hunter-gatherers demanded collective efforts. However, the erection of monumental architecture clearly did. The effort required for building this monumental architecture was not directed in an immediate and obvious way toward biological reproduction and thus must be understood in the context of the reproduction of social formations. Within the broader context of the commonalities of human biological needs, the people inhabiting Poverty Point, like all people, developed a unique culture which was driven by its own history and which must be understood in the light of this history.

References

Allen, Thurman
1990   Soils: Poverty Point. *Louisiana Archaeology* 13:163–200.
Allen, Thurman E., and B. Arville Touchet
1990   Geomorphic Evolution and Soils. In *Search*

for the Lost Sixth Ridge: The 1989 Excavations at Poverty Point, edited by J. L. Gibson, pp. 21–25. Report No. 9. Center for Archaeological Studies, University of Southwestern Louisiana, Lafayette.

Ames, Kenneth M.

1999   The Myth of the Hunter-Gatherer. *Archaeology* September/October:45–49.

2004   Supposing Hunter-Gatherer Variability. *American Antiquity* 69:364–374.

Anderson, David G.

2002   The Evolution of Tribal Social Organization in the Southeast. In *The Archaeology of Tribal Societies*, edited by W. A. Parkinson, pp. 246–277. Archaeological Series No. 15. International Monographs in Prehistory, Ann Arbor, Michigan.

2004   Archaic Mounds and the Archaeology of Southeastern Tribal Societies. In *Signs of Power: The Rise of Complexity in the Southeast*, edited by J. L. Gibson and P. J. Carr, pp. 270–299. University of Alabama Press, Tuscaloosa.

Arnold, Jeanne E.

1993   Labor and the Rise of Complex Hunter-Gatherers. *Journal of Anthropological Archaeology* 12:75–119.

1996a   The Archaeology of Complex Hunter-Gatherers. *Journal of Archaeological Method and Theory* 3:77–126.

1996b   Organizational Transformations: Power and Labor among Complex Hunter-Gathers and Other Intermediate Societies. In *Emergent Complexity: The Evolution of Intermediate Societies*, edited by J. E. Arnold, pp. 59–73. Archaeological Series No. 9. International Monographs in Prehistory, Ann Arbor, Michigan.

2000a   The Origins of Hierarchy and the Nature of Hierarchical Structures in Prehistoric California. In *Hierarchies in Action: Cui Bono?* edited by M. W. Diehl, pp. 221–240. Occasional Paper No. 27. Center for Archaeological Investigations, Southern Illinois University, Carbondale.

2000b   Revisiting Power, Labor Rights, and Kinship: Archaeology and Social Theory. In *Social Theory in Archaeology*, edited by M. B. Schiffer, pp. 14–30. University of Utah Press, Salt Lake City.

2001   Social Evolution and the Political Economy in the Northern Channel Islands. In *The Origins of a Pacific Coast Chiefdom: The Chumash of the Channel Islands*, edited by J. E. Arnold, pp. 267–296. University of Utah Press, Salt Lake City.

Arnold, Jeanne E. (editor)

1996   *Emergent Complexity: The Evolution of Intermediate Societies*. Archaeological Series No. 9. International Monographs in Prehistory, Ann Arbor, Michigan.

Barnard, A.

2004   Hunter-Gatherers in History, Archaeology and Anthropology: Introductory Essay. In *Hunter-Gatherers in History, Archaeology and Anthropology*, edited by A. Bernard, pp. 1–13. Berg, Oxford.

Berndt, C.

1994   Mythology. In *The Encyclopaedia of Aboriginal Australia: Aboriginal and Torres Strait Islander History, Society and Culture*, edited by D. Horton. Aboriginal Studies Press, Australian Institute of Aboriginal and Torres Strait Islander Studies, Canberra.

Bettinger, Robert L.

1987   Archaeological Approaches to Hunter-Gatherers. *Annual Review of Anthropology* 16:121–142.

1991   *Hunter-Gatherers: Archaeological and Evolutionary Theory*. Plenum Press, New York.

Binford, Lewis R.

2001   *Constructing Frames of Reference: An Analytical Method for Archaeological Theory Building Using Ethnographic and Environmental Data Sets*. University of California Press, Berkeley.

Blitz, John H.

1993   Locust Beads and Archaic Mounds. *Mississippi Archaeology* 28(1):20–43.

Buikstra, Jane E., and Douglas K. Charles

1999   Centering the Ancestors: Cemeteries, Mounds, and Sacred Landscapes of the Ancient North American Midcontinent. In *Archaeologies of Landscape: Contemporary Perspectives*, edited by W. Ashmore and A. B. Knapp, pp. 201–228. Blackwell, Oxford.

Burch, Ernest S., Jr.

1994   The Future of Hunter-Gatherer Research. In *Key Issues in Hunter-Gatherer Research*, edited by E. S. Burch, Jr., and L. J. Ellanna, pp. 451–455. Berg, Oxford.

Bushnell, David I., Jr.

1910   Myths of the Louisiana Choctaw. *American Anthropologist* 12:526–535.

Byrd, Kathleen M. (editor)

1991   *The Poverty Point Culture: Local Manifestations, Subsistence Practices, and Trade Networks*. Geoscience and Man No. 29. Geoscience Publications, Department of Geography and Anthropology, Louisiana State University, Baton Rouge.

Caldwell, Joseph R.

1958   *Trend and Tradition in the Prehistory of the Eastern United States*. Memoir No. 88. American Anthropological Association, Springfield, Illinois.

Carleton, K.
1996 Nanih Waiya: Mother Mound of the Choctaw. *Common Ground: Archeology and Ethnography in the Public Interest* 1(1). Electronic document, http://www.nps.gov/history/archeology/cg/vo11_num1/mother.htm.

Chapman, Jefferson
1981 *The Bacon Bend and Iddens Sites: The Late Archaic Period in the Lower Little Tennessee River Valley.* University of Tennessee, Department of Anthropology, Report of Investigations No. 31 and Tennessee Valley Authority Publications in Anthropology No. 25. Tennessee Valley Authority, Knoxville.

Chapman, Robert W.
1996 Problems of Scale in the Emergence of Complexity. In *Emergent Complexity: The Evolution of Intermediate Societies*, edited by J. E. Arnold. Archaeological Series No. 9. International Monographs in Prehistory, Ann Arbor, Michigan.
2003 *Archaeologies of Complexity.* Routledge, London.

Charles, Douglas K., and Jane E. Buikstra
1983 Archaic Mortuary Sites in the Central Mississippi Drainage: Distribution, Structure, and Behavioral Implications. In *Archaic Hunters and Gatherers in the American Midwest*, edited by J. L. Phillips and J. A. Brown, pp. 117–145. Academic Press, New York.

Charles, Douglas K., Jane E. Buikstra, and Lyle W. Konigsberg
1986 Behavioral Implications of Terminal Archaic and Early Woodland Mortuary Practices in the Lower Illinois Valley. In *Early Woodland Archaeology*, edited by K. B. Farnsworth and T. E. Emerson, pp. 458–474. Kampsville Seminars in Archeology Vol. 2. Center for American Archeology Press, Kampsville, Illinois.

Clark, John E.
2004 Surrounding the Sacred: Geometry and Design of Early Mound Groups as Meaning and Function. In *Signs of Power: The Rise of Complexity in the Southeast*, edited by J. L. Gibson and P. J. Carr, pp. 162–213. University of Alabama Press, Tuscaloosa.

Cobb, Charles R., and E. Drake
2008 The Colour of Time: Head Pots and Temporal Convergences. *Cambridge Journal of Archaeology* 18:85–93.

Coe, Joffre L.
1964 The Formative Cultures of the Carolina Piedmont. *Transactions of the American Philosophical Society* 54(5):1–130.

Connolly, Robert P.
2000 *2000 Annual Report: Station Archaeology Program at Poverty Point State Commemorative Area.* Louisiana Division of Archaeology, Baton Rouge.
2002 *2002 Annual Report: Station Archaeology Program at Poverty Point State Historic Site.* Louisiana Division of Archaeology, Baton Rouge.
2006 An Assessment of Radiocarbon Age Results from the Poverty Point Site. *Louisiana Archaeology* 27:1–14.

Corning, Peter A.
2001 Complexity Is Just a Word! *Institute for the Study of Complex Systems Commentaries.* Electronic document, http://www.complexsystems.org/commentaries/jan98.htm.

Crothers, George M.
2004 The Green River in Comparison to the Lower Mississippi Valley during the Archaic: To Build Mounds or Not to Build Mounds. In *Signs of Power: The Rise of Complexity in the Southeast*, edited by J. L. Gibson and P. J. Carr, pp. 86–96. University of Alabama Press, Tuscaloosa.

DeBoer, W. R.
2005 Colors for a North American Past. *World Archaeology* 37:66–91.

Flanagan, James G.
1989 Hierarchy in Simple "Egalitarian" Societies. *Annual Review of Anthropology* 18:245–266.

Ford, James A.
1954 Additional Notes on the Poverty Point Site in Northern Louisiana. *American Antiquity* 19(3):282–285.
1955a Poverty Point Excavations. *Science* 122(3169):550–551.
1955b The Puzzle of Poverty Point. *Natural History* 64(9):466–472.
1969 *A Comparison of Formative Cultures in the Americas: Diffusion or the Psychic Unity of Man.* Smithsonian Contributions to Anthropology No. 11. Smithsonian Institution Press, Washington, D.C.

Ford, James A., and Clarence H. Webb
1956 *Poverty Point, a Late Archaic Site in Louisiana.* Anthropological Papers Vol. 46, Pt. 1. American Museum of Natural History, New York.

Fritz, Gayle J., and Tristram R. Kidder
1993 Recent Investigations into Prehistoric Agriculture in the Lower Mississippi Valley. *Southeastern Archaeology* 12:1–14.

Gibson, Jon L.

1973   *Social Systems at Poverty Point: An Analysis of Intersite and Intrasite Variability.* Ph.D. dissertation, Southern Methodist University. University Microfilms, Ann Arbor, Michigan.

1986   Earth Sitting: Architectural Masses at Poverty Point, Northeastern Louisiana. *Louisiana Archaeology* 13:201–237.

1987   The Poverty Point Earthworks Reconsidered. *Mississippi Archaeology* 22(2):14–31.

1994   Before Their Time? Early Mounds in the Lower Mississippi Valley. *Southeastern Archaeology* 13:162–186.

1999   *Poverty Point: A Terminal Archaic Culture in the Lower Mississippi Valley.* 2nd ed. Anthropological Study No. 7. Department of Culture, Recreation and Tourism, Louisiana Archaeological Survey and Antiquities Commission, Baton Rouge.

2000   *The Ancient Mounds of Poverty Point: Place of Rings.* University Press of Florida, Gainesville.

2004   The Power of Beneficent Obligation in First Mound-Building Societies. In *Signs of Power: The Rise of Complexity in the Southeast*, edited by J. L. Gibson and P. J. Carr, pp. 255–269. University of Alabama Press, Tuscaloosa.

2006   Navel of the Earth: Sedentism at Poverty Point. *World Archaeology* 38:311–329.

2007   "Formed from the Earth of That Place": The Material Side of Community at Poverty Point. *American Antiquity* 72:509–523.

Gibson, Jon L., and Philip J. Carr

2004   Big Mounds, Big Rings, Big Power. In *Signs of Power: The Rise of Complexity in the Southeast*, edited by J. L. Gibson and P. J. Carr, pp. 1–9. University of Alabama Press, Tuscaloosa.

Grantham, B.

2002   *Creation Myths and Legends of the Creek Indians.* University Press of Florida, Gainesville.

Grier, Colin

2006   Affluence on the Prehistoric Northwest Coast of North America. In *Beyond Affluent Foragers: Rethinking Hunter-Gatherer Complexity*, edited by C. Grier, J. Kim, and J. Uchiyama, pp. 126–135. Oxbow Books, Oxford.

Guenther, M.

1999   From Totemism to Shamanism: Hunter-Gatherer Contributions to World Mythology and Spirituality. In *The Cambridge Encyclopedia of Hunters and Gatherers*, edited by R. B. Lee and R. Daly, pp. 426–433. Cambridge University Press, Cambridge.

Haag, William G.

1990   Excavations at the Poverty Point Site, 1972–1975. *Louisiana Archaeology* 13:1–36.

Hall, Robert L.

1997   *An Archaeology of the Soul: North American Indian Belief and Ritual.* University of Illinois Press, Urbana.

Hayden, Brian

1994   Competition, Labor, and Complex Hunter-Gatherers. In *Key Issues in Hunter-Gatherer Research*, edited by J. Ernst, S. Burch, Jr., and L. J. Ellanna, pp. 223–242. Berg, Oxford.

1995   Pathways to Power: Principles for Creating Socioeconomic Inequalities. In *Foundations of Social Inequality*, edited by T. D. Price and G. M. Feinman, pp. 15–86. Plenum Press, New York.

1996   Thresholds of Power in Emergent Complex Societies. In *Emergent Complexity: The Evolution of Intermediate Societies*, edited by J. E. Arnold, pp. 50–58. Archaeological Series No. 9. International Monographs in Prehistory, Ann Arbor, Michigan.

Helfert, M. R.

1978   *Climate and Climatic Normals of Monroe, Louisiana, 1887–1977.* Occasional Publications of the Northeast Louisiana University Climatic Research Center No. 1. Northeast Louisiana University, Monroe.

Hoskins, J. A.

1986   So My Name Shall Live: Stone Dragging and Grave Building in Kodi, West Sumba. *Bijdragen tot de Taal-, Land- en Volkenkunde* 142:31–51.

Ingold, Tim

1988   Notes on the Foraging Mode of Production. In *Hunters and Gatherers 1: History, Evolution, and Social Change*, edited by T. Ingold, D. Riches, and J. Woodburn, pp. 269–285. Berg, Oxford.

Jackson, H. Edwin

1986   Sedentism and Hunter-Gatherer Adaptations in the Lower Mississippi Valley: Subsistence Strategies during the Poverty Point Period. Unpublished Ph.D. dissertation, Department of Anthropology, University of Michigan, Ann Arbor.

1989   Poverty Point Adaptive Systems in the Lower Mississippi Valley: Subsistence Remains from the J. W. Copes Site. *North American Archaeologist* 10:173–204.

1991a   Bottomland Resources and Exploitation Strategies during the Poverty Point Period: Implications of the Archaeobiological Record from the J. W. Copes Site. In *The Poverty*

Point Culture: Local Manifestations, Subsistence Practices, and Trade Networks, edited by K. M. Byrd, pp. 131–157. Geoscience and Man No. 29. Louisiana State University, Baton Rouge.

1991b The Trade Fair in Hunter-Gatherer Interaction: The Role of Intersocietal Trade in the Evolution of Poverty Point Culture. In *Between Bands and States*, edited by S. A. Gregg, pp. 265–286. Occasional Papers No. 9. Center for Archaeological Investigations, Southern Illinois University, Carbondale.

Jennings, Jesse D.
1964 The Desert West. In *Prehistoric Man in the New World*, edited by J. D. Jennings and E. Norbeck, pp. 149–174. University of Chicago Press, Chicago.

Jordan, P.
2008 Hunters and Gatherers. In *Handbook of Archaeological Theories*, edited by R. A. Bentley, H. D. G. Maschner, and C. Chippindale, pp. 447–465. AltaMira Press, Lanham, Maryland.

Kelly, R. L.
1995 *The Foraging Spectrum*. Smithsonian Institution Press, Washington, D.C.

Kidder, Tristram R.
2002 Mapping Poverty Point. *American Antiquity* 67:89–101.
2006 Climate Change and the Archaic to Woodland Transition (3000–2600 cal BP) in the Mississippi River Basin. *American Antiquity* 71:195–231.

Kidder, Tristram R., Katherine A. Adelsberger, Lee J. Arco, and Timothy M. Schilling
2008 Basin Scale Reconstruction of the Geological Context of Human Settlement: An Example from Northeast Louisiana, USA. *Quaternary Science Reviews* 27:1255–1270.

Kidder, Tristram R., Lee J. Arco, Anthony L. Ortmann, Timothy M. Schilling, Caroline Boeke, Rachel Bielitz, and Katherine A. Adelsberger
2009 *Poverty Point Mound A: Final Report of the 2005 and 2006 Field Seasons*. Louisiana Division of Archaeology and the Louisiana Archaeological Survey and Antiquities Commission, Baton Rouge.

Kidder, Tristram R., Anthony L. Ortmann, and Thurman Allen
2004 Mounds B and E at Poverty Point. *Southeastern Archaeology* 23:98–113.

Kim, Jangsuk, and Colin Grier
2006 Beyond Affluent Foragers. In *Beyond Affluent Foragers: Rethinking Hunter-Gatherer Complexity*, edited by C. Grier, J. Kim, and

J. Uchiyama, pp. 192–200. Oxbow Books, Oxford.

Knight, Vernon J., Jr.
1986 The Institutional Organization of Mississippian Religion. *American Antiquity* 51:675–687.
2006 Symbolism of Mississippian Mounds. In *Powhatan's Mantle: Indians in the Colonial Southeast*, revised ed., edited by P. H. Wood, G. A. Waselkov, and M. T. Hatley, pp. 421–434. University of Nebraska Press, Lincoln.

Koyama, Shuzo, and Junzo Uchiyama
2006 Why "Beyond Affluent Foragers"? Looking Back at the Original Affluent Foragers Concept. In *Beyond Affluent Foragers: Rethinking Hunter-Gatherer Complexity*, edited by C. Grier, J. Kim, and J. Uchiyama, pp. 1–3. Oxbow Books, Oxford.

Lankford, George E. III
1987 *Native American Legends: Southeastern Legends—Tales from the Natchez, Caddo, Biloxi, Chickasaw, and Other Nations*. August House, Little Rock, Arkansas.

Lourandos, Harry
1988 Paleopolitics: Resource Intensification in Aboriginal Australia and Papua New Guinea. In *Hunters and Gatherers 1: History, Evolution, and Social Change*, edited by T. Ingold, D. Riches, and J. Woodburn, pp. 148–160. Berg, Oxford.

Moore, Clarence B.
1913 Some Aboriginal Sites in Louisiana and Arkansas. *Journal of the Academy of Natural Sciences of Philadelphia* 16:7–99.

Morse, Dan F., and Phyllis A. Morse
1983 *Archaeology of the Central Mississippi Valley*. Academic Press, New York.

Nelson, Ben A.
1995 Complexity, Hierarchy and Scale: A Controlled Comparison between Chaco Canyon, New Mexico, and La Quemada, Zacatecas. *American Antiquity* 60:597–618.

Ortmann, Anthony L.
2007 The Poverty Point Mounds: Analysis of the Chronology, Construction History, and Function of North America's Largest Hunter-Gatherer Monuments. Unpublished Ph.D. dissertation, Department of Anthropology, Tulane University, New Orleans.

O'Shea, John M., and Alex W. Barker
1996 Measuring Social Complexity and Variation: A Categorical Imperative? In *Emergent Complexity: The Evolution of Intermediate Societies*, edited by J. E. Arnold, pp. 13–24. International Monographs in Prehistory, Ann Arbor, Michigan.

Panter-Brick, Catherine, Robert H. Layton, and Peter Rowley-Conwy

2001 Lines of Inquiry. In *Hunter-Gatherers: An Interdisciplinary Perspective*, edited by C. Panter-Brick, R. H. Layton, and P. Rowley-Conwy, pp. 1–11. Cambridge University Press, Cambridge.

Pauketat, Timothy R.

2000 The Tragedy of the Commoners. In *Agency of Archaeology*, edited by M. A. Dobres and J. E. Robb, pp. 113–129. Routledge, London.

Price, T. Douglas

1981 Complexity in "Non-Complex" Societies. In *Archaeological Approaches to the Study of Complexity*, edited by S. van der Leeuw, pp. 55–99. Universiteit van Amsterdam, Amsterdam.

1995 Social Inequality at the Origins of Agriculture. In *Foundations of Social Inequality*, edited by T. D. Price and G. M. Feinman, pp. 129–146. Plenum Press, New York.

2002 Afterword: Beyond Foraging and Collecting; Retrospect and Prospect. In *Beyond Foraging and Collecting: Evolutionary Change in Hunter-Gatherer Settlement Systems*, edited by B. Fitzhugh and J. Habu, pp. 413–425. Kluwer Academic/Plenum, New York.

2003 Emerging Ideas about Complexity Emerging. In *Theory, Method, and Practice in Modern Archaeology*, edited by R. J. Jeske and D. K. Charles, pp. 51–67. Praeger, Westport, Connecticut.

Price, T. Douglas, and Gary M. Feinman

1995 Foundations of Prehistoric Social Inequality. In *Foundations of Social Inequality*, edited by T. D. Price and G. M. Feinman, pp. 3–11. Plenum Press, New York.

Richards, Colin

2004 Labouring with Monuments: Constructing the Dolmen at Carreg Samson, South-West Wales. In *The Neolithic of the Irish Sea: Materiality and Traditions of Practice*, edited by V. Cummings and C. Fowler, pp. 72–80. Oxbow Books, Oxford.

Rowley-Conwy, Peter

2001 Time, Change and the Archaeology of Hunter-Gatherers: How Original Is the 'Original Affluent Society'? In *Hunter-Gatherers: An Interdisciplinary Perspective*, edited by C. Panter-Brick, R. H. Layton, and P. Rowley-Conwy, pp. 39–72. Cambridge University Press, Cambridge.

Russo, Michael

1994 A Brief Introduction to the Study of Archaic Mounds in the Southeast. *Southeastern Archaeology* 13:89–93.

1996 Southeastern Preceramic Archaic Ceremonial Mounds. In *Archaeology of the Mid-Holocene Southeast*, edited by K. E. Sassaman and D. G. Anderson, pp. 259–287. University Press of Florida, Gainesville.

2004 Measuring Shell Rings for Social Inequality. In *Signs of Power: The Rise of Complexity in the Southeast*, edited by J. L. Gibson and P. J. Carr, pp. 26–70. University of Alabama Press, Tuscaloosa.

Russo, Michael, and G. Heide

2001 Shell Rings of the Southeast US. *Antiquity* 75:491–492.

Sahlins, Marshall D.

1968 Notes on the Original Affluent Society. In *Man the Hunter*, edited by R. B. Lee and I. Devore, pp. 85–89. Aldine, Chicago.

Sassaman, Kenneth E.

2004 Complex Hunter-Gatherers in Evolution and History: A North American Perspective. *Journal of Archaeological Research* 12:227–280.

2005 Poverty Point as Structure, Event, Process. *Journal of Archaeological Method and Theory* 12:335–364.

Saunders, Joe W.

2004 Are We Fixing to Make the Same Mistakes Again? In *Signs of Power: The Rise of Complexity in the Southeast*, edited by J. L. Gibson and P. J. Carr, pp. 146–161. University of Alabama Press, Tuscaloosa.

Saunders, Joe W., and Thurman Allen

1994 Hedgepeth Mounds: An Archaic Mound Complex in North-Central Louisiana. *American Antiquity* 59:471–489.

Saunders, Joe, Thurman Allen, Dennis LaBatt, Reca Jones, and David Griffing

2001 An Assessment of the Antiquity of the Lower Jackson Mound. *Southeastern Archaeology* 20:67–77.

Saunders, Joe W., Rolfe D. Mandel, C. Garth Sampson, Charles M. Allen, E. Thurman Allen, Daniel A. Bush, James K. Feathers, Kristen J. Gremillion, C. T. Hallmark, H. Edwin Jackson, Jay K. Johnson, Reca Jones, Roger T. Saucier, Gary L. Stringer, and Malcolm F. Vidrine

2005 Watson Brake, a Middle Archaic Mound Complex in Northeast Louisiana. *American Antiquity* 70:631–668.

Saunders, Joe W., Rolfe D. Mandel, Roger T. Saucier, E. Thurman Allen, C. T. Hallmark, Jay K. Johnson, Edwin H. Jackson, Charles M. Allen, Gary L. Stringer,

Douglas S. Frink, James K. Feathers, Stephen Williams, Kristen J. Gremillion, Malcolm F. Vidrine, and Reca B. Jones

1997 A Mound Complex in Louisiana at 5400–5000 Years before the Present. *Science* 277: 1796–1799.

Saunders, Rebecca

1994 The Case for Archaic Period Mounds in Southeastern Louisiana. *Southeastern Archaeology* 13:118–134.

Schambach, Frank F.

1998 *Pre-Caddoan Cultures in the Trans-Mississippi South.* Research Series No. 53. Arkansas Archeological Survey, Fayetteville.

Shnirelman, Victor A.

1992 Complex Hunter-Gatherers: Exception or Common Phenomenon? *Dialectical Anthropology* 17:183–196.

Swanton, John R.

1907 Mythology of the Indians of Louisiana and the Texas Coast. *Journal of American Folklore* 1907:285–289.

1917 Chitimacha Myths and Beliefs. *Journal of American Folklore* 30:474–478.

1929 *Myths and Tales of the Southeastern Indians.* Bulletin No. 88. Bureau of American Ethnology, Washington, D.C.

1931 *Source Material for the Social and Ceremonial Life of the Choctaw Indians.* Bulletin No. 103. Bureau of American Ethnology, Washington, D.C.

Thompson, Richard C., Robert A. Muller, and Stephen H. Crawford

1983 *Climate at the Northeast Research Station, St. Joseph, Louisiana, 1931–1980.* Bulletin No. 755. Louisiana Agricultural Experiment Station, Baton Rouge.

Trigger, Bruce G.

1990 Monumental Architecture: A Thermodynamic Explanation of Symbolic Behavior. *World Archaeology* 22:119–132.

Tuzin, Donald F.

2001 *Social Complexity in the Making: A Case Study among the Arapesh of New Guinea.* Routledge, London.

Ward, Heather D.

1998 The Paleoethnobotanical Record of the Poverty Point Culture: Implications of Past and Current Research. *Southeastern Archaeology* 17:166–174.

Webb, Clarence H.

1970 Intrasite Distribution of Artifacts at the Poverty Point Site, with Special Reference to Women's and Men's Activities. *Southeastern Archaeological Conference Bulletin* 12:21–34.

1982 *The Poverty Point Culture.* 2nd ed. Geoscience and Man No. 17. Geoscience Publications, Department of Geography and Anthropology, Louisiana State University, Baton Rouge.

Webb, Clarence H., James A. Ford, and Sherwood M. Gagliano

1963 Poverty Point and the American Formative. Ms. on file, Poverty Point State Historic Site, Epps, Louisiana.

Weems, Tracey A., Emmett E. Reynolds, E. Thurman Allen, Charles E. Martin, and Ronnie L. Venson

1977 *Soil Survey of West Carroll Parish, Louisiana.* U.S. Department of Agriculture, Soil Conservation Service, Washington, D.C.

Widmer, Randolph J.

2004 Explaining Sociopolitical Complexity in the Foraging Adaptations of the Southeastern United States: The Rules of Demography, Kinship, and Ecology in Sociocultural Evolution. In *Signs of Power: The Rise of Complexity in the Southeast*, edited by J. L. Gibson and P. J. Carr, pp. 214–233. University of Alabama Press, Tuscaloosa.

Willey, Gordon R.

1957 Review of *Poverty Point, a Late Archaic Site in Louisiana*, by J. A. Ford and C. H. Webb. *American Antiquity* 23:198–199.

Winterhalder, Bruce

2001 The Behavioral Ecology of Hunter-Gatherers. In *Hunter-Gatherers: An Interdisciplinary Perspective*, edited by C. Panter-Brick, R. H. Layton and P. Rowley-Conwy, pp. 12–38. Cambridge University Press, Cambridge.

Winters, Howard D.

1968 Value Systems and Late Archaic Trade Cycles. In *New Perspectives in Archaeology*, edited by S. R. Binford and L. R. Binford, pp. 175–222. Aldine, Chicago.

4

Practicing Complexity (Past and Present) at Kolomoki

Thomas J. Pluckhahn

As Susan Alt notes in the introduction, and as many of the contributors to this book illustrate through case studies, the complexity of the societies we examine archaeologically was continually produced and reproduced through practice—the day-to-day actions and interactions of people in the past. Of course, in another sense, complexity is also produced and reproduced through the practice of archaeologists in the present (Chapman 2003:192). Over the past few decades, the practice of North American archaeologists— particularly the accumulation of new data—has forced us to reconsider complexity, especially the categorical terms we have used in its description. These critiques have generally proceeded from two directions. In some cases, new archaeological discoveries have revealed a previously unappreciated degree or kind of complexity among societies long considered exemplary models of relatively "simple" evolutionary types. In southeastern North America, for example, the discovery of early monumental construction has forced archaeologists to rethink the presumed "band" or "tribal" organization of Archaic period societies, as described in this volume by Kidder and by Randall and Sassaman (see also Russo 1991; Sassaman 2004, 2005; Saunders et al. 1997; Saunders 1994).

In other cases, further study has achieved the opposite effect, providing insight into the manner in which societies have been forced—sometimes on the presence of only one or two facets of material culture—into models of more "complex" (especially politically hierarchical) societies for which they are, perhaps, poorly suited. This chapter is an example of the latter critique, focusing on the material culture complexes known as Swift Creek and Early Weeden Island, dating to the Middle Woodland period (roughly AD 100 to 600) and centered along the Gulf Coast and adjacent interior portions of Florida, Alabama, and Georgia (Figure 4.1)—an area herein referred to as the Deep South. I concentrate on what is arguably the largest settlement from this complex, the Kolomoki site (9ER1), in the lower Chattahoochee River Valley of southwestern Georgia.

The Middle Woodland societies of the Deep South are perhaps best known for their distinctive mortuary ceremonialism, specifically the caches of ceramic vessels—many in the form of zoomorphic effigies—found on the margins of burial mounds (Moore 1900, 1901, 1902, 1903a, 1903b, 1905, 1907b, 1918; Sears 1953, 1956; Willey 1949). Less well known is the fact that this area witnessed some of the earliest and most intensive platform mound construction north of Mexico (Anderson and Mainfort 2002; Jefferies 1994; Knight 1990, 2001; Pluckhahn 1996). Along with the mound construction came the earliest widespread appearance of sedentary villages in the Southeast, many consisting of distinctive circular arrangements around central plazas (Bense 1998; Milanich et al. 1997; Pluckhahn 2003; Russo et al. 2006; Stephenson et al. 2002; Willey 1949:403).

The Kolomoki site exemplifies these seemingly precocious characteristics. The site plan at Kolo-

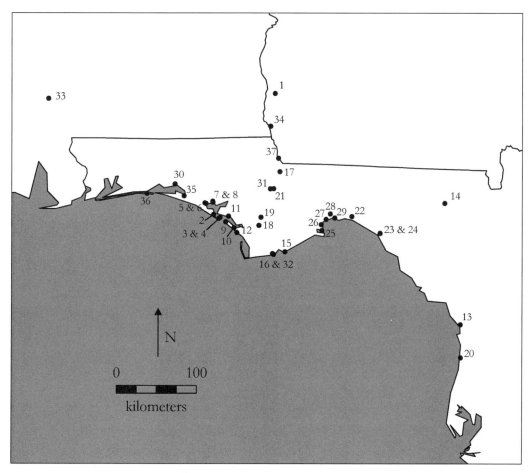

FIGURE 4.1. Location of Kolomoki and other sites mentioned in the text. (1) Kolomoki; (2) Sowell; (3) Davis Point (West); (4) Davis Point (East); (5) West Bay P.O.; (6) West Bay Creek; (7 & 8) Burnt Mill Creek Mounds; (9) Pearl Bayou; (10) Strange's Bayou; (11) Laughton's Bayou; (12) Hare Hammock; (13) Crystal River; (14) McKeithen; (15) Porter's Bar; (16) Tucker; (17) Aspalaga; (18) Burgess Landing; (19) Chipola Cutoff; (20) Bayport; (21) Bristol; (22) Lewis Place; (23 & 24) Warrior River Mounds; (25) Marsh Island; (26) Hall; (27) Mound Field; (28) Bird Hammock; (29) St. Marks; (30) Basin Bayou; (31) Davis' Field; (32) Cool Spring; (33) Carney's Bluff; (34) Shoemake Landing; (35) Point Washington; (36) Buck Mound; (37) Hare's Landing.

moki during the Middle Woodland included a central east–west axis defined by four mounds. Two of these were burial mounds (D and E), each with multiple interments and large caches of ceramic vessels (Figure 4.2). Another is a large platform mound (A) approximately 17 m tall (Pluckhahn 2003:193). Historical accounts suggest that these mounds may have been surrounded by a low earthen embankment (Palmer 1884; see also Pluckhahn 2003:53–57; Trowell 1998). Systematic sampling of the village at Kolomoki has revealed a roughly circular artifact scatter covering nearly a square kilometer and centered on a ca. 7-ha plaza.

Because of the amount of inhabited area, I have suggested that Kolomoki may have had a resident population of as many as 300 people during the Middle Woodland period (Pluckhahn 2003:191).

For archaeologists of the middle twentieth century, Kolomoki and the Middle Woodland societies of the Deep South presented a conundrum. While the presence of Hopewellian artifacts in many of the burial mounds clearly suggested a Middle Woodland date, other features—such as the presence of plazas and flat-topped mounds— did not accord well with the established cultural, historical, and neo-evolutionary sequences for

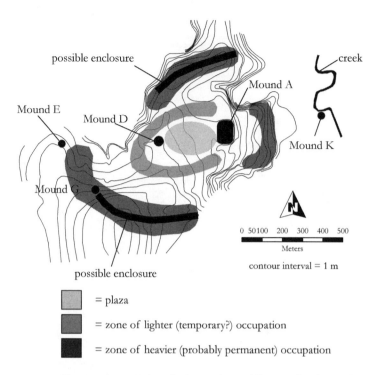

FIGURE 4.2. The site plan at Kolomoki during the Middle Woodland period.
Based on Pluckhahn (2003) and Sears (1956).

the region. Instead, these traits suggested an association with the chiefdom-level societies of the Temple Mound, or Mississippian, period. Some archaeologists proposed hyperdiffusionist explanations for these anomalies, interpreting the platform mounds of the Gulf Coast as evidence of contact with more "advanced" cultures of Mesoamerica (Ford 1969; McMichael 1960, 1964). Others, however, simply insisted that these sites *must* be Mississippian (Bullen 1951, 1953, 1966; Sears 1956; Smith 1951). In the absence of reliable radiocarbon dating, they built their cases mainly through regional sequence comparisons, ethnographic analogies, and appeals to neoevolutionary types.

The Kolomoki case illustrates the manner in which complexity is negotiated in both the past and the present. I begin with a critique of previous characterizations of complexity at Kolomoki. This serves as a point of departure for my own model of complexity in this region, which draws inspiration from recent interpretations of Hopewell societies in the Midwest (Brown 2006; Carr and Case 2006; Thomas et al. 2006). My argument

is not that Kolomoki and the Middle Woodland societies of the Gulf Coast were not complex, but that the character of their complexity is obscured under typologies emphasizing political hierarchy (Yoffee 2005:2). Using analogies that are more restricted, drawn from societies of comparable organization, and better supported by the archaeological record, I argue that complexity at Kolomoki and related settlements of the Middle Woodland period on the Gulf Coast may have been largely ritually based and more horizontal than vertical, with leadership vested in religious specialists perhaps drawn from a clan, sodality, or similarly cross-cutting social collective.

Complexity at Kolomoki:
A History of Archaeological Practice

For the sake of brevity, I begin the introduction to previous research at Kolomoki with the late 1940s, when William Sears began excavations for his dissertation at the University of Michigan (Sears 1950). Excavations in Mound E, a conical monument of earth and stone, revealed a central grave pit containing poorly preserved human remains and numerous shell beads (Sears 1951). Above and surrounding this central grave, Sears encountered additional interments, many of which included cymbal-shaped ornaments of copper and meteoric iron. Correspondence from the time indicates that Sears immediately discerned the Hopewellian affiliations of these grave goods (William H. Sears to James B. Griffin, August 18, 1949, University of Michigan Museum of Anthropology, Ann Arbor). He also recognized the pottery from the mound as variants of Woodland period types recently identified by Gordon Willey (Willey 1945, 1949; Willey and Woodbury 1942).

Sears faced a problem, however, in the form of Mound A at Kolomoki—the 17-m-tall, flat-topped pyramid. As noted above, according to the thinking of the day, mounds like this dated exclusively to the Mississippian period, when complex chiefdoms erected similar monuments across the Southeast. How could the Woodland occupation of the site be reconciled with this monumental earthwork? Sears (1953:20–23) solved the problem by dismissing similarities to Hopewell and by assigning the ceramics from Kolomoki to newly devised types that he placed coeval with more established Mississippian categories (Sears 1956, 1992).

When Sears's limited work in the village and Mound A failed to produce evidence clinching the connection between Kolomoki and Mississippian chiefdoms, he turned to Mound D, the largest of the burial mounds at the site. Briefly, excavations in Mound D revealed a complex series of deposits that began with the placement of five individuals in stone-lined graves (Sears 1953, 1956). A wooden scaffold and low earthen mound (the "primary mound") were built over these burials. To this surface were added the burials of two females and one male, the latter buried with a number of shell beads and covered by a framework of poles described by Sears as a "litter." These burials were covered by a small platform mound (the "core mound") that was subsequently enlarged to a larger platform (the "yellow brown stage"). The surface and margins of this third mound stage were elaborated by a series of log-lined pits and shallow graves containing a mix of secondary bundle burials, cremations, extended skeletons, and isolated crania. Before the mound was capped with a layer of red clay, a

FIGURE 4.3. Excavation of the ceramic cache in Mound D, ca. 1950. Reproduced courtesy of the Laboratory of Archaeology, University of Georgia, Athens.

cache of approximately 75 ceramic vessels and a few more isolated crania were added to the east side (Figure 4.3).

To Sears's (1956:96) way of thinking, Mound D provided the supporting evidence he needed for his argument for "a heavily class structured society" at Kolomoki. The ceremony that produced the mound was likened point by point to the elaborate funeral for the Natchez noble Tattooed Serpent witnessed by Le Page du Pratz in 1725 (Swanton 1911), in which a number of retainers were ritually killed (Sears 1952, 1954, 1956:98).[1] Commonalities in these burial ceremonies, argued Sears, implied similarity in their "total social systems" (Sears 1956:98). At the top of the Kolomoki hierarchy was the "priest chief"—represented by the male "litter" burial—and "an assortment of lesser politico-religious dignitaries," signified mainly by the females interred nearby (Sears 1956:98). Below this, Sears imagined a class of laborers and possibly another class of slaves, as indicated by the many bundle burials, cremations, and isolated crania. A 1951 article in *Time* spelled out Sears's vision to great dramatic effect:

> At last came a fearful day when a reigning priest-chief died. A frenzy of slaughtering and burying swept over the village. First the villagers laid the dead priest in his ceremonial litter at the end of their wide plaza. Near him they buried four men and two women, sacrifices or suicides, and covered the women's bodies with flat stones. Then, out of the temples and huts came all the appurtenances of their gruesome religion: the strange sacred pots, 75 of them, along with baskets of skulls and bundles of human bones. As they laid down these sacred deposits, the villagers built great fires and tossed into them dozens of newly dead bodies. Other victims were buried unburned. Before the pious orgy was over, the mound contained 50 skulls and perhaps 100 whole or partly cremated bodies. (*Time* 1951)

From his analogy with the Natchez, Sears inferred that Kolomoki had a population in the low thousands, supported by corn agriculture. Although he was originally somewhat circumspect in describing the extent of Kolomoki's power, in later publications Sears described Kolomoki as the capital of a "priest state" that extended from Kolomoki at the north to the Gulf Coast on the south, and from the Aucilla River on the east to Pensacola Bay on the west (Sears 1968:144), an area stretching approximately 200 by 300 miles.

Sears's assignment of Kolomoki to the Mississippian period was never widely accepted by archaeologists (for discussions, see Knight and Schnell 2004; Pluckhahn 2003:4–6, 2007). However, scholars have continued to cite Sears's reconstruction of the Mound D ceremony relatively uncritically (e.g., Milanich et al. 1997:191–195; Steinen 1995, 1998, 2006). In addition, perhaps because of the dramatic power of his ethnographic analogy, Sears's characterization of Kolomoki as a possible chiefdom (albeit not a state) has persisted in both popular and academic literature (Anderson 1998; Milanich et al. 1997; Steinen 1995, 1998, 2006). For example, Steinen (1998, 2006) has recently described Kolomoki as a "proto-chiefdom" that maintained a "religious hegemony" over a wide area.

There are obvious reasons to question Sears's interpretation of Mound D, and thus also his reconstruction of political complexity at Kolomoki and across the broader region. First, the interpretation of many of the interments in Mound D as sacrifices is problematic (Brose 1979:144; Ford 1956; Milanich et al. 1997:193–194). There was, for example, no evidence of the sort of mass grave that might suggest ritual sacrifice; most of the graves received some sort of special treatment, and even the isolated crania that Sears interpreted as trophies were frequently interred with Hopewellian trade goods (mostly copper and iron cymbals), an association Sears (1953:22) admitted was "difficult to understand."[2]

Likewise, there is reason to doubt the claim that Mound D was erected in a short period of time to honor a single individual. While it is true that a few of the burials are distinguished by differential processing and partitioning, this is a common pattern during the Middle Woodland period mounds in the region: primary, extended burials in submound pits and tombs, with the later addition of secondary interments in various stages of disarticulation (Brose 1979; Smith 1986: 47–48; Walthall 1979; Willey 1949:405).[3] And in contrast with his claim elsewhere that Mound D was erected in a continuous ceremony lasting as little as a few days, Sears (1954:342–343) reported that several of the large log-lined burial crypts in the upper reaches of the mound must have been added later, as "ceremonial afterthoughts."

Moreover, although the presumed "paramount" burial in Mound D included a number of conch shell beads, these were found in nine other graves within the mound (including several of the crania interpreted as trophies; Sears 1953:11–23; see Table 4.1), suggesting that they were not an exclusive badge of authority. In fact, none of the grave goods from Mound D were exclusive to any single interment, with the exceptions of a stone chisel from one grave and three ordinary projectile points from another. The largest offerings in Mound D—and in similar mounds throughout the region—invariably consist of the seemingly nonspecific caches of pottery, aptly described by Moore (1902:161) as placed "for the dead in common" (see also Willey 1949:405).

Thus far, I have limited my discussion to the

TABLE 4.1. Frequency of Grave Goods in Mound D at Kolomoki.

Type of Grave Good	Frequency (no. of graves)
Stone chisel	1
Projectile points	1
Copper cymbal	4
Pearl bead	4
Iron cymbal	6
Mica ornament or sheet	5
Conch shell beads	10

Source: Based on Sears 1953.

problems in Sears's interpretation of social stratification in Mound D at Kolomoki.[4] As I have argued elsewhere (Pluckhahn 2003), however, there are a number of other reasons to suggest that Kolomoki and related sites of the Middle Woodland period along the Gulf Coast are a poor fit for our traditional notion of a chiefdom, if it is defined as a regional polity with inherited positions of authority and pronounced differences in wealth and status. For example, at the time when mound construction and population were at their peak, Kolomoki was separated from its nearest neighboring mound site by a distance of more than 70 km, too far for any type of political administrative settlement hierarchy (Pluckhahn 2003:205).[5] Although the similarities in burial mounds (with their caches of zoomorphic ceramic vessels) point to a fairly intense social network centered on a broadly shared religious tradition, there is little reason to suppose that this was the result of some sort of top-down "religious hegemony" (sensu Steinen 2006:188).

In regard to status differentiation, systematic investigations of the village at Kolomoki—including more than 1,300 shovel tests and controlled surface collections—have failed to divulge significant variation in household status during the Middle Woodland period (Pluckhahn 2003:126–145). None of the elaborate effigy vessels or finished ornaments of stone, shell, and copper that were found in Mounds D and E have been found in the village. Although few other sites in the region have been systematically studied, the same pattern appears to hold: nonlocal artifacts and ef-

figy vessels are invariably limited to mounds and almost never found in village contexts (Milanich et al. 1997:69).

Additionally, Sears's supposition—based on analogy with Mississippian and early historic native societies of the Southeast—that Kolomoki and the Middle Woodland sites of the Deep South were agriculturally based has not been supported by subsequent archaeological investigations (Milanich et al. 1997; Ruhl 2000). Recent investigations at Kolomoki have yielded maize at approximately 10 percent ubiquity for all features from which flotation samples were drawn (curiously, starchy seeds and squash are less common; Pluckhahn 2003:Table 7.1). Although this figure suggests that horticulture may have made a more significant contribution to the diet than many archaeologists after Sears have supposed, the focus was clearly still on wild plants and animals.

Finally, in the 50 years that have elapsed since Sears's work at Kolomoki, the idea that platform mounds were exclusive to the Mississippian period has proved increasingly untenable. In addition to Mound A at Kolomoki, examples have been documented at at least 12 other Middle and Late Woodland sites in the Deep South alone (Knight 1990:168–69; Pluckhahn 2010). Knight's (1990, 2001) review of the features found on the summits of Woodland platform mounds indicates that structures are extremely rare, suggesting that these mounds were generally not substructures for elite residences or temples. Instead, the vast majority reveal evidence only for scattered pits and large posts, many of which appear to have been periodically removed and replaced in a manner suggestive of rituals of renewal.

The persistence of Sears's interpretations in light of these inconsistencies is a testament to three things: first, the evocative power of his analogy; next, the seductive convenience of essentialist types like "chiefdom"; and finally, the all-too-common archaeological equation of monumental construction with vertical political hierarchy. But if the time has finally come to recognize that Sears's ethnographic analogy is overextended, his use of types like "chiefdom" and "state" misplaced, and the equation of monumental architecture with political stratification simplistic, what can we say about complexity in their stead? How do we explain the florescence of mound construction and mortuary ceremonialism in the absence of the sort of pronounced vertical hierarchy that Sears envisioned?

Toward a New Understanding of the Practice of Complexity at Kolomoki

Rather than a unique and exceptional example of extreme social stratification, the monuments at Kolomoki must be understood within their historical context, as part of a larger florescence of mortuary ceremonialism in the Deep South during the Middle Woodland period. Moore and his crew excavated at least 92 mounds in the region with either Swift Creek or Weeden Island components or both, and these appear to have been the dominant components on mound sites in the region (Moore 1900, 1901, 1902, 1903a, 1903b, 1905, 1907a, 1907b, 1918; see also Brose and White 1999; Mitchem 1999; Sheldon 2001). Many of the mounds excavated by Moore also contained caches of ceramic vessels on their eastern margins, like those in Mounds D and E at Kolomoki. Mound D at Kolomoki is perhaps the largest and most elaborate of the burial mounds in the immediate region, but several of the Middle Woodland mounds excavated by Moore contained comparable quantities and varieties of burials and accouterments (for a comparison, see Brose 1979). The appearance of these spatially discrete cemeteries may be related to the need to integrate larger populations, as has been documented for other societies in the early stages of village development (for Formative Oaxaca, see Whalen 1983: 38; for Natufian and Prepottery Neolithic Levant, see Kuijt 1996).

As an alternative to Sears's view of a sharply defined political hierarchy, I have suggested that Kolomoki must be understood from a historical processual perspective that recognizes an inherent tension between competition and cooperation (Pluckhahn 2003, 2010). The absence of marked differentiation in the village attests to a tradition of relative egalitarianism as reproduced through everyday domestic practices. Corporate burial mounds and similar public works attest to the reproduction of this tradition at a grander scale through communal ritual practices. At the same time, however, the scale and continuity of monumental construction at sites such as Kolomoki

suggest the presence of some type of centralized authority—a subset of the population that was perhaps attempting to reinterpret such communal ritual practices for its own aggrandizement.

What might this authority have looked like? In the remainder of this chapter, I offer some hypothetical reconstructions. My argument is twofold. First, because of the preponderance of ceremony that is evident at Kolomoki and related settlements of the Deep South, I suggest that leadership was vested primarily in religious specialists. This is not a novel suggestion. Writing of the Woodland period in his landmark 1952 synthesis of eastern U.S. archaeology, Griffin (1952:359) observed, "It can certainly be said that the development of the earthwork pattern is along ceremonial lines devoted to the religious concepts and beliefs of the group and that this was probably dominated by male shamans who were promulgating the interpretation of the relationship of man to the universe for the population as a whole. This suggests the development of a specialized priesthood." Griffin's interpretation finds a parallel in Sears's (1956) inference of a "priest chief" at Kolomoki. It is also echoed in past and present interpretations of shamans in Adena and Hopewell societies (Brown 2006; Carr and Case 2006; Otto 1975; Romain 2009; Webb and Baby 1957).

However, bearing in mind the apparent communal nature of the burial mounds and relative paucity of markers of personal status, I suggest that power was not vested in a single individual as Griffin, Sears, and some later researchers have maintained. Instead, I argue that these religious specialists may have been drawn from a larger, more collective social formation such as a clan, moiety, or sodality. Positions of authority at Kolomoki and related Middle Woodland settlements of the Deep South may thus have combined elements that could be described as both horizontal and vertical, egalitarian and ranked.

Like Sears, I draw primarily from the remains of Mound D and similar burial mounds in the region. Also like Sears, I base my speculation largely on ethnographic analogy. However, I attempt to draw analogies that are more narrowly focused, come from societies of comparable social organization, and can be "triangulated" with other aspects of the material record (Brown 2006; Wylie 2002:127–135, 179–184).

FIGURE 4.4. Human effigy vessels from Middle Woodland sites in the Deep South (not to scale). (a, b) Kolomoki Mound D (Sears 1953:55, 59); (c) Larger Mound Near Burnt Mill Creek (Moore 1902:143); (d) Mound Near Basin Bayou (Moore 1901:458); (e) Mound Near Aspalaga (Moore 1903b:486); (f) Mound on the Lewis Place (Moore 1918); (g) Larger Mound Near Hare Hammock (Moore 1902:201); (h) Mound A, Warrior River (Moore 1902:332); (i) Smaller Mound Near Burnt Mill Creek (Moore 1902:148); (j) Buck Mound (Milanich 1994:193); (k) Mounds Near Carney Bluff (Moore 1905:256); (l) Mound Near Davis Point (Moore 1918:546).

The Case for Religious Specialists: "Lugubrious Little Statuettes"

Perhaps the most compelling evidence for religious specialists at Kolomoki and related sites in the Deep South is a class of effigy vessels representing human forms. All or portions of 17 of these human effigy vessels have been recovered from 15 sites in the region (Table 4.2). Twelve of the effigies are sufficiently complete to allow comparison (Figure 4.4). Consistent with the notion that these effigies portray individuals who played a distinct social role such as a ritual specialist,

they exhibit remarkable similarity in sexual characteristics, dress, and posture (with the exception of two anomalous forms, Figure 4.4j and 4.4l). First, where there are indications as to sex, all the effigies appear to represent males. In two cases this is indicated by the depiction of male genitalia, while on several other effigies the presence of male genitalia is hinted at by a protuberance in the area of the groin. None of the effigies has any obvious suggestions of female genitalia.

All the human effigies are minimally dressed, with the majority depicted wearing only a

TABLE 4.2. Effigy Vessels from Kolomoki and Other Middle Woodland Sites of the Deep South.

Site	Effigy form[a]	Source	Site	Effigy form[a]	Source
Kolomoki Mound D	human* bird [crested]* panther* fish (with bird?)* deer* panther human with birds [ibis?] and fish* deer owl* woodpecker* duck* duck* bird [turkey vulture?]* woodpecker?* bobcat* owl* opossum* quail?* woodpecker* duck [roseate spoonbill?] owl* rattlesnake	Sears 1953	Mound near Davis Point	human [legs and lower torso]* bird [turkey vulture?] rattlesnake* bird [crested]	Moore 1902:176–184
			Mound near Pearl Bayou	1 duck [roseate spoonbill?]	Moore 1902:183–188
			Mound B near Laughton's Bayou	horned owl* bird [unidentified]	Moore 1902:189–192
			Mound near Strange's Landing	bird [with bill]* bird [lacks bill or crest]	Moore 1902:192–196
			Larger mound near Hare Hammock	bird human* duck [roseate spoonbill?] bird [2 heads: 1 crested and 1 not]*	Moore 1902:197–209
Kolomoki Mound E	bird bird bird deer duck* duck*	Sears 1951	Cool Spring Mound	frog [form unspecified]	Moore 1902:216
			Mound near Porter's Bar	beaver [tail only] dog	Moore 1902:238–249
Basin Bayou	possible duck [roseate spoonbill?] human*	Moore 1901:455–458	Tucker	duck [roseate spoonbill?] wildcat or panther bird [pigeon or dove]* horned owl	Moore 1902:259–265
Mound near Point Washington	owl human	Moore 1901:465–472	Mound at Marsh Island	bird [turkey vulture?]*	Moore 1902:274–281
Mound near West Bay P.O.	panther? bird [roseate spoonbill?]	Moore 1902:130–140	Hall Mound	bird* bird* bird* [turkey vulture] with incised rattlesnake horned owl* human [legs and feet only]* turkey vulture [two heads]	Moore 1902:282–303
Larger mound near Burnt Mill Creek	human* bird [crested]*	Moore 1902:140–146			
Smaller mound near Burnt Mill Creek	human*	Moore 1902:146–151			
Sowell Mound	bird bird [crested]	Moore 1902:167–174			

Site	Effigy form[a]	Source	Site	Effigy form[a]	Source
Mound near Mound Field	unidentified [bird?]* bird owl* bird horned owl* deer* horned owl* bird [missing head; possible dove or pigeon]* bird [roseate spoonbill?] unidentified [frog?]	Moore 1902:306–320	Mound Below Hare's Landing	human* long-billed water-bird* [ibis?] quadruped* [deer?] bird* [turkey vulture?]	Moore 1907b:429–437
			Mound near Shoemake Landing	owl*	Moore 1907b:429–441
			Mound near West Bay Creek	four duck heads [roseate spoonbills?]	Moore 1918:542–543
Mound near St. Marks	ibis [roseate spoonbill?]	Moore 1902:320–325	Mound near Davis Point [East]	human*	Moore 1918:546–548
Mound near the Aucilla River	turkey or turkey vulture bird*	Moore 1902:327–330	Mounds in Bird Hammock (Mound A)	unidentified* [owl?] unidentified* [bob-cat or panther?]	Moore 1918:561–562
Warrior River Mound A	vulture human* bird [turkey vulture?]	Moore 1902:331–337	Site on the Lewis Place	human*	Moore 1918:564–567
Warrior River Mound B	bird	Moore 1902:337–344	Larger mound near Carney's Bluff	human*	Moore 1905:255–258.
Mound near Burgess Landing	wood duck	Moore 1903b:443–445	McKeithen	quail?* owl?* turkey vulture bird turkey vulture turkey vulture two birds and two dogs turkey vulture ibis roseate spoonbill	Milanich et al. 1997:151–160
Mound near Chipola Cut-Off	bird [roseate spoonbill?] bird* bird fish	Moore 1903b:445–466			
Mound in Davis' Field	bird* bird* [pigeon, quail, or dove?]	Moore 1903b:468–473			
Mound at Bristol	turkey vulture* bird [ibis?]	Moore 1903b:474–480	Mound near Crystal River	human* [face only]	Moore 1903a:379–413
			Mound near Bayport	two duck heads [roseate spoonbills?]	Moore 1903a:415–424
Mound near Aspalaga	human*	Moore 1903b:481–488	Buck Mound	human* turkey vulture owl	Lazarus 1979

[a] Asterisk indicates "effigies in the round" (Sears 1953) or pedestaled effigies (lacking standard orifices or vessel forms); all others are "derived" effigies (bowls with standard orifices and vessel forms, with effigy features added as adornos or molded into body of vessel).

breech-cloth. However, several of the effigies have specialized attire or accouterments. One of the human effigies from Kolomoki (Figure 4.4a), for example, depicts a man with what appears to be a wood ibis on each shoulder, each with a fish in its mouth (Milanich et al. 1997:182). This juxtaposition may have been a deliberate attempt to symbolically unite creatures from three distinct cosmological realms, as described in more detail below. The second human effigy from Kolomoki (Figure 4.4b) has a forelock in the form of the head of a roseate spoonbill, a species whose symbolic importance is also addressed below. Two of the effigies from other sites (Figure 4.4e, 4.4i) appear to have had the same or similar forelocks. If this is the case, the relatively consistent expression of this feature suggests that it could represent a sort of badge of office.

Virtually all the figures are either kneeling or squatting. These positions are consistent with a common shamanic practice of adopting an uncomfortable stance for long periods of time to show balance and strength (VanPool and VanPool 2007:67) or to induce an altered state of consciousness (Carr and Case 2006:196; Reilly 1989).[6] All the effigies are depicted with their hands on their chests or legs. In the case of 7 of the 12 complete effigies (Figure 4.4c–4.4l), the effect is strikingly similar: arms tightly clasped to the chest and clenched fists or interlocking fingers meeting squarely. The eyes on most of the figures appear to be either shut (in some cases tightly so) or perhaps hollow. Mouths are typically shut with pursed lips. In two cases (Figure 4.4j, 4.4k) the teeth are shown tightly clenched, providing resemblances with Adena and Hopewell figures that have been interpreted as shamans (Carr and Case 2006:194–197; Webb and Baby 1957; Otto 1975). The overall effect of solemnity prompted Caldwell (1958:57) to refer to these vessels as "lugubrious little statuettes with folded arms." Similarly, Milanich and colleagues (1997:182) described the figures as having a "pouting expression."

The nonhuman effigies from Kolomoki and related Middle Woodland sites of the Deep South provide supporting evidence for the possible existence of shaman-like religious specialists. Although a variety of other animals are represented, birds predominate, making up 17 of the 28 recognizable animal effigies from Mounds D and E at Kolomoki. Across the broader region, for 14 of the 39 mound caches with recognizable zoomorphic animal effigies,[7] birds are the only animals represented. Avian imagery would have been particularly fitting for religious specialists and their ritual practices, as a number of authors have suggested for societies widely varied in time and space (for Hopewell groups in the Midwest, see Carr and Case 2006:192; for the Casas Grandes culture of northern Mexico, see VanPool 2003, VanPool and VanPool 2007; for the Great Basin region, see Pearson 2002:134; for Bronze Age cultures of central Asia, see Devlet 2001:44). These researchers point to ethnographic studies suggesting that shaman-like religious specialists often experience "magical flight" (Eliade 1964) while in altered states of consciousness. Such experiences may include transformation into a bird in flight as part of "shamanic journeys" (Harner 1981) between the mundane and spirit worlds (Carr and Chase 2006:192). Many of the bird effigy vessels found at Kolomoki's Mound D and other burial mounds of the Deep South exhibit incised and punctate motifs that seem to emphasize wings and flight (Willey 1949:407).

Birds may have also been important symbols of one realm of what has been described as the "shamanic universe" (Pearson 2002:69; VanPool and VanPool 2007:21; Whitley 2000): a cosmos divided into an upper world of the sky and heavens (often associated with birds), a middle world in which people reside, and a lower world (often represented by water, amphibians, and reptiles). Whether this cosmology is typical of shamans in general (see Kehoe [2000] for a cogent argument to the contrary), the tripartite division and symbolic associations are consistent with the cosmology of many of the historic tribes in the Southeast (Hudson 1976:122–126), which presumably had some basis in antiquity. Shamans are often reported to derive power from their abilities to travel between worlds, and we thus might expect to see representations of these realms in ritual contexts where religious specialists presumably had a hand (VanPool and VanPool 2007:127–130), the pottery caches in burials mounds being a good example. If the bird effigies at Kolomoki and other Middle Woodland sites in the region indeed represented the upper world, they might have been opposed with underworld species represented in forms such as fish, frogs, and snakes. Effigies taking the form of terrestrial animals such as deer, bobcats, and humans could be seen as symbolic of the middle world.

The shamanic journey between realms may be represented metaphorically in the juxtaposition of animals from different realms, as in the case of the previously described effigy vessel from Kolomoki showing a man with a bird and fish on each shoulder. Likewise, a vessel from the Hall Mound consists of a bird effigy form with an incised rattlesnake design on its lower half. In a similar vein, several of the bird species that are most common in the effigy vessels from the Deep South—ibises, ducks, and roseate spoonbills—could have been deemed important because they inhabit both the sky and the watery surface of the earth (Hudson 1976:140–141; Milanich et al. 1997:171–172). The importance of spoonbills to Hopewell societies in the Midwest is well documented (Carr 2006:593–594; Milanich et al. 1997:172; Moorehead 1922). The roseate spoonbill's combination of red and white plumage may have been an additional factor in its importance in the Southeast, given the significance of these colors for the representation of earth and sky (respectively) among native peoples of the historic era (Milanich et al. 1997:167–168). Turkey vultures—another bird species that is frequently represented in the effigy vessels of the Deep South—may have been associated with ritual specialists for a very different reason. Hudson (1976:129–130) notes that the turkey vulture was a symbol of healing for the Cherokee because of its ability to "expose itself to dead things with impunity." Milanich has reasonably suggested that turkey vultures would have been a fitting symbol for religious specialists in a society where defleshing figured prominently in mortuary rites (Milanich and Ruhl n.d.; Milanich et al. 1997:196–197).

Finally, the structured nature of the ceramic caches also suggests that they were deposited in ritual performances directed by specialists. The caches were generally placed on the east side of burial mounds, in the direction of the rising sun. In the case of Mound D at Kolomoki, as well as several other mounds in the region, this would have also been the direction of the plaza, where participants could have assembled to view the performances. Moore (1902:334) noted that the

pots often seemed to be deliberately placed such that the finest effigies were positioned to the exterior and would have been the most conspicuous. In a number of cases, some of the pots appear to have been deliberately broken and the fragments scattered in different areas of the cache (Lazarus 1979:17–18; Moore 1902:130; Sears 1953:26). Sometime after the caches were deposited, they were covered by a layer of earth. We can definitively state that in at least one case (Mound E at Kolomoki) the process was repeated a second time in the same mound (Sears 1951), and there are reasons to suspect that the same might have been the case with some of the mounds excavated by Moore (e.g., Moore 1907b:430). The consistency and redundancy in the structure of these cache deposits—including the ritual objects themselves, their treatment, and the accompanying ceremonial architecture—suggest the development of what Rappaport (1999:35–36) has described as a "liturgical order," or a formal, more or less invariant, sequence of ritual acts that encapsulates shared understandings about the natural and supernatural worlds.

My argument that the human effigies from Kolomoki and other sites in the region may depict religious specialists draws from cross-cultural research on shamans (e.g., Winkelman 1990, 1992). General critiques of the application of the term "shaman" beyond societies of the circumpolar region (e.g., Kehoe 2000) are too lengthy to review here. More relevant is Whalen's (2008) recent argument that shamans are characteristic of simpler societies and thus not a fitting analogy for more complex social formations. There is some validity to this argument; Winkelman's (1990, 1992) cross-cultural research indicates that shamans are part-time specialists principally associated with hunting and gathering societies. They are generally independent practitioners, with power based on personal charisma, and typically employ trances and possession to communicate with spirits (Hayden 2003:46–47; Miller and Taube 1993:152; Winkelman 1990, 1992). More sedentary, horticulturally based societies, with greater political integration above the local community, are more likely to have full-time religious specialists (shaman-healers, healers, and priests, in Winkelman's terminology). Full-time specialists, who often wield considerable political power, typically do not rely on trances and spirit possession. As with any evolutionary typology, however, these are broad generalizations that permit numerous exceptions. Several ethnographically documented agricultural societies—including the historic Creek Indians of the Southeast—held positions that combined elements of shamans and priests (Winkelman 1990:346). More important, as Winkelman (1990:345) notes, "one would expect that the shamans would occupy roles similar to priests as those roles first begin to develop in societies." It would not be surprising if such was the case for the religious specialists at Kolomoki and the Middle Woodland societies of the Deep South as they devoted more time to horticulture and began living in larger and more permanent villages.

The Case for Collective and Cross-Cutting Ritual Authority

Although I have interpreted the human effigies as representations of religious specialists, the ritual need not have been under the exclusive control of individuals. As I argued above, there is a relative paucity of individual markers of status in these burial mounds, as well as in the remains of ordinary domestic activities in the village middens. This would seem to suggest that ritual authority was shared among members of a more collective social formation, such as a clan, moiety, or sodality. This does not preclude some degree of hierarchical organization as well, given that these types of social groups are frequently internally ranked. The human effigies from Kolomoki and other Middle Woodland sites in the Deep South could thus represent higher-ranking members of such larger collectives.

As Sears (1956:98) himself suggested, the seemingly totemic zoomorphic vessels practically beg for analogy with clans. Comparison of 20 Creek clan eponyms in use during the late nineteenth and early twentieth centuries (Swanton 1912, 1928, 1946) with the zoomorphic effigy pots from Kolomoki and related sites of the Middle Woodland period in the Deep South reveals some interesting similarities (Table 4.3).[8] All the animals represented in effigy form have analogs with Creek clan eponyms except one—the opossum. Nine of the 20 Creek clan names are represented in the effigy vessels, very close to the average of 10 clan

TABLE 4.3. Comparison of Selected Creek Clan Eponyms with Animals Represented in Middle Woodland Effigy Vessels.

Creek Clan eponym	Represented in effigy form?
Raptorial bird	no
Nonraptorial bird	yes
Turkey	yes
Raccoon	no
Snake	yes
Rabbit	no
Skunk	no
Squirrel	no
Daddy longlegs	no
Porcupine	no
Beaver	yes
Turtle	no
Fish	yes
Otter	no
Alligator	no
Toad	yes
Canine	yes
Bear	no
Deer/elk/moose	yes
Feline	yes

names noted for tribes in the eastern Woodlands (Thomas et al. 2006:343). One troubling aspect of this analogy is the aforementioned disproportionate representation of birds in the effigy assemblages from Kolomoki and other sites in the region; even if we recognize that the general category of "birds" may represent more than one clan eponym, they would appear to be overrepresented for a society with a healthy demographic profile and a functioning clan system (Thomas et al. 2006:361). It seems possible that a clan represented by birds enjoyed privileged participation in funerary ceremonies; Thomas and colleagues (2006:361–362) make a parallel argument for the incommensurate representation of bear parts in some Hopewell mounds, suggesting that members of a bear clan may have had an advantage over others in ritual matters. In the case of Kolomoki and the Middle Woodland sites of the Deep

South, however, it is unlikely that a single clan could have so thoroughly monopolized control over ritual performances across such a broad area.

Another possibility is that ceremonies at Kolomoki were organized by some larger kin-based social group such as a phratry or moiety, again as symbolized by birds. Choctaw villages of the early historic era, for example, were divided into moieties, each of which had responsibility for processing the dead of the opposite moiety (Swanton 1931:170–194). This task was left to specialists known as "bone pickers," who were typically the oldest and most respected members of the moiety. As several authors have suggested (Pluckhahn 2003:192; Russo et al. 2006:102–103), circular or U-shaped village plans found at Kolomoki and other Middle Woodland sites in the region would seem to support a dualistic social division along the lines of a moiety. At present, however, there is little evidence to link representations of birds (or other animals) to "halves" of villages at these sites. And again, it seems unlikely that a single moiety or similar kin-based social formation would be so consistently overrepresented in ritual contexts across a broad region.

A more likely alternative may be that ceremonies at Kolomoki and related sites were instead structured around some type of sodality. A general analogy might be provided by the religious sodalities of western Puebloan groups such as the Hopi and Zuni. Many of these societies cross-cut kin groups, thus integrating and reinforcing communal relations within villages (Kantner 2004:252). Some societies had tribe-wide membership (Cordell 1984:12).

Puebloan sodalities also integrated communities across larger regions (Adams and La-motta 2006; Schaafsma et al. 2002; Walker and Skibo 2002; Ware and Blinman 2000). Prospective members of "borrowed" sodalities were traditionally trained and initiated in the communities where those sodalities originated (Ware and Blin-man 2000:393). A number of archaeologists have suggested that the Kachina cult—the most public and the farthest-reaching of the religious sodalities—may have arisen as a mechanism to integrate the larger numbers of people that began to aggregate on the margins of the Colorado Plateau sometime around the thirteenth century (Adams and Lamotta 2006; Schaafsma and Schaafsma

1974; Ware and Blinman 2000). Similar organizational structures may have facilitated the unprecedented size of villages at Kolomoki and other settlements of the Middle Woodland period in the Deep South.

While communal, integrative, and egalitarian in many regards, however, the sodalities of Puebloan groups were also hierarchically structured internally. Particular clans often "owned" the ceremonies, ceremonial facilities, and ritual paraphernalia (Kantner 2004:252; Whitely 1987). Moreover, as McGuire and Saitta (1996:210) note, "the leaders of these groups were usually from high-ranked clans, and these leaders controlled the esoteric knowledge necessary for the societies and sodalities to survive" (see also Whitely 1987).

If the ceremonies that are embodied in Mound D and similar monuments of the Deep South were directed by a sodality resembling those of the Hopi and Zuni, that might better account for the similarities in ritual practices and ceremonial architecture that developed across the region during the Middle Woodland period. Sodalities may have spanned a number of communities. Moreover, members of the sodality could take the ceremonies to their home villages, perhaps after a period of initiation in the community where the sodality originated. The avian effigies so prevalent at Kolomoki and other Middle Woodland sites in the Deep South could have been symbolic not only of the group but also of general cosmological principles and specific ritual practices that the members of this sodality were charged with as part of community rituals. Higher-ranking members of the sodality could have adopted some of these avian symbols for personal adornment or as badges of office, as indicated by the human effigies shown with bird symbolism.

Conclusion

Complexity is constructed through practices in both the past and the present. One form of archaeological practice in the middle twentieth century equated particular forms of monumental architecture (platform mounds and plazas) with a specific period (Mississippian) and a corresponding model of complexity (chiefdom). This was the interpretive path followed by Sears in his work at Kolomoki. Lacking the evidence to prove that the platform mounds at the site were built in the Mississippian period, Sears turned to the rituals embodied in Mound D, likening them to the funeral ceremonies of the historic-era Natchez. He extended this analogy further to characterize Kolomoki as a chiefdom with inherited leadership and pronounced social stratification, and ultimately extended the comparison further still to describe Kolomoki as the capital of a small regional state.

Sears's interpretation was contested by several of his peers even at the time it was proposed, as alluded to above and as described in greater detail elsewhere (Knight and Schnell 2004; Pluckhahn 2007). In this chapter I have described the ways in which I believe Sears's interpretation is inconsistent with archaeological data both old and new. More broadly, as archaeological practice has changed, his vision of the complexity of the Middle Woodland societies appears increasingly rigid and simplistic. In the past 30 years it has become axiomatic that complexity can be manifested in ways other than political hierarchy, and that the categories we have used to describe variation in complexity may obfuscate more than explain (Chapman 2003; Crumley 1987, 1995; Feinman and Neitzel 1984; Yoffee 1993, 2005).

While I do not dismiss the notion that there were hierarchical elements to the organization of Middle Woodland societies, I suggest that these were less overt than Sears imagined. The absence of marked personal differentiation in both village and mound remains suggests to me that inequalities were plural, subtle, and contested. Specifically, I have posited a model of complexity that sees social differentiation as largely ritually based and more horizontal than vertical, with leadership vested in religious specialists drawn from a clan, sodality, or similarly cross-cutting social collective. Of course, my own interpretation of complexity—like that of Sears—is historically situated and subject to continued negotiation through archaeological practice.

Acknowledgments

I extend my appreciation to Susan Alt for the opportunity to participate in this endeavor. I thank David Anderson and an anonymous reviewer for helpful comments. An earlier version of this chapter elicited comments and criticisms from Kent Flannery, Joyce Marcus, and John O'Shea, for which I am also grateful. Of course, any mistakes are mine alone.

Notes

1. Sears (1951) first proposed an analogy with the Natchez in print in his report summarizing excavations in Mound E, but he did not develop the comparison in detail until subsequent publications (1952, 1954, 1956). In his use of ethnographic analogy to describe Kolomoki, Sears was undoubtedly influenced by Taylor (1948), whose call for a "conjunctive approach" was published in the same year that Sears began fieldwork at Kolomoki. Tooker (1963), among others, has noted some of the problems in Natchez social organization as described by Swanton (1911) (the model on which Sears's analogy was based).

2. Although trophy skulls have been documented from Hopewell sites in the Midwest (Seeman 1988, 2007), such has not been demonstrated for the isolated crania that are commonly found in Middle Woodland mounds in the Southeast (e.g., Walthall 1979). Indeed, there are few indications of warfare in the region during this period (Knight 2001:

327). Ford (1956), in his review of Sears's reports for *American Anthropologist*, dryly noted that Sears's analogy with the Natchez and the associated presumption of human sacrifice was "not entirely far-fetched" but went on to comment that "another possibility is that most of the skeletons may have been taken from houses of the dead where they were stored until the proper moment." The human remains from Kolomoki are too fragmentary and poorly preserved to resolve the issue definitively.

3. The framework of poles that Sears interpreted as a litter was curiously positioned above the presumed "paramount" burial rather than below (as in the case of the famous litter burials at the Mississippian Spiro site [Brown 1996]). Coverings of pole, thatch, or bark are relatively common on Middle Woodland interments (Brose 1979:144; for examples, see Brown 1979, Mainfort 1986, Toth 1979, and Walthall 1979). They are rarely (if ever) interpreted as chiefly litters.

4. Apart from these particulars, Sears's list of similarities between the Natchez and Mound D ceremonies includes several that are hopelessly vague. For example, "burial in mounds" and "erection of platform for mortuary rites" (Sears 1956:98) could describe almost any mound complex in the eastern United States.

5. Even nonmound settlements appear to have been

rare in Kolomoki's hinterland (Steinen 1976a, 1976b, 1995).

6. Indeed, the existence of pre-Mississippian platform mounds was acknowledged even in the landmark cultural historical synthesis of the lower Mississippi Valley by Phillips, Ford, and Griffin (1951), although Griffin (Sears's graduate adviser) dissented from his coauthors on this point (see Phillips et al. 1951:441 n. 35).

7. Milanich and colleagues (1997:182) have suggested that these figures may be "direct representations of the charnel house dead" (presumably meaning their corpses). Disregarding the fact that no definitive evidence for charnel houses has been discovered at any of the Middle Woodland sites in the Deep South (Knight 2001:323), the possibility that some of the human effigies represent the dead bodies of individuals buried in the mounds (rather than or in addition to ritual specialists) cannot be ruled out. This is clearly not the case with the two effigies from Kolomoki, however, which are shown in active poses. Several of the other effigies also seem to be maintaining postures unlike those of corpses.

8. I have excluded effigy adornos that were not found attached to a whole vessel or a substantial vessel fragment. I have also omitted a possible representation of either a ram's horn or grub worm from Pierce Mound A (DeBoer 2004; Milanich 1994:139; Moore 1902:220–222). Swanton (1912, 1928, 1946) noted 34 clan names among the Creek Indian groups with whom he worked. For purposes of analysis, I have discounted those eponyms that could not be accurately translated, as well as those that were represented by totems other than animals or by animals that were introduced to the region after the Middle Woodland period. My analysis should not be construed to imply that there is necessarily a direct lineal relationship between the Creek and the Middle Woodland societies of the Deep South. It is instead a practical consideration; the ethnographic record is richer in regard to clan names of the Creek than it is for other historic tribes in the Southeast.

References

Adams, Charles E., and Vincent M. Lamotta
2006   New Perspectives on Ancient Religion: Katsina Ritual and the Archaeological Record. In *Religion in the Prehispanic Southwest*, edited by Christine S. VanPool and Todd L. VanPool, pp. 53–66. AltaMira Press, Walnut Creek, California.

Anderson, David G.
1998   Swift Creek in a Regional Perspective. In *A World Engraved: Archaeology of the Swift Creek Culture*, edited by M. Williams and D. T. Elliott, pp. 274–300. University of Alabama Press, Tuscaloosa.

Anderson, David G., and Robert C. Mainfort, Jr.
2002   An Introduction to Woodland Archaeology in the Southeast. In *The Woodland Southeast*, edited by David G. Anderson and Robert C. Mainfort, Jr., pp. 1–19. University of Alabama Press, Tuscaloosa.

Bense, Judith A.
1998   Santa-Rosa Swift Creek in Northwestern Florida. In *A World Engraved: Archaeology of the Swift Creek Culture*, edited by M. Williams and D. T. Elliott, pp. 247–273. University of Alabama Press, Tuscaloosa.

Brose, David S.
1979   An Interpretation of the Hopewellian Traits in Florida. In *Hopewell Archaeology: The Chillicothe Conference*, edited by D. S. Brose and N. Greber, pp. 141–149. Kent State University Press, Kent, Ohio.

Brose, David S., and Nancy Marie White
1999   Introduction: Clarence B. Moore's Work in Northwest Florida, 1901–1918. In *The Northwest Florida Expeditions of Clarence Bloomfield Moore*, edited by David S. Brose and Nancy Marie White, pp. 1–41. University of Alabama Press, Tuscaloosa. Reprint of works published in 1901, 1902, 1903, 1907, and 1918.

Brown, James A.
1979   Charnel Houses and Mortuary Crypts: Disposal of the Dead in the Middle Woodland Period. In *Hopewell Archaeology: The Chillicothe Conference*, edited by D. S. Brose and N. Greber, pp. 211–219. Kent State University Press, Kent, Ohio.
1996   *The Spiro Ceremonial Center: The Archaeology of Arkansas Valley Caddoan Cultures in Eastern Oklahoma, Volumes 1 and 2*. Memoir No. 29. University of Michigan Museum of Anthropology, Ann Arbor.
2006   The Shamanic Element in Hopewellian Period Ritual. In *Recreating Hopewell*, edited by Douglas K. Charles and Jane E. Buikstra, pp. 475–488. University Press of Florida, Gainesville.

Bullen, Ripley P.
1951   The Enigmatic Crystal River Site. *American Antiquity* 17:142–143.
1953   The Famous Crystal River Site. *Florida Anthropologist* 6:9–37.
1966   Stelae at the Crystal River Site, Florida. *American Antiquity* 31(6):861–865.

Caldwell, Joseph R.

1958   *Trend and Tradition in the Prehistory of the Eastern United States*. Memoir No. 88. Society for American Archaeology, Menasha, Wisconsin.

Carr, Christopher

2006   Rethinking Interregional Hopewellian "Interaction." In *Gathering Hopewell: Society, Ritual, and Ritual Interaction*, edited by Christopher Carr and D. Troy Case, pp. 575–623. Springer, New York.

Carr, Christopher, and D. Troy Case

2006   The Nature of Leadership in Ohio Hopewellian Societies. In *Gathering Hopewell: Society, Ritual, and Ritual Interaction*, edited by Christopher Carr and D. Troy Case, pp. 177–237. Springer, New York.

Chapman, Robert

2003   *Archaeologies of Complexity*. Routledge, London.

Cordell, Linda S.

1984   *Prehistory of the Southwest*. Academic Press, Orlando, Florida.

Crumley, Carol

1987   A Dialectical Critique of Hierarchy. In *Power Relations and State Formation*, edited by T. Patterson and C. Gailey, pp. 115–159. American Anthropological Association, Washington, D.C.

1995   Heterarchy and the Analysis of Complex Societies. In *Heterarchy and the Analysis of Complex Societies*, edited by R. Ehrenreich, C. Crumley, and J. Levy, pp. 1–6. Archeological Papers No. 6. American Anthropological Association, Washington, D.C.

DeBoer, Warren B.

2004   Little Bighorn on the Scioto: The Rocky Mountain Connection to Ohio Hopewell. *American Antiquity* 69(1):85–108.

Devlet, Ekaterina

2001   Rock Art and the Material Culture of Siberian and Central Asian Shamanism. In *The Archaeology of Shamanism*, edited by Neil Price, pp. 43–55. Routledge, London.

Eliade, Mircea

1964   *Shamanism: Archaic Techniques of Ecstasy*. Princeton University Press, Princeton.

Feinman, Gary M., and Jill Neitzel

1984   Too Many Types: An Overview of Sedentary Prestate Societies in the Americas. *Advances in Archaeological Method and Theory* 7:39–102.

Ford, James A.

1956   Review of *Excavations at Kolomoki: Season I—1948, Excavations at Kolomoki: Season II—1950, Mound E*, and *Excavations at Kolomoki: Season III and IV, Mound D*, by William H. Sears. *American Anthropologist* 58:198–200.

1969   *A Comparison of Formative Cultures in the Americas*. Smithsonian Contributions to Anthropology Vol. 11. Smithsonian Institution Press, Washington, D.C.

Griffin, James B.

1952   Culture Periods in Eastern United States Archeology. In *Archeology of Eastern United States*, edited by James B. Griffin, pp. 352–364. University of Chicago Press, Chicago.

Harner, Michael J.

1981   *The Way of the Shaman: A Guide to Power and Healing*. Harper and Row, New York.

Hayden, Brian

2003   *Shamans, Sorcerers, and Saints: A Prehistory of Religion*. Smithsonian Institution Press, Washington, D.C.

Hudson, Charles

1976   *The Southeastern Indians*. University of Tennessee Press, Knoxville.

Jefferies, Richard W.

1994   The Swift Creek Site and Woodland Platform Mounds in the Southeastern United States. In *Ocmulgee Archaeology, 1936–1986*, edited by D. J. Hally, pp. 71–83. University of Georgia Press, Athens.

Kantner, John

2004   *Ancient Puebloan Southwest*. Cambridge University Press, Cambridge.

Kehoe, Alice Beck

2000   *Shamans and Religion: An Anthropological Exploration in Critical Thinking*. Waveland Press, Prospect Heights, Illinois.

Knight, Vernon J., Jr.

1990   *Excavation of the Truncated Mound at the Walling Site: Middle Woodland Culture and Copena in the Tennessee Valley*. Report of Investigations No. 56. Division of Archaeology, Alabama State Museum of Natural History, University of Alabama, Tuscaloosa.

2001   Feasting and the Emergence of Platform Mound Ceremonialism in Eastern North America. In *Feasts: Archaeological and Ethnographic Perspectives on Food, Politics, and Power*, edited by Michael Dietler and Brian Hayden, pp. 311–333. Smithsonian Institution Press, Washington, D.C.

Knight, Vernon James, Jr., and Frank T. Schnell

2004   Silence over Kolomoki: A Curious Episode in the History of Southeastern Archaeology. *Southeastern Archaeology* 23(1):1–11.

Kuijt, Ian

1996   Negotiating Equality through Ritual: A Consideration of Late Natufian and Prepottery Neolithic A Period Mortuary Practices. *Journal of Anthropological Archaeology* 15: 313–336.

Lazarus, Yulee W.
1979   *The Buck Burial Mound: A Mound of the Weeden Island Culture.* Temple Mound Museum, Fort Walton Beach, Florida.

Mainfort, Robert C., Jr.
1986   *Pinson Mounds: A Middle Woodland Ceremonial Center.* Research Series No. 7. Tennessee Department of Conservation, Division of Archaeology, Nashville.

McGuire, Randall H., and Dean J. Saitta
1996   Although They Have Petty Captains, They Obey Them Badly: The Dialectics of Prehispanic Western Pueblo Social Organization. *American Antiquity* 61(2):197–216.

McMichael, Edward V.
1960   *The Anatomy of a Tradition: A Study of Southeastern Stamped Pottery.* Ph.D. dissertation, Department of Anthropology, Indiana University, Bloomington. University Microfilms, Ann Arbor, Michigan.
1964   Veracruz, the Crystal River Complex, and the Hopewellian Climax. In *Hopewellian Studies*, edited by Joseph R. Caldwell and Robert L. Hall, pp. 123–132. Scientific Papers Vol. 12. Illinois State Museum, Springfield.

Milanich, Jerald T.
1994   *Archaeology of Precolumbian Florida.* University Press of Florida, Gainesville.

Milanich, Jerald T., Ann S. Cordell, Vernon J. Knight, Jr., Timothy A. Kohler, and Brenda J. Sigler-Lavelle
1997   *Archaeology of Northern Florida, AD 200–900: The McKeithen Weeden Island Culture.* Academic Press, New York. Originally published 1984.

Milanich, Jerald T., and Donna L. Ruhl
n.d.   Weeden Island Culture. Electronic document, http://picturesofrecordwired.com, accessed August 12, 2004.

Miller, Mary, and Karl Taub
1993   *An Illustrated Dictionary of the Gods and Symbols of Ancient Mexico and the Maya.* Thames and Hudson, London.

Mitchem, Jeffrey M.
1999   Introduction: Clarence B. Moore's Work in Western and Central Florida, 1895–1921. In *The West and Central Florida Expeditions of Clarence Bloomfield Moore*, edited by Jeffrey M. Mitchem, pp. 1–48. University of Alabama Press, Tuscaloosa. Reprint of works published in 1895, 1900, 1902, 1903, 1905, 1907, 1918, 1919, and 1921.

Moore, Clarence Bloomfield
1900   Certain Antiquities of the Florida West-Coast. *Journal of the Academy of Natural Sciences of Philadelphia, Second Series* 11(3): 350–394.
1901   Certain Aboriginal Remains of the Northwest Florida Coast. Part I. *Journal of the Academy of Natural Sciences of Philadelphia, Second Series* 11(4):421–497.
1902   Certain Aboriginal Remains of the Northwest Florida Coast. Part II. *Journal of the Academy of Natural Sciences of Philadelphia, Second Series* 12(2):127–358.
1903a   Certain Aboriginal Remains of the Central Florida West Coast. *Journal of the Academy of Natural Sciences of Philadelphia, Second Series* 12:361–438.
1903b   Certain Aboriginal Remains of the Apalachicola River. *Journal of the Academy of Natural Sciences of Philadelphia, Second Series* 12(3):440–494.
1905   Certain Aboriginal Remains of the Lower Tombigbee River. *Journal of the Academy of Natural Sciences of Philadelphia, Second Series* 13(2):246–278.
1907a   Crystal River Revisited. *Journal of the Academy of Natural Sciences of Philadelphia, Second Series* 13(3):406–425.
1907b   Mounds of the Lower Chattahoochee and Lower Flint Rivers. *Journal of the Academy of Natural Sciences of Philadelphia, Second Series* 13(3):426–457.
1918   The Northwestern Florida Coast Revisited. *Journal of the Academy of Natural Sciences of Philadelphia, Second Series* 16(4):514–581.

Moorehead, Warren K.
1922   *The Hopewell Mound Group of Ohio.* Publication No. 211, Field Museum of Natural History. Anthropological Series 6(5):73–184.

Otto, Martha Potter
1975   A New Engraved Adena Tablet. *Ohio Archaeologist* 25(2):31–36.

Palmer, Edward
1884   Mercier Mounds, Early County, Georgia. Report prepared for the Bureau of Ethnology Mound Survey, Smithsonian Institution. On file at the National Anthropological Archives, American Museum of Natural History, Smithsonian Institution, Washington, D.C.

Pearson, James L.
2002   *Shamanism and the Ancient Mind: A Cognitive Approach to Archaeology.* AltaMira Press, Walnut Creek, California.

Phillips, Phillip, James A. Ford, and James B. Griffin
1951   *Archaeological Survey in the Lower Mississippi*

Alluvial Valley, 1940–1947. Papers of the Peabody Museum of American Archaeology and Ethnology. Harvard University, Cambridge.

Pluckhahn, Thomas J.

1996   Joseph Caldwell's Summerour Mound and Late Woodland Platform Mounds in the Southeastern United States. *Southeastern Archaeology* 15(2):191–210.

2003   *Kolomoki: Settlement, Ceremony, and Status in the Deep South, AD 350 to 750*. University of Alabama Press, Tuscaloosa.

2007   "The Mounds Themselves Might Be Perfectly Happy in Their Surroundings": The "Kolomoki Problem" in Notes and Letters. *Florida Anthropologist* 60(2–3):63–76.

2010   The Sacred and the Secular Revisited: The Essential Tensions of Early Village Societies in the Southeastern U.S. In *Becoming Villagers*, edited by Matthew S. Bandy and Jake R. Fox, pp. 100–118. University of Arizona Press, Tucson.

Rappaport, Roy A.

1999   *Ritual and Religion in the Making of Humanity*. Cambridge University Press, New York.

Reilly, F. Kent III

1989   The Shaman in Transformation Pose: A Study of the Theme of Rulership in Olmec Art. *Record of the Art Museum, Princeton University* 48(2):4–21.

Romain, William F.

2009   *Shamans of the Lost World: A Cognitive Approach to the Prehistoric Religion of the Ohio Hopewell*. AltaMira Press, Walnut Creek, California.

Ruhl, Donna L.

2000   Archaeobotany at Bernath Place (8SR986) and Other Santa Rosa/Swift Creek–Related Sites in Coastal and Non-coastal Southeastern U.S. Locations. *Florida Anthropologist* 53(2–3):190–202.

Russo, Michael

1991   *Archaic Sedentism on the Florida Coast: A Case Study from Horr's Island*. Ph.D. dissertation, Department of Anthropology, University of Florida, Gainesville. University Microfilms, Ann Arbor, Michigan.

Russo, Michael, Margo Schwadron, and Emily M. Yates

2006   Archeological Investigation of the Bayview Site (8BY137), a Weeden Island Ring Midden, Tyndall Air Force Base, Panama City, Florida. National Park Service, Southeast Archeological Center, Tallahassee. Submitted to Tyndall Air Force Base, Panama City, Florida.

Sassaman, Kenneth

2004   Complex Hunter-Gatherers in Evolution and History: A North American Perspective. *Journal of Archaeological Research* 12(3):227–280.

2005   Poverty Point as Structure, Event, Process. *Journal of Archaeological Method and Theory* 12(4):335–365.

Saunders, R.

1994   The Case for Archaic Period Mounds in Southeastern Louisiana. *Southeastern Archaeology* 13:118–134.

Saunders, J. W., R. D. Mandel, R. T. Saucier, E. T. Allen, C. T. Hallmark, J. K. Johnson, E. H. Jackson, C. M. Allen, G. L. Stringer, D. S. Frink, J. K. Feathers, S. Williams, K. J. Gremillion, M. F. Vidrine, and R. Jones

1997   A Mound Complex in Louisiana at 5400–5000 Years before Present. *Science* 277:1796–1799.

Schaafsma, C. F., J. R. Cox, and D. Wolfman

2002   Archaeomagnetic Dating. In *The Joyce Well Site: On the Frontier of the Casas Grandes World*, edited by James M. Skibo, Eugene B. McCluney, and William H. Walker, pp. 129–148. University of Utah Press, Salt Lake City.

Schaafsma, Polly, and Curtis F. Schaafsma

1974   Evidence for the Origins of the Pueblo Kachina Cult as Suggested by Southwestern Rock Art. *American Antiquity* 39(4):535–545.

Sears, William H.

1950   *The Prehistoric Cultural Position in the Southeast of Kolomoki, Early County, Georgia*. Ph.D. dissertation, University of Michigan, Ann Arbor. University Microfilms, Ann Arbor, Michigan.

1951   *Excavations at Kolomoki: Season II, 1950*. University of Georgia Press, Athens.

1952   An Archaeological Manifestation of a Natchez-Type Burial Ceremony. *Florida Anthropologist* 5(1–2):1–7.

1953   *Excavations at Kolomoki: Seasons III and IV, Mound D*. University of Georgia Press, Athens.

1954   The Sociopolitical Organization of Pre-Columbian Cultures on the Gulf Coastal Plain. *American Anthropologist* 56(3):339–346.

1956   *Excavations at Kolomoki: Final Report*. University of Georgia Press, Athens.

1968   The State and Settlement Patterns in the New World. In *Settlement Archaeology*, edited by K. C. Chang, pp. 134–153. National Press Books, Palo Alto, California.

1992   Mea Culpa. *Southeastern Archaeology* 11(1):66–71.

Seeman, Mark F.
1988   Ohio Hopewell Trophy-Skull Artifacts as
        Evidence for Competition in Middle Wood-
        land Societies circa 50 BC–AD 350. *American
        Antiquity* 53(3):565–577.
2007   Predatory War and Hopewell Trophies. In
        *The Taking and Displaying of Human Body
        Parts as Trophies by Amerindians*, edited
        by Richard J. Chacon and David H. Dye,
        pp. 167–189. Springer, New York.
Sheldon, Craig T., Jr.
2001   Introduction. In *The Southern and Central
        Alabama Expeditions of Clarence Bloom-
        field Moore*, edited by Craig T. Sheldon, Jr.,
        pp. 1–114. University of Alabama Press, Tus-
        caloosa. Reprint of works published in 1899,
        1901, 1903, 1904, 1907, and 1918.
Smith, Bruce D.
1986   The Archaeology of the Southeastern United
        States: From Dalton to DeSoto, 10,500 to
        500 BP. *Advances in World Archaeology* 5:1–91.
Smith, Hale G.
1951   Crystal River Revisited, Revisited, Revisited.
        American Antiquity 17:143–144.
Steinen, Karl T.
1976a   Archaeological Reconnaissance in Early
        County, Georgia: A Model of Settlement Pat-
        terning. *Early Georgia* 4(1–2):68–75.
1976b   The Weeden Island Ceramic Complex: An
        Analysis of Distribution. Unpublished Ph.D.
        dissertation, Department of Anthropology,
        University of Florida, Gainesville.
1995   *Woodland Period Archaeology of the Geor-
        gia Coastal Plain*. Georgia Archaeological
        Research Design Paper No. 12, University of
        Georgia Laboratory of Archaeology Series
        Report No. 36. Athens.
1998   Kolomoki and the Development of Sociopo-
        litical Organization on the Gulf Coast Plain.
        In *A World Engraved: Archaeology of the Swift
        Creek Culture*, edited by M. Williams and
        D. T. Elliott, pp. 181–196. University of Ala-
        bama Press, Tuscaloosa.
2006   Kolomoki: Cycling, Settlement Patterns, and
        Cultural Change. In *Recreating Hopewell*,
        edited by Douglas K. Charles and Jane E.
        Buikstra, pp. 178–189. University Press of
        Florida, Gainesville.
Stephenson, Keith, Judith A. Bense, and Frankie Snow
2002   Aspects of Deptford and Swift Creek of the
        South Atlantic and Gulf Coastal Plains. In
        The Woodland Southeast, edited by David
        G. Anderson and Robert C. Mainfort, Jr.,
        pp. 318–351. University of Alabama Press,
        Tuscaloosa.

Swanton, John R.
1911   *Indian Tribes of the Lower Mississippi Valley
        and Adjacent Coast of the Gulf of Mexico.*
        Bureau of American Ethnology Bulletin
        No. 43. Smithsonian Institution, Washing-
        ton, D.C.
1912   A Foreword on the Social Organization of
        the Creek Indians. *American Anthropologist*
        14(4):593–599.
1928   Social Organization and Social Usages of the
        Indians of the Creek Confederacy. In *Annual
        Report of the Bureau of American Ethnology,
        1924–1925*, pp. 23–472. Smithsonian Institu-
        tion, Washington, D.C.
1931   *Source Material for the Social and Ceremonial
        Life of the Choctaw Indians.* Bureau of Ameri-
        can Ethnology Bulletin No. 103. Smithsonian
        Institution, Washington, D.C.
1946   *Indians of the Southeastern United States.*
        Bureau of American Ethnology Bulletin
        No. 137. Smithsonian Institution, Washing-
        ton, D.C.
Taylor, Walter W.
1948   *A Study of Archaeology.* Memoirs No. 69.
        American Anthropological Association,
        Menasha, Wisconsin.
Thomas, Chad R., Christopher Carr, and
Cynthia Keller
2006   Animal Totemic Clans of Ohio Hopewellian
        Peoples. In *Gathering Hopewell: Society, Rit-
        ual, and Ritual Interaction*, edited by Chris-
        topher Carr and D. Troy Case, pp. 339–385.
        Springer, New York.
Time
1951   Funeral in Georgia. November 12.
Tooker, Elisabeth
1963   Natchez Social Organization: Fact or Anthro-
        pological Folklore? *Ethnohistory* 10(4):358–
        372.
Toth, Alan
1979   The Marksville Connection. In *Hopewell
        Archaeology: The Chillicothe Conference*,
        edited by D. S. Brose and N. Greber, pp. 188–
        199. Kent State University Press, Kent, Ohio.
Trowell, Christopher T.
1998   A Kolomoki Chronicle: The History of a
        Plantation, a State Park, and the Archaeologi-
        cal Search for Kolomoki's Prehistory. *Early
        Georgia* 26(1):12–81.
VanPool, Christine S.
2003   The Shaman-Priests of Casas Grandes. *Amer-
        ican Antiquity* 68(4):696–717.
VanPool, Christine S., and Todd L. VanPool
2007   *Signs of the Casas Grandes Shamans.* Univer-
        sity of Utah Press, Salt Lake City.

Walker, W. H., and J. M. Skibo
2002   Joyce Well and the Casas Grandes Religious Interaction Sphere. In *The Joyce Well Site: On the Frontier of the Casas Grandes World*, edited by James M. Skibo, Eugene B. McCluney, and William H. Walker, pp. 167–176. University of Utah Press, Salt Lake City.

Walthall, John A.
1979   Hopewell and the Southern Heartland. In *Hopewell Archaeology: The Chillicothe Conference*, edited by D. S. Brose and N. Greber, pp. 200–208. Kent State University Press, Kent, Ohio.

Ware, John A., and Eric Blinman
2000   Cultural Collapse and Reorganization: The Origin and Spread of Pueblo Ritual Sodalities. In *The Archaeology of Regional Interaction: Religion, Warfare, and Exchange across the American Southwest*, edited by Michelle Hegmon, pp. 381–409. University Press of Colorado, Boulder.

Webb, William S., and Raymond S. Baby
1957   *The Adena People*. Ohio State University Press and Ohio Historical Society, Columbus.

Whalen, Michael E.
1983   Reconstructing Early Formative Village Organization in Oaxaca, Mexico. *American Antiquity* 48(1):17–43.
2008   Review of *Signs of the Casas Grandes Shamans*, University of Utah Press, Salt Lake City. *American Antiquity* 73(1):167–168.

Whitely, Peter M.
1987   The Interpretation of Politics: A Hopi Conundrum. *Man* 22(4):696–714.

Whitley, David S.
2000   *The Art of the Shaman: Rock Art of California*. University of Utah Press, Salt Lake City.

Willey, Gordon R.
1945   The Weeden Island Culture: A Preliminary Definition. *American Antiquity* 10(3):225–254.
1949   *Archeology of the Florida Gulf Coast*. Smithsonian Miscellaneous Collections No. 113. Smithsonian Institution, Washington, D.C.

Willey, Gordon R., and Richard B. Woodbury
1942   A Chronological Outline for the Northwest Florida Coast. *American Antiquity* 7:232–254.

Winkelman, Michael James
1990   Shamans and Other "Magico-Religious" Healers: A Cross-Cultural Study of Their Origins, Nature, and Social Transformations. *Ethos* 18(3):308–352.
1992   *Shamans, Priests, and Witches: A Cross-Cultural Study of Magico-Religious Practitioners*. Arizona State University, Tempe.

Wylie, Allison
2002   *Thinking from Things: Essays in the Philosophy of Archaeology*. University of California Press, Berkeley.

Yoffee, Norman
1993   Too Many Chiefs? (or, Safe Texts for the '90s). In *Archaeological Theory: Who Sets the Agenda?* edited by N. Yoffee and A. Sherratt, pp. 60–78. Cambridge University Press, Cambridge.
2005   *Myths of the Archaic State: Evolution of the Earliest Cities, States and Civilizations*. Cambridge University Press, New York.

5

Sacrificing Complexity

Renewal through Ohio Hopewell Rituals

Bretton Giles

Archaeological investigations of Ohio Hopewell complexity have focused on the analysis of burials and suggest that fleeting mortuary events reflect the social organization of these communities. However, the ritual landscape enacted by Ohio Hopewell peoples is replete with imagery that emphasizes containment and movement as elements of fluid processes rather than static events. I explore how Ohio Hopewell communities enacted a dynamic sacrificial economy in which persons, objects, and spaces served as containers that were transformed in order to open up spaces for renewal. I argue that baroque, as opposed to romantic, complexity more appropriately captures particular aspects of Ohio Hopewell communities.

This chapter delves into how Ohio Hopewell communities unraveled the ties between the living and dead by enacting the transience of bodies, objects, and structures in ways that opened up space for renewal, ca. 50 BC to AD 500. The complexity associated with these sacrificial regimes is located in how they set in motion and imply reciprocal obligations between heterogeneous sets of agents. These ritual regimes operate by separating the social persona of the deceased (and other things) into their constituent parts so as to redistribute particular aspects of them (Küchler 1997). Such transformations are often associated with the belief that the body and other objects serve as containers for various aspects of more complex (differentiated) social personas (Kan 1989; Küchler 2002). Inheriting particular parts

of this social persona requires distancing the corpse's pollution, while reestablishing ancestral and social connections (sensu Kan 1989; Küchler 2002). This ritual work often stresses the reciprocal obligations different persons and kin groups have to one another, the deceased, and important other-than-human persons. These processes, in turn, produce heterogeneous "agents" who contribute to one another's lives and might be aptly described as "table companions" (Kwa 2002).

This is especially relevant for the Woodland communities of the central Ohio River Valley, which tend to "fragment under scrutiny and dissolve into fluid groups of people, seemingly on the move," since these people seem to have cultivated social bonds through feasting and other ritual exchanges (Clay 2002:165). This spatial and political fluidity probably contributed to the diverse array of ritual practices that were enacted. Yet it is also vital to realize these communities' ritual regimes (like other sacrificial economies) probably established continuity with the ancestral past by recycling intangible names, knowledge, and prerogatives, as well as material things (Harrison 1992; Küchler 1997; von Gernet 1994). This recycling may contribute to the "fractal quality" of Woodland ritual practices in the central Ohio River Valley, in which basic patterns are often repeated in innovative ways at different scales (Clay 2002), just as novel combinations are formed from a limited set of elements in baroque music (Kwa 2002:26).

This heterogeneity marks an important distinction between romantic and baroque complexity. While romantic complexity sees the (often functional) integration of people, objects, and phenomena (Kwa 2002:24), baroque philosophers stress the importance of perspective and see an underlying heterogeneity (complexity) at multiple analytical scales (Law 1992; Rescher 1991; Serres 1995).[1] A passage from Leibniz's *Monadology* articulates this concept of heterogeneity or complexity at different scales: "Every bit of matter can be conceived as a garden full of plants or a pond full of fish. Each branch of the plant, each member of the animal, each drop of its bodily fluids, is also such a garden or such a pond" (Leibniz in Rescher 1991:228). The point is that even the body is composed of a bundle of "political" relations. This boundary between people and things blurs in many gift-giving societies because the gifts and products of persons' labor continue to be associated with them throughout their lives (Strathern 1988).

But persons and things are not indistinguishable; rather, it is that both contribute to larger wholes that are composed of many parts (sensu DeLanda 2006). Ohio Hopewell charnel houses are a useful example because they were composed of not only poles, bark, and other things, but also the people who maintained and traversed them. Thus, every person is part of and contributes to his or her kin groups (houses), just as these sodalities often have reciprocal obligations to one another. These complex wholes are often conceived by indigenous communities (including Native Americans) as interwoven (or enfolded) microcosms-macrocosms (Peat 2002:6–7). We thus need a multiscalar approach to understand Ohio Hopewell complexity, one that assesses how social agents were composed of diverse assemblages of material and immaterial things, as well as how they contributed to larger wholes linked through the flow of shared substances, such as food, smoke/tobacco, gifts, collaborative labor, speeches, and ritual performances.

The Woodland Communities of Southern Ohio

While earlier perspectives argued that Ohio Hopewell earthworks were produced by hierarchical societies with corn-based agricultural economies, permanent villages, and centralized redistribution, archaeologists began reassessing the social and economic organization of these communities in the 1960s and 1970s (see Brose and Greber 1979; Struever 1964; Struever and Houart 1972). It became clear that the sub-mound buildings were not domiciles, but charnel structures for processing the dead (Brown 1979). Settlement surveys have also found little evidence of domestic dwellings among Hopewell earthworks. Instead, they have documented the presence of small, dispersed occupations that can be characterized as either sedentary farmsteads or nodes in a more itinerant hunter-gatherer lifeway (compare Pacheco and Dancey 2006 with Cowan 2006; Yerkes 2006). Analyses of subsistence also show continuity with earlier Archaic subsistence adaptations, increased utilization of indigenous domesticates, and minimal evidence of maize (Smith 1992; Wymer 1992, 1997).

Ohio Hopewell mound building also has considerable continuity with the Archaic traditions, since Eastern Woodland people began building earthworks thousands of years earlier (Russo 1996). Although the majority of Middle Archaic mounds were not constructed as places to inter the dead (Russo 1996), some midwestern communities constructed small tumuli to bury their dead by the Late Archaic (Charles and Buikstra 1983; Seeman 1986). In the central Ohio River Valley, people began building small mounds over the dead and ritual caches during the Late/Transitional Archaic period at such places as the Kline, Medcalf, Mimmey, Munson Springs, R. P. Swartz, and Corwin mounds (Figure 5.1; Greber 1991; Pacheco and Burks 2008; Richards and Shane 1974; Seeman 1986:568–569; Stout and Bravard 1973). Some Transitional Archaic/Early Woodland mounds cover large caches of ritual paraphernalia, as exemplified by the cache of Turkey Tail points covered by the R. P. Swartz mound (Greber 1991; Shetrone 1923) or placed with burials under the Medcalf mound (Seeman 1986:570). The ritual caches deposited by subsequent Woodland peoples built on these earlier sacrificial traditions.

After ca. 500 BC, many Early and Middle Woodland communities in the central Ohio River Valley also built ceremonial structures, buildings, and/or enclosures that served as a stage for processing the dead (Brown 1979; Clay 2002; Hays

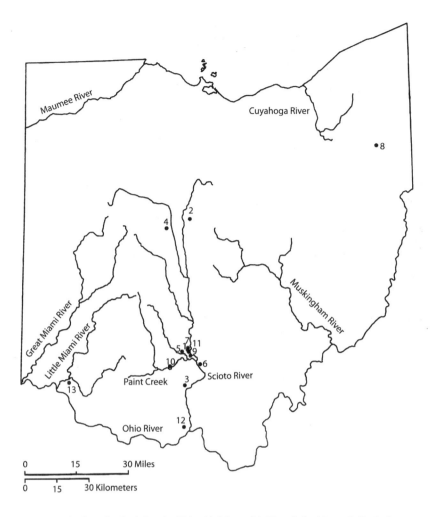

FIGURE 5.1. Archaeological sites in Ohio. (1) Adena; (2) Alum Lake Mounds (includes the Bagley and La Moreaux Mounds); (3) Corwin Mound; (4) Darby Creek Mounds; (5) Hopewell; (6) Liberty; (7) Mound City; (8) North Benton Mound; (9) R. P. Swartz Mound; (10) Seip; (11) Shriver; (12) Tremper; (13) Turner.

1995; Seeman 1986). Clay (2002) argues that these structures were built by fluid amalgamations of people who came together to create contexts for particular ritual events, only to subsequently dismantle them and mound the space over. Sometimes a number of sequential structures were constructed and dismantled before the area was mounded over, although not all these structures were covered with mounds (Clay 1998). Some early examples were probably windbreaks, racks, or scaffolding used to store corpses during their decomposition and before their final interment, such as the post-mold patterns found underneath

the Bagley and La Moreaux mounds (Hays 1995: 223). The use of submound pits to store and allow the dead to decompose at the Alum Lake and Darby Creek mounds probably paralleled this practice (Aument 1990; Hays 1995:220–222).

Beginning around 500 BC, a circular shape started to be employed in the central Ohio River Valley. Small circular ditches and embankments were constructed that have often been dubbed "ceremonial circles." Circular, paired post structures have also been identified at the base of some of these mounds (Clay 1998:6). Clay (1987:46) has suggested that the comparable size and organization of these paired post structures and small circular earthworks may imply their functional similarity and use. Yet he has also raised the question of why circular ditches and embankments were often constructed around or over paired post structures if they were equivalent ritual spaces (Clay 1998:18).

It certainly appears that these structure/earthworks were sequential constructions in some instances, but in other cases it appears that multiple circular spaces were ritually defined at the same time, producing concentric rings or sets of nested containers. Nevertheless, both these circular ritual spaces were probably ultimately used to process the dead, since burial mounds were constructed within or over both (Clay 1987:46; Seeman 1986). This construction of circular ritual spaces appears to have become a resilient, iconic practice for people in the central Ohio River Valley (Clay 2002).

The shift from circular to oblong structures along the Scioto was associated with important changes in the spatial organization of these ritual regimes (Brown 1979, 2004). In general, the quadrilateral plan of Ohio Hopewell charnel houses was probably more conducive to the permanent allocation of roofed space for particular ritual activities (Brown 2004:149). Thus, the use of oblong buildings probably contributed to a shift from vertically stacking burials in accretional mounds to the horizontal use of space in Ohio Hopewell charnel houses (Brown 2004; Clay 1986, 1987; Prufer 1964). It probably also allowed the stacking of bodies within a standing structure such as in the Seip-Pricer submound building (Brown 2004:149).

Nevertheless, Ohio Hopewell ritual regimes continued to feature secondary burial rites that occurred after the dead were cremated or allowed to decompose. Cremating the dead predominated at Tremper and Mound City (Mills 1916, 1922; Brown 1979, 2004), but primary interment was also employed at some later Ohio Hopewell mortuary complexes (Mills 1907; Moorehead 1922; Shetrone 1926; Willoughby and Hooton 1922). Given the demands of hosting these large gatherings and Hopewell people's dispersed land-use strategies (cf. Pacheco and Dancey 2006; Cowan 2006), the extended burials probably had adequate time to decompose. Ohio Hopewell com-

munities also defleshed particular people. Some skeletal elements were modified and even transformed into ritual objects (Johnston 2002; Seeman 1988).

Besides processing the dead, Ohio Hopewell people enacted other rites of ritual riddance that removed from circulation a plethora of ceremonial paraphernalia by depositing it in these charnel houses before mounding them over (Brown 1979, 2004; Clay 2002; Greber 1996). Many Ohio Hopewell ritual caches were placed in close proximity to prepared fired clay basins, including two famous caches from Mound City and Tremper that included "killed" platform pipes (Mills 1916:284, 1922:436; Squier and Davis 1998 [1848]: 153). Ohio Hopewell people also placed "killed" objects, cremations, pots, ashes, and elaborate ritual caches directly in fired clay basins at such places as Hopewell, Seip, and Turner (Greber and Ruhl 1989; Moorehead 1922; Shetrone 1926; Shetrone and Greenman 1931; Willoughby and Hooton 1922).

Finishing the Dead
in Sacrificial Economies

Why is it important that Ohio Hopewell communities constructed and dismantled various "things" as part of their mortuary regime? Since many sacrificial regimes are concerned with "finishing the dead," such as the potlatches of the Northwest Coast (Kan 1989; Seguin 1984) and the malanggan rites of New Ireland (Küchler 2002), comparing these rites of ritual riddance with the Ohio Hopewell sacrificial economy provides a useful entry point. These elaborate secondary burial rites occur after the initial disposal of the body and deal with the perceived state of disorder that emerges at death because of the presence of "left over" animated substances that are associated with the deceased. These rites serve to reclaim and channel this "left over" animated substance into new containers in order to enact renewal (Küchler 1997).

The importance of potlatches in finishing the dead has often been underestimated because they always follow the death of a prominent person and are held to honor his or her memory (Kan 1989; Seguin 1984). Yet potlatches only culminate a funerary regime that emphasizes how material release facilitates reincarnation. For this renewal to occur, the corpses of people and animals must be treated properly. Each fish must be totally consumed and its bones returned to water or burned so that it can be reborn, because bodies serve only as "passing" containers for souls (Seguin 1984: 119). This belief partially explains why the Tlingit describe the human body as a house for the spirit and alludes to how the flesh was deemed "a container or a cover for some other components of the person" (Kan 1989:49–50). It also points to how the body and the house operated as intertwined microcosms in Northwest Coast societies (MacDonald 1981). This rich metonym highlights how the body and house conceal and hold things that must be revealed or released only under special circumstances (Kan 1989:63). Some of the essential things each of these "containers" hold are the immortal names and crests of the matrilineage that carry claims to ritual knowledge, positions, and prerogatives (Kan 1989:52).

The process of finishing the dead began with rites that celebrated the deceased, after which they were cremated with some personal possessions/gifts in order to separate the perishable flesh from its permanent components (Kan 1989). The final ritual event that finished the dead was the potlatch, during which the hosts fed, entertained, and presented their guests with gifts (Kan 1989). Tsimshian potlatches, for example, symbolically "eat" the wealth of the matrilineage in order to empty it of the influence of the dead (Seguin 1984). They return the worldly and otherworldly contributions that had been made to deceased individuals by their paternal relatives, who in turn provide a new container for the deceased and move the remains to the "village" of the dead (Kan 1989). Only after these rites were completed could an heir reclaim the deceased person's titles, crests, and prerogatives.

The malanggan of New Ireland are also associated with "finishing the dead." This ritual work begins by effacing all trace of the deceased from the landscape, a process timed to correspond with the decomposition of the corpse (Küchler 2002:85). It culminates with the sacrifice of a carved wooden malanggan effigy, reminiscent of a body wrapped in images. Each image or motif has its own history/future, for which the sculptures only serve as a temporary container. The ownership, use, and inheritance of land were also tied to the transmission of these motifs. When revealed, the odor/form of the carved effigy stimulates a moment of fleeting recollection (Küchler 2002:151). The malanggan is then killed and its image conveyed to the mourners, while the empty statue is placed in the forest to decompose or is traded to Europeans. Its decomposition arrests the odor of the dead in the spiritual domain of moroa, stimulating the turning of the seasons and enabling agricultural renewal. In becoming image, malanggan are subject to an intellectual system of ownership and serve as a means of transmitting names believed to be an augmentable source of "regenerative life force" (Küchler 2002:150).

Both these mortuary regimes distance the dead and maintain continuity with past. They separate the deceased into his or her constituent parts so as to purify, redistribute, and/or reclaim particular aspects of them. This process of dissolution illustrates that a person is not an indivisible whole, but a composite separable into a number of constituent parts. Their destruction separates the tangible from the insubstantial with the invisible forces arrested in the ethereal odors and smoke that result from these processes, where they would not haunt or harm the living (Küchler 1997:44). Yet these intangibles constitute an important offering to spiritual personages, one that placates them and anticipates a return. Rendering these sacrificial "objects" absent also severs their image and memory from material form.

This process enables an economy of transmission to emerge because intangible images, rituals, names, and knowledge are inherently alienable and reproducible in the manifold combinations they can produce. The cyclical exchange of this "intangible" ritual knowledge, prerogatives, and imagery through systems of intellectual ownership is the stuff from which reproductive ideologies are fabricated because it stresses how material release facilitates renewal (Küchler 1997). In fact, the aforementioned rites of renewal are quite similar to Iroquoian, Algonquian, and Siouan adoption/mourning rituals that "raised or kept alive the name in order to symbolically reincarnate a dead relative" (Hall 1987:188). These sacrificial regimes produce complex social agents, composed of a variety of differentiated parts, who are obliged by reciprocal obligations to contribute to one another's existence.

Sacrificing Complexity

In contrast, anthropological approaches to complexity have often attempted to group societies in various conceptual schemes, which designate particular features of their political organization as characteristic of idealized categories and then place each society along a continuum of sociopolitical complexity (e.g., Service 1962; Fried 1967). Following Binford's (1971) work, mortuary analyses became a privileged method for inferring social organization. As opposed to analyzing mortuary regimes as long-term integrated social processes (see Parker Pearson 1999), these approaches crystallize particular aspects of funerary rites as representative of social organization, especially the moment when objects are placed with the corpse. The results are then used to ascertain whether the society was egalitarian, ranked, or stratified (see Tainter 1978). We should distance ourselves from these typological, pyramid schemes because they produce an idealized social order that does not mirror a living, moving society. Instead, we need to focus on how communities establish, maintain, and remember the bonds that tie them together (Serres 1995). Thus, Ohio Hopewell complexity is not only reflected in the objects placed with the dead, but more actively resided in the reciprocal obligations these communities established and maintained through sacrificial and gift-giving regimes.

Models of Ohio Hopewell Complexity

I explore in the next sections how Ohio Hopewell societies constructed and deconstructed complex wholes, including the human body, charnel houses, and fired clay basins, through gift-giving and sacrificial regimes. The complexity of these sacrificial regimes is located in how they set in motion and implied reciprocal obligations between heterogeneous sets of social and "spiritual" agents. I argue that fired clay basins, charnel houses, and earthen embankments each served as contingent containers that contributed to the existence of others at the same time they enacted important ritual transformations. To understand Ohio Hopewell complexity, I employ a multi-scalar analysis that assesses how social agents were composed of diverse assemblages of material and immaterial things and contributed to larger wholes through the flow of shared sub-

stances, such as food, smoke, gifts, heat, collaborative labor, and ritual performances.

(Re)Making and Unmaking Ohio Hopewell Communities as Complex "Wholes"

While there is a great deal of variability in Early and Middle Woodland mortuary regimes, Mound City presents a useful entry point into how Ohio Hopewell communities constructed complex "wholes" at multiple scales. Mound City was part of an elaborate built landscape along the Scioto. It consisted of a large rectangular enclosure with rounded corners that enclosed at least 24 mounds (see Brown 2004:152). In the mid-nineteenth century, Squier and Davis (1998) also mapped two mounds outside the enclosure, which suggests that Mound City was an even larger, more historically complicated site (Figure 5.2; Brown 2004). The two gates in the enclosure's wall were asymmetrically positioned along its east and west sides.

Excavations at Mound City have shown that all the mounds appear to have covered the remains of dismantled charnel houses (Brown 2004:153). The charnel houses at Mound City were commonly constructed as rounded-corner, relatively rectangular (or flat-sided elliptical) buildings with clearly defined doorways located opposite one another (Brown 2004:157–159). Nevertheless, the general shape of the most carefully constructed buildings, such as the submound building under Mound 13, provided a template for the fired clay basins they contained, as well as the form of the larger ritual enclosure. The reiterative use of this design created a series of nested containers, or a "building of buildings" (Brown 2004:159). The regularity of this spatial layout implies that the meaning attached to the shape of these containers was important (see Brown 2004:159, 162).

Yet Mound City is not an isolated example, because earlier "Adena" enclosures in its immediate vicinity were also constructed as nested containers (houses). These earlier enclosures, such as Adena and Shriver, emphasize sets of concentric circles instead of the template employed at Mound City (Brown 2004:151). While not all Early to Middle Woodland sites were constructed as "nested houses," these examples show how particular shapes were used to analogically link ritual spaces.

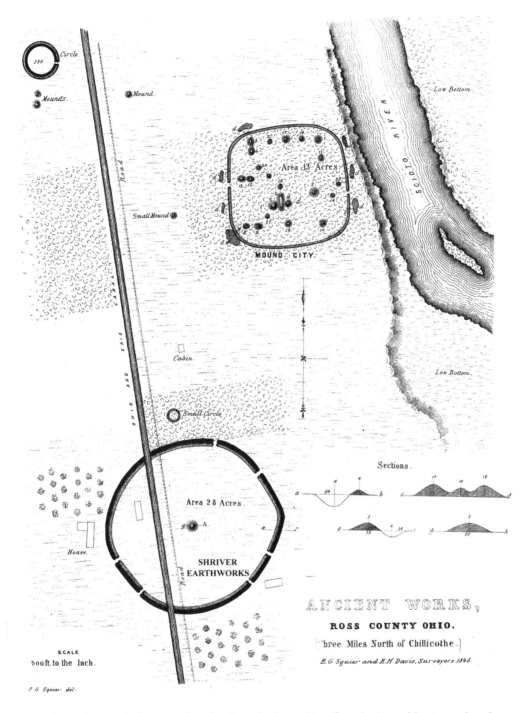

FIGURE 5.2. Mound City and Shriver Earthworks, along the Scioto River (from Squier and Davis 1998 [1848]: Plate XIX).

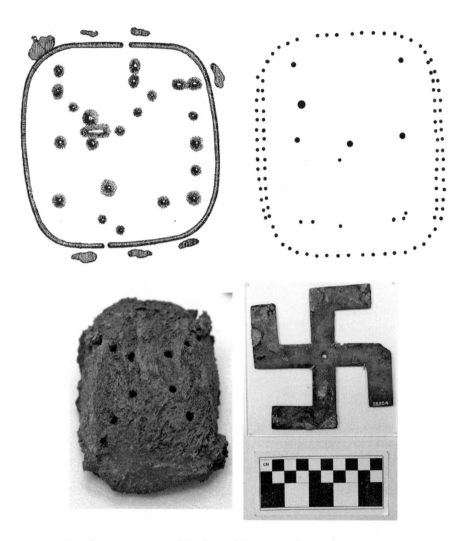

FIGURE 5.3. Visual representations of the form of the Mound City enclosure: Squier and Davis's map of Mound City from Figure 5.2; a schematic diagram of the submound building under Mound 10 at Mound City; a copper turtle shell rattle found with Burial 12 under Mound 7 at Mound City; and a copper swastika from the cache of copper artifacts in Hopewell Mound 25 (after Brown 2004:Fig. 5). The relative size of the postmolds is not accurate in the diagram of the submound building under Mound 10 at Mound City; it is meant only as a schematic visual illustration of their spatial organization.

It therefore seems relevant that the form of fired clay basins, charnel houses, and the enclosure at Mound City parallels the shape of the 18 copper turtle rattles associated with Burial 12 under Mound 7 (Figure 5.3; Mills 1922:494). This similarity may not be a coincidence since the world was considered by the Iroquois, Delaware, Shawnee, and other Algonquian tribes to lie on the back of a turtle (Lankford 2007:22). Ohio

Hopewell buildings would have also looked like turtles' shells, since they were probably domed structures (Brown 2004:153). Covering these buildings with mounds would have once again created another domed vault. This pattern fits with shamanic beliefs that model the cosmos as either a dwelling or a living being, or both (MacDonald 1981:227). Significantly, the carapaces of these copper turtle rattles were pierced with four sets of three holes. These twelve holes form a cross motif, albeit one with acute angles. Cross and quartered-circle motifs occur frequently in Ohio Hopewell iconography, but in some cases the lines intersect at right angles (Figure 5.3). Nevertheless, both have commonly been interpreted as world symbols (Greber and Ruhl 1989:87–88).

Osage people referred to these quartered circles as Ho'-e-ga, which La Flesche translated as "an enclosure in which all life takes on bodily form" (1932:63). The Osage therefore conceptualized the body as a contingent container composed of multiple contributions, a notion succinctly captured by defining Ho'-e-ga as the "snare of life" (Bailey 1995:31). Yet the Osage do not use Ho'-e-ga as a vague term; rather, they employ it to refer to particular sacred "things." Significantly, they call the earth's surface Ho'-e-ga because it is the space where all life takes on bodily form, which implies that the quartered circle is an Osage world symbol. However, they also use Ho'-e-ga to refer to the child in the Wa'-wa-tho (peace/adoption) ceremony, the sacred eagle, and their ceremonial hearths (see Bailey 1995; Hall 1997).

These associations in Osage beliefs are reminiscent of the common cross-cultural practice of employing relational notions of the body, house, and settlement as elements in a microcosmic repertoire (sensu Ellen 1986:3). It is therefore pertinent that "the Osage image of the universe is seen in their village arrangement (La Flesche 1921:50–51), in the organization of their House of Mystery (La Flesche 1925:84), and in the rush mat that held the sacred hawk (La Flesche 1930:682–83)" (Bailey 1995:289 n. 19). In other rituals, the Osage conceived of a symbolic man, who "stood for the unification of the two great tribal divisions, representative of the sky with its cosmic bodies and the Earth, the earth into which life descends to take on bodily forms" (Bailey 1995:137). All life was believed to be produced by the interaction of the sky (father) and the earth (mother), analogous to the reciprocal obligations that the Osage earth and sky moieties had to each other (La Flesche in Bailey 1995:31). Consequently, Ho'-e-ga relationally defines the earth as a container analogous to the bodies of humans and animals, whose life consists of a marked cycle of birth, maturity, old age, death, and rebirth. The importance assigned to these life cycles is not specific to the Osage,

but common to most Native American religions (Hultkrantz 1987).

Scioto communities at Mound City and other Ohio Hopewell sites may have employed a similar relational microcosmic repertoire, since such beliefs are often associated with the construction of nested containers as documented by various ethnographic and archaeological case studies (see, for example, Carsten and Hugh-Jones 1995; Ellen 1986; Gillespie 2000; Hugh-Jones 1995; Waterson 1990). The quartered circles, prominently displayed by Scioto peoples on a variety of Ohio Hopewell ritual paraphernalia, may also suggest ritual themes analogous to the Osage Ho'-e-ga (cf. Lankford 2007). Since microcosms and macrocosms are relational constructs that depend on where you enter (Ellen 1986:3), let us walk through the door of a Mound City charnel house.

Ohio Hopewell Charnel Houses

Inside these charnel houses, Ohio Hopewell peoples stored their dead as they moved through the various stages of their dissolution (Brown 1979, 2004; Greber 1983). Yet these mortuary regimes, like those of the Huron and other Native American communities, were probably marked by a distinct ambivalence because it was important both to maintain a safe distance from the dead and literally to reincorporate valued attributes of their persona into living people (Hall 1976, 1997). These buildings were also places where Ohio Hopewell people performed other rites of ritual riddance, including the deposition of "killed ceremonial objects" and ritual feasting (Brown 2004). Yet like the dead, these charnel houses were dismantled and often covered with a mound at the end of their life, although some of the most important were rebuilt (Brown 2004). While this is physically how Scioto peoples used these charnel houses, I posit that the human body served as a model for the symbolism of these contingent containers (sensu Miller 1980).

In particular, the use of Ohio Hopewell charnel houses may have been linked to how a person's skin operates as a permeable boundary. For example, the skin holds in and protects its contents at the same time as it communicates what is inside (Anzieu 1989; Gell 1993). Thus, the shape and form of these charnel houses probably signaled what they contained (i.e., the dead), while "protecting" and isolating their contents. This containment focused on the putrescence of the corpse in order to curtail the movement of the malevolent spirits/souls associated with the dead (Hall 1976; Hultkrantz 1953). In fact, Hall (1976) has stated that Eastern Woodland peoples widely believed that a circular shape, analogous to many Early and Middle Woodland charnel structures, offered protection from otherworldly forces.[2] Other "sacred" shapes were also considered ritually potent; for example, when Cherokee conjurers watched over and protected a corpse, they raked coals and hot ashes into small rectangular hearths with raised ridges for walls. The Cherokee considered these ritual hearths analogous to other sacred enclosures such as the square-ground mound, house, or yard, which were constructed by many communities in the Southeast (Witthoft 1983:71).

It also seems likely that these charnel structures symbolized a higher level of communal relations to these dispersed peoples, since they resulted from collective investment (cf. Carr 2005; Greber 1983; Greber and Ruhl 1989). The social relations encompassed by this "house" may have varied significantly (compare Clay 1987 and 1998 with Greber 1997), but even kin groups or sodalities consist of diverse groups whose associations often cross-cut other identities (Carr 2005). Likewise, the diverse physical composition of these houses, consisting of clay floors, wooden posts, fired clay basins, and other features, may have also symbolized how unity can be fashioned from diversity, similar to the symbolism of historic Calumet pipes (Hall 1997:51; see also Bailey 1995:34–35). These buildings may have also indexed social alliances that stressed the importance of reciprocal relations because some of these charnel houses were linked through portals or passageways (Carr 2005). These connected spaces may have also served in ritually complementary ways such as at Mound City (Brown 2004:157–159), while in other cases they may have signified specific alliances (sensu Carr and Case 2005).

Like the body, Early and Middle Woodland charnel houses consumed the dead in order to turn them into sustenance that ensured the life and continuity of the community. This process both contained and allowed the pollution of the death to escape, leaving behind the immortal durable parts of these persons (sensu Hertz 1960). The consumption of the dead by charnel houses was enacted through the processing of the deceased in these places. It seems likely that this began when local relatives and other people closely associated with the deceased placed the corpse in the ritual enclosure, since the body's decomposition and/or cremation in these places was probably important.[3] Unfettering of the moorings between the living and dead was probably believed to occur in the liminal period following death (Hertz 1960; van Gennep 1970) because many Native American peoples considered death a lengthy process marked by rites of separation, transition, and reincorporation (Straus 1977, 1978; von Gernet 1994:43).

While there was considerable diversity in how the dead were processed and interred during the Early–Middle Woodland period, Scioto peoples probably enacted the importance of material release through either ritual decomposition or cremation. For example, the dead were allowed to ritually decompose in many Early Woodland charnel structures, along the lines presented in Hertz's (1960) classic discussion of secondary burial rites. This dissolution signaled material release and the end of the corpse's ritual pollution (Hertz 1960; Metcalf and Huntington 1991). The "clean" bones of the deceased were then frequently collected, although some isolated elements often remained (Aument 1990; Clay 1998; Hays 1995). Cross-culturally, cremation is often considered an alternative to decomposition that accelerates material release (Hertz 1960; Miller 2001a). Scioto people almost exclusively cremated the dead at Mound City and Tremper, probably fairly soon after death (Brown 1979, 2004; Mills 1922; Squier and Davis 1998 [1848]), since these corpses appear to have been burned in the flesh (Baby 1954; Konigsberg 1985). Cremation was also the predominant method of processing the dead at many other Ohio Hopewell sites (Fischer 1974). Yet primary interments were present at Hopewell, Edwin Harness, Seip, and Turner (Mills 1907; Moorehead 1922; Shetrone and Greenman 1931; Willoughby and Hooton 1922). But given the organizational demands of hosting increasingly larger secondary burial rites, these extended burials probably had adequate time to decompose. Other idiosyncratic mortuary rites such as crushing skulls at North Benton probably also signified material release (Magrath 1945).

The material release of various portions of the deceased through their decomposition or cremation probably distanced their pollution and safely arrested it in places where it would not haunt or harm the living (Küchler 1997:48). The odor and flesh of the dead may have been considered a vital offering to otherworldly persons (sensu Küchler 1997), including the charnel house and the raptorial birds, who fed on the bodies.[4] These offerings may have "returned" the contributions or gifts that otherworldly persons made to human life (Straus 1977). The process purified and left behind the immortal durable parts of the person, that is, their bones, names, knowledge, positions, and prerogatives. In some cases, the deceased's heir probably reclaimed these names, positions, or prerogatives through mourning/adoption rituals (Hall 1997).

These Early and Middle Woodland charnel structures also followed a similar trajectory to that of a human life because they had complicated ceremonies at their birth and death (Brown 2004; Greber 1983). Thus, razing a significant charnel house and constructing a new one might have been considered analogous to symbolic rebirth of important persons through Eastern Woodlands mourning/adoption rituals (sensu Hall 1997; von Gernet 1994). Notably, at their death some of these Early/Middle Woodland charnel structures were burned (Mills 1916; Webb and Baby 1957; Webb and Snow 1974), while in other cases only particular posts were burned and the rest were simply pulled (Greber 1983:29). These differences may relate to the cyclicality of these ritual regimes or lack thereof. The only structure at Tremper, for example, was burned (Mills 1916), but in places where multiple charnel houses were constructed, only some of the posts were burned and the rest pulled, such as at Seip, Liberty, and Mound City (Greber 1983: 29). The construction of multiple charnel houses and mounds at these places indicates the cyclicality of these ritual regimes, which was absent at Tremper. If we use cremation as an analogue, perhaps only the decomposing posts were burned and the others were recycled to provide continuity between these structures, as in Northwest Coast ritual practices (Kan 1989:64). This continuity was often reinforced through the use of an idealized architectural template like the one employed at Mound City (Brown 2004).

In general, the symbolism of Ohio Hopewell charnel houses probably emphasized how a united social body or a complex whole is created from the reciprocal obligations of diverse agents. These obligations probably prescribed how the living should care for bodies of the dead, as well as what they should give the dead for their journey, as in Winnebago funerary rites (see Radin 1970). This ritual work almost certainly implied reciprocal relations beyond the immediate sodality, obligations that were probably fulfilled by the guests at elaborate secondary burial rites (see below). Other ritual sacrifices were probably also performed for the significant other-than-human persons, who made "life" possible. In turn, the dead and these important other-than-human persons returned various gifts that enabled life. These gifts may have included the mourning/adoption rituals that symbolically reincarnated important individuals by transferring their names, positions, and/or knowledge to the living (Hall 1987:188).

Ohio Hopewell Fired Clay Basins

Another important architectural feature in most Ohio Hopewell charnel houses was the fired clay basin, which was usually oriented along the same axis as the structure that enclosed it (Brown 2004). These basins were often constructed as a mirror image of the charnel house in which they were contained, as well as possibly a representation of the earth/cosmos (see above). Like the earth, these clay basins were continually in a state of consuming and transforming the materials they were fed, such as wood, animal fat, and blood. In return, these fires provided light, supplied warmth, and cooked food that enabled the life of these communities. These clay basins were therefore not static, self-contained entities, but agents of transformation that enabled the life of others through the flow of shared substances, such as heat, life, health, smoke, and food. Like other Ohio Hopewell contingent containers, these fired clay basins had a distinctive life cycle that was marked or commemorated at different stages. And sometimes important sacrificial caches were placed within or next to them at their death.

At Mound City, Liberty, and Seip, Ohio Hopewell peoples usually produced these ceremonial hearths as rectangular basins with rounded corners, mirroring the shape and orientation of the charnel house in which they were contained (see Brown 2004; Greber 1983, 1996).[5] They were produced from puddled clay, a mixture of clay and water, at the same time as the floor of the charnel structure.[6] These fired clay basins were usually between three and six feet in length (Seeman 2004:68), but their size gradient varies at different Ohio Hopewell sites, perhaps implying differences in their use (Greber 1996:159; Konigsberg 1985).

Although these fired clay basins were molded from the earth, their life probably began when they were first kindled because fire was believed by many southeastern Native people to be associated with the sky (upper world) and thought to possess a life of its own (Hudson 1976:126).[7] This parallels the Osage belief that life comes from the sky and descends to take material form on the earth, caught in Ho'-e-ga, or the "snare of life" (Bailey 1995:31). Many southeastern Native peoples also considered the sacred fire the principal symbol of purity, the center of community life, and the ally and earthly representation of the sun (Hudson 1976:126, 318; Lankford 1987:54). Dire consequences could occur if the "sacred fire" were sullied (see Lankford 1987:56–57).

Southeastern peoples therefore fed fire only particular substances such as wood and blood, and they were careful not to extinguish fire with water, its opposite (Hudson 1976:128). The Cherokee, for example, believed that blood was to fire as saliva was to water, so it was important not to spit in the fire. The sacred hearth thus contained fire just as the body held in blood. It was consequently acceptable to place meat in the fire, and successful Cherokee hunters would give/sacrifice a small portion of their kill to the fire (Hudson 1976:126; 1984:12).[8] People were therefore responsible for keeping fire and water apart, "except in funerary ceremonies in an act that symbolized death" (Hudson 1976:317–318). This symbolic death enacted through quenching these ritual hearths with water may have been an important rite of reversal, which had a special place in Ohio Hopewell mortuary ritual (see below).

Consequently, Ohio Hopewell ceremonial hearths were probably fed a steady diet of various (possibly symbolically charged) woods, as well as probably blood, meat, food, tobacco, and other flammable materials. In addition, many of these basins appear to have been used to contain intense fires in which were burned (at least at some Ohio Hopewell sites) the bodies of the dead, as well as ritual paraphernalia (Seeman 2004:68). The use of these ceremonial hearths to cremate the dead is supported by the pieces of these basins that Mills (1922) found mixed in with cremations at Mound City, but the contextual evidence at other sites is more ambiguous and the associated basins are smaller (Konigsberg 1985). Brown (2004) has also argued that feasts were held in some mortuary contexts at Mound City, while Seeman (1979b) presented widespread (if often decontextualized) evidence of feasting at other Ohio Hopewell sites. The presence of feasting in these mortuary contexts suggests that some of these ceremonial basins might have been used in the preparation of food.

Although the association between cremation and cooking might appear incongruous, burning the body may have been symbolically likened to cooking food, since both purified things that were consumed to ensure the continued existence of the community. The smoke was probably believed to carry back the contributions from the upper world/sky, leaving behind the durable portions of the person, his or her burned ashes/bones, which were returned to the earth during secondary burial (mounding) rites. Cremation would have also allowed fairly rapid burial rites to be scheduled so that a person's successor could quickly replace him or her through mourning/adoption rites.[9] It may have also alleviated the smell of the corpse and hastened the person's transmogrification to other realities (Miller 2001a). For example, the Maricopa from the Southwest cremate their dead so that they could enter the afterworld because otherwise they smelled bad, while the Mohave and Pomo note that fire improves the smell and prefer cooking (cremation) to putrefaction (Miller 2001a:125).

It is probably also important that other objects were burned (sacrificed) in these ceremonial hearths. There are at least two possible explanations for sacrificing objects during these mortuary rituals. As Hertz (1960:46) pointed out, the secondary disposal of the dead is often connected to ritual sacrifice by the notion that objects must be destroyed in this world so that they can pass to the next. Winnebago mourning and burial rites, for example, offered the deceased a burning brand, food, and tobacco to take on their journey and to give to the important personages they encountered along the way (see Radin 1970). Similarly, the Huron dead would not depart from the land of the living until they collected the gifts bestowed on them at the "Feast of the Dead" (von Gernet 1994:43). In other cases, sacrificial rites are more distinctly rites of ritual riddance that "kill" objects that have become polluted or dangerous as a result of the contact they effect with otherworldly beings, as is commonly believed by many indigenous people in the Pacific (Küchler 1997:40).

Ohio Hopewell fired clay basins were extensively used, cared for, and periodically cleaned out, since they were baked bright red, often to a depth of several feet. Yet many of these ceremonial hearths were deeply fissured and cracked, characteristics that archaeologists have interpreted as evidence of long-term usage (Brown 2004:155; Seeman 2004:69). However, it is possible that Ohio Hopewell people "killed" or extinguished some of these hearths by dousing them with water, an act that would very likely have cracked them (sensu Hudson 1976:317–318, 335). While the notion that Ohio Hopewell people "killed" these basins is tentative, it is important to take note of other rites of reversal that occurred in these contexts. For example, Scioto people at Mound City created a "ceremonial basin" that paralleled the form of these clay hearths from the burned organic and ceremonial refuse under Mound 13 (Mills 1922:448–451).[10] The charnel houses that contained these clay basins were also dismantled, which would have paralleled ceremonially killing these hearths by dousing them with water, an act in southeastern funerary rites that symbolized death (sensu Hudson 1976:317–318, 335).

Fragments of broken or shattered basins were also included as offerings in intact basins (Seeman 2004:69), similar to the placement of cremations and other mortuary objects in these hearths (Greber 1996). Sometimes Scioto people also placed important ritual caches within or

near some of these "fixed" basins, including the cache of effigy pipes and other ritual paraphernalia found under Mound 8 at Mound City (Squier and Davis 1998 [1848]:153). Scioto people also burned vast amounts of ritual paraphernalia in two altars (fired clay basins) that were eventually covered by Hopewell Mound 25 (see Greber and Ruhl 1989:76–81). In fact, virtually all the large Ohio Hopewell ceremonial caches appear to have been placed within or near one of these basins, although most of these hearths were "empty" (Greber 1996:159).

New ceremonial basins were sometimes constructed adjacent to or even directly over an older ceremonial basin (Seeman 2004:69).[11] At Mound City, these new hearths were constructed in tandem with an entirely new charnel house and appear to have symbolically renewed the ritual space (Brown 2004). This symbolic renewal appears to have occurred only in the most important charnel houses, as marked by the presence of large ritual caches. This renewal of particular spaces would have enhanced the continuity between ritual cycles, while marking an end and a new beginning.

Thus, Ohio Hopewell fired clay basins seem to have acted like charnel houses, as living entities and agents of transformation who contributed to the flow of shared substances through these communities. These hearths probably were used to heat/feed the community, to supply the dead with various killed or insubstantial things, and to "kill" particular polluted things in rites of ritual riddance (Küchler 1997). This highlights how these fired clay basins transformed the various things they consumed in order to ensure the life of the community, but in turn their lives ended in an event sometimes marked by elaborate ritual interments (caches). However, the most important ceremonial hearths may have been reincarnated in a new material form, just as mourning/adoption "requickened" the dead in the Eastern Woodlands (see Hall 1987, 1997).

Ohio Hopewell Mounds and Enclosures

Ohio Hopewell mounds and earthen embankments also served as contingent containers through which transformation was achieved. In the most obvious sense, these mounds and enclosures were constructed as containers that covered and enveloped liminal places symbolically associated with death in order to enact a ceremonial renewal of the earth (Hall 1997; Knight 2006). This mound building probably occurred during secondary burial rites that were scheduled well in advance. The scheduled events were probably large, diverse, interregional gatherings and feasts that were hosted by the Ohio Hopewell communities, similar to the historic Feast of the Dead in the Great Lakes (Carr 2005; see also Hickerson 1960, 1963; von Gernet 1994). Yet sponsoring these ritual gatherings and feasts probably also enacted renewal in a less obvious sense by redistributing the hosts' food, tobacco, and other gifts into new "containers," the bodies of their guests. These events thus transformed food, pots, tobacco, and other comestibles into spatially expansive social relations and interpersonal remembrance (sensu Munn 1986).

The construction of an Ohio Hopewell mound appears to have begun with rites of ritual riddance, which often included razing and/or dismantling a charnel structure (Clay 2002). As noted above, Ohio Hopewell people destroyed these charnel houses by either burning the entire structure or burning only particular poles and pulling the rest. Sometimes it appears that Scioto people started to mound over these areas while the charnel structure was still burning or at least smoldering (see Greber 1991:9; Greber and Ruhl 1989:44). Other times, small mounds were built over important burials and/or ceremonial hearths while the area was still covered by a charnel house. This mounding seems to have been an aspect of ritual riddance, since it appears to have been essential to separate and cover ceremonial remains, possibly because they were believed to be dangerous or polluting to the living (sensu Küchler 1997). These acts of ritual riddance were probably carefully choreographed with quite a bit of pageantry, and were at least partially intended to entertain the large audiences that attended these secondary burial rites, since mound building appears to have occurred as part of (or very soon after) other important ritual performances.

The notion that Ohio Hopewell mound building occurred as part of secondary burial rites that were scheduled well in advance explains how these communities assembled the labor force necessary to construct the earthworks. Using catch-

ment analyses and ethnographic comparisons, Bernardini (2004) has shown that Ohio Hopewell earthworks and mounds were apparently constructed by multiple spatially overlapping communities. While Carr has used this evidence to argue that multiple communities with overlapping territories used mound and earthwork complexes (Ruby et al. 2005:159–166), I believe it is more likely, based on ethnographic comparisons, that the deceased individual's local relatives and other closely linked people first placed and processed the corpse in these ritual enclosures (sensu Greber 1991, 1997). They then commemorated the dead and reincorporated them into the community at secondary burial rites when the labor of large aggregate groups of people was marshaled to construct the Ohio Hopewell embankments and mounds (sensu Bernardini 2004). However, membership in these various sodalities may have overlapped considerably, necessitating the renegotiation of social relations at these mortuary events (Clay 1987, 1998).

Shifts in mound construction from the Early to Middle Woodland transition in the central Scioto River Valley also point to changes in how continuity with the ancestral past was established (Seeman and Branch 2006; Branch 2000). This transition marked a shift from a more spatially dispersed mound building on hilltops and ridges to larger, more historically complicated, multiple mound centers that were located on broad terraces directly above the floodplain (Seeman and Branch 2006). Seeman and Branch (2006:121) argue that this shift occurs because "Adena" mounds served as a stage for cyclical ritual activities, while Hopewell structures fix and remember an event in space. But this dichotomy is based on Branch's characterization of "Adena" mounds as accretional structures that were used through time and thus the result of cyclical ritual activities. Yet many of the activities at the different stages of "Adena" mounds were highly variable; it is very often the primary interments at the base of these mounds that share the most similarities (Hays 1995:356).

In contrast, Scioto communities at many large Ohio Hopewell complexes used ritual spaces quite consistently in a highly cyclical manner. Scioto people at Mound City repetitively and sequentially constructed, used, and dismantled oblong charnel houses with rounded corners (Brown 1979, 2004). Scioto peoples terminated the ritual use of these different precincts by mounding these spaces over, not once but repetitively, more than 24 times at Mound City alone (see Brown 2004:152–155). Sequential buildings were also constructed in some of these spaces before they were eventually covered with a mound, similar to some other Early and Middle Woodland sites (Brown 2004:153–155; see also Clay 1987, 1998, 2002).[12] These repetitive ritual cycles were also enacted at other Ohio Hopewell mound sites, where large oblong buildings with rounded corners constitute a fairly standardized template (Brown 1979, 2004), such as Seip and Liberty (Greber 1979, 1983, 1996).[13] These repetitive ritual regimes suggest that Ohio Hopewell communities enacted a cyclical and consequentially regenerative mounding that highlights the role of these rites in enacting renewal (see Knight 2006; Miller 2001b). Ohio Hopewell mound construction did not therefore inscribe the landscape as a static aide-mémoire, but rather offered templates that were used in a dynamic process of memory work (sensu Küchler 1993).

Ohio Hopewell mound building also returned the durable parts of the dead to the earth by covering these liminal places with mounds in an act of world renewal (Byers 2004; Hall 1997; Knight 2006; Miller 2001b). This act was probably analogous to the rebirth of the earth in spring, as well as the reincarnation of important persons through mourning/adoption rites of "requickening" (Hall 1997). This symbolic act probably transformed liminal places associated with death into new "earth islands" and/or symbolic wombs that covered old surfaces to literally create new places (sensu Knight 2006:428). Yet the physical presence of the mound still marked this sequence of events. In this way, the dead were safely distanced from the living, while maintaining their presence on the landscape. Ohio Hopewell mounds also stabilized liminal places by literally containing them under mounds and within ritually efficient enclosures (sensu Miller 2001b).

Ohio Hopewell secondary burial rites likely also served as an opportunity to "work out" competing claims on the social persona of the dead and its economic consequences (Clay 1998:14), as well as to fulfill other reciprocal obligations.

For example, more recent excavations have suggested the importance of feasting at Mound City, since the deer bones associated with particular ritual deposits in several different spatial locales appear to have been associated with feasting (Brown 2004:155, 159). During these feasts, the hosts of these Ohio Hopewell ceremonies probably fed, entertained, and gifted their guests. Given ethnographic parallels, these feasts were presumably significant in forgetting the dead and emptying these houses of their pollution by returning the contributions "others" made to the life of the deceased (Battaglia 1992; Kan 1989; Küchler 2002). These events probably also entailed other reciprocal obligations as well because the guests at these secondary burial feasts helped construct earthworks that constituted the final containers for their dead.[14] The guests may have also played a crucial role in mourning and adoption rituals through which the dead were "requickened" or reincarnated by passing their name, title, and/or other important ritual prerogatives to their successors (cf. Hall 1997 and Küchler 1997). In turn, Ohio Hopewell communities probably also offered other, more intangible things such as songs, masked performances, and dances that referred to their connections to the dead and important other-than-human persons (Morrison 2000).

Feasting and gift giving likely also contributed to establishing even larger social wholes composed of all the participants at these secondary burial events. Although bonds of friendship cannot be purchased through vulgar economic exchanges, giving gifts and maintaining reciprocal relations often serve to transform the value of food, comestibles, and other objects into enduring social relationships (Battaglia 1992; Munn 1986; Shoemaker 2004). This flow of food, tobacco, and other gifts appears to be recorded at many Hopewell sites (see Seeman 1979a, 1995) and constitutes patterns of exchange that probably had continuity with earlier Archaic practices (Brose 1990).

Conclusion

It is important to realize that Ohio Hopewell complexity lies in the reciprocal obligations established and maintained by these communities through the flow of tangible and intangible "things." This flow of "things" served in Ohio

Hopewell mortuary regimes to perpetuate life cycles and enact renewal, marking the movement from "womb to tomb" (sensu Parker Pearson 1999:25). These Ohio Hopewell rites both distanced the dead and emptied their sponsors of the dead person's influence by returning the gifts that had been made to them, contributions that had enabled their life. This process separated the deceased and other things into their constituent parts so as to purify and redistribute particular aspects of them (Küchler 1997). These material and immaterial things were then recycled into "new" agents, vessels, or containers, that is, bodies, houses, and communities. Yet each of these agents (persons, houses, fires, and communities) had the obligation to contribute to and provision these larger wholes by sharing their labor, food, light, heat, and after death their ancestral legacy, probably including important names, positions, prerogatives, rituals, and knowledge.

Consequently, Ohio Hopewell communities were linked through the flow of shared substances, such as food, smoke (tobacco), gifts, collaborative labor, speeches, and ritual performances. The ritual elaboration of these reciprocal relations suggests that maintaining continuity was important, since Early and Middle Woodland communities in the central Ohio River Valley either lived in dispersed farmsteads or engaged in even more itinerant hunter-gatherer lifeways (Cowan 2006; Pacheco and Dancey 2006; Yerkes 2006). Maintaining continuity in a fragmented world is an important rationale for the sacrificial rites enacted by the indigenous peoples of the Northwest Coast and New Ireland (see Kan 1986, 1989; Küchler 1997, 2002). However, these are not "functional" relations of interiority as theorized by romantic complexity (DeLanda 2006:9; Kwa 2002). Rather, Ohio Hopewell communities constructed relations of exteriority in which the properties of these wholes resulted from each of its different parts exercising their capabilities (DeLanda 2006:11). This produced heterogeneous sets of "agents," who contribute to each other's ex-

istence and can be aptly described as "table companions" (Kwa 2002). Yet personal ambition is not necessarily suppressed by these ritual regimes, but rather remains in an uneasy tension with communal obligations (Kan 1989; Küchler 2002).

While it is possible to emphasize the alterity of these sacrificial regimes, simplistically attributing these rites of ritual riddance to non-Western "others" disregards the complicated relationship between idolatry and iconoclasm in Western discourses (Gross 1985; Küchler 1997). Serres, for example, has characterized scholarly discourses as sacrificial or parasitic economies in which we often symbolically "kill" our intellectual ancestors and distance our work from its familial ties (2007 [1992]; Serres and Latour 1995). How else to characterize Marx turning Hegel's dialectics on its head? Or the way we routinely attack and kill the intellectual legacy of our ancestors and colleagues? Serres's analogy also emphasizes how we steal (consume) or more hopefully use data and ideas from other people, places, and times, as reflected in our bibliographies. Thus, the question is not whether we should eat, but how we should eat well or ethically (Wolfe 2007:xvi). Should we kill our intellectual ancestors or acknowledge their importance in order to create larger communities bound together by the flow of data, knowledge, and ideas? Obviously, disagreeing with and critiquing the work of others is important, but we also must establish reciprocal obligations with one another and the communities we study. Personal ambitions often rest uneasily with these goals.

Yet each of our offerings always produces a complex whole that enacts a form of renewal. It provides food for thought, some of which we distance ourselves from and some of which we recycle and mobilize in our subsequent work. It is an efficacious representation, a ritual sacrifice. Perhaps our notions of complexity will always revolve around particular ways in which we are similar to other societies (sensu Chapman 2003:7).

Acknowledgments

I express my gratitude to the Ohio Historical Society, the British Museum, the Field Museum, and the Hopewell Culture National Historical Park for granting access to their collections from the Hopewell, Mound City, and Tremper sites. In particular, Martha Otto, Bradley Lepper, Jamie Kelly, and Ian Taylor were very kind, patient, and tolerant in guiding me through the collections at these institutions. I also thank Charlie Cobb, David Anderson, Kim Vivier, and the anonymous reviewers for their comments and insights on a draft of this chapter.

Notes

1. This perspectivism emphasizes "the truth of relativity and not a relativity of truth" (Deleuze 1993:21).
2. In some mortuary rites, the widow and close relatives of the deceased would even walk a circuit around the corpse so that the spirit of the departed would not bother them (Voegelin 1944:388–399).
3. Alternately, the deceased may have sometimes been processed elsewhere and interred on the floor of these charnel houses during secondary burial rites. This redeposition may have occurred when (1) the corpse decomposed elsewhere and was later interred as a bundle burial or (2) an individual was cremated and the remains were collected and then deposited in another place.
4. For the Northern Cheyenne, "the final locale of the life principal is in the marrow-filled bones of the skeleton after the flesh has fallen away or been eaten by carnivorous birds.... Following scaffold burial, reburial of bones was common in the old days, and marked the end of the process of death" (Straus 1977:327).
5. Rectangular basins with rounded corners also predominated at Hopewell and Turner, but some circular basins were found at Hopewell (Squier and Davis 1998 [1848]; Mills 1922) and a few oblong basins with trefoil corners were constructed at Turner (Greber 1996; Willoughby and Hooton 1922). The relationship between the circular basins at Hopewell and the oblong basins with trefoil corners at Turner and the charnel structures that probably enclosed them cannot be well established at these sites because the early archaeological excavations did not adequately document the spatial patterning of post molds (see Brown 2004).
6. These fired clay basins and the clay floors of these houses were probably constructed after the area was extensively prepared. At Edwin Harness, Scioto people stripped off the topsoil down to the B horizon and leveled out the exposed surface before they started constructing the clay floor and charnel house (Greber 1983:23).
7. The Cherokee, for example, referred to fire as an old woman and fed her a portion of each meal (Hudson 1976:126).
8. Similarly, it was important not to mix blood and water, an activity whose consequences are chronicled in the "Twins myths." In these myths "thrown away boy" was born from his twin's blood and umbilical cord, which their parents threw into the river. While "thrown away boy" and his twin were heroes in these myths, they also killed their father and sacrificed their mother, marking both their ritual power and their ambiguity.
9. Otherwise, it is often important to allow the body to completely decompose before secondary burial rites (Hertz 1960).
10. Four important cremations and associated ritual paraphernalia were placed in this pseudo fired clay basin, after which the entire area was covered with large sheets of mica. Mills dubbed these burials the Great Mica Grave (1922:448–451).
11. In addition, some of these important broken basins were "fixed" with the application of additional puddled clay. However, these "fixed" hearths were never relit or reused.
12. Although some of these charnel houses were certainly used at the same time, differences in their relative age suggest a dynamic history at Mound City (Brown 2004).
13. Similar charnel houses were probably also present at Hopewell and Turner, but early excavations at these sites did not consistently identify house patterns (see Moorehead 1922; Shetrone and Greenman 1931; Willoughby and Hooton 1922).
14. An ethnographic example from the Northwest Coast is the reciprocal obligation of the guests to construct a new container for the deceased's remains and then move them into the village of the dead (Kan 1989).

References

Anzieu, Didier
1989   *The Skin Ego*. Translated by Chris Turner. Yale University Press, New Haven.

Aument, Bruce W.
1990   Mortuary Variability in the Middle Big Darby Drainage of Central Ohio between 300 BC and 300 AD. Unpublished Ph.D. dissertation, Ohio State University, Columbus.

Baby, Raymond
1954   *Hopewell Cremation Practices*. Papers in Archaeology No. 1. Ohio Historical Society, Columbus.

Bailey, Garrick A.
1995   *The Osage and the Invisible World: From the Works of Francis La Flesche*. University of Oklahoma Press, Norman.

Battaglia, Debbora
1992   The Body in the Gift: Memory and Forgetting in Sabarl Mortuary Exchange. *American Ethnologist* 19(1):3–18.

Bernardini, Wesley

2004   Hopewell Geometric Earthworks: A Case Study in the Referential and Experiential Meaning of Monuments. *Journal of Anthropological Archaeology* 23:331–356.

Binford, Lewis

1971   Mortuary Practices: Their Study and Their Potential. In *Approaches to the Social Dimensions of Mortuary Practices*, edited by James A. Brown. *Memoirs of the Society for American Archaeology* 25:6–29.

Branch, James R.

2000   Patterns of Mound Distribution: The Cultural Landscape of Ross County, Ohio. Unpublished master's thesis, Kent State University, Kent, Ohio.

Brose, David S.

1990   Towards a Model of Exchange Values for the Eastern Woodlands. *Midcontinental Journal of Archaeology* 15(1):100–136.

Brose, David, and N'omi Greber

1979   *Hopewell Archaeology: The Chillicothe Conference*. Kent State University Press, Kent, Ohio.

Brown, James

1979   Charnel Houses and Mortuary Crypts: Disposal of the Dead in the Middle Woodland Period. In *Hopewell Archaeology: The Chillicothe Conference*, edited by David Brose and N'omi Greber, pp. 211–219. Kent State University Press, Kent, Ohio.

2004   Mound City and Issues in the Developmental History of Hopewell Culture in the Ross County Area of Southern Ohio. In *Aboriginal Ritual and Economy in the Eastern Woodlands: Essays in Memory of Howard Dalton Winters*, edited by Anne-Marie Cantwell, Lawrence A. Conrad, and Jonathan E. Reyman, pp. 147–168. Kampsville Studies in Archeology and History Vol. 5. Center for American Archeology, Kampsville, Illinois.

Byers, A. Martin

2004   *The Ohio Hopewell Episode: Paradigm Lost and Paradigm Gained*. University of Akron Press, Akron, Ohio.

Carr, Christopher

2005   The Tripartite Ceremonial Alliance among Scioto Hopewellian Communities and the Question of Social Ranking. In *Gathering Hopewell: Society, Ritual, and Ritual Interaction*, edited by Christopher Carr and D. Troy Case, pp. 258–338. Kluwer Academic/Plenum, New York.

Carr, Christopher, and D. Troy Case

2005   The Nature of Leadership in Ohio Hopewellian Societies: Role Segregation and the Transformation from Shamanism. In *Gathering Hopewell: Society, Ritual, and Ritual Interaction*, edited by Christopher Carr and D. Troy Case, pp. 177–237. Kluwer Academic/Plenum, New York.

Carsten, Janet, and Stephen Hugh-Jones

1995   Introduction: About the House—Lévi-Strauss and Beyond. In *About the House: Lévi-Strauss and Beyond*, edited by Janet Carsten and Stephen Hugh-Jones, pp. 1–46. Cambridge University Press, Cambridge.

Chapman, Robert

2003   *Archaeologies of Complexity*. Routledge, London.

Charles, Douglas K., and Jane E. Buikstra

1983   Archaic Mortuary Sites in the Central Mississippi Drainage: Distribution, Structure, and Behavioral Implications. In *Archaic Hunters and Gatherers in the American Midwest*, edited by James L. Phillips and James A. Brown, pp. 117–145. Academic Press, New York.

Clay, R. Berle

1986   Adena Ritual Spaces. In *Early Woodland Archaeology*, edited by Kenneth Farnsworth and Thomas Emerson, pp. 581–595. Center for American Archeology, Kampsville, Illinois.

1987   Circles and Ovals: Two Types of Adena Ritual Space. *Southeastern Archaeology* 6(1): 46–55.

1998   The Essential Features of Adena Ritual and Their Implications. *Southeastern Archaeology* 17:1–21.

2002   Deconstructing the Woodland Sequence from the Heartland: A Review of Recent Research Directions in the Upper Ohio Valley. In *The Woodland Southeast*, edited by David G. Anderson and Robert C. Mainfort, Jr., pp. 162–184. University of Alabama Press, Tuscaloosa.

Cowan, Frank L.

2006   A Mobile Hopewell? Questioning Assumptions of Ohio Hopewell Sedentism. In *Recreating Hopewell: New Perspectives on Middle Woodland in Eastern North America*, edited by Douglas K. Charles and Jane E. Buikstra, pp. 26–49. University Press of Florida, Gainesville.

DeLanda, Manuel

2006   *A New Philosophy of Society: Assemblage Theory and Social Complexity*. Continuum Books, New York.

Deleuze, Gilles
1993   *The Fold: Leibniz and the Baroque*. Translated by Tom Conley. University of Minnesota Press, Minneapolis.

Ellen, Roy
1986   Microcosm, Macrocosm, and the Nuaulu House: Concerning Reductionist Fallacy as Applied to Metaphoric Levels. *Bijdragen Tot de Taal-, Land- en Volkenkunde* 142:1–30.

Fischer, Fred W.
1974   Early and Middle Woodland Settlement, Subsistence, and Population in the Central Ohio River Valley. Unpublished Ph.D. dissertation, Washington University, St. Louis.

Fried, Morton H.
1967   *The Evolution of Political Society: An Essay in Political Anthropology*. Random House, New York.

Gell, Alfred
1993   *Wrapped in Images: Tattooing in Polynesia*. Clarendon Press, Oxford.

Gillespie, Susan D.
2000   Maya "Nested Houses": The Ritual Construction of Place. In *Beyond Kinship: Social and Material Reproduction in House Societies*, edited by Rosemary Joyce and Susan Gillespie, pp. 135–160. University of Pennsylvania Press, Philadelphia.

Greber, N'omi
1979   A Comparative Study of Site Morphology and Burial Patterns at Edwin Harness Mound and Seip Mound 1 and 2. In *Hopewell Archaeology: The Chillicothe Conference*, edited by David Brose and N'omi Greber, pp. 27–38. Kent State University Press, Kent, Ohio.

1983   *Recent Excavations at the Edwin Harness Mound, Liberty Works, Ross County, Ohio*. Midcontinental Journal of Archaeology Special Paper No. 5. Kent State University Press, Kent, Ohio.

1991   A Study of Continuity and Contrast between Central Scioto Adena and Hopewell Sites. *West Virginia Archaeologist* 43:1–26.

1996   A Commentary on the Contexts and Contents of Large to Small Ohio Hopewell Deposits. In *A View from the Core: A Synthesis of Ohio Hopewell Archaeology*, edited by Paul J. Pacheco, pp. 128–149. Ohio Archaeological Council, Columbus.

1997   Two Geometric Enclosures in the Paint Creek Valley: An Estimate of Possible Community Changes through Time. In *Ohio Hopewell Community Organization*, edited by William S. Dancey and Paul J. Pacheco,

pp. 207–230. Kent State University Press, Kent, Ohio.

Greber, N'omi, and Katherine Ruhl
1989   *The Hopewell Site: A Contemporary Analysis Based on the Work of Charles Willoughby*. Westview Press, Boulder, Colorado.

Gross, Kenneth
1985   *Spenserian Poetics: Idolatry, Iconoclasm, and Magic*. Cornell University Press, Ithaca, New York.

Hall, Robert L.
1976   Ghosts, Water Barriers, Corn and Sacred Enclosures in the Eastern Woodlands. *American Antiquity* 41(3):360–364.

1987   Calumet Ceremonialism, Mourning Ritual, and Mechanism of Inter-Tribal Trade. In *Mirror and Metaphor: Material and Social Constructions of Reality*, edited by Daniel W. Ingersoll, Jr., and Gordon Bronitsky, pp. 29–43. University Press of America, Boston.

1997   *An Archaeology of the Soul: North American Indian Beliefs and Ritual*. University of Illinois Press, Urbana.

Harrison, Simon
1992   Ritual as Intellectual Property. *Man* 27(2): 225–244.

Hays, Christopher
1995   Adena Mortuary Patterns and Ritual Cycles in the Upper Scioto Valley, Ohio. Unpublished Ph.D. dissertation, Binghamton University, Binghamton, New York.

Hertz, Robert
1960   *Death and the Right Hand*. Translated by Rodney and Claudia Needham. Free Press, Glencoe, Illinois.

Hickerson, Harold
1960   The Feast of the Dead among the Seventeenth Century Algonkians of the Upper Great Lakes. *American Anthropologist* 62(1): 81–107.

1963   The Sociohistorical Significance of Two Chippewa Ceremonials. *American Anthropologist* 65(1):67–85.

Hudson, Charles
1976   *The Southeastern Indians*. University of Tennessee Press, Knoxville.

1984   *Elements of Southeastern Indian Religion*. Iconography of Religions, Section X: North America. E. J. Brill, Leiden.

Hugh-Jones, Stephen
1995   Inside-Out and Back-to-Front: The Androgynous House in Northwest Amazonia. In *About the House: Lévi-Strauss and Beyond*, edited by Janet Carsten and Stephen

Hugh-Jones, pp. 226–252. Cambridge University Press, Cambridge.

Hultkrantz, Åke

1953   *Conceptions of the Soul among North American Indians: A Study of Religious Ethnology.* Monograph Series No. 1. Ethnographical Museum of Sweden, Stockholm.

1987   *Native Religions of North America.* Harper and Row, San Francisco.

Johnston, Cheryl A.

2002   Culturally Modified Human Remains from the Hopewell Mound Group. Unpublished Ph.D. dissertation, Ohio State University, Columbus.

Kan, Sergei

1986   The Nineteenth-Century Tlingit Potlatch: A New Perspective. *American Ethnologist* 13(2): 191–212.

1989   *Symbolic Immortality: The Tlingit Potlatch of the Nineteenth Century.* Smithsonian Institution Press, Washington, D.C.

Knight, Vernon J.

2006   Symbolism of Mississippian Mounds. In *Powhatan's Mantle: Indians in the Colonial Southeast,* revised ed., edited by G. A. Waselkov, P. H. Wood, and T. Hatley, pp. 421–434. University of Nebraska Press, Lincoln.

Konigsberg, Lyle

1985   Demography and Mortuary Practice at Seip Mound One. *Midcontinental Journal of Archaeology* 10(1):123–148.

Küchler, Susanne

1993   Landscape as Memory: The Mapping of Processes and Its Representation in a Melanesian Society. In *Landscape: Politics and Perspectives,* edited by B. Bender, pp. 85–106. Berg, Providence, Rhode Island.

1997   Sacrificial Economy and Its Objects: Rethinking Colonial Collecting in Oceania. *Journal of Material Culture* 2(1):39–60.

2002   *Malanggan: Art, Memory, and Sacrifice.* Berg, Oxford.

Kwa, Chunglin

2002   Romantic and Baroque Conceptions of Complex Wholes in the Sciences. In *Complexities: Social Studies of Knowledge Practices,* edited by John Law and Annemarie Mol, pp. 23–52. Duke University Press, Durham, North Carolina.

La Flesche, Francis

1921   The Osage Tribe: Rite of Chiefs, Sayings of the Ancient Men. In *Thirty-Sixth Annual Report of the Bureau of Ethnology,* pp. 35–604.

1925   The Osage Tribe: Rite of Vigil. In *Thirty-Ninth*

Annual Report of the Bureau of Ethnology, pp. 31–630.

1930   The Osage Tribe: Rite of Wa-xo-be. In *Forty-Fifth Annual Report of the Bureau of Ethnology,* pp. 523–833.

1932   *A Dictionary of the Osage Language.* Bureau of American Ethnology, Bulletin No. 59. Washington, D.C.

Lankford, George E.

1987   *Native American Legends, Southeastern Legends: Tales from the Natchez, Caddo, Biloxi, Chickasaw, and Other Nations.* American Folklore Series. August House, Little Rock, Arkansas.

2007   Some Cosmological Motifs in the Southeastern Ceremonial Complex. In *Ancient Objects and Sacred Realms: Interpretations of Mississippian Iconography,* edited by F. Kent Reilly III and James F. Garber, pp. 8–38. University of Texas Press, Austin.

Law, John

1992   *Notes on the Theory of the Actor-Network: Ordering, Strategy and Heterogeneity.* Centre for Science Studies, Lancaster University. Electronic document, http://comp.lancs.ac.uk/sociology/soc054jl.html.

MacDonald, George F.

1981   Cosmic Equations in Northwest Coast Indian Art. In *The World Is as Sharp as a Knife: An Anthology in Honour of Wilson Duff,* edited by Donald N. Abbot, pp. 225–238. British Columbia Provincial Museum, Victoria.

Magrath, William H.

1945   The North Benton Mound: A Hopewell Site in Ohio. *American Antiquity* 11(1):40–47.

Metcalf, Peter, and Richard Huntington

1991   *Celebrations of Death: The Anthropology of Mortuary Ritual.* Cambridge University Press, Cambridge.

Miller, Jay

1980   The Matter of the (Thoughtful) Heart: Centrality, Focality or Overlap. *Journal of Anthropological Research* 36(3):338–342.

2001a   Ashes Ethereal: Cremation in the Americas. *American Indian Culture and Research Journal* 25(1):121–137.

2001b   Instilling the Earth: Explaining Mounds. *American Indian Culture and Research Journal* 25(3):161–177.

Mills, William C.

1907   Explorations of the Edwin Harness Mound. *Ohio Archaeological and Historical Quarterly* 16:113–193.

1916   Exploration of the Tremper Mounds. *Ohio*

Archaeological and Historical Quarterly 25: 262–398.

1922   Exploration of the Mound City Group. *Ohio Archaeological and Historical Quarterly* 31: 423–584.

Moorehead, Warren K.

1922   *The Hopewell Mound Group of Ohio*. Publication No. 211. Field Museum of Natural History, Chicago.

Morrison, Kenneth M.

2000   The Cosmos as Intersubjective: Native American Other-Than-Human Persons. In *Indigenous Religions: A Companion*, edited by Graham Harvey, pp. 23–36. Cassel, New York.

Munn, Nancy D.

1986   *The Fame of Gawa: A Symbolic Study of Value Transformation in a Massim (Papua New Guinea) Society*. Duke University Press, Durham, North Carolina.

Pacheco, Paul J., and Jarrod Burks

2008   Early Ceremonialism in Context: Results of the LCALS Research at the Munson Springs Site (33LI251). In *Transitions: Archaic and Early Woodlands Research in the Ohio Country*, edited by Martha P. Otto and Brian G. Redmond, pp. 159–182. Ohio University Press, Columbus.

Pacheco, Paul J., and William S. Dancey

2006   Integrating Mortuary and Settlement Data on Ohio Hopewell Society. In *Recreating Hopewell: New Perspectives on Middle Woodland in Eastern North America*, edited by Douglas K. Charles and Jane E. Buikstra, pp. 3–25. University Press of Florida, Gainesville.

Parker Pearson, Mike

1999   *The Archaeology of Death and Burial*. Texas A&M University Press, College Station.

Peat, F. David

2002   *Blackfoot Physics*. Weiser Books, Boston.

Prufer, Olaf

1964   The Hopewell Complex of Ohio. In *Hopewellian Studies*, edited by J. Caldwell and R. Hall, pp. 35–83. Scientific Papers No. 12. Illinois State Museum, Springfield.

Radin, Paul

1970   *The Winnebago Tribe*. University of Nebraska Press, Lincoln.

Rescher, Nicholas

1991   *G. W. Leibniz's Monadology: An Edition for Students*. University of Pittsburgh Press, Pittsburgh.

Richards, Ed, and Orrin C. Shane III

1974   Tuscarawas County's Kline Mound. *Ohio Archaeologist* 24(3):4–8.

Ruby, Bret, Christopher Carr, and Douglas Charles

2005   Community Organization in the Scioto, Mann and Havanna Hopewellian Regions. In *Gathering Hopewell: Society, Ritual, and Ritual Interaction*, edited by Christopher Carr and D. Troy Case, pp. 119–176. Kluwer Academic/Plenum, New York.

Russo, Michael

1996   Southeastern Archaic Mounds. In *Archaeology of the Mid-Holocene Southeast*, edited by Kenneth Sassaman and David Anderson, pp. 259–287. University Press of Florida, Gainesville.

Seeman, Mark

1979a   *The Hopewell Interaction Sphere: The Evidence of Interregional Trade and Structural Complexity*. Prehistory Research Series No. 5. Indiana Historical Society, Indianapolis.

1979b   Feasting with the Dead: Ohio Hopewell Charnel House Ritual as a Context for Redistribution. In *Hopewell Archaeology: The Chillicothe Conference*, edited by David Brose and N'omi Greber, pp. 39–46. Kent State University Press, Kent, Ohio.

1986   Adena "Houses" and Their Implications for Early Woodland Settlement Models in the Ohio Valley. In *Early Woodland Archaeology*, edited by Kenneth Farnsworth and Thomas Emerson, pp. 564–580. Center for American Archeology, Kampsville, Illinois.

1988   Ohio Hopewell Trophy-Skull Artifacts as Evidence for Competition in Middle Woodland Societies, circa 50 BC–AD 350. *American Antiquity* 53(3):565–577.

1995   When Words Are Not Enough: Hopewell Interregionalism and the Use of Material Symbols at the GE Mound. In *Native American Interactions: Multiscalar Analyses and Interpretations in the Eastern Woodlands*, edited by M. S. Nassaney and K. E. Sassaman, pp. 122–143. University of Tennessee Press, Knoxville.

2004   Hopewell Art in Hopewell Places. In *Hero, Hawk and Open Hand: American Indian Art of the Ancient Midwest and South*, edited by Richard Townsend, pp. 57–71. Art Institute of Chicago and Yale University Press, New Haven.

Seeman, Mark, and James L. Branch

2006   The Mounded Landscapes of Ohio: Hopewell Patterns and Placements. In *Recreating Hopewell: New Perspectives on Middle Woodland in Eastern North America*, edited by Douglas K. Charles and Jane E. Buikstra, pp. 106–121. University Press of Florida, Gainesville.

Seguin, Margaret
1984   Lest There Be No Salmon: Symbols in Tradi-
        tional Tsimshian Potlatch. In *The Tsimshian:
        Images of the Past, Views from the Present*,
        edited by M. Seguin, pp. 110–136. University
        of British Columbia Press, Vancouver.

Serres, Michel
1995   *The Natural Contract*. Translated by Elizabeth
        MacArthur and William Paulson. University
        of Michigan Press, Ann Arbor.
2007   [1992] *The Parasite*. Translated by Lawrence
        Schehr. University of Minnesota Press, Min-
        neapolis.

Serres, Michel, with Bruno Latour
1995   *Conversations on Science, Culture and Time*.
        University of Michigan Press, Ann Arbor.

Service, Elman R.
1962   *Primitive Social Organization: An Evolution-
        ary Perspective*. Random House, New York.

Shetrone, Henry C.
1923   The Spetnagel Cache of Flint Spear Points.
        Ohio Archaeological and Historical Quarterly
        32:638–640.
1926   Explorations of the Hopewell Group of Pre-
        historic Earthworks. *Ohio Archaeological and
        Historical Quarterly* 34:154–168.

Shetrone, Henry C., and Emerson F. Greenman
1931   Explorations of the Seip Group of Prehistoric
        Earthworks. *Ohio Archaeological and Histori-
        cal Quarterly* 40:343–509.

Shoemaker, Nancy
2004   *A Strange Likeness: Becoming Red and White
        in Eighteenth-Century North America*.
        Oxford University Press, New York.

Smith, Bruce
1992   *Rivers of Change: Essays on Early Agriculture
        in Eastern North America*. Smithsonian Insti-
        tution Press, Washington, D.C.

Squier, Ephraim, and Edwin H. Davis
1998   [1848] *Ancient Monuments of the Mississippi
        Valley*. Edited by David J. Meltzer, Smithson-
        ian Institution Press, Washington, D.C.

Stout, Charles B., and Dudley C. Bravard
1973   A Red Ocher Mound. *Artifacts* 3(2):13–15.

Strathern, Marilyn
1988   *Gender of the Gift*. University of California
        Press, Berkeley.

Straus, Anne S.
1977   Northern Cheyenne Ethnopsychology. *Ethos*
        5(3):326–357.
1978   The Meaning of Death in Northern Cheyenne
        Culture. *Plains Anthropologist* 32(79):1–6.

Struever, Stuart
1964   The Hopewell Interaction Sphere in
        Riverine–Western Great Lakes Culture His-
        tory. In *Hopewellian Studies*, edited by Joseph
        Caldwell and Robert L. Hall, pp. 86–106. Sci-
        entific Papers No. 12. Illinois State Museum,
        Springfield.

Struever, Stuart, and Gail Houart
1972   An Analysis of the Hopewell Interaction
        Sphere. In *Social Exchange and Interaction*,
        edited by E. N. Wilmsen, pp. 47–147. Anthro-
        pological Papers No. 46. University of Michi-
        gan Museum of Anthropology, Ann Arbor.

Tainter, Joseph A.
1978   Mortuary Analyses and the Study of Prehis-
        toric Social Systems. *Advances in Archaeolog-
        ical Method and Theory* 1:105–141.

van Gennep, Arnold
1970   *The Rites of Passage*. Translated by M. B. Vize-
        dom and B. L. Caffee. University of Chicago
        Press, Chicago.

Voegelin, Erminie W.
1944   Mortuary Customs of the Shawnee and
        Other Eastern Tribes. *Prehistoric Research
        Series* 2(4):227–444. Indiana Historical Soci-
        ety, Indianapolis.

von Gernet, Alexander
1994   Saving the Souls: Reincarnation Beliefs of the
        Seventeenth-Century Huron. In *Amerindian
        Rebirth: Reincarnation Beliefs among North
        American Indians and Inuit*, edited by Anto-
        nia Mills and Richard Slobodin, pp. 38–54.
        University of Toronto Press, Toronto.

Waterson, Roxanna
1990   *The Living House: An Anthropology of Archi-
        tecture in Southeast Asia*. Oxford University
        Press, Oxford.

Webb, William S., and Raymond S. Baby
1957   *The Adena People No. 2*. Ohio Historical Soci-
        ety, Columbus.

Webb, William S., and Charles E. Snow
1974   *Adena People*. University of Tennessee Press,
        Knoxville.

Willoughby, Charles C., and Earnest A. Hooton
1922   *The Turner Group of Earthworks Hamilton
        County, Ohio*. Papers of the Peabody
        Museum of American Archaeology and
        Ethnology Vol. 8, No. 3. Harvard University,
        Cambridge.

Witthoft, John
1983   Cherokee Beliefs Concerning Death. *Journal
        of Cherokee Studies* 2(2):68–72.

Wolfe, Cary
2007   Introduction to New Edition: Bringing the
        Noise; The Parasite and the Multiple Gene-
        alogies of Posthumanism. In *The Parasite*,
        by Michel Serres, pp. xi–xxviii. University
        of Minnesota Press, Minneapolis.

Wymer, Dee Ann

1992   Trends and Disparities: The Woodland Paleoethnobotanical Record of the Mid-Ohio Valley. In *Cultural Variability in Context: Woodland Settlements of the Mid-Ohio Valley*, edited by Mark F. Seeman, pp. 65–76. Midcontinental Journal of Archaeology Special Paper No. 7. Kent State University Press, Kent, Ohio.

1997   Paleoethnobotany in the Licking River Valley, Ohio: Implications for Understanding Ohio Hopewell. In *Ohio Hopewell Community Organization*, edited by William S. Dancey and Paul J. Pacheco, pp. 153–175. Kent State University Press, Kent, Ohio.

Yerkes, Richard W.

2006   Middle Woodland Settlements and Social Organization in the Central Ohio Valley: Were the Hopewell Really Farmers? In *Recreating Hopewell: New Perspectives on Middle Woodland in Eastern North America*, edited by Douglas K. Charles and Jane E. Buikstra, pp. 50–61. University Press of Florida, Gainesville.

6

Mobile Farmers and Sedentary Models

Horticulture and Cultural Transitions
in Late Woodland and Contact Period New England

Elizabeth S. Chilton

In New England the relationship between subsistence and social complexity is a topic that is at once poorly understood and hotly debated. There are several reasons for this: first, archaeological evidence indicates that there was an enormous amount of diversity among the Native groups of the Northeast both before and after European contact, and archaeologists have yet to come to terms with that diversity. Second, there is no general agreement among archaeologists on the relationship among subsistence choices, sedentism, and sociopolitical organization. While some archaeologists believe there is a dependent relationship among farming, sedentism, and social complexity, others emphasize alternative trajectories of human history. Finally, there are many assumptions but a lack of consensus about definitions of "social complexity," making discussions of the matter all the more difficult. In this chapter I review the current evidence for subsistence and settlement during the Late Woodland period (AD 1000–1500) in New England (Figure 6.1). I then discuss the implications of these data for understanding social complexity in general and contemporary Native issues in New England in particular.

Mobile Farmers:
The Archaeological Evidence

Native peoples of New England began to grow maize by AD 1000; this date is based primarily on AMS dates for maize since we lack stable isotope or other comparable data for the region (Chil-

ton 2006). Around this time maize farming was apparently incorporated into what was essentially a hunting and gathering lifestyle, and while maize seems to have been ideologically and socially important to Native peoples, it did not apparently serve as a staple crop, as it clearly was for the Iroquois of upstate New York at that time (see Snow 1994). By the Late Woodland period (AD 1000–1500), the Iroquois of upstate New York were living as sedentary maize farmers, shifting settlements only every 20–50 years, and living in fortified villages containing many larger longhouses (see Snow 1994). The Iroquois represent what many North American archaeologists have come to think of as the "nature state" (Hart 1999) for maize horticulturalists: sedentary, intensive farmers, with marked intergroup conflict and a relatively rigid social organization.

Given that the New England archaeological evidence did not seem to fit the mold for the Iroquoian model of maize farming, in 1999 I proposed a model suggesting that Native peoples of New England at the time of European initial contact were "mobile farmers" (Chilton 1999, 2002). In the next section I present the evidence in support of the mobile farming model.

Late Woodland Period Settlement
in New England

There is no archaeological evidence for year-round settlement during the Late Woodland period in New England, except perhaps along the coast in some protected harbors (Bernstein

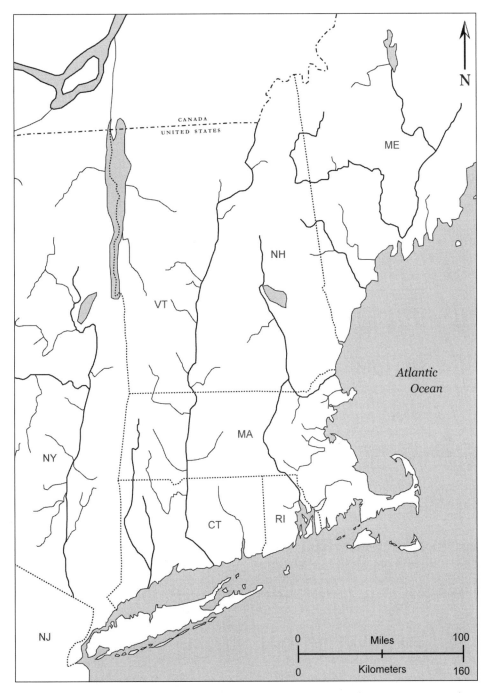

FIGURE 6.1. Map of New England, defined here as the modern U.S. states of Connecticut, Massachusetts, Rhode Island; southern New Hampshire, Maine, and Vermont; and eastern and coastal New York (map drawn by Kathryn Curran).

et al. 1997; Bernstein 1993, 1999; Gwynne 1982). These coastal year-round or nearly year-round settlements date back as early as the Late Archaic (3000–1000 BC; Gwynne 1982). In those cases, diet seems to have been centered on maritime resources, and the appearance of these more sedentary settlements correlates more with the establishment of shellfish beds and not the adoption of maize horticulture (Bernstein et al. 1997; Bernstein 1993, 1999; Ceci 1979–80). Late Woodland period settlements in the interior of New England are generally small and dispersed and seem to have been occupied for no more than a season or two at a time (Chilton 1996, 1999). Structures on these sites are small and ephemeral and do not support a model of sedentism. There are a few cases of "longhouse" structures in New England, but either they are isolated structures or the dating is questionable (e.g., the Goldkrest site in New York [Largy et al. 1999] and the Tracy Farm site in Maine [Cowie 2000]). No evidence for precolonial clusters of large, permanent structures or anything resembling a fortified village has been reported in the New England interior.

Late Woodland Period Subsistence in New England

As discussed previously, there is clear evidence for the adoption of maize horticulture by AD 1000 (Chilton 2006). However, archaeobotanical and faunal data from Late Woodland sites in New England indicate a varied diet consisting of a wide variety of nuts, seeds, fruits, fish, shellfish, reptiles, and both large and small mammals (see Hart 1999; Hart and Rieth 2002; Hart 2008). In terms of sheer quantity of archaeobotanical remains, nuts often predominate (e.g., Chilton et al. 2000; Heckenberger et al. 1992), which is certainly not the case for Iroquoian sites from upstate New York from the same time period (see Snow 1994).

Ceramics can serve as a proxy for subsistence since they are used for food collection, preparation, storage, and, most important, cooking. Analysis of archaeological ceramics found in the New England interior indicates that they were manufactured in a wide variety of social and environmental contexts, lending further support to a certain degree of mobility throughout the year (Chilton 1996, 1998). The morphology of the pots also suggests that they are not specialized cook-

ing pots but were used for cooking and storing a wide variety of substances (Chilton 1996, 1998). In contrast, Iroquoian ceramics embody their use as specialized cooking pots for maize (Chilton 1996, 1998).

Human osteological evidence is sparse, but it suggests that Native people ate a varied diet and generally had very good health throughout the Late Woodland period. There do not appear to be significant changes in dental or dietary health beginning with the Late Woodland period or at any point in prehistory. Likewise, there does not appear to be any disparity in accumulation of wealth as evidenced by the treatment of the dead or the contents or layout of dwellings.

Stable isotope analysis of human remains from the New England coast indicates that although maize was present, it did not constitute a large portion of the diet before European colonization (Little and Schoeninger 1995). Because it is often not practical, possible, or ethical to conduct stable isotope analysis on human remains, archaeologists have sometimes analyzed the remains of domesticated animals to serve as an indicator of the presence of maize (e.g., Allitt et al. 2008). While the stable isotope analysis of dog remains may provide a reasonable proxy for human diet, a sufficient sample of late prehistoric dog remains from the New England interior has not yet been identified. In a collaborative project that I undertook a few years ago, there was apparently quite a bit of variability in the amount of maize consumed by dogs in the Northeast (Chilton et al. 2001), although this was a relatively small sample.

Political Organization and Social Complexity

In contrast to the fairly structured tribal political organization of the Iroquois, the Late Woodland and early Colonial period Algonquians of New England apparently shared a loosely organized and flexible political organization. Instead of well-defined tribes, there were a series of related communities with fluid social and political boundaries (Bruchac and Chilton 2003; Johnson 1993). Colonists and ethnohistorians mapped out what they thought were distinct Native communities or tribes in western Massachusetts (Pocumtuck at Deerfield, Norwottuck at Northampton and Hadley, Agawam in the Springfield area, and

Woronoco in Westfield), but recent research has shown that these "tribes" were actually Algonquian place-names (Bruchac and Chilton 2003). From ethnohistorical and archaeological research, we know that (1) groups congregated and dispersed in response to seasonal movements for subsistence and social purposes, and (2) patterns of residence and the reckoning of kin were more flexible than those of the Iroquois (see Johnson 1993). Kinship appears to have been more bilateral than exclusively matrilineal, allowing kinship ties to be situational. The advantage to this social strategy is that in the face of political disagreements, people could literally "vote with their feet." Such a strategy likely dispelled tensions that otherwise could have led to violence. It is perhaps for this reason that there is no evidence for warfare prior to European colonization in New England.

There is no evidence for social hierarchy among Late Woodland Algonquian peoples. The size and shape of the house structures show a great deal of diversity with respect to season and group size, indicating that families may often have constructed their own houses. There is no evidence for status seeking in the form of aggrandizing feasts or accumulations of wealth, nor is there evidence for craft specialization. But does the absence of these things indicate a lack of social complexity for the Late Woodland Algonquian peoples? Before addressing this question, I first examine a case study from the interior of New England.

The Pine Hill Site,
Deerfield, Massachusetts

Having previously worked exclusively in upstate New York, I assumed, when I began my research in the Connecticut River Valley in the late 1980s, that our fieldwork would reveal large or at least well-defined Late Woodland period villages. I was surprised to discover that there were relatively few Late Woodland period sites known in the middle or Massachusetts portion of the Connecticut Valley. I assumed that archaeologists had simply been digging in the wrong places or that the sites had been destroyed by the Connecticut Valley's broad and winding floodplain.

Excavations at the Pine Hill site in Deerfield, Massachusetts, challenged these assumptions

(Chilton et al. 2000). Pine Hill is the largest Late Woodland period site professionally excavated in the middle Connecticut River Valley, and radiocarbon dating suggests that the main use of the site was between AD 1400 and 1600. The site was excavated over several summers as part of the UMass Amherst Field School in Archaeology between 1989 and 1997. We identified 21 storage or food-processing features and recovered more than 200 kernels of charred, eight-row maize. However, instead of large, permanent houses or villages, we found an overlapping pattern of small, seasonal encampments. Archaeobotanical and osteological evidence from the site included a diverse array of animal and plant species, including butternut, hickory nut, squirrel, moose, huckleberry, and raspberry. These remains indicated that the late summer and fall were the likely periods of site use over time (Chilton et al. 2000).

Even though we found the highest number of maize kernels that I had ever encountered from one site, it was clear that the number of maize kernels preserved on an archaeological site does not necessarily correlate directly with the importance of that plant for prehistoric peoples. For example, all the 200+ maize kernels came from one feature and could represent one only cob. In fact, we had far more butternut shells and squirrel bone fragments at the site than maize kernels. It is clear that we needed to look beyond a simple quantification of the archaeobotanical remains in order to make interpretations of diet.

Ceramics and Social Messaging

As an outgrowth of my dissatisfaction with regional ceramic typologies, I undertook a ceramic attribute analysis of pottery from the Pine Hill site as part of my dissertation research (Chilton 1996, 1998). As part of this research I examined technical and stylistic attributes for 56 vessel lots from the site. I then compared the results from the Pine Hill site with vessel lots from the Guida Farm site, in Westfield, Massachusetts, and the Klock site, an Iroquoian site in the Mohawk Valley. The results of this analysis strongly indicated that Iroquoian pots were functionally ideal cooking pots for maize. In contrast, Algonquian pots from Pine Hill and Guida Farm were more diverse in nearly every attribute analyzed but were otherwise not ideal cooking pots. I suggested that this reflected a lack of subsistence specialization for New England Algonquians and that the diversity of pottery from the Connecticut River Valley indicated settlement mobility and fluidity of social boundaries. I also argued that the relative homogeneity of Iroquoian pottery marked a need for social signaling within a highly structured and predictable social organization. For New England Algonquians, however, I suggested that the great diversity in all attributes of ceramics indicated a more complex, fluid, and creative medium for mitigating social relationships. One could certainly say that the types of social messages being communicated through ceramic styles was more "complex" for Algonquian peoples, but what is the meaning of that complexity?

High Culture and Mobile Farming

New England is often considered by archaeologists working outside the region to be a kind of cultural backwater. As Dena Dincauze put it 30 years ago (1980:29), "the Northeast has traditionally been considered a marginal, culturally retarded outlier of the eastern United States." As stated above, within the Northeast, the Iroquois have long served as the benchmark or exemplars of Late Woodland society. Marge Bruchac and I refer to this as a kind of "Irocentrism" (Bruchac and Chilton 2003). Many assume that "like water, high culture flows downhill" (Dietler 1998:296), meaning that, for example, the more civilized Iroquoian way of life would have naturally "flowed downhill" to the more "simple" and mobile farmers of New England. This follows an implicit, ethnocentric notion that "civilized" (i.e., densely settled, sedentary, hierarchical) societies are somehow superior to mobile, less hierarchical societies. There is also an erroneous—but prevalent—assumption that civilized societies are more "complex" than heterarchical, mobile societies. Social and physical mobility, especially in the context of a horticultural economy and population increase, must have been enormously complex in terms of kinship, leadership, land rights, and distribution of wealth. Wengrow (2001) even argues that with state formation comes the evolution of social "simplicity," at least in terms of the organization of labor (see also Yoffee 2005). I would argue that stratified societies are in many ways simpler than egalitarian societies in terms of their rigidity and in their more explicit and predictable—if not contested—social relations.

As archaeologists, we must be self-conscious about our assumptions about social evolution and colonial encounters. Otherwise, as Dietler (2005: 34) points out, we "risk unconsciously imposing the attitudes and assumptions of ancient colonists, filtered and reconstituted through a modern interpolating prism of colonial ideology…back onto the ancient situation." In his example Dietler discusses how Hellenophilia and Romanophilia have dominated European self-identity since the Renaissance, and how the obsession with Greek and Roman historical trajectories served to justify the following colonial era and likewise have infiltrated archaeological interpretations of the ancient world (Dieter 2005).

Why should we expect the Algonquian-speaking peoples of New England to have adopted maize horticulture into their diet and into their lives in exactly the same way as did the Iroquoian-speaking people of upstate New York? Certainly these groups had different histories, lived in different natural and cultural environments, and had different decisions to make in their own social contexts about acting and reacting to new technologies, plants, and social conditions.

It is probably true that instead of being implicitly ethnocentric, many New England archaeologists believe that Native peoples in the region must have been settled horticulturalists (despite the extant archaeological evidence) because they want to be able to argue for the social complexity of the region's peoples. Many want to elevate the region's archaeology—to "center" New England, as Dincauze put it (1993). In doing so, many archaeologists strive to demonstrate that New England peoples were not passive reactors to the Iroquois or to Europeans and that, in fact, they were evolutionarily "complex" before European contact (Chilton 2005). Certainly—and wrongly—New England's Native peoples have historically been relegated to the cultural backwaters of evolution, being classified as neither bands nor tribes nor states, and denied "evolutionary complexity." But do societies require intensive horticulture to be sedentary? Does sedentism in and of itself indicate social complexity? And does complexity require social hierarchy? When one reviews the archaeological literature, it is clear that the answer to all these questions is a resounding "no."

Over the past decade or so, anthropologists have begun to outline models of "transegalitarian societies," or "intermediate societies," which are neither egalitarian nor politically stratified (see Arnold 1996; Hayden and Adams 2004; Hayden 2001). Models of increasing social complexity should, therefore, include the potential for horizontal complexity or heterarchy (see Coupland 1996; Creamer 1996; Crumley 1987). There are numerous archaeological examples of societies that are at once essentially egalitarian yet quite large and socially complex, or cases of alternating episodes of horizontal expansion and vertical reorganization in the formation of what we might call chiefdoms. Ultimately, each society must be examined individually, and we must strive to explore the relationship between the local and the global and to "develop methodologies for coming to grips with local agency, culture, and history" (Dietler 2005:68). The archaeology of New England presents us with a set of data that does not easily fit the typological mold of social evolution. Rather than see it as an exception or failure, we should see it as an opportunity to learn about alternative human histories and to examine our assumptions and existing models.

Native American Heritage in the Twenty-First Century

The issue of maize adoption and, more importantly, settlement mobility for New England's Native peoples is more than simply academic curiosity or professional debate. A strategy of mobile farming with fluid social boundaries has significant implications for how New England peoples have been viewed and treated since European contact. The English clearly did not understand the type of horticulture that was being practiced by New England peoples. Many of the New England planting fields would have seemed quite disorderly to Europeans, who at the time of contact were accustomed to mono-crop, intensive farming. In fact, Europeans believed that New England's Native peoples were not "improving" the land and used this as an implicit justification for the taking of land. For example, John Locke (1980 [1698]:343) wrote that "in the beginning, all the world was America," by which he meant that America is an Edenic wilderness, free for the taking and improving. Colonial Europeans either did not understand or chose not to acknowledge the more egalitarian social organization of New England peoples. This in turn affected the ways that Europeans treated Native peoples during the contact period and led to their near invisibility in historical writings after the end of the seventeenth century (Bruchac and Chilton 2003). This lack of understanding and misrepresentation has had a profound effect on land claims, federal recognition, and repatriation under the Native American Graves Protection and Repatriation Act (Public Law 101-601). Archaeologists have been complicit in these historical misunderstandings through their insistence on normative models of social evolution.

To conclude, judging by the evidence we have at hand, precontact New England provides us with an example of a society that is at once complex but not necessarily socially stratified, committed to horticulture but not necessarily living in year-round settlements, engaged in complex social messaging through material culture but without craft specialization. Thus, regional archaeologists have much to contribute to worldwide discussions on the causes, effects, and even the very definitions of social complexity.

References

Allitt, Sharon, R. Michael Stewart, and Timothy Messner
2008   The Utility of Dog Bone (*Canis familiaris*) in Stable Isotope Studies for Investigating the Presence of Prehistoric Maize (*Zea mays* ssp. *mays*): A Preliminary Study. *North American Archaeologist* 29(3–4):343–367.

Arnold, Jeanne E. (editor)
1996   *Emergent Complexity: The Evolution of Inter-mediate Societies.* International Monographs in Prehistory, Ann Arbor, Michigan.

Bernstein, David J.
1993   *Prehistoric Subsistence on the Southern New England Coast.* Academic Press, San Diego.
1999   Prehistoric Use of Plant Foods on Long Island and Block Island Sounds. In *Current Northeast Paleoethnobotany*, edited by J. P.

Hart, pp. 101–119. Bulletin No. 494. New York State Museum, Albany.

Bernstein, David J., M. J. Lenardi, D. Merwin, and S. Zipp
1997   *Archaeological Investigation on the Solomon Property, Mount Sinai, Town of Brookhaven, Suffolk County, New York.* Institute for Long Island Archaeology, Department of Anthropology, State University of New York, Stony Brook.

Bruchac, Marge M., and Elizabeth S. Chilton
2003   From Beaver Hill to Bark Wigwams: Reconsidering Archaeology and Historical Memory in the Connecticut River Valley. Paper presented at the Society for Historical Archaeology, Providence.

Ceci, Lynn
1979–   Maize Cultivation in Coastal New York:
1980   The Archaeological, Agronomical and Documentary Evidence. *North American Archaeologist* 1(1):45–74.

Chilton, Elizabeth S.
1996   Embodiments of Choice: Native American Ceramic Diversity in the New England Interior. Unpublished Ph.D. dissertation, University of Massachusetts, Amherst.
1998   The Cultural Origins of Technical Choice: Unraveling Algonquian and Iroquoian Ceramic Traditions in the Northeast. In *The Archaeology of Social Boundaries,* edited by M. Stark, pp. 132–160. Smithsonian Institution Press, Washington, D.C.
1999   Mobile Farmers of Pre-contact Southern New England: The Archaeological and Ethnohistorical Evidence. In *Current Northeast Paleoethnobotany,* edited by J. P. Hart, pp. 157–176. Bulletin No. 494. New York State Museum, Albany.
2002   "Towns They Have None": Diverse Subsistence and Settlement Strategies in Native New England. In *Northeast Subsistence-Settlement Change: AD 700–1300,* edited by J. P. Hart and C. B. Rieth, pp. 265–288. Bulletin No. 496. New York State Museum, Albany.
2005   Farming and Social Complexity in the Northeast. In *North American Archaeology,* edited by T. P. and D. D. Loren, pp. 138–160. Blackwell Studies in Global Archaeology. Blackwell, Malden, Massachusetts.
2006   The Origin and Spread of Maize (*Zea mays*) in New England. In *Histories of Maize: Multidisciplinary Approaches to the Prehistory, Biogeography, Domestication, and Evolution of Maize,* edited by J. Staller, R. Tykot, and B.

Benz, pp. 539–547. Academic Press, Burlington, Massachusetts.

Chilton, Elizabeth S., Tonya B. Largy, and Kathryn Curran
2000   Evidence for Prehistoric Maize Horticulture at the Pine Hill Site, Deerfield, Massachusetts. *Northeast Anthropology* 59:23–46.

Chilton, Elizabeth S., Nikolas van der Merwe, Ninian Stein, and Kimberly O. Allegretto
2001   Canine Proxies for Native American Diets. Paper presented at the Society for American Archaeology, New Orleans.

Coupland, Gary
1996   This Old House: Cultural Complexity and Household Stability on the Northern Northwest Coast of North America. In *Emergent Complexity: The Evolution of Intermediate Societies,* edited by Jeanne E. Arnold, pp. 74–90. Archaeological Series No. 9. International Monographs in Prehistory, Ann Arbor, Michigan.

Cowie, Ellen R.
2000   *Archaeological Investigations at the Tracy Farm Site (69.11 ME) in the Central Kennebec River Drainage, Somerset County, Maine (Revised from 9/99).* 2 vols. Archaeological Research Center, University of Maine, Farmington.

Creamer, Winifred
1996   Developing Complexity in the American Southwest: A Case from the Pajarito Plateau, New Mexico. In *Emergent Complexity: The Evolution of Intermediate Societies,* edited by Jeanne E. Arnold, pp. 107–127. Archaeological Series No. 9. International Monographs in Prehistory, Ann Arbor, Michigan.

Crumley, Carole L.
1987   A Dialectical Critique of Hierarchy. In *Power Relations and State Formation,* edited by Thomas C. Patterson and Christine W. Gailey, pp. 155–169. American Anthropological Association, Washington, D.C.

Dietler, Michael
1998   Consumption, Agency, and Cultural Entanglement: Theoretical Implications of a Mediterranean Colonial Encounter. In *Studies in Culture Contact: Interaction, Culture Change, and Archaeology,* edited by James G. Cusick, pp. 288–315. Occasional Paper No. 25. Center for Archaeological Investigations, Southern Illinois University, Carbondale.
2005   The Archaeology of Colonization and the Colonization of Archaeology: Theoretical Challenges from an Ancient Mediterranean

Colonial Encounter. In *The Archaeology of Colonial Encounters*, edited by Gil J. Stein, pp. 33–68. School of American Research Press, Santa Fe.

Dincauze, Dena F.

1980   Research Priorities in Northeast Prehistory. In *Proceedings of the Conference on Northeastern Archaeology*, Vol. 19, edited by J. A. Moore, pp. 29–48. Department of Anthropology, University of Massachusetts, Amherst.

1993   Centering. *Northeast Anthropology* 46:33–37.

Gwynne, Margaret A.

1982   The Late Archaic Archaeology of Mount Sinai Harbor, New York: Human Ecology, Economy and Residence Patterns on the Southern New England Coast. Unpublished Ph.D. dissertation, State University of New York, Stony Brook.

Hart, John P.

1999   Maize Agriculture Evolution in the Eastern Woodlands of North America: A Darwinian Perspective. *Journal of Archaeological Method and Theory* 6(2):137–180.

Hart, John P. (editor)

1999   *Current Northeast Paleoethnobotany*. Bulletin No. 494. New York State Museum, Albany.

2008   *Current Northeast Ethnobotany II*. Bulletin No. 512. New York State Museum, Albany.

Hart, John P., and Christina Reith (editors)

2002   *Northeast Subsistence-Settlement Change: AD 700–AD 1300*. Bulletin No. 496. New York State Museum, Albany.

Hayden, Brian

2001   The Dynamics of Wealth and Poverty in the Transegalitarian Societies of Southeast Asia. *Antiquity* 75:571–581.

Hayden, Brian, and Ron Adams

2004   Ritual Structures in Transegalitarian Communities. In *Complex Hunter-Gatherers: Evolution and Organization of Prehistoric Communities on the Plateau of Northwestern*

North America, edited by William Prentiss and Ian Kuijt, pp. 84–102. University of Utah Press, Salt Lake City.

Heckenberger, M. J., J. B. Petersen, and N. Asch Sidell

1992   Early Evidence of Maize Agriculture in the Connecticut River Valley of Vermont. *Archaeology of Eastern North America* 20: 125–149.

Johnson, Eric S.

1993   Some by Flatteries and Others by Threatening: Political Strategies in Seventeenth Century Native New England. Unpublished Ph.D. dissertation, Department of Anthropology, University of Massachusetts, Amherst.

Largy, Tonya B., Lucianne Lavin, Marina E. Mozzi, and Kathleen Furgerson

1999   Corncobs and Buttercups: Plant Remains from the Goldkrest Site. In *Current Northeast Paleoethnobotany*, edited by J. P. Hart, pp. 69–84. Bulletin No. 494. New York State Museum, Albany.

Little, Elizabeth A., and Margaret J. Schoeninger

1995   The Late Woodland Diet on Nantucket Island and the Problem of Maize in Coastal New England. *American Antiquity* 60(2):351–368.

Locke, John

1980   [1698] *Second Treatise of Government*. Hackett, Indianapolis.

Snow, Dean R.

1994   *The Iroquois*. Blackwell, Cambridge, Massachusetts.

Wengrow, David

2001   The Evolution of Simplicity: Aesthetic Labour and Social Change in the Neolithic Near East. *World Archaeology* 33(2):168–188.

Yoffee, Norman

2005   *Myths of the Archaic State: Evolution of the Earliest Cities, States and Civilizations*. Cambridge University Press, Cambridge.

7

Confounding Kinship

Ritual Regional Organization
in Northern Michigan, AD 1200–1600

Meghan C. L. Howey

For almost 150 years, anthropology has had a deep and complex relationship with kinship. With Morgan (1997 [1871], 1985 [1877]) and Maine (1970 [1861]), "the invention of kinship was virtually the invention of anthropology itself" (Trautmann 2001:268). These founding figures argued that the divide between class-based (civitas) and kin-based (societas) societies was the *fundamental* change in human development. From this birth, kinship became the major topic of anthropological study and remained so for close to 100 years.

In the 1970s, emboldened by Schneider (1968), a wide array of scholars critiqued the ethnocentric, biological prioritizing perspective inherent in kinship studies, and kinship was left for dead. Kinship is being resuscitated in anthropology today, but in a metamorphosed form (sensu Godelier 2004) that broadens the kinship concept to include an array of key social relations (Peletz 1995). Although considered important, kinship-by-procreation is increasingly recognized crossculturally as insufficient for making persons fully acceptable in society, and scholars are considering constructed, context-based relationships essential as well (Shimizu 1991:396).

Concurrently in archaeology, recent decades have seen an active engagement in the "unpacking of the evolutionary portmanteau" as applied to social organization (McIntosh 1999:4). As several chapters in this book point out, this has called into question traditional typologies that rely on a suite of "bipolar traits" (Berreman 1978:226) to categorize what a society *is* (Feinman and Neitzel 1984; O'Shea and Barker 1996). Archaeologists have built sophisticated theoretical understandings of social complexity—the emergence of permanent hierarchical leadership and ascribed inequality (Arnold 2000:17). This includes deeper appreciation for the array of trajectories toward complexity (Chapman 2003; Pauketat 2001), the multiple sources of power and authority that can be used to construct and maintain permanent inequalities (Blanton et al. 1996; Feinman et al. 2000; Yoffee 2005), and the notion that political arrangements in complex societies are not necessarily organized in a top-down fashion (see Crumley's concept of heterarchy [1987, 1995] and contributions in McIntosh [1999]). This work has also taken aim at what constitutes "class-based" society (civitas). In *Myths of the Archaic State*, Yoffee illustrates that in the earliest states social systems were not organized without kinship rules (Yoffee 2005:17), calling into question the utility of a view of class-based societies as lacking substantial kin-based structures.

Within this important theory-building lies an oversight. Even when there is an appreciation for the complicated inequalities such societies can have (e.g., Flanagan 1989; Paynter 1989; Wiessner 2002), "simple" societies remain largely conceived of and treated as "kin-based" social structures (societas). Thus, the concept that kinship played *the* primary role in structuring past "small-scale" societies has been largely unpacked. If archaeologists have shown that "class-based" societies were much more complicated than "class-based" can iterate, don't we have reason also to question how, if even, and to what extent "small-scale" societies were organized primarily on kin-relations? In this chapter I contend that as we continue our efforts to confound long-standing static models of human communities, we must grapple with questions of the place and primacy we give biological kinship in our studies of "small-scale" societies.

To engage this process, I use a case from a time and place occupied by communities that epitomize what people conceive of when they use the concept "kin-based" society (societas), the late Late Woodland/Late Prehistoric period (AD 1200–1600) in northern Michigan (referred to herein as simply the Late Prehistoric). Examining this specific archaeological record, I aim to illustrate how social actors in "small-scale" societies can readily construct, negotiate, and deploy media of relations beyond biological kinship, most notably ritual affiliation, to gain direct control over their contexts and resources and to create meaning and order in their lives (Peletz 1995).

Anthropological Kinship's Birth, Death, and Resurrection

Again, one need look no further than to the grandfather of social evolution, Lewis Henry Morgan, to see where anthropological kinship came from (see Lekson, this volume, for more on the continuing influence of Morgan in the discipline). His book *Systems of Consanguinity and Affinity of the Human Family* (1997 [1871]) was the first systematic, cross-cultural analysis of kinship nomenclature (Feinberg 2001:1). Around the same time, the divide between class-based (civitas) and kin-based (societas) societies as the *fundamental* change in human development was formulated by Maine (1970 [1861]) and Morgan (1985 [1877]).

For the next 100 years, kinship studies dominated cultural anthropology, cross-cutting theoretical developments, and every major figure in the field considered the topic. There was widespread interest in the recurrence of patterns of kinship terms (which Morgan inferred had evolutionary significance), and generations of fieldworkers represented the kinship systems of the people they studied in conventionalized diagrams. These various schools and scholars reified the civitas and societas divide. Neo-evolution embraced it. Marxism, interested in social change based on internal conflicts of the forces of relations and production and shifts in property relations from communal to private, held class to be the key social unit of analysis (Chapman 2003:59). Durkheim's mechanical solidarity viewed kinship as the means by which social and moral order emerged in societies lacking centralized political institutions.

Major debates over kinship occurred between two primary camps in anthropology: descent theorists and alliance theorists. Descent theorists, such as Meyer Fortes (1967 [1959], 1969, 1970 [1953]) and E. E. Evans-Pritchard (1940, 1951), promoted unilineal descent as the basic organizing principle of many societies, particularly important to the stability of "simple" societies. Alliance theorists, headed by Claude Lévi-Strauss and his *Elementary Structures of Kinship* (1969 [1949]), argued instead that the organizing principle of societies was not patrilineal descent but marriage exchange of women (Watanabe 2004:163). Nevertheless, even Lévi-Strauss's structuralism grew from a concern with how kinship relations (marriage exchange and affinal ones) structured "simple" societies and the transition from kin-based to state-ordered, class-stratified societies (Watanabe 2004:163; Peletz 1995). Further, alliance theory's move away from descent was actually far less profound than it seems, as "the focus was still on unilineally bounded groups and their external relations and reproduction through time. In short, descent-based social units still constituted the point of departure and ultimate loci of investigation [in alliance theory]" (Peletz 1995: 350). Both descent and alliance theorists, then, gave primacy to biological kin-relations, particularly in organizing "simple" societies.

At this point David Schneider entered the scene. He "suggested that the fundamental and implicit assumption on which the entire analysis of kinship (from Maine and Morgan to Fortes and Lévi-Strauss) rested was that 'blood is thicker than water'" (Carsten 2000:695). Schneider declared that anthropological kinship was invalidly founded on Euro-American notions of biological reproduction and insisted that other cultures do not necessarily construct their social relations in these terms (Schneider 1968, 1984). Arguing that kinship as used in anthropology was an English term and imposition, he made the bold move to declare that in the way Morgan and his followers had used it, kinship did not exist in any human society. After Schneider's declarations, many dropped the investigation of the topic, agreeing that old kinship studies had let Euro-American ideas of genealogical relatedness direct the questions asked about other societies and had imposed a biological evolutionary and Western-based concept on people who did not necessarily construct their lives and relationships in these terms.

Following years of silence on the topic, some cultural anthropologists began to reevaluate old kinship studies and develop new ways to think cross-culturally about relationships between people, heeding Schneider's warnings at the same time. In a detailed reevaluation of one of the foundational kinship studies in modern cultural anthropology, Evans-Pritchard's *The Nuer*, McKinnon (2000) finds a major paradox: "despite Evans-Pritchard's effort to link the lineage structure to the tribal structure as its skeletal backbone in the political context, the lineage always vanishes to be replaced by the territorial (*cieng*)" (McKinnon 2000:55). She concludes that among the Nuer, held up for years as a classic example of a "simple" (stateless) society based on biological unilineal descent, it is in fact nearly impossible to disarticulate the idea of lineage from that of local community (McKinnon 2000:55). This reevaluation seems to show that what Schneider had warned was true: working within the purview of Western notions of biological relatedness as foundational to societies, kinship studies had in a sense "forced" data to fit into these models, overlooking how people may have constructed their relationships in other ways.

From such reevaluations a new approach to kinship has emerged, one which acknowledges that most communities have systems of relationships that are defined at least partially in genealogical terms, but which remains suspicious of the primacy and universality previously accorded biological kinship. These new approaches expand the idea of kinship in terms of *relatedness*—a term that can encompass a variety of bases and media of relationships—and avoid assigning more or

less importance to one medium over another without careful investigation of a specific setting (Carsten 2000:700; see also Carsten, ed. 2000; Feinberg and Ottenheimer 2001; Franklin and McKinnon 2001; Stone 2001).

Implications for the Archaeology of "Small-Scale" Societies

The archaeology of "simple" societies has yet to seriously consider the potential elusiveness of biological kinship, in terms of both material evidence and conceptual utility. In the era of the deconstruction of kinship, close to 40 years ago, Allen and Richardson (1971) spoke directly to archaeologists. They warned that archaeology relied too heavily on the assumption of a high adherence in past cultures to the "dogma of descent" and that using such simplified assumptions to construct connections between artifact production and kinship was "questionable (at best)" (Allen and Richardson 1971:51). They stated, simply, that claims of archaeological identification of descent patterns are spurious (Allen and Richardson 1971:51). However, even in a relatively recent and significant treatise on social complexity and change, we see the argument that "even with the passing of the traditional functionalist notion of kinship as forming a moral system for the ordering of social relationships, the dominance of kinship relations in the structuring of political and economic relations in many small-scale societies has served to retain its status as one of the irreducible principles of social structure," and that identifying the kinship structure of a past "simple" society will have major value for understanding the political and economic structure of that society (Rowlands 1998:143).

Indeed, it seems that many of us who work on "small-scale" societies continuously default to this idea of kinship as an "irreducible principle," using terms like "corporate," "descent," and "kin" when discussing our findings, but what specifically is our evidence of these biological processes and groupings? Is it possible that because we are working on small-scale societies, we are assuming, based on the widespread idea that such societies were kin-based, that our material evidence reflects biological kinship patterns?

Anthropology's reformulation of kinship has

shown that kinship-by-procreation is often insufficient for creating order in social worlds and that while the facts of biology are fixed, the lived experience of them can be fluid, negotiated, and monopolized. Moreover, constructed and shared media of relations are critical to ordering the social, economic, and ideological lives of communities. In this light, it is clear that by uncritically evaluating the idea of "small-scale" societies as kin-based, we impose biological relationships as primary. Moreover, we risk overlooking evidence of media of relations that could have been as important as or more important than genealogy in ordering past life. Having unpacked the problems with evolutionary types, archaeology stands ready to unpack the idea that kinship-by-procreation was the ultimate means that "stateless" societies used to organize their worlds.

To borrow a metaphor from Mayan ethnographer John Watanabe (2004:165) to offer my sense for how to undertake this unpacking, "small-scale" societies (like all societies) are constituted by a social fabric of interwoven relationships between individuals and groups. The strands of relatedness in this fabric consist of the vertical warp of genealogical descent, and the horizontal woof is the array of other bases of interaction, relation, and alliance enacted by people. The warp and woof cannot be separated, but as the fabric is formed, we can imagine that there are moments when one becomes more critical to holding together the overall fabric than the other and that these moments can fluctuate during construction as well. As archaeologists studying past "small-scale" communities, we should not assume that the warp of biology was more critical than the woof of socially negotiated relations (or that it was not a socially negotiated/contested relation itself), which is what we risk when we apply the concept "kin-based" uncritically. By discerning conflicting and connecting patterns of warp and woof in "small-scale" societies, we can see how people used different relationships and identities strategically to assert direct control over their worlds. With this in mind, we may just find other kinds of society in the past, and as Chapman so eloquently puts it, it is the search for the other that is one of archaeology's greatest challenges (Chapman 2003:196).

Ritual Relatedness in
Late Prehistoric Northern Michigan

The Late Prehistoric period (AD 1200–1600) in northern Michigan provides a useful case for examining issues surrounding the concept of kin-based in interpreting the archaeology of "small-scale" societies. I argue that kinship was far from a static, universal ordering principle of life across this region occupied by "small-scale" communities; rather, multiple variables of relatedness were subject to monopolization and negotiation by social strategizers. Extending the fabric metaphor, the warp of descent (traditional kinship) was presumably present, but during the Late Prehistoric the archaeological record indicates that people invested large amounts of their time, physical effort, resources, and mental energy into creating places for ritual interaction between different levels of community not related specifically to biological descent. Ritual relations played a principal role in ordering the world; people's designing of and participation in a regional ritual system determined how their labor was allocated (or at least impinged on when and to what ends it was allocated), framed what resources they had access to, and defined their social relationships—directing who they saw, when, and where. Native American communities in northern Michigan actively emphasized different types of ritual relatedness to negotiate the social, economic, and ideological setting of the Late Prehistoric.

The Late Prehistoric Setting

The Late Prehistoric period in northern Michigan was marked by a major resource shift: maize (*Zea mays*) began to be cultivated in a limited manner in the Great Lakes region around AD 500–600 (Crawford et al. 1997:116), but between ca. AD 1000 and 1200, maize became increasingly adopted by established forager communities along the coasts of the Great Lakes, where the lake effect sufficiently extended the growing season. While the initial adoption of maize was important, it was this later change in the status of maize (ca. AD 1000–1200) that led to "major restructuring of patterns of settlement, territoriality, subsistence and social scheduling" (O'Shea 2003:3). That is, this economic shift resulted in, but was also facilitated by, social shifts allowing maize production

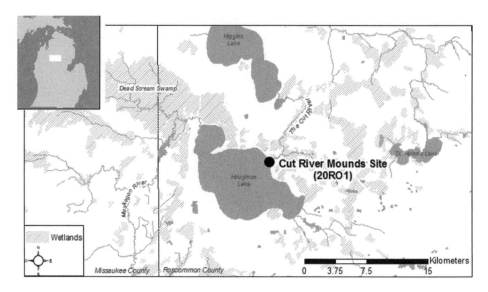

FIGURE 7.1. Location of the Cut River Mounds site in inland Michigan.

to develop into a dependable and significant economic activity. To ensure the success and productivity of maize agriculture, coastal communities developed more intensive local interactions and restricted ranges of movement. As they did, they began to develop stronger senses of local territory and identity. As spatial proximity became increasingly important in the new economic and social setting, coastal farmers began claiming and marking their territories and forming spatially restricted and regionally distinctive identities. The emergence of strong and distinctive new ceramic stylistic traditions reflects this consolidation of coastal, maize-producing communities during the Late Prehistoric period (Hambacher 1992; Lovis 1973; Milner 1998; O'Shea and Milner 2002; Stothers 1999).

Before the changes in the Late Prehistoric period, communities both in the interior and along the coasts had been rather homogeneous (O'Shea 2003:70), all practicing a broad-spectrum foraging economy. Within this pattern, groups could move easily between the different resource zones of the inland and Great Lakes coasts. During Late Prehistory, inland groups, living outside the lake-effect farming zone, were circumscribed to the interior by the developments along the coasts. Interior hunting and gathering groups were forced to respond to these new social circumstances as their access to coastal resources

became increasingly limited by alliances that excluded them.

Intracommunity Ritual Relations

One response to the changing socioeconomic world of the Late Prehistoric period by Native American communities was the construction of ceremonial monuments at important localized resource zones. Through this effort, Late Prehistoric groups accomplished several things: (1) they marked critical resource zones as exclusive to their local territories; (2) they protected the resources at these places against outside interests and secured these rich resource bases for their own communities; and (3) they created nexuses that required people from throughout the local area to come together for ritual (and associated economic) renewal in the landscape. With such strategic monumental investment in local places, intracommunity ritual affiliations played a major role in ordering Late Prehistoric life.

The Cut River Mounds site (20RO1), in Markey Township, Roscommon County, Michigan (23N03W), offers an example of this process in the interior. It is located at the confluence of Houghton Lake and the Cut River, which connects Higgins and Houghton lakes, Michigan's largest inland lake system (Figure 7.1). This confluence has long been renowned as a prime fishing spot, particularly for its spring spawning runs of wall-

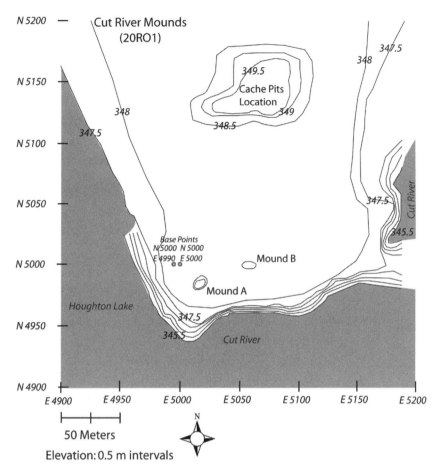

FIGURE 7.2. Topographic map of the Cut River Mounds site.

eye. Spring-spawning species native to Michigan's inland lakes prefer to spawn up riverine tributaries that converge with lakes in a shallow lacustrine habitat (Jones et al. 2003). Cut River, the widest tributary point on Michigan's largest and very shallow inland lake, Houghton Lake, thus forms a critical locale for seasonal spawning activity, creating a unique, abundant, reliable, and seasonally predictable resource zone in the inland landscape.

The site, the first reported in Roscommon County (20RO1), was originally recorded as having three mounds. Today only two are preserved, one large and one small, referred to herein as Mound A and Mound B, respectively (Figure 7.2). The mounds that gave the site its name are located on the north side of the confluence. Here the land rises roughly 2 m from the river/lake shore, and the mounds are positioned on this elevated bank.

The bank is extremely flat, and the first notable rise in the landscape lies roughly 100 m north of the confluence, where there is a small, 50-m-long and 50-m-wide shelf elevated roughly 2 m from the surrounding landscape. On this shelf, the closest higher ground, is a series of cache pits. No professional archaeological work had been conducted at the site before my research program.

The excavations, radiometric dates, and analyses of lithic, ceramic, and subsistence remains demonstrate that Cut River Mounds was a multicomponent site dating from the Middle Woodland (radiocarbon date of 1570 ± 60 BP, calibrated to AD 380–620) through the Late Prehistoric period (ca. AD 1200–1600). The largest component recovered was a dense early Late Woodland occupation, dated across the site to AD 780–1040. The occupation remains from this period indicate that people aggregated seasonally at the site to extract its rich spawning fish resource base. The characteristics of the early Late Woodland materials, particularly lithics and ceramics, demonstrate that the communities aggregating at the site in the early Late Woodland came from a wide geographic range and had direct access to the coasts of the Great Lakes. Briefly, there were very high proportions of lithics (and evidence of primary reduction of these raw materials) made of two distinct Michigan chert sources located on the coasts of the Great Lakes—Bayport chert from the Saginaw Bay area and Norwood chert from northwestern Michigan along northern Lake Michigan—suggesting direct access to these materials. The ceramic styles indicate a broad geographic range as well.

Both mounds were added on top of the dense early Late Woodland debris after AD 1200, when the social and economic sphere in northern Michigan was changing with the rise in the dominance of maize along the coasts and emerging exclusive social systems. An AMS date from occupation directly below Mound A's construction dated to 890 ± 40 BP, calibrated to AD 1030–1240. At Mound B from the same context, directly below mound construction, came an AMS date of 930 ± 40 BP, calibrated to AD 1020–1200. The addition of the mounds was imperative given the economic, social, and ideological milieu of this later period. By commemorating the site through the addition of ceremonial monuments, inland tribal communities marked this critical resource zone as an exclusive part of their territory and also created a formal space for intracommunity interaction. This level of local interaction was increasingly essential for balancing the resource uncertainty faced by groups restricted to the interior resource zone during their annual rounds. Within the circumscribed social setting of the period, informal interaction with groups from and/or direct movement into different resource zones (particularly Great Lakes coastal zones)—strategies the inland groups previously relied on to balance resource shortfalls—were no longer options.

Analysis of the ceramic and lithic materials from the site confirmed that the communities using the site in the Late Prehistoric period were no longer coming from throughout Michigan, with direct access to the Great lakes, as had occurred

in the early Late Woodland period. The lithic evidence shows a marked reduction in the lithic assemblage of the primary cherts from the coasts of the Great Lakes and an increase in local ceramics. The site was now used by groups circumscribed to the interior (for details, see Howey 2006).

As well as adding the mounds, these inland Late Prehistoric communities incorporated this site into their seasonal rounds in different ways than the nonlocal groups that used the site in the early Late Woodland. In the earlier period, groups visited the site chiefly for the prime seasonal resource, the spawning runs. In the later period, inland groups circumscribed to the interior resource zone capitalized on the other resource potentials offered at the site. They harvested the wild floral and faunal resources offered in the surrounding wetlands and forests. They transformed the high ground near the site into a storage complex, storing food resources as well as ritual paraphernalia for events at the mounds in a series of cache pits, which extended the availability of harvested resources throughout the annual round (Figure 7.2).

The site was a key locale in the regional landscape for centuries, heavily used for its seasonal spawning runs by diverse groups during the early Late Woodland period. In the Late Prehistoric period, this once open resource zone was transformed into an intracommunity ceremonial monument center by people circumscribed to interior Michigan. Transforming the Cut River site into a ritual center at once provided a nexus of ritual renewal for the newly forming social fabric of the local inland community and a means of buffering the inland economy by securing dispersed groups access to the resources of this site, particularly the influx of dense spawning runs. In this context, we see that inland forager communities actively commanded intracommunity ritual affiliations to direct local economics, including determining resource access and seasonal extraction activities, as well as social life.

Intersocietal Ritual Relations

While Late Prehistoric period communities increased their internal coherence and exclusivity, using intracommunity ceremonial monuments like the Cut River Mounds to organize local life across northern Michigan (there is evidence of

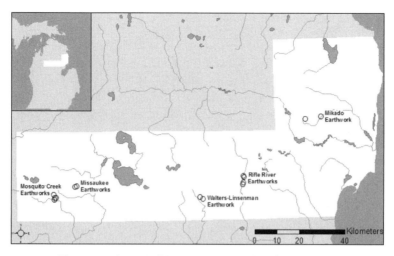

FIGURE 7.3. The series of Late Prehistoric circular earthwork enclosures running east-west across north-central Lower Michigan.

similar monuments in coastal areas), inland and coastal communities also invested substantial time, energy, labor, and resources into the planning, design, construction, and maintenance of multiple monumental ceremonial precincts for large-scale intersocietal ritual events. Both inland and coastal groups occupied environmental settings riddled with risk and uncertainty, making interaction and access to outside resources very important. Periodic aggregations between groups from these different settings would have provided important opportunities for resource pooling and exchange, as well as for establishing social contacts with (and gaining access to the resources of) the social systems outside each group's own resource zone.

A series of Late Prehistoric (ca. AD 1200–1600) circular earthwork enclosures runs east-west across north-central Michigan (Figure 7.3; Carruthers 1969; Cleland 1965; Cornelius and Moll 1961; Dustin 1932; Greenman 1926, 1927a; Moll et al. 1958). Despite the fact that these circular ditch and embankment structures were built on a larger, more permanent, and more elaborate scale than other sites in northern Michigan during the Late Prehistoric period, limited excavations, all of which were conducted only inside the enclosures themselves, have not resulted in any strong conclusions about their function. The default interpretation is that they are fortifications (e.g., Krakker 1999; Zurel 1999). However, the ex-

tant data from this cluster of enclosures do not support this interpretation, as all have breaches through their embankments, not all (none conclusively) have palisades, and habitation debris is light.

Through detailed work on one of these enclosure sites—the Missaukee Earthworks site—an analysis of ceramic style across assemblages from these enclosures, a GIS-based model of site accessibility and movement, and the incorporation of ethnohistoric information, I have developed an understanding of these sites as monumental centers laid out as ritual precincts in a regional ritual circuit. These sites served as ceremonial locales for periodic intersocietal ritual aggregation between coastal farmers and inland foragers in the Late Prehistoric regional landscape (Howey and O'Shea 2006; Howey 2006, 2007).

The Missaukee Earthworks site (20MA11-12), one site within this cluster, consists of a pair of enclosures in Aetna Township, Missaukee County, Michigan (22NR06W) (Figure 7.3). The site is situated in the interior of the Lower Peninsula in a position removed from the major waterscapes of this interior region, 20 km southwest of Michigan's largest inland lake system, Houghton Lake (80 km^2) and Higgins Lake (39 km^2), and 8 km west of the Muskegon River, Michigan's fifth largest river, which has its headwaters in these lakes and drains into Lake Michigan. The large Dead Swamp emerges in this headwater region, and its low marshes fill the vicinity of the Missaukee Earthworks site. The site dates to the Late Prehistoric period, ca. AD 1200–1450. Fitting (1970) reports a radiocarbon date for the site of 750 ± 150 BP as 1200 ± 75 AD (M-790) (Fitting used a calibration of some kind, but it seems the range was rounded; the calibrated range of this date using the intcal04 curve is AD 1070–1320). An AMS date run on residue recovered from a pottery fragment at the site yielded a date of 600 ± 40 BP, calibrated to AD 1290–1420 (Howey 2006:228).

The highest feature on the landscape is a glacial esker, and at its highest point is a shallow, basin-shaped area. It is here that the two earthworks were constructed, 653.5 m apart on an east-west line. An unusual upland spring and adjoining wetland lie immediately to the southwest of the eastern earthwork.

Each enclosure had two planned entryways made up of a breach in the embankment about 2 m wide and a raised platform running from the breach across the ditch onto flat land outside the enclosure. One opening on each enclosure roughly aligns with the other, and the second opening on each enclosure aligns in the same direction (the azimuth of the western one is 336°; the eastern one, 334°). The westernmost earthwork was assigned state site number 20MA11 and has a diameter of 48 m. There is a large boulder in the center of this enclosure. The easternmost earthwork, assigned state site number 20MA12, has a diameter of 53 m (Figure 7.4).

There are other features at the site in addition to the enclosures themselves. Conical burial mounds are located symmetrically at opposite ends of the site; two are located northeast of the eastern earthwork, and one is located southwest of the western earthwork (Figure 7.4; Greenman 1927b). The area also contains hundreds of abandoned subterranean storage pits (all the excavated ones have been empty). Some occur in small clusters of 4 to 10 pits, and a large concentration of more than 100 pits was reported in the central portion of the site (Greenman 1926:2).

Extensive shovel testing around the two Missaukee enclosures revealed a pattern of concentrated and localized activity: small clusters of dense cultural debris separated by extensive areas with no cultural debris. This pattern indicates a highly structured and prescribed use of space in the area around the earthworks, suggesting ceremonial use rather than standard habitation debris. The analysis of materials from excavation at four of these dense debris loci suggests that the spatially bounded activity areas outside the earthworks had distinctive ritual functions as well (Howey 2006).

A cross section done on an old cut in the western enclosure also indicates a ceremonial role for the enclosures. This cross section ran 10 m from inside the enclosure to a location beyond the edge of the outside ditch, and it confirms that this enclosure is a ditch-and-embankment structure with an embankment 4 m wide and at its maximum 0.5 m high. Dirt was removed from a ditch, piled on the extant ground surface immediately next to the ditch, and mounded and spread to form this humped embankment. The construction ditch has a shallow U-shape, being 2 m wide and 1 m deep at its maximum depth. This construction process indicates that the enclosure was built in a single episode rather than accumulatively. Further, no palisade was found on top of the enclosure; Greenman (1926) also reported a lack of a palisade. Thus, the enclosures were not defensive structures.

During the cross-sectioning excavations, all removed dirt was screened. Only one artifact, a single ceramic sherd, was recovered, and it came from the ditch. This finding indicates two important things: (1) the earthwork was not constructed on and/or with previous occupation debris, and (2) the ditch was not a repository for trash from the activities inside the enclosure. These were clean constructions, both during the construction process, when clean materials were used, and afterward, when the ditch was explicitly maintained to be free from trash.

Together the results of this testing program suggest that the earthworks, along with nearby mounds and clusters of cache pits, constituted a coherent ritual precinct. The layout of the ritual precinct at the Missaukee Earthworks involved (1) spatially distinct, activity-specific stations outside the earthworks that were used repetitively; (2) large clusters of cache pits (for storage/provisioning); and (3) open space inside the earthworks, the locus of distinct ritual action

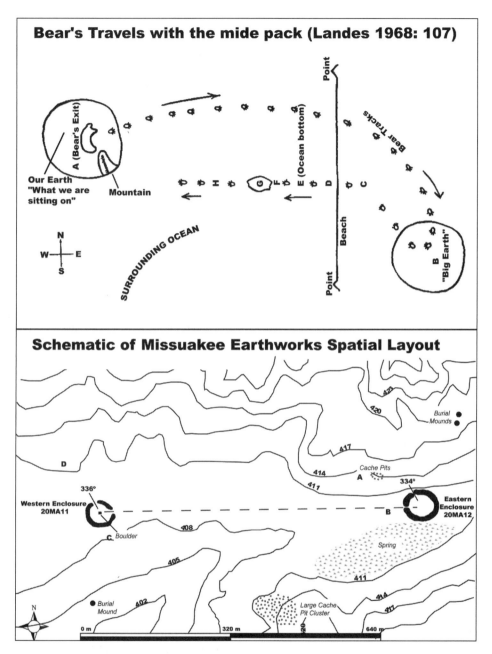

FIGURE 7.4. Comparison of the diagram of Bear's travels with the mide pack used during the teaching of the mide origin myth, as recounted by Will Rogers, or Hole-in-the-Sky (Landes 1968:107), with the schematic of the Missaukee Earthworks ritual precinct developed from the extensive shovel testing and excavation at the site. Both figures are oriented north-south. To facilitate reading, I deleted the original labeling and retyped it verbatim.

(Figure 7.4). Further, the high proportion of lithics made on two distinct Michigan chert sources, again Bayport chert from the Saginaw Bay area and Norwood chert from northwestern Michigan along northern Lake Michigan, as well as the presence of inland and coastal Late Prehistoric ceramic styles, demonstrates that the Missaukee Earthworks attracted both coastal and inland peoples (Howey 2006; Howey and O'Shea 2006). The ritual gatherings at the Missaukee Earthworks, drawing communities from coastal farming zones and the interior, would have provided key moments for facilitating interaction and exchange between these distinct social systems.

An ethnohistoric convergence (detailed in Howey and O'Shea 2006; Figure 7.4) bolstered our understanding of the Missaukee Earthworks as a specifically planned and coherently constructed ritual precinct. The Midewiwin (Grand Medicine Society) is a ceremonial complex whose importance among the Algonquin-speaking people of the Great Lakes region was noted frequently throughout the historical era (see Densmore 1929; Hoffman 1891; Kinietz 1947; Landes 1968; Warren 1984 [1885]). The telling of a version of the origin of the Midewiwin was required at every Midewiwin ceremony among the Ojibwa (Densmore 1929; Hoffman 1891; Landes 1968; Warren 1984 [1885]). A common account of the origin of the Midewiwin describes Bear as the servant who delivered the great mystery of the Midewiwin to the Native Americans. The Bear origin narrative told to Landes by Will Rogers, or Hole-in-the-Sky, at Red Lake reservation near Bemidji, Minnesota, in 1932–1933 and the associated sketch of Bear's travels with the mide pack, a sacred bundle holding the medicine for the people, (Landes 1968:107) provide a detailed comparative ethnohistorical source for the prehistoric Missaukee Earthworks site.

When the physical layout of the Missaukee Earthworks site is compared with Rogers's diagram, as is done in Figure 7.4, the similarities are remarkable (see Howey and O'Shea 2006). With a cursory glance it is clear that the respective size and location of the two earths and the enclosure circles, the location of water, the topographic setting, and even the directional orientation of the features all match. Along Bear's pathway between the two earths there are even specific stops,

matching the prescribed use of the space outside the enclosures found in the archaeological survey. The correspondences between the major components of the Missaukee Earthworks site and the diagram of Bear's journey, detailed in Howey and O'Shea (2006), demonstrate that the site was likely constructed as a monumental rendition of Bear's journey with the mide pack.

This insight opened new avenues for understanding the other Late Prehistoric earthworks in north-central Michigan, which share many layout similarities with Missaukee (twinning, boulder, water features), as similarly planned intersocietal ritual sites. Indeed, when one examines the ceramics from the small collections available from the other enclosures, it is clear that they too drew groups from the inland and the coast, although, interestingly, the ceramics also suggest some geographic ordering to the use of these enclosures. That is, these sites have inland-made ceramics and show variation in the amount of ceramics made by groups from different coastal regions of the Great Lakes, differences that are seemingly proportional to distance from the given Great Lake, suggesting that the use of the enclosures may have been arranged geographically. A GIS model of mobility and site accessibility in the Late Prehistoric shows that these enclosures were in positions that were uniquely accessible by both coastal and inland polities, which further supports the interpretation of these enclosures as connected ritual centers (see Howey 2007 for details).

These enclosures were monumentally constructed and designed ritual centers for coastal-inland interaction, and together they formed a regional ritual circuit that ordered social relationships, economic activities, and ideology in northern Michigan, from the changes that began ca. AD 1200 until European contact (ca. AD 1600). This ritual system was so important, so foundational in ordering the world, during this time that elements of it have shaped the historic and modern Midewiwin ceremonial (Howey and O'Shea 2006). If we consider the importance of these ritual centers, it seems clear that the ritual medium, not the medium of biological kinship, was the important focus: much of people's annual economic activity was directed toward it, their access to outside resources was dependent on it, and their social relationships were forged within it.

Some Concluding Thoughts

This brief look into the Late Prehistoric period in northern Michigan provides insight into some of the ways people in "small-scale" societies can differentially prioritize types of relatedness, in this case, ritual relationships, to maximize control over their worlds. In saying this, I do not intend to promote the idea that people in "small-scale" societies do not value biological relatedness or use family connections in their lives. Rather, my aim is to encourage archaeologists who look at the material records left by "small-scale" societies to avoid defaulting to a static view of these communities as "kin-based." The case presented here should lead us to question embedded ideas of biological kinship as primary and fixed in non-complex societies and to consider the ways social actors construct multiple means of relatedness to navigate their social contexts. Cases presented in other chapters of this volume add further perspective to this conclusion. For instance, in Chapter 3 Kidder concludes that the labor directed to the construction of the monuments at Poverty Point was not about biological reproduction, but about the reproduction of social formations. In Chapter 2 Randall and Sassaman explore the ways Archaic hunter-gatherer communities on the St. Johns River embedded their social order in ritual shell mound monuments. In Chapter 5 Giles demonstrates how Hopewell operated through an intricate system of reciprocal obligations, many of which were deeply ritualistic.

By considering multiple means of relatedness, we paint more complicated, but more accurate, pictures of the past and avoid re-creating and rediscovering Maine and Morgan's societas time and again. As we expand archaeologies of Native North America, we will learn more about the interesting worlds people crafted, about the social fabrics they wove which intertwined biology, family, ritual, territory, food, resources, ideas, labor, and so on. Future work, then, offers us the chance to greatly confound as well as build our understandings of relatedness and, ultimately, our conceptions of complexities in North America and beyond.

References

Allen, W. L., and J. B. Richardson III
1971   The Reconstruction of Kinship from Archaeological Data: The Concepts, the Methods, and the Feasibility. *American Antiquity* 36(1): 41–53.

Arnold, J. E.
2000   Revisiting Power, Labor Rights, and Kinship: Archaeology and Social Theory. In *Social Theory in Archaeology*, edited by M. B. Schiffer, pp. 14–30. Foundations of Archaeological Inquiry, J. Skibo, general editor. University of Utah Press, Salt Lake City.

Berreman, G.
1978   Scale and Social Relationships. *Current Anthropology* 19(2):225–245.

Blanton, R. E., S. A. Kowalewski, P. N. Peregrine, and G. M. Feinman
1996   Dual-Processual Theory for the Evolution of Mesoamerican Civilization. *Current Anthropology* 37(1):1–14.

Carruthers, P. J.
1969   The Mikado Earthwork 20AA5. Unpublished Master's thesis, University of Calgary, Calgary, Alberta.

Carsten, J.
2000   "Knowing Where You've Come From": Ruptures and Continuities of Time and Kinship in Narratives of Adoption Reunions. *Journal of the Royal Anthropological Institute* 6(4): 687–703.

Carsten, J. (editor)
2000   *Cultures of Relatedness: New Approaches to the Study of Kinship*. Cambridge University Press, Cambridge.

Chapman, R.
2003   *Archaeologies of Complexity*. Routledge, London.

Cleland, C. E.
1965   Field Notes from 1965 Season at the Missaukee Earthworks. Copy on file at the University of Michigan Museum of Anthropology, Great Lakes Range, Ann Arbor.

Cornelius, E. S., and H. W. Moll
1961   The Walters-Linsenman Earthwork Site. *Totem Pole* 44(9).

Crawford, G. W., David G. Smith, and Vandy E. Bowyer
1997   Dating the Entry of Corn (*Zea mays*) into the Lower Great Lakes Region. *American Antiquity* 62(1):112–119.

Crumley, C. L.
1987   Dialectical Critique of Hierarchy. In *Power*

Relations and State Formation, edited by
T. C. Patterson and C. W. Gailey, pp. 155–169.
American Anthropological Association,
Washington, D.C.

1995   Heterarchy and the Analysis of Complex
Societies. In *Heterarchy and the Analysis of
Complex Societies*, edited by R. M. Ehrenreich,
C. L. Crumley, and J. E. Levy, pp. 1–5. Archeo-
logical Papers No. 6. American Anthropolog-
ical Association, Arlington, Virginia.

Densmore, F.

1929   *Chippewa Customs*. U.S. Government Print-
ing Office, Washington, D.C.

Dustin, F.

1932   *Report on the Indian Earthworks in Ogemaw
County, Michigan*. Scientific Publications
No. 1. Cranbrook Institute of Science, Bloom-
field Hills, Michigan.

Evans-Pritchard, E. E.

1940   *The Nuer: A Description of the Modes of Livelihood and Political Institutions of a Nilotic
People*. Clarendon Press, Oxford.

1951   *Kinship and Marriage among the Nuer*.
Oxford University Press, London.

Feinberg, R.

2001   Introduction: Schneider's Cultural Analysis
of Kinship and Its Implications for Anthropological Relativism. In *The Cultural Analysis
of Kinship: The Legacy of David M. Schneider*,
edited by R. Feinberg and M. Ottenheimer,
pp. 1–32. University of Illinois Press, Urbana.

Feinberg, R., and M. Ottenheimer (editors)

2001   *The Cultural Analysis of Kinship: The Legacy
of David M. Schneider*. University of Illinois
Press, Urbana.

Feinman, G. M., K. G. Lightfoot, and S. Upham

2000   Political Hierarchies and Organizational
Strategies in the Puebloan Southwest. *American Antiquity* 65(3):449–470.

Feinman, G. M., and J. Neitzel

1984   Too Many Types: An Overview of Seden-
tary Prestate Societies in the Americas. In
*Advances in Archaeological Method and
Theory*, Vol. 7, pp. 39–102. Academic Press,
New York.

Fitting, J. E.

1970   *The Archaeology of Michigan: A Guide to the
Prehistory of the Great Lakes Region*. Natural
History Press, Garden City, New York.

Flanagan, J. G.

1989   Hierarchy in Simple "Egalitarian" Societies.
Annual Review of Anthropology 18:245–266.

Fortes, M.

1967   [1959] *The Web of Kinship among the Tallensi:
The Second Part of an Analysis of the Social*

Structure of a Trans-Volta Tribe. Oxford University Press, London.

1969   *Kinship and the Social Order: The Legacy of
Lewis Henry Morgan*. Aldine, Chicago.

1970   [1953] The Structure of Unilineal Descent
Groups. In *Time and Social Structure, and
Other Essays*, by M. Fortes. Athlone Press,
London.

Franklin, S., and S. McKinnon (editors)

2001   *Relative Values: Reconfiguring Kinship Studies*. Duke University Press, Durham, North
Carolina.

Godelier, M.

2004   *Métamorphoses de la parenté*. Fayard, Paris.

Greenman, E. F.

1926   Field Notes from 1926 Season at the Missaukee Earthworks. Original on file at the University of Michigan Museum of Anthropology, Great Lakes Range, Ann Arbor.

1927a   The Earthwork Inclosures of Michigan.
Unpublished Ph.D. dissertation, University
of Michigan, Ann Arbor.

1927b   Michigan Mounds, with Special Reference to
Two in Missaukee County. *Michigan Academy of Science, Arts and Letters Papers* 7:1–9.

Hambacher, M.

1992   The Skegemog Point Site: Continuing Studies in the Cultural Dynamics of the Carolin-
ian-Canadian Transition Zone. Unpublished
Ph.D. dissertation, Michigan State University,
East Lansing.

Hoffman, W. J.

1891   The Midewiwin or "Grand Medicine Society"
of the Ojibwa. In *7th Annual Report of the
Bureau of American Ethnology for the Years
1885–1886*, pp. 143–300. Smithsonian Institution, Washington, D.C.

Howey, M. C. L.

2006   Ritual, Resources and Regional Organization
in the Upper Great Lakes, AD 1200–1600.
Unpublished Ph.D. dissertation, University
of Michigan, Ann Arbor.

2007   Using Multi-criteria Cost Surface Analysis
to Explore Past Regional Landscapes: A Case
Study of Ritual Activity and Social Interaction in Michigan, AD 1200–1600. *Journal of
Archaeological Science* 34(11):1830–1846.

Howey, M. C. L., and J. M. O'Shea

2006   Bear's Journey and the Study of Ritual in
Archaeology. *American Antiquity* 71(2):
261–282.

Jones, M. L., J. K. Netto, J. D. Stockwell, and J. B. Mion

2003   Does the Value of Newly Accessible Spawning Habitat for Walleye (*Stizostedion vitreum*)
Depend on Its Location Relative to Nursery

Habitats? *Canadian Journal of Fisheries and Aquatic Sciences* 60(12):1527–1539.

Kinietz, W. Vernon

1947   *Chippewa Village: The Story of Katikitegon.* Cranbrook Institute of Science, Bloomfield Hills, Michigan.

Krakker, J.

1999   Late Woodland Settlement Patterns, Population, and Social Organization Viewed from Southern Michigan. In *Retrieving Michigan's Buried Past: The Archaeology of the Great Lakes State*, edited by J. R. Halsey and M. D. Stafford, pp. 228–243. Cranbrook Institute of Science, Bloomfield Hills, Michigan.

Landes, Ruth G.

1968   *Ojibwa Religion and the Midéwiwin.* University of Wisconsin Press, Madison.

Lévi-Strauss, Claude

1969   [1949] *The Elementary Structures of Kinship* (*Les structures élémentaires de la parenté*). Revised ed. Translated by J. H. Bell and J. R. von Sturmer; edited by R. Needham. Eyre and Spottiswoode, London.

Lovis, W. A.

1973   Late Woodland Cultural Dynamics in the Northern Lower Peninsula of Michigan. Unpublished Ph.D. dissertation, Michigan State University, East Lansing.

Maine, H. S., Sir

1970   [1861] *Ancient Law: Its Connection with the Early History of Society and Its Relation to Modern Ideas.* Introduction and notes by F. Pollock. Beacon Press, Gloucester, Massachusetts.

McIntosh, S. K. (editor)

1999   *Beyond Chiefdoms: Pathways to Complexity in Africa.* Cambridge University Press, Cambridge.

McKinnon, S.

2000   Domestic Exceptions: Evans-Pritchard and the Creation of Nuer Patrilineality and Equality. *Cultural Anthropology* 15(1):35–83.

Milner, C. M.

1998   Ceramic Style, Social Differentiation, and Resource Uncertainty in the Late Prehistoric Upper Great Lakes. Unpublished Ph.D. dissertation, University of Michigan, Ann Arbor.

Moll, H. W., N. G. Moll, and E. S. Cornelius

1958   Earthwork Enclosures in Ogemaw, Missaukee and Alcona Counties, Michigan. *Totem Pole* 41(3).

Morgan, L. H.

1985   [1877] *Ancient Society, or Researches in the Lines of Human Progress from Savagery through Barbarism to Civilization.* Reprint with a foreword by E. Tooker. University of Arizona Press, Tucson.

1997   [1871] *Systems of Consanguinity and Affinity of the Human Family.* Reprint with a foreword by E. Tooker. University of Nebraska Press, Lincoln.

O'Shea, J. M.

2003   Inland Foragers and the Adoption of Maize Agriculture in the Upper Great Lakes of North America. *Before Farming: The Archaeology of Old-World Hunter-Gatherers* 2(3): 1–21.

O'Shea, J., and A. W. Barker

1996   Measuring Social Complexity and Variation: A Categorical Imperative? In *Emergent Complexity: The Evolution of Intermediate Societies*, edited by J. E. Arnold, pp. 13–24. International Monographs in Prehistory, Ann Arbor, Michigan.

O'Shea, J. M., and C. M. Milner

2002   Material Indicators of Territory, Identity, and Interaction in a Prehistoric Tribal System. In *The Archaeology of Tribal Societies*, edited by W. A. Parkinson, pp. 200–226. International Monographs in Prehistory, Ann Arbor, Michigan.

Pauketat, T. R.

2001   Practice and History in Archaeology: An Emerging Paradigm. *Anthropological Theory* 1(1):73–98.

Paynter, R.

1989   Archaeology of Equality and Inequality. *Annual Review of Anthropology* 18:369–399.

Peletz, M. G.

1995   Kinship Studies in Late Twentieth-Century Anthropology. *Annual Review of Anthropology* 24:343–372.

Rowlands, M. J.

1998   Kinship, Alliance and Exchange in the European Bronze Age. In *Social Transformations in Archaeology: Global and Local Perspectives*, by K. Kristiansen and M. J. Rowlands, pp. 142–175. Routledge, London.

Schneider, D. M.

1968   *American Kinship: A Cultural Account.* Prentice-Hall, Englewood Cliffs, New Jersey.

1984   *A Critique of the Study of Kinship.* University of Michigan Press, Ann Arbor.

Shimizu, A.

1991   On the Notion of Kinship. *Man* 26(3):377–403.

Stone, L. (editor)

2001   *New Directions in Anthropological Kinship.* Rowman and Littlefield, Lanham, Maryland.

Stothers, D. M.

1999   The Late Woodland Models for Cultural Development in Southern Michigan. In *Retrieving Michigan's Buried Past: The Archaeology of the Great Lakes State*, edited by J. R. Halsey and M. D. Stafford, pp. 194–211. Cranbrook Institute of Science, Bloomfield Hills, Michigan.

Trautmann, T.

2001   The Whole History of Kinship Terminology in Three Chapters: Before Morgan, Morgan and After Morgan. *Anthropological Theory* 1(2):268–287.

Warren, William W.

1984   [1885] *History of the Ojibway People*. Minnesota Historical Society Press, St. Paul.

Watanabe, J.

2004   Some Models in a Muddle: Lineage and House in Classic Maya Social Organization. *Ancient Mesoamerica* 15(1):159–166.

Wiessner, P.

2002   Vines of Complexity: Egalitarian Structures and the Institutionalization of Inequality among the Enga. *Current Anthropology* 43(2):233–269.

Yoffee, N.

2005   *Myths of the Archaic State: Evolution of the Earliest Cities, States and Civilizations*. Cambridge University Press, Cambridge.

Zurel, R. L.

1999   Earthwork Enclosure Sites in Michigan. In *Retrieving Michigan's Buried Past: The Archaeology of the Great Lakes State*, edited by J. R. Halsey and M. D. Stafford, pp. 244–248. Cranbrook Institute of Science, Bloomfield Hills, Michigan.

8

Complexity in Action(s)

Retelling the Cahokia Story

Susan M. Alt

The historical reality is continuous and infinitely complex; and cold hard facts into which it is said to be analyzed are not concrete portions of reality but only aspects of it.
(Becker 1910)

The question of complexity remains troubling in North American archaeology, particularly for places like Cahokia, the largest precolumbian center in North America. In this chapter I review why this is so, and I retell the Cahokia story as a way to demonstrate an alternative approach to complexity. This approach ignores the more common goal of categorization and instead seeks complexity in the day-to-day actions of people as well as in extraordinary events. Such a retelling views complexity as engendered through actions and events as well as created through the interconnections of individuals, objects, and places. This is because political and social complexity are, in fact, intertwined. They are part of the fabric of the everyday lived experience, not just certain political moments or organizations. Taking cues from current social theory, I reevaluate how complexity was created and experienced by the people of the Cahokia polity and suggest why this more practice-historical approach provides a richer understanding of the past.

Given its enormous earthen pyramids and sprawling plazas, the Cahokia site, located in Collinsville, Illinois (Figure 8.1), is easily identifiable as a major center. Even today, cut into pieces by highways and modern development, Cahokia still maintains an imposing presence. But what this place represents in terms of polity and complexity has been a matter of contentious debate for decades. Characterizations range from viewing Cahokia as a communal place of great equality (Saitta 1994) to assigning it a role as a Mesoamerican city (e.g., Kehoe and Bruhns 1992; O'Brien 1989; Saitta 1994). This variability in interpretation is not, I believe, a surprising outcome since analysis and interpretation treats complexity as a series of traits and requires that all polities fit into a categorical system that flattens variation and dismisses that which is unique. Thus, when a place such as Cahokia does not comfortably fit the expected trajectory for a chiefdom or a state, interpretive chaos can and often does ensue.

Here I attempt to tell a new kind of Cahokia story by sidestepping the typical analytical reliance on the categorical. I evaluate complexity at Cahokia and its surroundings by measuring discrete actions, events, and the spaces wherein complexity was created and enacted. While this is a more historical approach, it also focuses on the *ways* in which Cahokians were complex rather than simply asking "was Cahokia complex?" (cf. Nelson 1995). Instead of identifying a few traits and assigning categories or subcategories, I evaluate the material evidence of what people did and how they did it and try to understand the details of how life in Cahokian towns may have engendered complexity, or not. I further recognize that

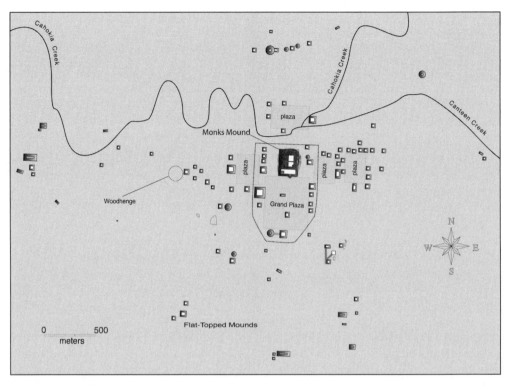

FIGURE 8.1. Map of Cahokia.

The Old Cahokia Story
(or Why No One Can Agree on Complexity)

complexity may be uneven, that some events, procedures, and processes may engender more complexity than others. Thus, this approach, focused on daily performance, operationalizes the recognition that complexity is lived and practiced.

Cahokia has long been proffered as a case study in the development of political complexity despite the disparate views of complexity at Cahokia (e.g., Neitzel 1999). The basic Cahokia story is that an indigenous midwestern Late Woodland period town underwent massive changes and grew exponentially in size and population during a short time span (covering a generation or two) around AD 1050 (Emerson 1997a; Milner 1998; Pauketat 2007). Also accepted by most is that the changes included a demographic reorganization. Instead of living in scattered small villages in the floodplain around Cahokia, called the "American Bottom," people moved to Cahokia or other mound centers, and a few chose to live in independent farmsteads or hamlets. During this time, the

mounds and plazas were built, new technologies were devised, and pottery and housing styles all changed. New types of buildings, pots, and other types of material goods appeared. These changes and innovations have been considered markers of a new type of polity (Emerson 1997a, b; Fowler 1975; Hall 1973; Kelly 1990; Milner 1998; Muller 1997; Pauketat 1994, 1998, 2004).

The preceding gloss of the Cahokia story can be told with little disagreement from Cahokia researchers. However, how Cahokia is *interpreted* is an entirely different matter (contrast Emerson 1997b; Fowler 1974; Hall 1991; Kelly 1991; Mehrer 1995; Milner 1998; Muller 1997; O'Brien 1989; Pauketat 2004, 2007; Saitta 1994). Understanding Cahokia becomes contentious when analysts begin to assign meanings or try to make categorical statements about complexity.

Since the 1950s, Cahokia debates have centered on identifying stimuli that would have instigated the changes that transformed an agricultural village into a major Mississippian center. The debates have revolved around the question of whether change was internally or externally motivated (Bareis and Porter 1984; Fowler 1973; Frei-muth 1974; Hall 1965, 1966, 1975, 1991; Kelly 1980, 1991, 1992; Porter 1969, 1974; Vogel 1975). Porter (1974) and Perino (1959) asserted that Mississippian traits developed elsewhere and were carried to the American Bottom by foreigners. Hall (1965, 1966) and Kelly (1980, 1991), on the other hand, argued for local in situ developmental scenarios. So did intruders impose elements of a more complex society or did they emerge sui generis?

It would have been simple to lay the blame on intrusive Mississippians (Perino 1959; Porter 1974), but there were none (at least none who brought in fully formed Mississippian culture). Currently, it is more commonly thought that the Cahokians were the first Mississippians (Brown 2007; Pauketat and Emerson 1997), but how and why did they become Mississippian? If complexity emerged in situ, then according to most analysts there must have been a prime mover behind the changes, something like the adoption of agriculture, competition with outsiders, ambitious leaders, or the control of trade routes (Dincauze and Hasenstab 1989; Hall 1975; Kelly 1990, 1991; Peregrine 1992; Porter 1969, 1974). Other analysts posited that the transformation to greater complexity was part of a normal evolutionary trajectory, something to be expected as the typical progress of a healthy society (Fowler 1973, 1975, 1978, 1997).

With evidence pointing to a "Big Bang" (a term implicating a sudden transformation from village to center; Pauketat 1994), it became clear that the rise of Cahokia as a major center could not be evaluated as the gradual evolution of complexity through time. It was also demonstrated that most of the innovations that are counted as elements of the Big Bang had precursors in earlier times (Bareis and Porter 1984; Pauketat 1994; Pauketat and Emerson 1997). For example, after the Big Bang, currently dated to the decade or two around ca. AD 1050, pottery was typically made using shell temper. However, shell-tempered pots had also been made, although rarely, in the later phases of the preceding Late Woodland period. Thus, shell temper could be seen to represent an internal change in use frequencies, not a new or imposed technology (see Bareis and Porter 1984; Feathers 1990; Feathers and Peacock 2008; J. Kelly 2000). So it was determined that there were no outside invaders. It was further discovered that reliance on corn agriculture preceded the Big Bang (Bareis and Porter 1984). And finally, Cahokia lacked evidence of violent encounters as well as extensive trade networks (Emerson et al. 2003; Milner 1998; Pauketat and Emerson 1997). It seemed that none of the typical prime movers could account for the changes at Cahokia. These determinations only made understanding complexity at Cahokia that much more controversial.

By the 1980s, in conjunction with the aforementioned studies, most researchers designated Cahokia a Mississippian chiefdom (see Smith 1978), a label that is, in fact, comfortable for many analysts (see, for example, Anderson 1994b; Beck 2003; Milner 1998; Muller 1997). Still, considerable discomfort surrounded the determination of how complex a chiefdom it was (Cobb 2003). In fact, Cahokia was called a state by a few (Kehoe and Bruhns 1992; O'Brien 1989), a recently revived claim (Pauketat 2007). So the question of what to make of Cahokian complexity remained, and remains, unanswered—although clearly not for a lack of trying.

Today there is a vast literature on Cahokia. In this literature one faction, called minimalists, argues that Cahokia was nothing more than a typical southeastern chiefdom (Stoltman 1991). Others are called exaggerationalists if they argue for greater complexity (Muller 1997). Too many on both sides warrant their arguments by appeals to the categorical and a focus on traits and categories rather than on the actual doings of the people of the Cahokia polity. Attempts to address the complexity arguments usually involve invoking subtypes: was it a simple, complex, paramount, group-oriented, individualizing, corporate, network, apical, or constituent chiefdom (Anderson 1994a; Beck 2003; Blanton et al. 1996; D'Altroy and Earle 1985; Johnson and Earle 1987; Renfrew 1974; Steponaitis 1978; Stoltman 1991; Wright 1984)? But subcategories do not resolve the question, how complex was Cahokia? They simply change the language and recapitulate the same problems inherent to defining an entire society on the basis of a few traits. The central questions—how was polity constituted, how much power and authority was wielded over whom and across what distances—remain topics lacking a suitable method of engagement.

Why Categorizing Does Not Work

As implied above, the debates over Cahokian complexity do not arise because we do not have data concerning the workings of Cahokia, but rather the reverse. The problem is that we have been doing our jobs well and the data have outgrown our traditional categorical approaches. The disagreements between so-called minimalists and exaggerationalists or in situ versus intrusive constructs are a by-product of using outdated models for discussions about precolumbian places. In the past, categories such as chiefdom or state could be useful because, with little data at hand, we could group societies into gross categories that focused on similarities and provided points of reference for comparisons. But since these terms came into vogue, there has been a great deal of research that has generated more data, and these data provide a basis to argue for greater diversity than a categorical approach can accommodate. Calling a polity a chiefdom is no longer terribly informative because we are actually uncovering detailed histories for past peoples and places such as Cahokia (as well as others). Thus, in such cases, the old categories not only fail to provide guidance but instead act as constraints. With a categorical approach, differences between polities are hard to evaluate because the categorical procedure was rigged to ignore diversity: anything unique is typically ignored or at best filed away as an anomaly or outlier rather than viewed as a clue to a different way of being complex. Characteristics of polities that fall outside expectations are too often dismissed out of hand. And of course, in ignoring certain lines of evidence simply because they do not fit, we risk creating false characterizations of the people and places we study.

Redefining Complexity

There is, of course, nothing new in arguing against categorical approaches for understanding human history. There is a large and ever growing literature on the topic (for examples, see Bawden 1989; Cobb 2003; Crumley 1995; Curet 2003; Drennan 1991; Feinman and Neitzel 1984; Hodder 1986; Kristiansen 1991; McGuire 1983; Pauketat 2007; Paynter 1989; Shanks and Tilley 1987; Spencer 1987; Upham 1987, 1990; Yoffee 1993, 2005). But concepts such as complexity are also problematic because they suffer from uncertain definitions, reductionist procedures, and relationships with evolutionary models (see introduction, this volume; Chapman 2003; Smith 2003; Yoffee 2005). For example, complexity is often treated as a property that is inherent to a state, institution, or group. Complexity, as used in archaeology, has historically been understood in terms of progress and social evolution (Chapman 2003).

However, complexity is not a thing. It is not even an inherent property of things. Complexity can be difficult to define, whether in math, physics, or the social sciences. Much like the old saw about pornography, analysts claim to know complexity when they see it (Cilliers 1998; Finkenthal 2008), which is perhaps an indication that the concept is hopelessly culture-bound and situationally specific.

Most attempts to define complexity list properties such as multiple parts, interrelations, dependency, unpredictability, heterogeneity, intricacy, complication, and combined effects that produce a whole that is greater than its parts. We can take from this a sense, then, that complexity is dependent on a variety of interrelated conditions and is ever in process (Cilliers 1998; Finkenthal 2008; Law and Mol 2006).

The subcategories of organizations or institutions defined to prop up categories of political types are equally constraining. For example, the palace has been offered as a signifier for complexity and an indicator for a type of political organization, namely, the state (Flannery 1998). On the basis of this observation we now have arguments that the Harappa, the Olmec, or the Cahokians were not state societies because they did not have palaces (Flannery 1998; Possehl 1997). Thus, a palace, meant to serve as a sign that complex actions may be occurring, instead becomes treated as if it were, in and of itself, complexity (Christie and Sarro 2006). A palace is no longer a sign but has become, in effect, the signified (Preucel 2006).

Instead, complexity derives from the activities that occur within a palace, activities that could also occur in places that look nothing like a palace. This, then, is where I would shift the focus: away from traits like palaces to what people actually did in the past. Recovering evidence of past actions, even day-to-day actions, is what archae-ologists can do (Shennan 1993). That is not to say that this is a simple task, certainly not as easy as identifying a trait and letting it stand in for com-plex actions. Such a plan requires a great deal of fine-grained data, but then numerous details and fine-grained analyses have been accumulating through the practice of archaeology over the past decades.

Complexity is engendered through people's interactions with one another as well as their engagement with the material world. These inter-actions create interdependent relationships of meaning and action that change the whole and yet are inseparable from the whole (Cilliers 1998; Hannerz 1992; Law and Mol 2006; Sawyer 2005). Thus, in social memory, cultural identity, and rit-ual practice we have better avenues of research for explaining social complexity (e.g., Mills 2004; Mills and Walker 2008; Patterson 2004; Spiel-mann 2002; Van Dyke 2003). As other chapters in this book demonstrate, such studies shift the em-phasis away from categories, elites, and political economy and toward the ways in which all people lived economies or practiced politics or created social networks. In eastern North America such studies dovetail with suggestions that heterarchy, communalism, and gender were as important as hierarchy in Mississippian developments (e.g., Anderson 1994b; Crumley 1995; L. Kelly 2000a; King 2003; Mehrer 2000; Nassaney 2001; Saitta 1994; Sullivan and Rodning 2001; Trubitt 2000; Yoffee et al. 1999).

In the terms of contemporary theories of prac-tice, agency, and landscape, daily practices—or what people do and how they do it—are inextri-cably associated with and shaped by the cultural landscapes and histories of places, bodies, and portable objects (Ashmore 2002; Bradley 2000; Dobres and Robb 2000; Meskell 2004; Meskell and Joyce 2003; Soja 1996). Any place, body, or cultural object is part of a continually renegoti-ated field or landscape of social action that takes material form and occupies space (e.g., Lightfoot et al. 1998). Such fields have thick histories, with meanings that derive from those histories (which is to say the "genealogies" of practices, the "bi-ographies" of portable things, the chaînes opéra-toires of technologies, and the "experiences" of

particular places, monuments, and architecture generally [see Bradley 2000; Clark 2004; Costin 1998; Dobres and Robb 2000; Hodder and Cess-ford 2004; Joyce 2000; Kopytoff 1986]).

As the discussion above implies, complexity is not solely the province of the elite, nor is it to be located only in centers or palaces. In fact, Yoffee (2005) would label such developments "simplifi-cations." The creation of complexity, on the other hand, is a multisited process, engaged in by all people across a region and beyond. Here I illus-trate my point by telling a new kind of Cahokia story that examines complexity through the in-teractions between Cahokians and local villag-ers and investigates how practices, actions, and events illustrate the ways that people created and lived complexity in the American Bottom region of Illinois about 1,000 years ago.

A New Cahokia Story

Complexity in the practical, everyday terms I suggest above is best measured archaeologically through the variability of practices evident across a landscape and the relationships between per-sons, places, and things. For this reason, I now turn to a locality located in the uplands to the east of Cahokia that has been termed the Richland complex (Figure 8.2; Alt 2001, 2002a; Pauketat 2003). With this case study I demonstrate how an examination of the microdetails of what people actually did, and how they did it, can illuminate complexity. To explicate complexity on a polity-wide level, I then discuss detailed analyses of how people founded villages, made choices in orga-nizing their settlements, utilized available tech-nologies, practiced a variety of occupations, and managed special events.

Excavation and analysis of several villages in the Richland complex explicitly focused on doc-umenting the daily lives of the village inhabitants (Alt 2001, 2002a and b, 2006a and b; Pauketat 2002, 2003). Excavations directed by T. Pauketat and myself as well as excavations conducted by the Illinois Transportation Archaeological Re-search Program have provided a sample of over 250 houses and many more hundreds of pits at the Halliday, Grossmann, Pfeffer, Emerald, and Hal Smith sites (Figure 8.2; Alt 2001, 2002a and b, 2006a and b, 2008; Hargrave et al. 2000; Howe

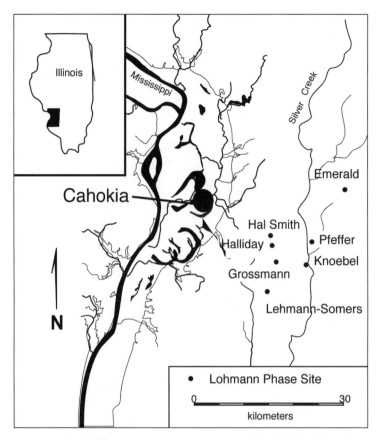

FIGURE 8.2. Map of the American Bottom and sites in the Richland complex.

2000; Jackson 2000; Kruchten 2000; Kruchten and Alt 2003; Pauketat 2003). Two other villages, the Knoebel site and the Lehmann-Somers site, provide over 150 more houses and pits to add to the discussion (Alt 2002b; Bareis 1976; Kelly and Powell 2000; Kinsella 2002).

All but one of the villages discussed (Knoebel) were newly settled or resettled at about AD 1050, the very time that Cahokia was being reconfigured as a major center. Interestingly, the settling of new rural districts, or as Yoffee phrases it, "the ruralization that follows urbanization," is not uncommon and often follows the rise of large cities (Yoffee 2005:60).

Village Life

Investigations at several Richland complex villages (the Halliday, Knoebel, Hal Smith, Pfeffer, and Grossmann sites; see Figure 8.2) revealed that the people who lived in these neighboring upland villages did not all do things in the same way, that

is, one Mississippian settlement or household was not necessarily a blueprint for another (Alt 2001, 2002a and b, 2006a and b, 2008; Hargrave et al. 2000; Howe 2000; Jackson 2000; Kelly and Powell 2000; L. Kelly 2000a; Kinsella 2002; Kruchten 2000; Kruchten and Alt 2003; Pauketat 2003). People in this region seem to have organized villages and built houses according to principles based on particular individual histories rather than on a generic Cahokian Mississippian plan.

Differential construction techniques, such as variable use of wall trenches or single post wall construction, and variety in building sizes, shapes, locations, and grouping choices all point to disparate origins for many residents of the Cahokia region. Distant origins are also implicated in the choices people made in pottery production as well as in lithic tool manufacture (Alt 2006a, b). While in some cases it seemed that people tried to emulate a Cahokian aesthetic in their products, analysis of stylistic and manufacturing details

Artifact Densities

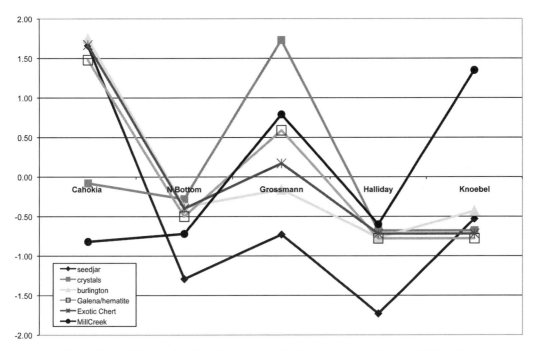

FIGURE 8.3. Comparison of the distribution of exotics at Cahokia, the American Bottom, Richland complex farming villages (Halliday and Knoebel), and Grossmann (data compiled from Alt 2002a and b, 2006a and b; Emerson and Jackson 1984; Jackson 1992; Holley 1989; Pauketat 1998; on file, University of Illinois).

implies differentially internalized technological and aesthetic templates for how a house or pot or scraper should be made (Alt 2001, 2002a and b, 2006a and b).

Evidence for specific distant origins for people was found to cluster in different villages: for example, the Halliday village contained evidence that strongly suggests a southeastern Missouri "Varney" origin for many inhabitants, and the Knoebel village contained evidence of southwestern Indiana "Yankeetown" traditions (Alt 2006a, b).[1] Overall, in architecture and village organization, the farming villages looked more like pre-Mississippian villages than like Mississippian towns. They lacked mounds and other types of public architecture. Houses were organized in old-fashioned courtyard configurations. Village residents persisted in using older styles of construction such as single post wall constructions at the same time as they were emulating more up-to-date Cahokian-like pottery technologies (Alt 2001, 2002a and b, 2006a and b).

The people of the various villages engaged in a number of activities that were similar to each other as well as some that were not. For example, all the villages contained evidence for farming in a much more intensified manner than that seen at the floodplain settlements. This is apparent in significant quantities of Mill Creek chert debris from hoe maintenance (see Figure 8.3) as well as the presence of generous storage facilities for agricultural products. But some villagers also engaged in specialized productive activities, clearly manufacturing more cordage or beads than would be needed on a household level (Alt 1999, 2001, 2002a and b, 2006a and b; Pauketat 2002). At the same time, display objects, ornaments, and exotics were very rare in all but one of the Richland complex locations (Figure 8.3).

Villagers engaged in specialized production in varying ways, but it should be noted that not all people engaged in some sort of specialized productive activity. Each village seemed to have a particular specialty, and thus not all villages produced the same materials. At Halliday and Knoebel, fiber production was identified through high densities of spindle whorls and a large number of pans that may relate to the soaking and dyeing of fibers (Alt 1999). The Pfeffer and Lehmann-Somers sites contained concentrations of microdrills used for shell working and the production of marine shell beads (Kelly and Powell 2000; Kinsella 2002; Koldehoff et al. 1993; Kruchten 2000). On the other hand, there was no evidence for specialized production at Hal Smith (although very little of this site has been excavated; on file, University of Illinois). Of interest is that these productive activities, of both foodstuff and other goods, were apparently implicated in the creation of many new kinds of interactions in the Cahokia region and may have even provoked the development of a new kind of settlement.

Thus, village life seemed to have centered on agricultural pursuits, but some people at each village were engaged in more specialized production of such things as fabric, beads, and celts. Each cluster or courtyard grouping of houses possessed its own storage hut, either free-standing (Halliday and Pfeffer) or attached to another structure (Knoebel), as well as some external storage pits. Courtyards, likely places of communal gathering, were kept clean. Debris was swept into middens that regularly occurred behind the courtyard groups. Things like cooking pots were made by households as needed, as were expedient lithic tools. Specialized tools and equipment were rare, although, for example, the people of Halliday made and kept a few ceramic chunkey stones during a time when stone ones were used exclusively by Cahokian elites. Evidence for special events, magico-ritual items, or public architecture was extremely rare in the villages. However, the village at Grossmann stood out as a very different sort of place precisely because of how much it varied from the previously discussed patterns (Figure 8.4; Alt 2002a and b, 2006a).

The Grossmann Site
and the Rituals of Complexity

Evidence at the village at Grossmann suggests that Cahokian society was highly differentiated, multifaceted, and interconnected in a variety of ways. This evidence explicates how the many parts were interrelated and how bonds were created between very different groups of people. It

also points to the implications and consequences of those connections.

Dating between about AD 1075 and 1150, the Grossmann site was founded in the uplands 10 miles east of Cahokia in the middle of the Richland complex farming villages (Alt 2002a, 2006a). Grossmann was not settled at the same time as the other Richland complex villages but about a generation after the others were already in place. Also, Grossmann did not contain evidence indicating a foreign origin for its inhabitants, as did other Richland complex villages. Instead, the Grossmann site looked very Cahokian, a place that Emerson (1997a) would probably describe as a nodal center. Nodal settlements are defined as household, civic, or ceremonial settlements with heterarchical as well as hierarchical relationships. The nodes are considered constituents of a dispersed community pattern. For example, multiple homesteads comprised a dispersed village that was integrated though civic and ceremonial nodes (see Emerson 1997a). But Grossmann contained evidence of buildings, material culture, and special events that were found in both farmsteads and civic and ceremonial centers, and in other ways (to be explained below) were very unlike Emerson's descriptions for the various kinds of nodal centers found on the Cahokian landscape.

The Grossmann site was excavated in its entirety and was found to contain a dense stand of 113 structures and 95 pits. Unusual for an upland village, structures on the site included four large council houses or temples, three circular sweat lodges, three residences for leaders, and one charnel house (Figure 8.4). At least 24 of the remaining 102 structures were storage buildings, not residences (a more typical ratio would be one storage building for every seven or eight structures [Alt 2002b]). This wide range of building types as well as residues from ritual events indicated multiple kinds of integrative community practices and activities associated with the wider political economy. Presumably, Grossmann's people played host to particular religious and political events in the farming district, as well as acting as a clearinghouse for produce and goods passing between Cahokia and the uplands (Alt 2006a).

People at Grossmann did not just farm (although the village included farmers) and produce

FIGURE 8.4. Map of the Grossmann site.

craft goods. Unlike the farmers at the other Richland complex villages, the Grossman residents were not poor in exotic, ritual, or status items (Figure 8.3). Occupations at Grossmann also included ritual specialists who tended to places such as the temples, sweat lodges, and charnel houses. Some people, presumably leaders or religious specialists, wore status or ritual objects such as ear spools, lived in larger houses, possessed more exotic goods, and presumably presided over events at the meeting houses. Some were engaged in the acquisition, storage, and dispersal of the uplands produce. At least one-quarter of the buildings were storage huts, and about one-quarter of the vessels were also used for storage (Alt 2006a). Pottery did not indicate alien aesthetics but looked very Cahokian and included Ramey Incised, the definitive Cahokian vessel type (Pauketat and Emerson 1990). Overall, ceramic vessels had a rather unusual size profile with a large proportion of overly tiny and overly large vessels. There seemed more need here for storage and medicine jars than at the farming villages or other Cahokian residential locales (Figure 8.5).

Production at Grossmann did not indicate a single craft specialty as at some of the other local villages; rather, there was evidence of many different kinds of productive activities: fiber production, celt manufacture, tool and bead making, crystal production, and pigment processing. Evidence also suggests the production of ceremonial items (such as a carved red stone figurine and quartz crystals) as well as fineware and some unusual ceramic vessels. Production at Grossmann was not limited to workshop-like locales but seems to have been an integral part of the many

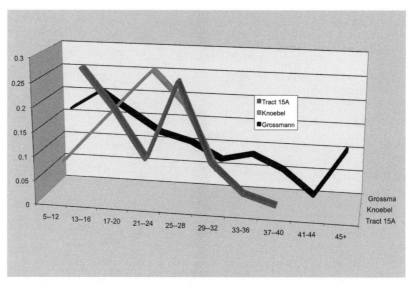

FIGURE 8.5. Comparison of jar size distribution at Tract 15A of Cahokia, Knoebel, and Grossmann (data compiled from Alt 2002a and b, 2006a and b; Pauketat 1998).

ceremonial events that occurred there. And the ceremonial events are critical to understanding the relationships of the people at Grossmann, the farming villages, and Cahokia.

While evidence from both architecture and ceramic vessels at Grossmann points to storage facilities in quantities exceeded only by those at the East St. Louis Mound Center (Fortier 2007; Pauketat 2005), there is also evidence as to how that storage was connected to Cahokia and the farming villages. Both the farming villages and Grossmann utilized storage huts rather than storage pits, a form more conducive to short-term storage than pits. I suspect that the farmers passed goods from their village storehouses to the ones at Grossmann. From Grossmann, material moved to areas such as the storage compound at the East St. Louis Mound center (located just outside downtown Cahokia). At East St. Louis, walled compounds contained little else but storage facilities (Fortier 2007; Pauketat 2005). This finding, along with a study by Lucretia Kelly (2000b), who found that the best cuts of meat were consumed at Cahokia while the less desirable parts were more common in the uplands, suggests that the rural villagers sent out their best to Cahokia. The evidence of how and why this occurred is understood through deposits at the Grossmann site

that contained debris from elaborate ritual and ceremonial events.

The evidence in the ritual deposits suggests that the farmers came together with religious and political leaders from Cahokia at the Grossman site, where they held public gatherings, both political and ritual in nature. Rituals of the sort that happened at Grossmann did not occur at any of the other contemporaneous rural locations. The rituals seem to have celebrated important elements of Mississippian religion, social life, agricultural practices, ancestors, and mythic figures. These rituals did not contain evidence of feasting (which did happen at other rural sites) but contained evidence of meaning-laden events that imparted the importance of productivity, the harvest, and most significantly, renewal. Important to keep in mind is that these events were politics in action, in themselves part of the creation and maintenance of community, polity, and complexity.

As part of these rituals and ceremonies, objects and buildings were "killed" and new objects and buildings were manufactured (Alt 2006a). For example, 70 celts were made by a number of different craftspeople from the surrounding agricultural settlements and deposited in a dedicatory pit (Pauketat and Alt 2004). Bags of corn and seeds were burned in conjunction with hoes, picks, points, other tools, and figurines. Crystals, galena, and hematite included in the deposits attest to the cosmological import of the events. All these items referenced past, present, and future. Curated objects such as Archaic period spear points referenced times past. Precious minerals referenced ongoing interactions with the sacred. Corn and seeds needed for future productivity were all burned, together with the debris of newly crafted objects as well as the tools used to make them (Table 8.1), following green corn ceremonialism, a necessary step to ensure the future (for details on green corn ceremonialism, see Witthoft 1949). The provisioning that went along with these events was not simply a way of supplying Cahokians with upland produce but was more importantly community and polity building through a reaffirmation of the cosmos, of the way that things should be, and of being Cahokian. The seemingly communal nature of the events may suggest that participation was voluntary; but other evidence, such as human legs that were buried away from the rest of the body in a pit, may argue otherwise (Alt 2006a, 2008).[2]

The disposition of some human remains adds to the layers of meaning at Grossmann. A few bodies were maintained with great care in a charnel house, a treatment that is not at all typical of the region and has been suggested only at mortuary mounds (e.g., Fowler et al. 1999). The persons curated in the tiny charnel structure were likely reminders of the Cahokian genealogy that warranted events that could be enacted at Grossmann but not at other places, such as the farming villages. But other contexts, such as a woman buried in the bottom of a pit with a broken celt, or the previously mentioned legs in a pit, suggest that perhaps there could have been repercussions for not complying with the status quo.

For the most part, evidence points to gatherings that were community- and polity-building events, but the events would have also emphasized and perhaps helped naturalize status differences. It would have been clear that some people contributed their products to fill the many storehouses at Grossmann or created objects to be sacrificed at the rituals, while other people collected and/or consumed those contributions. And then there were people who controlled the meeting houses, the temples, the sweat lodges, and the charnel houses. Those people wore the recovered ear spools, gorgets, and other insignia of office; on the other hand, the farmers lacked special goods of any kind. Inequality was also evident in the size and patterning of special buildings and elite residences in association with the special structures. It was also evident in the fact that at the other villages people did not build such structures; instead, they brought the fruits of their labors to Grossmann in order to participate in events ultimately associated with being Cahokian.

Here, in the details of living, farming, crafting, commemorating, and celebrating, is complexity-in-the-making. The architecture and events at Grossmann indicate a complex and multilayered place that was a piece of a much larger complex and multilayered regional history. On the one hand, Grossmann was a place to come for ritual and ceremony to celebrate the harvest and the renewal of life. On the other hand, Grossmann was a highly politicized place with storage facilities and workshop areas proclaiming and fulfilling the needs of the Cahokians. Embedded in this was a tension between the communal and repercussions for dissension, or perhaps for remaining an outsider. But none of this need have been accomplished by an overt imposition of Cahokian will and ideology on upland people of a sort that might have, at one time, justified calling Cahokia a "complex society." It was seemingly accomplished through rituals of inclusion thick with cosmological references, hierarchical relations, and history.

Conclusion

Inclusive rituals such as those at Grossmann that seem to have underwritten Cahokia might be dismissed by some as belonging in the realm of less complex polities (in the sense of Kelly 2002): states have politics, chiefdoms have rituals. Yet what would politics be without rituals? Great polities are built on the back of many kinds of rituals—town hall meetings, parades and Fourth of July fireworks, setting out the flag, the inauguration of a new president. Politics are, in fact, themselves only a certain kind of ritual (Kertzer 1988). Rituals, celebrations, and commemorations are

TABLE 8.1. Contents of Features with Special Deposits at the Grossmann Site.

Feature	Size (m)	Volume (m³)	Ceramics	Tools	Other (ritual/exotic/unusual)
PIT F 12	1.07 × 1.06	.28	8 jars 1 seedjar 1 bowl 1 beaker	1 abrader 1 hoe fragment	Human leg bones
PIT F 146	1.62 × 1.58	1.07	16 jars 5 funnels 1 jug 6 bowls (1 Ramey) 1 beaker	8 saw/sanders 1 Archaic biface 2 hoe fragments 6 celt flakes	Burned thatch Charred seeds Mud daubers 41 kaolin 3 galena
PIT F 159	1.3 × 1.3	1.42	12 jars Frog effigy handle 2 bowls 7 funnels 1 pan	2 abraders 3 hammers Hoe shatter	Burned walls Burned thatch Mud daubers Killed pots 2 galena 1 crystal
PIT F 206	.84 × .84	1.02		70 celts	
PIT F 209	1.6 × 1.51	1.86	7 jars 3 bowls (1 bilobed) 1 seedjar 1 jug 1 funnel 1 bottle 1 pan	4 hammer/grinders 3 abraders 1 grinder 1 Madison point	In situ burning Hematite 7 crystals
PIT F 220	2.42 × 1.35	2.47	8 jars 1 bowl	2 hammers 3 palettes	1 human burial 1 galena 1 limonite 1 red ochre 1 Hixton
PIT F 256	1.37 × 1.02	2.65	35 jars (1 minijar) 2 pinch pots 2 seedjars 1 beaker 3 bowls 3 funnels 6 bottle stoppers	1 abrader 1 grinder 1 hammer 1 sander 3 spindle whorls 1 pottery trowel 2 Cahokia points 1 Ramey knife	Yellow lining 1 hematite 1 red ochre 4 crystals 2 kaolin 6 celt flakes
PIT F 260	1.37 × 1.02	.82	3 jars 1 incised sherd	1 hammer	1 large crystal Figurine fragment Burned corn Burned thatch Burned seeds Mud daubers
PIT F 275	2.32 × 1.58	1.78	4 jars (1 is painted white) 1 bowl	1 abrader 1 grinder 12 sanders 2 palette/sanders 4 saw/sanders 1 biface fragment	Killed figurine Burned corn Burned seeds Burned fabric Mud daubers
PIT F 287	1.22 × 1.01	.78	11 jars 3 bowls 1 beaker	Celt butt 1 abrader/sander 2 hammer/grinder 1 spindle whorl	Burned nuts Burned seeds Bone 1 crystal Fabric-impressed clay

the glue that holds people together. Ritual allows the embodiment, actualization, and materialization of belief in practices that are at once traditional and discursive. Ritual happens, it is active, therefore it is reactive (Bell 1997; Geertz 1981; Tambiah 1990). Ritual can legitimate leadership, enforce ideologies, buy compliance, or incite resistance. Ritual, with its potential for multivocality and mitigation of social and political cleavages, can be a very complex endeavor, linking diverse peoples, ideas, and practices into a coherent cohesive community. Ritual is, in fact, another kind of politicking (Kelly and Kaplan 1990; Kertzer 1988).

It was within the complex processes of living their lives and how those lives came together, along with the politicization of religion, that farmers, immigrants, elites, religious specialists, craftsmen, and more created what we now call Mississippian society. The rituals at Grossmann served to integrate immigrant farmers with rural Cahokians as well as Cahokian elites and specialists. This was not a one-sided meeting but rather a give-and-take of ideas and customs as well as a setting ripe for the creation of new rituals and beliefs that might better speak to all. This multiplicity of population and events, the creation of elaborate rituals and a multilayered social fabric in order to integrate an ever growing polity, was highly complex, involving intricate connections as well as separations between the various elements of society.

There is complexity in how the linkages between people, places, occupations, and status were created at the same time as status and distance were maintained. There were, in fact, many "parts" or layers of belief that required negotiation and engendered compliance as well as resistance. It is in the interaction of all these realms that complexity was created in the Cahokia polity. But this is not the sense of complexity that gets you a "complex society" in current parlance (it was "not like us").

In the end, the Cahokia case points out that it is insufficient simply to say that the society was or was not complex without addressing the historical formation of complexity. Indeed, assigning a category to explain Cahokia, Grossmann, and the farmers would not really tell us anything new. Assigning a label would instead require ignoring the historical details, flattening diversity, and glossing over the complex connections between people, places, and things. What should matter in evaluating past polities is how people did what they did, whether other polities had comparable histories, and how various moments, institutions, or processes might have been complex.

Complexity should not be negated or assumed based on constructed categories. As the Cahokia case demonstrates, we can actually find the details of those processes and begin to write more thorough histories of the people we study. We have the details of past lives, and we can now better identify and explore the many dimensions and contingencies of such complexities. And those details rarely, if ever, fit our carefully constructed categories. What should take precedence are the real histories, the complexities of enactment and social experience. In other words, complexity is all in the details.

Notes

1. The Varney tradition, best exemplified by the Zebree site (Morse and Morse 1980), was a Late Woodland/early Mississippian tradition identified in southeastern Missouri. Varney wares are shell tempered with red slipped interiors and particular vessel morphology. Varney wares have been identified at many Cahokian communities but never in such high numbers as occurred at the Halliday site. The Yankeetown tradition, defined at the Yankeetown site (Blasingham 1953, 1965; see also Redmond 1990), was a Late Woodland through early Mississippian tradition identified in southwestern Indiana, southeastern Illinois, and northwestern Kentucky. Yankeetown wares have a grog paste as well as distinctive stamped, filleted, and incised decorative treatments.

2. There are suggestions of violent outcomes for persons in the Cahokia region. The best-known cases are the sacrificial burials at Mound 72 (Fowler et al. 1999), but less dramatic instances are known, such as a trussed woman tossed into a post pit at East St. Louis and pits with just legs at Cahokia (similar to the one at Grossmann) (Hargrave 2007; Hargrave et al. 2000; Lopinot et al. 1991; Pauketat 1998).

References

Alt, S. M.

1999 Spindle Whorls and Fiber Production at Early Cahokia. *Southeastern Archaeology* 18:124–134.

2001 Cahokian Change and the Authority of Tradition. In *The Archaeology of Traditions: Agency and History Before and After Columbus*, edited by T. Pauketat, pp. 141–156. University Press of Florida, Gainesville.

2002a Identities, Traditions and Diversity in Cahokia's Uplands. *Midcontinental Journal of Archaeology* 27:217–236.

2002b The Knoebel Site: Tradition and Change in the Cahokian Suburbs. Master's thesis, University of Illinois, Urbana.

2006a Cultural Pluralism and Complexity: Analyzing a Cahokian Ritual Outpost. Unpublished Ph.D. dissertation, University of Illinois, Urbana.

2006b The Power of Diversity: Settlement in the Cahokian Uplands. In *Leadership and Polity in Mississippian Society*, edited by B. M. Butler and P. D. Welch. Occasional Paper No. 33. Center for Archaeological Investigations, Southern Illinois University, Carbondale.

2008 Unwilling Immigrants: Culture, Change and the "Other" in Mississippian Societies. In *Invisible Citizens: Captives and Their Consequences*, edited by C. M. Cameron, pp. 289–308. University of Utah Press, Salt Lake City.

Anderson, D. G.

1994a Factional Competition and the Political Evolution of Mississippian Chiefdoms in the Southeastern United States. In *Factional Competition and Political Development in the New World*, edited by E. Brumfiel and J. Fox, pp. 61–76. Cambridge University Press, Cambridge.

1994b *The Savannah River Chiefdoms: Political Change in the Late Prehistoric Southeast.* University of Alabama Press, Tuscaloosa.

Ashmore, W.

2002 Decisions and Dispositions: Socializing Spatial Archaeology. *American Anthropologist* 104(4):1172–1183.

Bareis, C. J.

1976 *The Knoebel Site, St. Clair County, Illinois.* Illinois Archaeological Survey, Urbana.

Bareis, C. J., and J. W. Porter

1984 *American Bottom Archaeology.* University of Illinois Press, Urbana.

Bawden, G.

1989 The Andean State as State of Mind. *Journal of Anthropological Archaeology* 45:327–332.

Beck, R. A.

2003 Consolidation and Hierarchy: Chiefdom Variability in the Mississippian Southeast. *American Antiquity* 68(4):641–661.

Becker, C.

1910 Detachment and the Writing of History. *Atlantic Monthly* 106:524–536.

Bell, C. M.

1997 *Ritual: Perspectives and Dimensions.* Oxford University Press, New York.

Blanton, R., G. M. Feinman, S. Kowalewski, and P. Peregrine

1996 A Dual-Processual Theory for the Evolution of Mesoamerican Civilization. *Current Anthropology* 37:1–14.

Blasingham, E. J.

1953 Temporal and Spatial Distribution of the Yankeetown Cultural Manifestation. Master's thesis, Indiana University, Bloomington.

1965 Excavations of Yankeetown. Report to the National Park Service, NER-815. Loyola University, Chicago.

Bradley, R.

2000 *An Archaeology of Natural Places.* Routledge, London.

Brown, J. A.

2007 Sequencing the Braden Style within Mississippian Art and Iconography. In *Ancient Objects and Sacred Realms*, edited by F. K. Reilly III and J. F. Garber, pp. 213–246. University of Texas Press, Austin.

Chapman, R.

2003 *Archaeologies of Complexity.* Routledge, London.

Christie, J. J., and P. J. Sarro (editors)

2006 *Palaces and Power in the Americas.* University of Texas Press, Austin.

Cilliers, P.

1998 *Complexity and Postmodernism.* Routledge, London.

Clark, J. E.

2004 The Birth of Mesoamerican Metaphysics: Sedentism, Engagement, and Moral Superiority. In *Rethinking Materiality: The Engagement of Mind with the Material World*, edited by E. DeMarrais, C. Gosden, and C. Renfrew, pp. 205–224. McDonald Institute Monographs. Cambridge University Press, Cambridge.

Cobb, C. R.

2003 Mississippian Chiefdoms: How Complex? *Annual Review of Anthropology* 32(1):63–84.

Costin, C. L. (editor)

1998 *Craft and Social Identity.* Archeological

Papers No. 8. American Anthropological Association, Washington, D.C.

Crumley, C. L.
1995 Heterarchy and the Analysis of Complex Societies. In *Heterarchy and the Analysis of Complex Societies*, edited by R. Ehrenreich, C. L. Crumley, and J. Levy, pp. 1–6. Archeological Papers No. 6. American Anthropological Association, Washington, D.C.

Curet, L. A.
2003 Issues on the Diversity and Emergence of Middle-Range Societies of the Ancient Caribbean: A Critique. *Journal of Archaeological Research* 11(1):1–42.

D'Altroy, T., and T. Earle
1985 Staple Finance, Wealth Finance and Storage in the Inca Political Economy. *Current Anthropology* 26:187–206.

Dincauze, D. F., and R. J. Hasenstab
1989 Explaining the Iroquois: Tribalization on a Prehistoric Periphery. In *Center and Periphery*, edited by T. C. Champion. Unwin Hyman, London.

Dobres, M.-A., and J. E. Robb
2000 *Agency in Archaeology*. Routledge, London.

Drennan, R. D.
1991 Pre-Hispanic Chiefdom Trajectories in Mesoamerica, Central America and Northern South America. In *Chiefdoms: Power, Economy and Ideology*, edited by T. Earle, pp. 263–287. Cambridge University Press, Cambridge.

Emerson, T. E.
1997a *Cahokia and the Archaeology of Power*. University of Alabama Press, Tuscaloosa.
1997b Reflections from the Countryside on Cahokian Hegemony. In *Cahokia: Domination and Ideology in the Mississippian World*, edited by T. R. Pauketat and T. E. Emerson, pp. 190–228. University of Nebraska Press, Lincoln.

Emerson, T. E. and D. K. Jackson
1984 *The BBB Motor Site*. American Bottom Archaeology FAI 270 Series. University of Illinois Press, Urbana.

Emerson, T. E., R. Hughes, M. Hynes, and S. U. Wisseman
2003 The Sourcing and Interpretation of Cahokia-Style Figures in the Trans-Mississippi South and Southeast. *American Antiquity* 68(2):287–314.

Feathers, J. K.
1990 Explaining the Evolution of Prehistoric Ceramics in Southeastern Missouri. Unpublished Ph.D. dissertation, University of Washington, Seattle.

Feathers, J. K., and E. Peacock
2008 Origins and Spread of Shell Tempered Ceramics in the Eastern Woodlands: Conceptual and Methodological Frameworks for Analysis. *Southeastern Archaeology* 27(2):286–293.

Feinman, G. M., and J. Neitzel
1984 Too Many Types: An Overview of Sedentary Prestate Societies in the Americas. In *Advances in Archaeological Method and Theory*, Vol. 7, pp. 39–102. Academic Press, New York.

Finkenthal, M.
2008 *Complexity, Multi-disciplinarity and Beyond.* Peter Lang, New York.

Flannery, K. V.
1998 The Ground Plans of Archaic States. In *Archaic States*, edited by G. M. Feinman and J. Marcus, pp. 15–58. School of American Research Press, Santa Fe.

Fortier, A. C. (editor)
2007 *The Archaeology of the East St. Louis Mound Center, Part II: The Northside Excavations*. Research Reports No. 22. Illinois Transportation Archaeological Research Program, Urbana.

Fowler, M. L.
1973 *Cahokia: Ancient Capitol of the Midwest*. Module in Anthropology No. 48. Addison Wesley, Reading, Massachusetts.
1974 A Pre-Columbian Urban Center on the Mississippi. *Scientific American* 233(2):92–101.
1975 Chronology and Phases at Cahokia. In *Perspectives in Cahokia Archaeology*, edited by M. Fowler, pp. 15–31. Bulletin No. 10. Illinois Archaeological Survey, Urbana.
1978 Cahokia and the American Bottom: Settlement Archaeology. In *Mississippian Settlement Patterns*, edited by B. D. Smith, pp. 455–478. Academic Press, New York.
1997 *The Cahokia Atlas: A Historical Atlas of Cahokia Archaeology*. Studies in Archaeology No. 2. Illinois Transportation Archaeological Research Program, University of Illinois, Urbana.

Fowler, Melvin L., J. Rose, B. VanderLeest, and S. R. Ahler
1999 *The Mound 72 Area: Dedicated and Sacred Space in Early Cahokia*. Illinois State Museum Reports of Investigation No. 54. Illinois State Museum Society, Springfield.

Freimuth, G. A.
1974 The Lunsford-Pulcher Site: An Examination of Selected Traits and Their Social

Implications in American Bottom Prehistory. Pre-dissertation paper, University of Illinois, Urbana.

Geertz, C.

1981   *Negara: The Theater State in 19th Century Bali.* Princeton University Press, Princeton.

Hall, R. L.

1965   The Mississippian Heartland and Its Plains Relationship. Paper presented at the Second Plains Conference, Lincoln, Nebraska.

1966   Cahokia Chronology. Paper presented at the Annual Meeting of the Central States Anthropological Society, St. Louis, Missouri.

1973   An Interpretation of the Two Climax Model of Illinois Prehistory. Paper presented at the 9th International Congress of Anthropological and Ethnological Sciences, Chicago.

1975   Some Problems of Identity and Process in Cahokia Archaeology. Paper presented at the Advanced Seminar "Reviewing Mississippian Development," School of American Research, Santa Fe.

1991   Cahokia Identity and Interaction Models of Cahokia. In *Cahokia and the Hinterlands,* edited by T. E. Emerson and R. B. Lewis, pp. 3–34. University of Illinois Press, Urbana.

Hannerz, U.

1992   *Cultural Complexity: Studies in the Social Organization of Meaning.* Columbia University Press, New York.

Hargrave, E.

2007   Human Remains. In *The Archaeology of the East St. Louis Mound Center, Part II: The North Side Excavations,* edited by A. C. Fortier, pp. 77–83. Research Reports No. 22. Illinois Transportation Archaeological Research Program, Urbana.

Hargrave, E. A., K. Hedman, and T. Emerson

2000   Mortuary Tradition at Cahokia: A Comparison between Early Mississippian Upland Cemeteries and Cahokia. Paper presented at the Southeastern Archaeological Conference, Macon, Georgia.

Hodder, I.

1986   *Reading the Past.* Cambridge University Press, Cambridge.

Hodder, I., and C. Cessford

2004   Daily Practice and Social Memory at Çatalhöyük. *American Antiquity* 69:17–40.

Holley, G. R.

1989   *The Archaeology of the Cahokia Mounds ICT-II: Ceramics.* Illinois Cultural Resources Study 11. Illinois Historic Preservation Agency, Springfield.

Howe, J.

2000   Ceramic Diversity in the Uplands: American Bottom Chronology Reconsidered. Paper presented at the Southeastern Archaeological Conference, Macon, Georgia.

Jackson, D. K.

2000   The Mississippian Community at the Grossmann Site. Paper presented at the Southeastern Archaeological Conference, Macon, Georgia.

Jackson, D. K., A. C. Fortier and J. A. Williams

1992   *The Sponemann Site 2: The Mississippian and Oneota Occupations.* American Bottom Archaeology FAI-270 Reports. University of Illinois Press, Urbana.

Johnson, A., and T. Earle

1987   *The Evolution of Human Societies.* Stanford University Press, Stanford.

Joyce, R. A.

2000   Heirlooms and Houses: Materiality and Social Memory. In *Beyond Kinship: Social and Material Reproduction in House Societies,* edited by R. Joyce and S. D. Gillespie, pp. 189–212. University of Pennsylvania Press, Philadelphia.

Kehoe, A. B., and K. O. Bruhns

1992   Cahokia: A Mesoamerican City? Paper presented at the 25th Annual Chacmool Conference, Calgary, Alberta.

Kelly, J. D., and M. Kaplan

1990   History, Structure and Ritual. *Annual Review of Anthropology* 19:119–150.

Kelly, J. E.

1980   Formative Developments at Cahokia and the Adjacent American Bottom: A Merrell Tract Perspective. Unpublished Ph.D. dissertation, University of Wisconsin, Madison.

1990   The Emergence of Mississippian Culture in the American Bottom Region. In *The Mississippian Emergence,* edited by B. Smith, pp. 113–152. Smithsonian Institution Press, Washington, D.C.

1991   Cahokia and Its Role as a Gateway Center in Interregional Exchange. In *Cahokia and the Hinterlands,* edited by T. Emerson and R. B. Lewis, pp. 61–80. University of Illinois Press, Urbana.

1992   The Evidence for Prehistoric Exchange and Its Implications for the Development of Cahokia. In *New Perspectives on Cahokia,* edited by J. Stoltman, pp. 65–92. Prehistory Press, Madison, Wisconsin.

2000   The Nature and Context of Emergent Mississippian Cultural Dynamics in the Greater American Bottom. In *Late Woodland*

Societies: Tradition and Transformation across the Midcontinent, edited by T. E. Emerson, D. L. McElrath, and A. C. Fortier, pp. 163–175. University of Nebraska Press, Lincoln.

2002   The Pulcher Tradition and the Ritualization of Cahokia. *Southeastern Archaeology* 21(2): 136–148.

Kelly, J. E., and G. Powell
2000   Potential Implications of the New Whiteside School Investigations of an Early Mississippian Lohmann Phase Village. Paper presented at the Southeastern Archaeological Conference, Macon, Georgia.

Kelly, L. S.
2000a   Results of Preliminary Analysis of Faunal Remains from the Halliday Site. Paper presented at the Southeastern Archaeological Conference, Macon, Georgia.

2000b   Social Implications of Faunal Provisioning for the Cahokia Site: Initial Mississippian, Lohmann Phase. Unpublished Ph.D. dissertation, Washington University, St. Louis.

Kertzer, D. I.
1988   *Ritual, Politics, and Power*. Yale University Press, New Haven.

King, A. A.
2003   *Etowah: The Political History of a Chiefdom Capital*. University of Alabama Press, Tuscaloosa.

Kinsella, L.
2002   The Lithic Assemblage from the Lehmann-Somers Site. Paper presented at the 2002 Midwestern Archaeological Conference, Columbus, Ohio, October 3–6.

Koldehoff, B., T. R. Pauketat, and J. E. Kelly
1993   The Emerald Site and the Mississippian Occupation of the Central Silver Creek Valley. In *Highways to the Past: Essays on Illinois Archaeology in Honor of Charles J. Bareis*, edited by T. E. Emerson, A. C. Fortier, and D. L. McElrath, pp. 331–343. Special issue, *Illinois Archaeology* 5(1–2).

Kopytoff, I.
1986   The Cultural Biography of Things: Commoditization as Process. In *The Social Life of Things: Commodities in Cultural Perspective*, edited by A. Appadurai, pp. 64–91. Cambridge University Press, Cambridge.

Kristiansen, K.
1991   Chiefdoms, States, and Systems of Social Evolution. In *Chiefdoms: Power, Economy and Ideology*, edited by T. K. Earle, pp. 16–43. Cambridge University Press, Cambridge.

Kruchten, J.
2000   Early Cahokian Fluidity on the Fringe: Pfeffer Mounds and the Richland Complex. Paper presented at the Southeastern Archaeological Conference, Macon, Georgia.

Kruchten, J., and S. M. Alt
2003   Villages and Farmsteads: The Making of Mississippian Cahokia. Paper presented at the 49th Annual Midwest Archaeological Conference, Milwaukee, October 16–19.

Law, J., and A. M. Mol (editors)
2006   *Complexities: Social Studies of Knowledge Practices*. Duke University Press, Durham, North Carolina.

Lightfoot, K. G., A. Martinez, and A. M. Schiff
1998   Daily Practice and Material Culture in Pluralistic Settings: An Archaeological Study of Cultural Change and Persistence from Fort Ross, California. *American Antiquity* 63(2):199–224.

Lopinot, N. H., L. S. Kelly, G. R. Milner, and R. Paine
1991   *The Archaeology of the Cahokia Mounds ICT-II: Biological Remains*. Illinois Historic Preservation Agency, Springfield.

McGuire, R.
1983   Breaking Down Cultural Complexity: Inequality and Heterogeneity. In *Advances in Archaeological Method and Theory 6*, edited by M. B. Schiffer, pp. 91–142. Academic Press, New York.

Mehrer, M. W.
1995   *Cahokia's Countryside: Household Archaeology, Settlement Patterns and Social Power*. Northern Illinois University Press, De Kalb.

2000   Heterarchy and Hierarchy: The Community Plan as Institution in Cahokia's Polity. In *The Archaeology of Community: A New World Perspective*, edited by M. A. Canuto and J. Yaeger, pp. 44–57. Routledge, London.

Meskell, L. M.
2004   *Object Worlds in Ancient Egypt: Material Biographies Past and Present*. Berg, London.

Meskell, L. M., and R. A. Joyce
2003   *Embodied Lives: Figuring Ancient Maya and Egyptian Experience*. Routledge, London.

Mills, B.
2004   The Establishment and Defeat of Hierarchy: Inalienable Possessions and the History of Collective Prestige Structures in the Pueblo Southwest. *American Anthropologist* 106(2): 238–251.

Mills, B., and W. H. Walker (editors)
2008   *Memory Work: Archaeologies of Material Practices*. School for Advanced Research Press, Santa Fe.

Milner, G. R.
1998   *The Cahokia Chiefdom*. Smithsonian Institution Press, Washington, D.C.

Morse, D. F., and P. A. Morse
1980   *Zebree Archaeological Project*. Arkansas Archaeological Survey, Fayetteville.

Muller, J.
1997   *Mississippian Political Economy*. Plenum Press, New York.

Nassaney, M. S.
2001   The Historical-Processual Development of Late Woodland Societies. In *The Archaeology of Traditions: Agency and History Before and After Columbus*, edited by T. R. Pauketat, pp. 157–173. University Press of Florida, Gainesville.

Neitzel, J. E.
1999   *Great Towns and Regional Polities: In the Prehistoric American Southwest and Southeast*. Amerind Foundation, University of New Mexico Press, Albuquerque.

Nelson, B. A.
1995   Complexity, Hierarchy and Scale: A Controlled Comparison between Chaco Canyon, New Mexico, and La Quemada, Zacatecas. *American Antiquity* 60:597–618.

O'Brien, P. J.
1989   Cahokia: The Political Capitol of the Ramey State? *North American Archaeologist* 10(4):275–292.

Patterson, T. C.
2004   Class Conflict, State Formation and Archaism. *Journal of Social Archaeology* 4:288–306.

Pauketat, T. R.
1994   *The Ascent of Chiefs: Cahokia and Mississippian Politics in Native North America*. University of Alabama Press, Tuscaloosa.

1998   Refiguring the Archaeology of Greater Cahokia. *Journal of Archaeological Research* 6:45–89.

2002   A Fourth Generation Synthesis of Cahokia and Mississippianization. *Midcontinental Journal of Archaeology* 27:149–170.

2003   Farmers with Agency: Resettlement, Mississippianization and Historical Processes. *American Antiquity* 68:39–66.

2004   *Ancient Cahokia and the Mississippians*. Cambridge University Press, Cambridge.

2007   *Chiefdoms and Other Archaeological Delusions*. AltaMira Press, Walnut Canyon, California.

Pauketat, T. R. (editor)
2005   *The Archaeology of the East St. Louis Mound Center: Southside Excavations*. Research Reports No. 21. Illinois Transportation Archaeological Research Program, Urbana.

Pauketat, T. R., and S. M. Alt
2004   The Making and Meaning of a Mississippian Axe Head Cache. *Antiquity* 78:779–796.

Pauketat, T. R., and T. E. Emerson
1990   The Ideology of Authority and the Power of the Pot. *American Anthropologist* 93:919–941.

1997   *Cahokia: Domination and Ideology in the Mississippian World*. University of Nebraska Press, Lincoln.

Paynter, R.
1989   The Archaeology of Equality and Inequality. *Annual Review of Anthropology* 18:369–399.

Peregrine, P.
1992   *Mississippian Evolution: A World System Perspective*. Monographs in World Archaeology No. 9. Prehistory Press, Madison, Wisconsin.

Perino, G.
1959   Recent Information from Cahokia and Its Satellites. *Central States Archaeological Journal* 6(4):130–138.

Porter, J. W.
1969   The Mitchell Site and Prehistoric Exchange Systems at Cahokia: AD 100 ± 300. In *Explorations into Cahokia Archaeology*, edited by M. L. Fowler, pp. 137–164. Illinois Archaeological Survey, Urbana.

1974   Cahokia Archaeology as Viewed from the Mitchell Site: A Satellite Community at AD 1150–1200. Unpublished Ph.D. dissertation, University of Wisconsin, Madison.

Possehl, G. L.
1997   The Transformation of the Indus Civilization. *Journal of World Prehistory* 11(4):425–472.

Preucel, R. W.
2006   *Archaeological Semiotics*. Blackwell, Oxford.

Redmond, B. G.
1990   The Yankeetown Phase: Emergent Mississippian Cultural Adaptation in the Lower Ohio River Valley. Unpublished Ph.D. dissertation. Indiana University, Bloomington.

Renfrew, C.
1974   Beyond a Subsistence Economy: The Evolution of Social Organization in Prehistoric Europe. In *Bulletin of the American Schools of Oriental Research*, edited by C. Moore, Vol. 20, pp. 69–95.

Saitta, D. J.
1994   Agency, Class and Archaeological Interpretation. *Journal of Anthropological Archaeology* 13:201–227.

Sawyer, K. R.
2005   *Social Emergence: Societies as Complex Systems*. Cambridge University Press, Cambridge.

Shanks, M., and C. Tilley
1987   *Social Theory and Archaeology.* Polity Press, Cambridge.
Shennan, S. J.
1993   After Social Evolution: A New Archaeological Agenda? In *Archaeology Theory: Who Sets the Agenda?* edited by N. Yoffee and A. Sherratt, pp. 53–59. Cambridge University Press, Cambridge.
Smith, A. T.
2003   *The Political Landscape: Constellations of Authority in Early Complex Polities.* University of California Press, Berkeley.
Smith, B. D. (editor)
1978   *Mississippian Settlement Patterns.* Academic Press, New York.
Soja, E. W.
1996   *Thirdspace.* Blackwell, Oxford.
Spencer, C. S.
1987   Rethinking the Chiefdom. In *Chiefdoms in the Americas,* edited by R. D. Drennan and C. A. Uribe, pp. 369–389. University Press of America, Lanham, Maryland.
Spielmann, K. A.
2002   Feasting, Craft Specialization, and the Ritual Mode of Production in Small Scale Societies. *American Anthropologist* 104(1):195–207.
Steponaitis, V.
1978   Location Theory and Complex Chiefdoms. In *Mississippian Settlement Patterns,* edited by B. D. Smith, pp. 417–453. Academic Press, New York.
Stoltman, J. B.
1991   *New Perspectives on Cahokia: Views from the Periphery.* Prehistory Press, Madison, Wisconsin.
Sullivan, L. P., and C. B. Rodning
2001   Gender, Tradition, and the Negotiation of Power Relationships in Southern Appalachian Chiefdoms. In *The Archaeology of Traditions: Agency and History Before and After Columbus,* edited by T. R. Pauketat, pp. 107–120. University Press of Florida, Gainesville.
Tambiah, S. J.
1990   *Magic, Science, Religion and the Scope of Rationality.* Cambridge University Press, New York.
Trubitt, M. B. D.
2000   Mound Building and Prestige Goods Exchange: Changing Strategies in the Cahokia Chiefdom. *American Antiquity* 65:669–690.

Upham, S.
1987   Theoretical Consideration of Middle Range Societies. In *Chiefdoms in the Americas,* edited by R. D. Drennan and C. A. Uribe, pp. 343–367. University Press of America, Lanham, Maryland.
1990   Decoupling the Processes of Political Evolution. In *The Evolution of Politcal Systems: Sociopolitics in Small-Scale Sedentary Societies,* edited by S. Upham, pp. 1–17. School of American Research and Cambridge University Press, Cambridge.
Van Dyke, R. M.
2003   Memory and the Construction of Chacoan Society. In *Archaeologies of Memory,* edited by R. M. Van Dyke and S. E. Alcock, pp. 180–200. Blackwell, Oxford.
Vogel, J. O.
1975   Trends in Cahokia Ceramics: Preliminary Study of the Collections from Tracts 15A and 15B. In *Perspectives in Cahokia Archaeology,* edited by M. Fowler, pp. 32–125. Bulletin No. 10. Illinois Archaeological Survey, Urbana.
Witthoft, J.
1949   *Green Corn Ceremonialism in the Eastern Woodlands.* Occasional Contributions No. 13. Museum of Anthropology, University of Michigan, Ann Arbor.
Wright, H.
1984   Prestate Political Formations. In *On the Evolution of Complex Societies: Essays in Honor of Harry Hoijer,* edited by T. Earle. Undena Publications, Malibu, California.
Yoffee, N.
1993   Too Many Chiefs? (or, Safe Texts for the '90s). In *Archaeological Theory: Who Sets the Agenda?* edited by N. Yoffee and A. Sherratt, pp. 60–78. Cambridge University Press, Cambridge.
2005   *Myths of the Archaic State: Evolution of the Earliest Cities, States and Civilizations.* Cambridge University Press, Cambridge.
Yoffee, N., S. K. Fish, and G. R. Milner
1999   Comunidas, Ritualities, Chiefdoms: Social Evolution in the American Southwest and Southeast. In *Great Towns and Regional Polities in the Prehistoric American Southwest and Southeast,* edited by J. E. Neitzel, pp. 261–271. Amerind Foundation, University of New Mexico Press, Albuquerque.

9

Categories of Complexity
and the Preclusion of Practice

Jon Bernard Marcoux and Gregory D. Wilson

Archaeologists working in the southeastern United States have found it increasingly difficult to reconcile the temporal and geographical variability exhibited by Late Prehistoric Native American groups with classic trait-list definitions of Mississippian culture, such as corn agriculture, shell-tempered pottery, and mounds (e.g., Cobb 2003; Scarry 1996; Smith 1990). In response, many have searched for analytical frameworks that can make sense of this variability while retaining some unifying notion of Mississippian. Overwhelmingly, answers to this search have taken the form of comparative categorical models that extend a shared definition of Mississippian-ness founded on the concept of "chiefdom" and that characterize variability among groups in terms of similarities and differences in political economy (Anderson 1994; Beck 2003; King 2003; Steponaitis 1991). Most notable among these are the simple-complex-(paramount) chiefdom model, dual processual theory, and the apical-constituent chiefdom model. The reason for the popularity of these frameworks doubtless lies in their ability to "explain" a vast amount of diversity by compartmentalizing it into two or three different categories. We argue that such a perceived benefit can also be seen as a major flaw, as the ease with which the interpretations flow from these frames has been achieved at the expense of understanding the particular practices that actually generated complex power relations at the local level (Alt, this volume, Chapter 1). Instead of the safe interpretations these frames allow, we argue for riskier ones that attempt to account for "com-

plexity" in power relationships by using methods that move more slowly and resist the urge to jump from local to global understandings (Alt, this volume, Chapter 8).

In this chapter we explore how Mississippian mortuary practices could be treated using an alternative approach to categorical models. Our perspective is derived from actor-network theory, or the sociology of translation (Callon 1986; Latour 1991, 1992, 2005; Law 1992, 1997, 1999). This moniker and its acronym (ANT) refer to an extremely diverse and dynamic set of premises and approaches that have a common foundation in a post-structural rejection of essentialist divisions and a shared view that the social consists of performed networks of human and nonhuman "actors." The challenge laid out by ANT is to "reassemble the social" by tracing the associations between these heterogeneous entities rather than make the social a taken-for-granted starting point of analysis. After outlining actor-network theory, we briefly sketch out what an alternative ANT-like approach to Mississippian archaeological contexts might look like when applied to local mortuary practices at the Moundville site in west-central Alabama.

Critique of the Categorical

The simple-complex (paramount) chiefdom model, dual processual theory, and the apical-constituent chiefdom model are all part of a ramage that traces its descent from the neo-socioevolutionary schemas of "complexity" developed by Fried (1967) and Service (1962). Like their predecessors, these models present us with various ways of parsing out diversity along a single dimension that measures "complexity" as the degree of political centralization exhibited by a particular sociopolitical unit (see Yoffee 1993). Complexity in these models is tied to a particular notion of power that emphasizes how certain actors exercised power over other actors—usually phrased in terms of an elite-commoner dichotomy. The models seek to capture variability in this dichotomous power relationship by taking input consisting of settlement pattern, architectural, and mortuary data and sorting it into ostensibly defined categories. The simple-complex chiefdom model divides this variability vertically, dual process does so horizontally, and the apical-constituent model attempts to do both simultaneously (see Beck 2006; Blanton et al. 1996; Steponaitis 1991).

We contend that the central problem with these archaeological models lies in their essentialist foundations. There is a tautological logic that is inherent to these approaches in that they assume that the archaeological patterning in any given case can ultimately be lumped into one of two political-administrative categories (Pauketat 2007; Wilson et al. 2006; Yoffee 2005). The result of the search for material correlates of these categorical models is that not only mortuary events but also settlement patterns, architecture, mounds, and foodways have been treated as simple intermediaries that convey a single notion, that of political power. Indeed, in many studies the practices of entire communities are reduced to proxies for the political power exercised by a hypothetical chief and cadre of elites with only lip service, at best, paid to commoners (Yoffee 2005).

Very little space is given to the consideration of how the practices of individuals and social groups produce the social. What is more, one can see an instantaneous "jump" in these models from local to global interpretations in the form of a series of often implicit "if-then" statements. Everything becomes an example of the rule. A social group is either simple or complex...apical or constituent. Until we recognize this flaw, we are likely destined to continue to replace categorical models with other categorical models that offer yet more ready-to-use "frames" for our data.

Thinking Actor-Networks to Complexity

What would happen if we abandoned the search for macroscale categorical chiefdom models with which to understand Mississippian societies? What if we were instead to envision the complexity of power relations in these societies as the effect of associations—associations between many heterogeneous entities that required constant performance to maintain? In other words, what if we viewed "social structure" as a verb rather than a noun (Latour 2005; Law 1992:5)? This is the perspective followed by practitioners of actor-network theory, a dynamic corpus of ideas whose origins can be traced to studies in the sociology of scientific knowledge. ANT moves in the opposite direction of the categorical models in that it strives to talk about, appreciate, and practice complexity by emphasizing contingency, tension, movement, and fractionality rather than stability, structure, and fixity (Latour 1999:22; Law 1999:10; Anderson's [1994] work presents a notable exception for Mississippian societies).

In direct opposition to the categorical models, actor-network theory requires that researchers begin by not assuming that which they wish to explain, namely, the existence of social aggregates like elites and commoners, or the notion of society itself. We are told instead to begin with a clean slate and to describe what the actors themselves are "telling" us by mapping their oppositions and tracing their associations (Latour 2005:8; Law 1992:2). The aim is to explore how actors generate what we know as social structure. Applying this approach to the archaeological study of Mississippian mortuary practices will require a radical shift in perspective, one that follows from abandoning the a priori existence of any particular kind of hierarchical social structure.

The shift includes three major moves: (1) a move away from an ostensive to a performative definition of social groups, (2) a double move to recast agency to include human and nonhuman actors and to de-center singular agents, and (3) a move to consider conceptions of power other than hierarchy or "power over."

Move 1: Proponents describe ANT as a "ruthless application of semiotics" (Latour 2005:34–35; Law 1999:4). At the heart of the ANT is the notion that all entities are defined by their relation to other entities, and as such, they are constituted by the performance of those relationships. As Latour (2005:35) says, "For ANT if you stop making and remaking groups, you stop having groups." In the categorical models, we have ostensively defined entities like elites and commoners, social groups whose existence is seen as given and perpetual, even if those who fill the categories change through time. Hence, they inhabit both the beginning and end of any analysis; they are at once the explanandum and the explanans. In ANT, the existence of groups, their apparent stability, is what needs to be explained through the empirical analysis of their performance.

Move 2: One of the most notable and controversial aspects of ANT is the way agency is conceived of and deployed. The categorical models presented above have a very straightforward view of agency, one that privileges those seen as being in power (i.e., elites) and their intentional strategies. Recently, researchers have put forth a more inclusive view of agency, one that is cast in the agency/structure dichotomy of Giddens (1979) and Bourdieu (1977). This perspective stresses the intentional actions and unintentional consequences of strategically positioned actors (e.g., Dobres and Robb 2000; Hodder 2000; Pauketat 2000). ANT presents us with a third alternative whose attempt to be inclusive elides the agency/structure dichotomy entirely. At the heart of this move is the recognition that networks consist of both human and nonhuman "actors." The latter include materials such as texts, tools, architectures, and machines. More broadly, nonhuman actors might also include landscapes and spaces (Whitridge 2004). The key determinant to defining these nonhumans as "actors" is that they act as vehicles—costly means for extending the "life" of the associations that generate groups (Latour 1992). In ANT these human and nonhuman agents are both "sets of relations and nodes in those sets of relations" (Law 1991:173–176). The resulting focus of study, therefore, is not to define separately "agents" and "structures" but rather to analyze the durability of these "heterogeneous networks" in toto. This is very much a processual method because a network is never seen as being finished; instead, it is always moving, and as

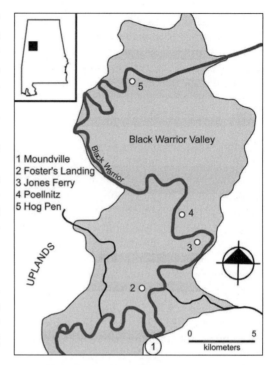

FIGURE 9.1. Early Mississippian mound centers in the northern Black Warrior Valley, Alabama.

analysts we are catching snapshots of networks in motion.

Move 3: Law's (1991) approach to power can be very helpful in our attempt to trace power relations among Mississippian groups. In addition to the typical political-economy approach to power, "power over," Law (1991:166–167) considers "power to"—the capacity to act as the non-zero-sum effect of relationships between entities (see also Barnes 1988; Foucault 1978). For any study of social complexity, this notion of "power to" adds a much needed complement to "power over" in that it helps us to remember that social collectivities are necessarily created and maintained through practices that beget solidarity. Both "power over" and "power to" can be stored and deployed by actors, but in the end, power is a function of a network of relations that are constantly contested and negotiated. As a consequence, when we are engaging with complexity, an ANT perspective encourages us to look at actors, their actions, and their relations, and to try to characterize the methods and the extent to which they have the ef-

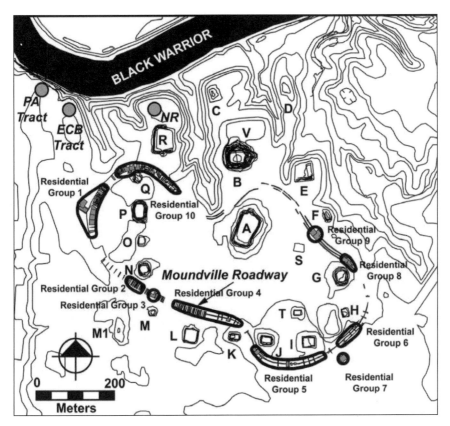

FIGURE 9.2. Geographic information system (GIS) representation of the Moundville site, featuring residential groups identified in the Moundville roadway and riverbank excavations.

fect of securing a store of "power to" and "power over" (Law 1991:176).

Together these three moves set forth a new challenge to the analyst—to explain social groups not by framing them within the context of some global social structure (e.g., elite, commoner, apical hierarchy, simple chiefdom, etc.) but by summing up their associations (Latour 1999:16–17).

Moundville's "Complex" History

Located in the Black Warrior Valley of west-central Alabama, Moundville was one of the largest and most complex Mississippian polities in the southeastern United States (Figure 9.1). The Moundville site is located on a high, flat terrace where the Black Warrior River cuts close to the Fall-Line Hills (Knight and Steponaitis 1998; Peebles 1978). Today the site consists of 29 mounds arranged around a rectangular plaza (Figure 9.2; Knight and Steponaitis 1998:3). In all, the Mound-

ville site was about 75 ha in size (Knight and Steponaitis 1998:3). The primary areas of residential occupation are located between the plaza and the palisade wall. Much of the central plaza appears to have been unoccupied. However, a number of small residential areas have been identified along the outside edges of the plaza as well as outside the limits of the palisade (Figure 9.2; Wilson 2008).

Over a century of archaeological investigation has revealed that throughout its long history of residential and ceremonial use, Moundville community space came to be highly charged with social meaning as different kin groups incorporated the landscape itself into the politics of identity formation (Knight 1998; Peebles 1971, 1978). For the purpose of the current study, we divide Moundville's residential and ceremonial history into two periods (Figure 9.3). The first period, which we call Consolidation and Emplacement, spans the late Moundville I phase to the early Moundville II phase (AD 1200 to 1300). The second period,

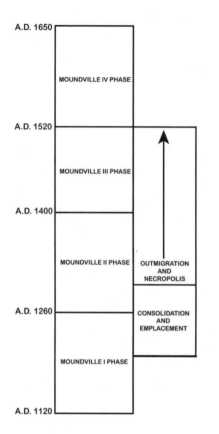

FIGURE 9.3. Mississippian period chronology for the Black Warrior Valley.

which we call Outmigration and Necropolis, corresponds with the late Moundville II and Moundville III phases (AD 1300 to 1550).

Consolidation and Emplacement

The decades bracketing AD 1200 correspond with the rapid political consolidation of the northern Black Warrior Valley and the rise of the Moundville site as a regional political and ceremonial center. During Moundville's first century and a half of occupation its inhabitants enlisted a variety of material entities, including mounds, plazas, and even small domestic structures, to embody and stabilize a network of kin-based social identity and ranking (Knight 1998; Wilson 2008). Archaeological excavations have revealed that construction began on Moundville's ceremonial precinct around AD 1200 in conjunction with a large-scale in-migration of the regional populace to the Moundville site. This ceremonial precinct

consisted of a minimum of 29 earthen mounds arranged in a very orderly manner around a rectangular central plaza (Figure 9.2; Peebles 1971, 1978). The largest mounds are located on the northern edge of the plaza, and they become increasingly smaller going either clockwise or counterclockwise around the plaza to the south. With few exceptions these earthen monuments are arranged in pairs of larger and smaller mounds. The largest of the paired mounds served as elevated platforms for the temples and homes of the ruling elite. Some smaller mounds also functioned as platforms for special-purpose buildings and contained cemeteries that included many high-status burials (Knight 1998, 2004).

Knight (1998) has interpreted these paired monuments as the political and ceremonial facilities for discrete kin groups such as the matriclans that comprised most Native American societies in the early Historic period throughout the southeastern United States. The decreasing size of these paired mounds from north to south is thought to demarcate the hierarchical ranking of these corporate kin groups around the central plaza. If Knight is correct, then the early Moundville community consisted of numerous, spatially discrete kin groups, each of which possessed its own monumental political and ceremonial facilities.

While larger kin groups endeavored to negotiate and perpetuate their corporate identities through the construction of earthen monuments, smaller subclan groups did so through the construction and in situ rebuilding of spatially discrete residential areas (Figure 9.4; Knight 1998; Wilson 2008; Wilson et al. 2006). The architectural analysis of hundreds of buildings and other domestic features throughout the Moundville site has revealed that its early Mississippian occupation was not spatially contiguous but separated into a number of spatially discrete residential groups (Wilson 2008; Wilson et al. 2006:52). Although Moundville's occupation during this period was nucleated, there were sizable unoccupied areas between residential groups. Rather than spread out or relocate when houses required repair or replacement, however, households opted to rebuild in place, reproducing particular architectural arrangements in particular places (Figure 9.4). The spatial distribution of these residential groups is consistent with broader social divisions

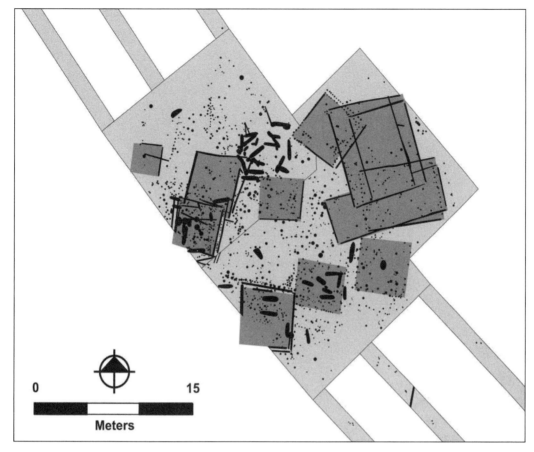

FIGURE 9.4. Late Mississippian burials superimposed on early Mississippian domestic structures at residential group 9.

in the Moundville community as represented in the arrangement and size of earthen monuments. Thus, each "clan" division at Moundville appears to have included numerous discrete "subclan" residential groups (Wilson 2008).

Outmigration and Necropolis

Sometime in the final decades of the thirteenth century Moundville ceased to be used as a nucleated residential center and was transformed into a necropolis where the rurally relocated occupants of the Black Warrior Valley buried their dead in a variety of different cemeteries (Knight and Steponaitis 1998:19; Steponaitis 1998:39–41). Most off-mound cemeteries at Moundville consist of tightly arranged rectilinear clusters of burials surrounded by a more dispersed pattern of associated burials (Figure 9.5; Wilson 2008; Wilson et al. 2010). A seriation of mortuary ceramics

and a close examination of feature superimposition indicate that most of these cemeteries represent the performance of mortuary events for some two centuries following Moundville's outmigration (Steponaitis 1983; Wilson 2008; Wilson et al. 2010). What was once a bustling town became a vacant ceremonial center occupied primarily by a small number of Moundville's elite and other religious specialists (Knight and Steponaitis 1998:17–21).

This outmigration corresponds with increasing population densities in the rural countryside of the Black Warrior Valley (Maxham 2004:129). Such a dramatic transformation of the regional landscape would have entailed important changes in the ways social groups used space and negotiated their corporate identities, for no longer did nucleated kin groups dwell in the shadow of earthen monuments, nor did families raise

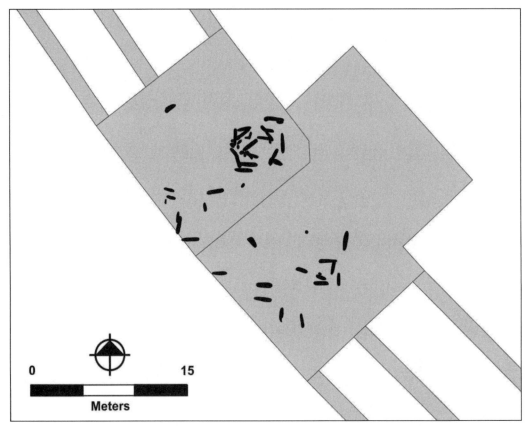

FIGURE 9.5. Arrangement of burials in a cemetery in residential group 9 (early Mississippian domestic structures are removed from the map).

buildings over the foundations of the homes of their parents and grandparents.

With its many dynamic intersections of human and nonhuman actors, Moundville's historical narrative provides boundless opportunities for ANT analyses. We focus on mortuary events associated with Moundville's transformation into a necropolis because they represent very clear material "snapshots" of networks being performed at a critical time in the polity's history. Particularly, we argue that the disjuncture in landscape and community that occurred with Moundville's large-scale outmigration led the Mississippian inhabitants of the Black Warrior Valley to implement new patterns of mortuary ceremonialism. Ultimately, the goal of these new mortuary practices was similar to that of the earlier residential emplacement strategies—to create durable networks of human and nonhuman actors that promoted kin-based solidarity and associated claims

to social and economic resources (see Law 2000 for a discussion of the "fluid" nature of networks).

ANT and Mortuary Analysis

The recognition of the strategic opportunities created by the death of an individual is nothing new (see Arnold 2002; Gillespie 2002; Joyce 2001; Meskell 2001; Parker Pearson 1999; and Silverman 2002 for a similar postprocessual take on mortuary practices). These events and their associated practices offer ideal settings for an ANT approach because they represent the type of "crisis" moments when networks become visible as they are deleted, renegotiated, replaced, and mobilized (Latour 1992:233, 2005:65; Law 1992:4–5). When someone dies, networks are altered and new networks are negotiated. Mortuary events are practices that embody this performance. Death events bring about the intersection of different networks. The "deaths" of old networks are memorialized, but in doing so mourners are also laying the foundations of new networks. What is too often mentioned uncritically in archaeological discourse is that Mississippian mortuary events included not only the deceased but also a host of other actors that were at that moment actively engaged in "performing" networks. We can view each mortuary context as a "setting" or a constructed collection of objects where each object is the effect of its relationship with other human and nonhuman objects. In other words, when looking at mortuary data, we should see the human remains, artifacts, burial location, and mourners not as reflections of some "thing" called social structure but instead as the variable effects of networks whose movements can be traced (Akrich and Latour 1992:259; Law 1999:3).

In our case study, examining Moundville cemeteries as sites of social production rather than correlates of a particular kind of social structure requires us to conduct an investigation of their composition and history. Whereas categorical models usually treat mortuary contexts en masse as ahistorical proxies for a particular type of social structure, in tracing networks we must turn up the magnification on these cemeteries in order to identify the disparate entities enrolled in each case. Only when we consider the histories of people, places, and things enchained within these cemeteries can we begin to determine the broader social relationships and meanings that were stabilized through the cemeteries and the mortuary practices that created them. Consequently, our study of mortuary practices at Moundville includes a "roll call" of the sorts of things being enchained; however, simply listing these participants is not nearly enough. As Latour (2005:128) states, "A good ANT account is a narrative or a description or a proposition where all the actors do something and don't just sit there." The something Latour refers to is the work that is being done by the participants in the network and the transformations that are taking place. Of great import to our consideration of Moundville is how transformative power relations (both "power to" and "power over") were negotiated through mortuary events. To investigate this process, we consider the size, location, composition, and use histories of various off-mound cemeteries at the Moundville site.

Power To: Network Objects and Off-Mound Cemeteries

Researchers have long recognized that mortuary ceremonies are performances in which people, places, and things are brought into transformative relationships involving the deceased, the living, and particular cultural notions of the soul and the afterlife (Hertz 1960; Metcalf and Huntington 1991:79–85). In terms of Moundville we consider two transformations particularly important in generative schemes of power (i.e., power to): (1) the transformation of the deceased individual into a network object—an effect of an array of relations (Law 2000:1)—symbolized by his or her status as an ancestor, and (2) the memorialization of an intimate shared history through the transformation of residential space into mortuary space.

The death of an individual in the Moundville chiefdom invariably constituted a threat to the stability of a host of networks. A prescriptive process of mortuary ceremonialism ameliorated this threat. An important component of this process was the burial furniture interred with some of the deceased. Most individuals in these cemeteries were buried with nothing or with only a ceramic serving container or two (Peebles 1974), but there are a few exceptions to this pattern in which individuals were interred with multiple items and/or elaborate display goods. Lankford (2007) and Steponaitis and Knight (2004) have recently argued that much of the iconography found on these display goods references mortuary themes involving death and the afterlife. Specifically, these iconographic items appear to have been part of a suite of mortuary practices intended to facilitate the passage of a deceased individual-cum-ancestor's soul to the Realm of the Dead (Figure 9.6). A corpus of five closely related motifs (the hand and eye, skull, bone, winged serpent, and raptor) are thought to reference the Path of Souls, a treacherous celestial journey along the Milky Way that the souls of the deceased must navigate to make their way to the Realm of the Dead. According to the religious beliefs of many native groups from the Plains and Eastern Woodlands, the corpse had to be prepared in a ceremonially prescribed manner to ensure that the soul of the deceased would complete this journey (Lankford 2007). Souls that traversed this path and its obstacles successfully

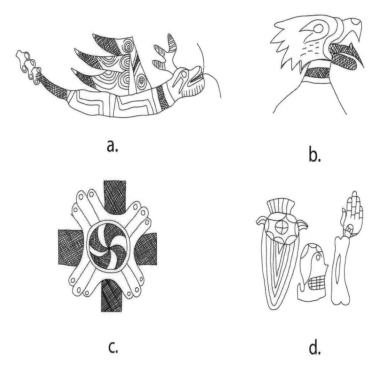

a.

b.

c.

d.

FIGURE 9.6. Iconographic designs linked to the Path of Souls: (a) winged serpent; (b) raptor; (c) center symbol, four quartered hands; (d) skull, bone, hand-and-eye (adapted from Lankford 2007).

became powerful allies to their living descendants, offering guidance and power. Souls that faltered along the path, on the other hand, sometimes returned to haunt the living or spent the rest of eternity in a liminal state (Lankford 2007). Through mortuary practices, mourners were attempting to stabilize a network in crisis through the transformation of an individual from a living actor to a nonhuman actor (i.e., an ancestor) who nevertheless remained an integral, if altered, network component (Law 2000; see also Giles, this volume).

One of the most important features of Moundville's small off-mound cemeteries is their location. Nearly every off-mound cemetery that has been excavated at Moundville superimposes spatially discrete early Mississippian residential groups (Wilson 2005). It follows that part of the broader meaning and purpose of these small cemeteries was to establish social and spatial continuity with ancestral residential space. Indeed, some clues in the spatial organization of these cemeteries indicate that they were strategically designed to invoke an early Mississippian residential past.

For example, the rectilinear arrangement of most burials in these cemeteries corresponds to the dimensions of early Mississippian domestic structures at Moundville (Wilson 2008). Thus, it is not unreasonable to speculate that these cemeteries served as a kind of metaphor for a house that embodied kin group identity while maintaining continuity with the residential origin and history of kin groups at Moundville.

From this perspective the mortuary rituals that took place during the fourteenth and early fifteenth centuries at Moundville involved commemorative ceremonies in which domestic groups re-presented their earlier history of residential occupation in a ceremonial capacity. By building the cemeteries directly on top of thirteenth-century residential areas and arranging the graves in a rectilinear house-like pattern, these groups intentionally and discursively enacted this earlier era in a ceremonially embodied form.

It is not surprising that specific Mississippian kin groups at Moundville used spatially discrete cemeteries to bury their dead. Drawing on global ethnographic data, Goldstein (1980) and Saxe (1970) have demonstrated that agricultural societies with lineal corporate rights over the use and inheritance of land often have cemeteries that are used exclusively by specific kin groups. Both scholars argue that these exclusive mortuary arrangements are part of broader strategies by which individuals seek to affirm their descent group membership and the land inheritance rights that come with it. The heritability of social and economic resources no doubt helped inspire the initial construction of Moundville's mound and plaza complex and the clan-based political and ceremonial order it embodied.

Power Over: Elites as an Obligatory Passage Point

While it is tempting to think of Moundville cemeteries as singular coherent units, we must remember that each is a collection of entities representing a convergence born out of the heterogeneous motivations and strategies of the mourners and other funerary attendees. The result of each and every mortuary event was a complex imbroglio motivated by grief, remembrance, claims of solidarity and difference, and aspirations to status and power.

Nevertheless, it is also important to note that some actors would have been better situated than others in regard to recruiting people, bodies, and things into playing particular roles within mortuary events held at Moundville cemeteries. For example, Knight et al. (2001) have interpreted certain Moundville hair ornaments made of embossed copper as symbols referencing the ability of certain religious specialists to perform celestial spirit journeys. These hair ornaments, known archaeologically as bi-lobed arrows, are thought to represent "a conventionalized bow and arrow composite that operates as an instrument of soul flight, by which the bearer magically projects soul essence into the upper world" (Figure 9.7; Knight et al. 2001:137). Bi-lobed arrow hair ornaments have been found in direct association with burials in mounds at Moundville and Etowah—burials that fit the typical definition of "high-status" individuals. These ornaments are also iconographically depicted as regalia worn by the Mississippian "elite" on rock art, embossed copper plates, stone palettes, and marine shell black drink cups and

gorgets at numerous sites in the southeastern and midwestern United States (Diaz-Granados 2004; Dye 2004:Fig. 1; King 2004:Fig. 11; Phillips and Brown 1978:Pl. 6, 19; Steponaitis and Knight 2004: Fig. 13).

With specialized knowledge of the Path of Souls, certain members of the Moundville community were well positioned to strategically (re)configure mortuary ritual. To the degree to which the regional populace was convinced that these individuals performed an essential role in the journey to the afterlife, mortuary ceremonialism at the Moundville site would have served as a kind of obligatory passage point. That is, if family members wanted to ensure that the souls of their deceased kin successfully navigated the treacherous journey and transformation into an ancestor, then it may have been necessary to consult with one of these religious specialists who knew the proper ways to prepare and inter the corpse and who could serve as a guide for the deceased along the Path of Souls. This ability to translate the interests of, and exert "power over," others within mortuary events may well have produced and legitimized decision-making authority that extended beyond the arena of funerary practice.

Discussion and Conclusion

Throughout the course of our research it became apparent that ANT does not offer nicely framed archaeological interpretations. Indeed, we found that it is quite easy to fail in creating a completely faithful ANT-style narrative. Instead, we realize that the best we can hope to do is to construct a description that appreciates the complexity of the transformations that took place through practices enacted in the past. When we examine Moundville cemeteries, it becomes obvious that when mourners performed mortuary rites, they were literally folding time and space. We can observe this in the enchainment of mythical places and times through iconographic references to the Path of Souls and the Realm of the Dead on display goods. We can also see this in the way that cemeteries were built directly over ancestral residential spaces within well-demarcated clan and subclan precincts. At such high magnification we can see how human remains, an ancestral residential past, display goods, serving containers, mourners, the Milky Way, and an array of

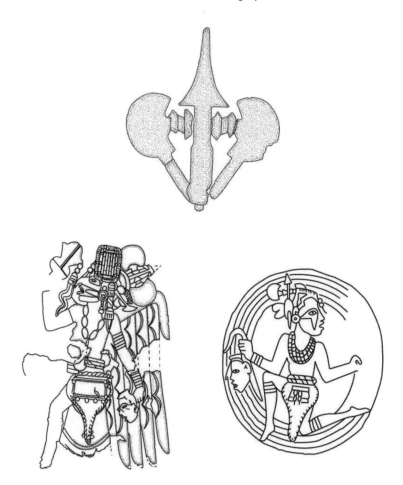

FIGURE 9.7. *Top:* Fragment of a copper bi-lobed arrow headdress element recovered from a burial context. *Bottom:* Depictions of mythical hero figures wearing bi-lobed arrow headdresses.

other cosmological entities were all recruited into playing specific roles within a network.

The key to our ANT analysis is that the processes of recruitment and reassembly that created Moundville cemeteries transformed all the various entities involved. Recognizing the various transformations returns movement and fluidity to social production—something that is sorely missing from static categorical models. Through their funerary practices, mourners were able to deploy generative effects of power. By transforming the deceased individual into a network object, mourners attempted to stabilize the crisis created in the aftermath of death. Individual cemeteries themselves were continually transformed through mortuary practices as they took on attributes of ruralized kin groups and various

cosmological entities through association with deceased community members, ancestral residential space, clan monuments, religious iconography, and the Path of Souls. Likewise, it can be said that the identities and interests of ruralized kin groups were transformed by Moundville cemeteries. Through association with centralized mortuary facilities, kin groups actively enlisted the past and the cosmologically distant via spatial associations with ancestral residential space, earthen monuments, and symbolic linkages to the Path of Souls. Finally, by virtue of having access to esoteric knowledge, certain members of society were able to exploit the transformations associated with death and mortuary rites in order to exert "power over" others.

Our principal goal in this chapter was to examine Moundville cemeteries as sites of social production rather than correlates of some pre-defined social structure. We hope we have been able to convey some sense of the complexity of this goal. In the end, we believe, the promise of ANT lies in posing challenges instead of offering easy solutions. In order to embrace these challenges, we need to identify the frames produced by past social groups rather than impose them, in an a priori fashion, on the archaeological record. In doing so, we must focus on the composition and generative practices of actors, places, and things themselves rather than simply contextualize these entities in reference to the social forces that surround them (Latour 2005).

Acknowledgments

Thanks to Susan Alt for inviting us to take part in this provocative volume. Special thanks to Pete Whitridge for many stimulating conversations about actor-network theory. We also thank Mary Hancock, Stuart Smith, Vincas Steponaitis, and Amber VanDerwarker for their comments on an earlier version of this chapter.

References

Akrich, Madleine, and Bruno Latour
1992   A Summary of a Convenient Vocabulary for the Semiotics of Human and Nonhuman Assemblies. In *Shaping Technology, Building Society: Studies in Sociotechnical Change*, edited by W. Bijker and J. Law, pp. 259–264. MIT Press, Cambridge, Massachusetts.

Anderson, David G.
1994   *The Savannah River Chiefdoms: Political Change in the Late Prehistoric Southeast.* University of Alabama Press, Tuscaloosa.

Arnold, Bettina
2002   A Landscape of Ancestors: The Space and Place of Death in Iron Age West-Central Europe. In *The Space and Place of Death*, edited by H. Silverman and D. Small, pp. 129–144. Archeological Papers No. 11. American Anthropological Association, Arlington, Virginia.

Barnes, Barry
1988   *The Nature of Power.* Polity Press, Cambridge.

Beck, Robin A., Jr.
2003   Consolidation and Hierarchy: Chiefdom Variability in the Mississippian Southeast. *American Antiquity* 68:641–661.

2006   Persuasive Politics at Cahokia and Moundville. In *Leadership and Polity in Mississippian Society*, edited by B. Butler and P. Welch, pp. 19–42. Occasional Paper No. 33. Center for Archaeological Investigations, Southern Illinois University, Carbondale.

Blanton, Richard E., Gary M. Feinman, Stephen A. Kowalewski, and Peter N. Peregrine
1996   A Dual Processual Theory for the Evolu-tion of Mesoamerican Civilization. *Current Anthropology* 37:1–14.

Bourdieu, Pierre
1977   *Outline of a Theory of Practice.* Cambridge University Press, New York.

Callon, Michele
1986   Some Elements of a Sociology of Translation: Domestication of the Scallops and the Fishermen of Saint Brieuc Bay. In *Power, Action and Belief: A New Sociology of Knowledge*, edited by J. Law, pp. 196–233. Routledge and Kegan Paul, London.

Cobb, Charles R.
2003   Mississippian Chiefdoms: How Complex? *Annual Review of Anthropology* 32:63–84.

Diaz-Granados, Carol
2004   Marking Stone, Land, Body, and Spirit: Rock Art and Mississippian Iconography. In *Hero, Hawk, and Open Hand: American Indian Art of the Ancient Midwest and South*, edited by R. F. Townsend and R. V. Sharp, pp. 139–150. Yale University Press, New Haven.

Dobres, Marcia-Anne, and John Robb
2000   Agency in Archaeology: Paradigm or Platitude? In *Agency in Archaeology*, edited by M. Dobres and J. E. Robb, pp. 3–18. Routledge, London.

Dye, D. H.
2004   Art, Ritual, and Chiefly Warfare in the Mississippian World. In *Hero, Hawk, and Open Hand: American Indian Art of the Ancient Midwest and South* edited by R. Townsend. Yale University Press.

Foucault, Michel
1978   *Discipline and Punish: The Birth of the Prison.* Penguin Books, London.

Fried, Morton
1967   *The Evolution of Political Society: An Essay in Political Anthropology.* Random House, New York.

Giddens, Anthony
1979   *Central Problems in Social Theory.* Macmillan, London.

Gillespie, Susan D.

2002   Body and Soul among the Maya: Keeping
        the Spirits in Place. In *The Space and Place of
        Death*, edited by H. Silverman and D. Small,
        pp. 67–78. Archeological Papers No. 11.
        American Anthropological Association,
        Arlington, Virginia.

Goldstein, Lynn

1980   *Mississippian Mortuary Practices: A Case
        Study of Two Cemeteries in the Lower Illinois
        Valley*. Archeology Program Scientific Papers
        No. 4. Northwestern University, Evanston,
        Illinois.

Hertz, Robert

1960   *Death and the Right Hand*. Translated by
        R. Needham and C. Needham. Free Press,
        Glencoe, Illinois.

Hodder, Ian

2000   Agency and Individuals in Long-Term Pro-
        cesses. In *Agency in Archaeology*, edited by
        M. Dobres and J. E. Robb, pp. 21–33. Rout-
        ledge, London.

Joyce, Rosemary A.

2001   Burying the Dead at Tlatilco: Social Memory
        and Social Identities. In *Social Memory, Iden-
        tity, and Death: Anthropological Perspectives
        on Mortuary Rituals*, edited by M. S. Ches-
        son, pp. 12–26. Archeological Papers No. 10.
        American Anthropological Association,
        Arlington, Virginia.

King, Adam

2003   *Etowah: The Political History of a Chiefdom
        Capital*. University of Alabama Press, Tusca-
        loosa.

2004   Power and the Sacred: Mound C and the
        Etowah Chiefdom. In *Hero, Hawk, and Open
        Hand: American Indian Art of the Ancient
        Midwest and South*, edited by R. F. Townsend
        and R. V. Sharp, pp. 151–166. Yale University
        Press, New Haven.

Knight, Vernon James, Jr.

1998   Moundville as a Diagrammatic Ceremonial
        Center. In *Archaeology of the Moundville
        Chiefdom*, edited by V. J. Knight, Jr., and V. P.
        Steponaitis, pp. 44–62. Smithsonian Institu-
        tion Press, Washington, D.C.

2004   Characterizing Elite Midden Deposits at
        Moundville. *American Antiquity* 69:304–
        321.

Knight, Vernon James, Jr., James A. Brown, and
George E. Lankford

2001   On the Subject Matter of Southeastern Cere-
        monial Complex Art. *Southeastern Archaeol-
        ogy* 20:129–141.

Knight, Vernon James, Jr., and Vincas P. Steponaitis

1998   A New History of Moundville. In *Archaeol-
        ogy of the Moundville Chiefdom*, edited by
        V. J. Knight, Jr., and V. P. Steponaitis, pp. 1–25.
        Smithsonian Institution Press, Washing-
        ton, D.C.

Lankford, George

2007   The "Path of Souls": Some Death Imagery in
        the Southeastern Ceremonial Complex. In
        *Ancient Objects and Sacred Realms: Interpre-
        tations of Mississippian Iconography*, edited
        by F. K Reilly III and J. F. Garber, pp. 174–212.
        University of Texas Press, Austin.

Latour, Bruno

1991   Technology Is Society Made Durable. In *A
        Sociology of Monsters: Essays on Power, Tech-
        nology and Domination*, edited by J. Law,
        pp. 103–131. Routledge, London.

1992   Where Are the Missing Masses? The Sociol-
        ogy of a Few Mundane Artifacts. In *Shaping
        Technology, Building Society: Studies in Socio-
        technical Change*, edited by W. Bijker and J.
        Law, pp. 225–258. MIT Press, Cambridge,
        Massachusetts.

1999   On Recalling ANT. In *Actor Network Theory
        and After*, edited by J. Law and J. Hassard,
        pp. 15–25. Blackwell and the Sociological
        Review, Oxford.

2005   *Reassembling the Social: An Introduction to
        Actor-Network-Theory*. Oxford University
        Press, Oxford.

Law, John

1991   Power, Discretion, and Strategy. In *A Sociol-
        ogy of Monsters: Essays on Power, Technology
        and Domination*, edited by J. Law, pp. 165–
        191. Routledge, London.

1992   *Notes on the Theory of the Actor-Network:
        Ordering, Strategy and Heterogeneity*. Centre
        for Science Studies, Lancaster University.
        Electronic document, http://www.comp
        .lancs.ac.uk/sociology/papers/Law-Notes
        -on-ANT.pdf.

1997   *Traduction/Trahison: Notes on ANT*. Centre
        for Science Studies, Lancaster University.
        Electronic document, http://www.comp
        .lancs.ac.uk/sociology/papers/Law-Traduct
        ion-Trahison.pdf.

1999   After ANT: Topology, Naming and Complex-
        ity. In *Actor Network Theory and After*, edited
        by J. Law and J. Hassard, pp. 1–14. Blackwell
        and the Sociological Review, Oxford.

2000   *Objects, Spaces, and Others*. Centre for Sci-
        ence Studies, Lancaster University. Electronic
        document, http://www.comp.lancs.ac.uk/

sociology/papers/Law-Objects-Spaces-Others.pdf.

Maxham, Mintcy
2004   Native Constructions of Landscapes in the Black Warrior Valley, Alabama, AD 1020–1520. Unpublished Ph.D. dissertation, Department of Anthropology, University of North Carolina, Chapel Hill.

Meskell, Lynn
2001   The Egyptian Ways of Death. In *Social Memory, Identity, and Death: Anthropological Perspectives on Mortuary Rituals*, edited by M. S. Chesson, pp. 27–40. Archeological Papers No. 10. American Anthropological Association, Arlington, Virginia.

Metcalf, Peter, and Richard Huntington
1991   *Celebrations of Death: The Anthropology of Mortuary Ritual.* 2nd ed. Cambridge University Press, Cambridge.

Parker Pearson, Michael
1999   *The Archaeology of Death and Burial.* Texas A & M University Press, College Station.

Pauketat, Timothy R.
2000   The Tragedy of the Commoners. In *Agency in Archaeology*, edited by M. Dobres and J. E. Robb, pp. 113–129. Routledge, London.
2007   *Chiefdoms and Other Archaeological Delusions.* AltaMira Press, Walnut Canyon, California.

Peebles, Christopher S.
1971   Moundville and Surrounding Sites: Some Structural Considerations of Mortuary Practices. In *Approaches to the Social Dimension of Mortuary Practices*, edited by J. A. Brown, pp. 68–91. Memoir No. 15. Society for American Archaeology, Washington, D.C.
1974   Moundville: The Organization of a Prehistoric Community and Culture. Unpublished Ph.D. dissertation, University of California, Santa Barbara.
1978   Determinants of Settlement Size and Location in the Moundville Phase. In *Mississippian Settlement Patterns*, edited by B. D. Smith, pp. 369–416. Academic Press, New York.

Phillips, Philip, and James A. Brown
1978   *Pre-Columbian Shell Engravings from the Craig Mound at Spiro, Oklahoma, Part 1.* Peabody Museum Press, Cambridge, Massachusetts.

Saxe, Arthur
1970   Social Dimensions of Mortuary Practices. Unpublished Ph.D. dissertation, Department of Anthropology, University of Michigan, Ann Arbor.

Scarry, John F.
1996   The Nature of Mississippian Societies. In *Political Structure and Change in the Prehistoric Southeastern United States*, edited by J. F. Scarry, pp. 12–24. University Press of Florida, Gainesville.

Service, Elman
1962   *Primitive Social Organization: An Evolutionary Perspective.* Random House, New York.

Silverman, Helaine
2002   Narratives of Identity and History in Modern Cemeteries of Lima, Peru. In *The Space and Place of Death*, edited by H. Silverman and D. Small, pp. 167–190. Archeological Papers No. 11. American Anthropological Association, Arlington, Virginia.

Smith, Bruce D. (editor)
1990   *Mississippian Emergence.* Smithsonian Institution Press, Washington, D.C.

Steponaitis, Vincas P.
1983   *Ceramics, Chronology, and Community Patterns: An Archaeological Study at Moundville.* Academic Press, New York.
1991   Contrasting Patterns of Mississippian Development. In *Chiefdoms: Power, Economy, and Ideology*, edited by Timothy K. Earle, pp. 193–228. Cambridge University Press, Cambridge.
1998   Population Trends at Moundville. In *Archaeology of the Moundville Chiefdom*, edited by V. J. Knight, Jr., and V. P. Steponaitis, pp. 26–43. Smithsonian Institution Press, Washington, D.C.

Steponaitis, Vincas P., and Vernon James Knight, Jr.
2004   Moundville Art in Historical and Social Context. In *Hero, Hawk, and Open Hand: American Indian Art of the Ancient Midwest and South*, edited by R. F. Townsend and R. V. Sharp, pp. 167–182. Yale University Press, New Haven.

Whitridge, Peter
2004   Whales, Harpoons, and Other Actors: Actor-Network Theory and Hunter-Gatherer Archaeology. In *Hunters and Gatherers in Theory and Archaeology*, edited by G. M. Crothers, pp. 445–474. Occasional Paper No. 31. Center for Archaeological Investigations, Southern Illinois University, Carbondale.

Wilson, Gregory D.
2005   Between Plaza and Palisade: Household and Community Organization at Early Moundville. Unpublished Ph.D. dissertation, Department of Anthropology, University of North Carolina, Chapel Hill.

2008   *The Archaeology of Everyday Life at Early Moundville.* University of Alabama Press, Tuscaloosa.

Wilson, Gregory D., Jon Bernard Marcoux, and Brad Koldehoff

2006   Square Pegs in Round Holes: Organizational Diversity between Early Moundville and Cahokia. In *Leadership and Polity in Mississippian Society*, edited by B. M. Butler and P. D. Welch, pp. 43–72. Occasional Paper No. 33. Center for Archaeological Investigations, Southern Illinois University, Carbondale.

Wilson, Gregory D., Vincas P. Steponaitis, and Keith Jacobi

2010   Social and Spatial Dimensions of Moundville Mortuary Practices. In *Mississippian Mortuary Practices: Beyond Hierarchy and the Representationist Perspective*, edited by L. P. Sullivan and R. C. Mainfort, Jr., pp. 74–89. University Press of Florida, Gainesville.

Yoffee, Norman

1993   Too Many Chiefs? (or, Safe Texts for the '90s). In *Archaeological Theory: Who Sets the Agenda?* edited by N. Yoffee and A. Sherrat, pp. 60–78. Cambridge University Press, Cambridge.

2005   *Myths of the Archaic State: Evolution of the Earliest Cities, States and Civilizations.* Cambridge University Press, Cambridge.

10

Landscapes of Complexity in the U.S. Southwest

The Hohokam, Chacoans, and Peer Polity Interaction

Jill E. Neitzel

Scattered across the landscape of the U.S. Southwest are innumerable ruins that range from huge, multistory buildings to simple, one-room field houses. For over a century, these diverse structures have fascinated both professional archaeologists and the general public as they have wondered how the buildings' occupants survived in the Southwest's unforgiving environment, what their cultures were like, and why these people ultimately abandoned their homes. Another issue that has dominated the attention of archaeologists over the past several decades has concerned how the occupants of these structures were organized. Two questions have been the focus of considerable research and debate: which, if any, prehispanic southwestern societies had complex sociopolitical organizations, and for those identified as complex, what was the nature and degree of this complexity?

Efforts to answer these questions have generally equated complexity with being hierarchically organized. Given the assumption that larger structures housed more people and entailed greater managerial requirements to build, the search for organizational hierarchies has concentrated on those parts of the Southwest with the most massive ruins. These investigations have produced a general, but not complete, consensus that the polities associated with these sites had a moderate degree of complexity—they were not egalitarian, nor were they states, but rather something in between.

An intriguing characteristic of the most com-

plex of these polities is that they were not singular entities surrounded by egalitarian groups. Rather, they stood in the midst of other, similarly organized polities, which all together encompassed broad regions. This correlation between complexity and regions has also been documented for middle-range societies in other parts of the world, but the question of why it exists has received relatively little attention. The one notable exception is Colin Renfrew's (1986) two-decades-old model of peer polity interaction.

In this chapter I use two cases from the American Southwest, the Hohokam of south-central Arizona and the Chacoans of northwest New Mexico (Figure 10.1), to update Renfrew's model. I begin with a review of early and more recent studies of complexity and regions in the Southwest. Then, after summarizing Renfrew's model, I suggest several revisions that incorporate newer theoretical and substantive developments in archaeology. With these modifications, I conclude that complexity was often associated with multiple, neighboring polities, for two reasons: (1) the preconditions for complexity encompassed broad regions, and (2) the leadership strategies employed in one polity could affect the strategies used in others.

Early Approaches to Complexity and Regions

Approaches to the study of complexity and regions changed from the early days of Southwest archaeology through the advent of the so-called

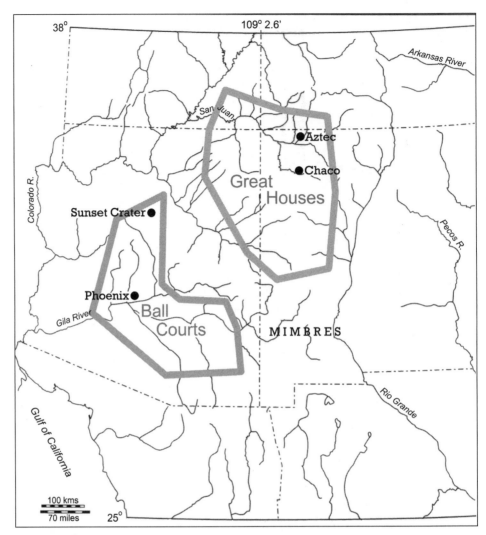

FIGURE 10.1. Distributions of Hohokam ball courts and Chacoan great houses in the U.S. Southwest (Lekson 2008:Fig. 5.2). Reprinted by permission from *A History of the Ancient Southwest*, by Stephen H. Lekson. Copyright © 2008 by the School for Advanced Research, Santa Fe.

new archaeology in the 1960s–1970s. An interest in regions came first and involved a succession of alternate approaches. Inquiries into how past peoples were organized developed later, leading eventually to the issue of complexity.

Initial Studies

During their first half century of research, Southwest archaeologists were interested in regions but generally did not consider the topic of organization at all. Early investigators used the distributions of painted ceramics and residential and nonresidential architecture to define broad areas

whose inhabitants were thought to have shared the same culture. For example, the Hohokam culture area was delineated in the desert and surrounding uplands of south-central Arizona by the limits of red-on-buff pottery, houses in pits, and ball courts (Figures 10.1 and 10.2; Gladwin and Gladwin 1929a, 1929b, 1930a, 1935). Whereas some researchers saw the late appearance of polychrome ceramics and platform mounds (Figure 10.3) as new Hohokam cultural traits, others interpreted these remains as part of a new culture area, known as the Salado (Gladwin and Gladwin 1930b; Haury 1945).[1] To the north, the Anasazi

FIGURE 10.2. Hohokam ball court under excavation at the site of Snaketown (Gladwin et al. 1937:Pl. VIII). Courtesy Arizona State Museum, University of Arizona. Photo #70572, photographer unknown.

culture area was mapped on the plateau of northern Arizona and New Mexico and southern Utah and Colorado based on the distributions of black-on-white pottery, pit houses, pueblos, and kivas (Kidder 1924, 1927).

Once the major Southwest culture areas were defined, researchers shifted their attention to culture history. They invested enormous effort into delineating each area's chronological sequence (Dean 1991:91; Hayes 1981:18) and making spatial subdivisions to accommodate the varied patterns of different kinds of remains. Hohokam subdivisions included the core area of the Lower Salt and Middle Gila River valleys (aka the Phoenix Basin), the Santa Cruz River valley (aka the Tucson Basin), and other, peripheral drainages. One of the Anasazi sub-areas was centered on Chaco Canyon, New Mexico, and was defined by the distribution of Chacoan great houses (Figures 10.1, 10.4). As with the original definition of the Hohokam and Anasazi culture areas, smaller-scale units in time and space were interpreted as representing groups of people who shared the same culture.

Hohokam and Chacoan archaeologists con-tinued to emphasize culture history through the mid-twentieth century even as criticisms began to be published. Critics noted how material remains were often difficult to classify using proposed sequences (Brew 1946) and how these sequences, no matter how refined, failed to produce insights into prehistoric life and culture change (Taylor 1948). Concurrently, a renewed interest among some cultural anthropologists in cultural evolution offered an alternative approach. While some neo-evolutionists examined the process of cultural evolution itself (e.g., Steward 1955; White 1959), others proposed typologies for classifying societies into developmental stages whose diagnostic characteristics included the distinction between egalitarian and hierarchical organizations (e.g., Fried 1967; Oberg 1955; Sahlins 1958; Service 1962; Steward 1949).

Impacts of the New Archaeology

Although neither criticisms of culture history nor proposals of new societal types had any immediate effects on how Hohokam or Chacoan archaeologists studied regions or complexity, they were precursors of the new archaeology,

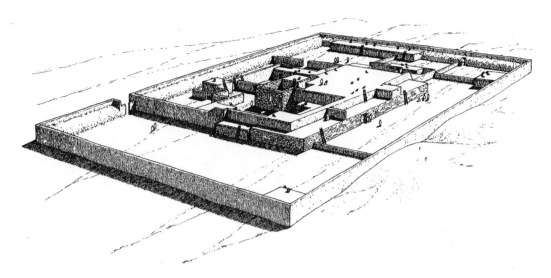

FIGURE 10.3. Reconstruction of Cline Terrace platform mound, Tonto Basin, Arizona (AD 1320–1420) (Jacobs 1997:frontispiece). Drawing by Glena Cain, from A Salado Platform Mound on Tonto Creek, by David Jacobs. Copyright © 1997 by Department of Anthropology, Arizona State University. Courtesy of Arleyn Simon.

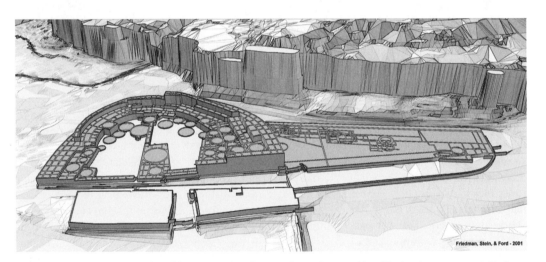

FIGURE 10.4. Reconstruction of Pueblo Bonito great house, Chaco Canyon, New Mexico (AD 1070–1115) (Stein et al. 2003:Fig. 4.21). Drawing by Richard Friedman, John Stein, and Dabney Ford, from Pueblo Bonito: Center of the Chacoan World, edited by Jill E. Neitzel, 2003. Courtesy of Richard Friedman.

which eventually had a tremendous impact. For example, Lewis Binford's (1962) advocacy of systems theory generated new ways of studying broad-scale patterns, ultimately leading both Hohokam and Chacoan researchers to discard the culture-area approach with its assumptions about shared norms in favor of the regional system concept, which allowed for variation in different characteristics (Wilcox 1979). Similarly,

Southwest archaeologists responded to Binford's (1962) call for archaeology to be anthropology with ground-breaking studies of social organization (Hill 1970; Longacre 1970), and to his identification of cultural evolution as archaeology's overarching goal with studies of long-term change that were processual rather than culture-historical (Plog 1974).

The topic of complexity began to be addressed

by Hohokam, Chacoan, and other Southwest archaeologists as they combined their developing interests in organization and change. The initial studies were profoundly influenced by ethnographic descriptions of the Hopi, Zuni, Tewa, Pima, and other Historic period indigenous groups as egalitarian (e.g., Eggan 1950; Parsons 1929; Russell 1908; Titiev 1944). Through analogy, many archaeologists assumed that the Southwest's ancestral populations were egalitarian as well (e.g., Haury 1976; Upham 1987; Vivian 1970; Woodbury 1961). The opposite conclusion—that some prehistoric societies were hierarchically organized—first appeared in a few sporadic studies (e.g., Clark 1969; Doyel 1974; Grebinger 1973; Griffin 1967; Judge 1979; Martin and Plog 1973), which were followed eventually by a cascade of publications that put complexity at the forefront of Southwest archaeology.

Much of this new research was centered at Arizona State University and Chaco Canyon. At ASU, Fred Plog's prior research focus on small sites was transformed in 1977 by a comment from his former professor, Near Eastern archaeologist Robert McCormick Adams. After visiting the huge Pueblo IV site of Chavez Pass, Adams told Plog and his graduate students that if they wanted to understand small sites, they would have to investigate big settlements such as Chavez Pass (J. L. Hantman, personal communication 2008; Upham 1982:xiii). By the end of that day, Plog had reassigned his students to new research topics related to the issue of complexity. This research benefited immeasurably by the addition of David Wilcox and Gary Feinman to the ASU faculty the following year. Wilcox (1976; Wilcox and Shenk 1977) had begun to evaluate the evidence for complexity among the Protohistoric Pueblos and the late Classic period Hohokam; and Feinman suggested that the incipient complexity evidenced at Formative period sites in Oaxaca, Mexico, might have counterparts in the Southwest. This intellectual crucible generated a series of publications that provoked much debate and further research (e.g., Cordell and Plog 1979; Lightfoot 1984; Lightfoot and Feinman 1982; Upham 1982; Wilcox 1979; Wilcox et al. 1981).

Concurrently, archaeologists associated with the National Park Service's multidisciplinary Chaco Project, which was initiated in 1971 with the goal of understanding Chaco culture, began to focus on the topic of complexity; and in 1981 they presented their findings for settlement patterns, architecture, burials, and artifacts to an overflow crowd at the Annual Meeting of the Society for American Archaeology (Judge and Schelberg 1984). Although their conclusions were not accepted by all (e.g., Toll 1985; Vivian 1990), the evidence for complexity among the Chacoans was convincing in its redundancy.

The only other Southwest case for which early efforts to study complexity produced such consistent results in diverse remains (e.g., irrigation canals, community and settlement patterns, burials) was the Hohokam (Doyel 1979, 1980; Wilcox 1991a). Hohokam and Chacoan researchers were the first Southwest archaeologists to link explicitly the topics of regions and complexity, and following the interests of the new archaeology, both initially attributed the development of complexity within their respective regions to the same causal variables—environmental variation, subsistence, and food exchange (Judge 1979; Plog 1980).

Recent Developments

Early studies of complexity were followed by more than a decade of increasingly heated debates about whether or not various Southwest cases were in fact complex. As more and more archaeologists participated in these sometimes acrimonious arguments, complexity emerged as the Southwest's dominant research issue and regions declined in importance, becoming just one of a number of scales where evidence of complexity was sought. The controversies eventually subsided as expanding databases, the updating of old approaches, the application of new perspectives, and comparative studies revealed more organizational diversity than could be accommodated by the simple complex/not complex dichotomy.

The Database

Concurrent with the complexity debates was an enormous increase in archaeological fieldwork. Some surveys and excavations, such as those sponsored by the National Park Service's Chaco Project, were prompted by the debates themselves (Mathien 2005), but most were cultural resource management (CRM) projects. Hohokam archaeology benefited from a virtual explosion of CRM research, some of unprecedented scale, financed by construction booms in the rapidly expanding cities of Phoenix and Tucson (Doelle 2007; Fish and Fish 2007).

The growing databases for the Hohokam, Chacoans, and other Southwest cases produced insights into multiple characteristics associated with complexity, such as demography, subsistence, exchange, settlement patterns, and burial practices. Furthermore, these data encompassed not just sites and regions but the entire gamut of spatial scales (see Neitzel 1999). Thus, while regions continued to be important, most notably in studies of settlement patterns, ceramic design, and long-distance trade, interest in a number of other scales grew, ranging from burial and household groups, community patterns, and irrigation systems to interregional interaction, the entire Southwest macroregion, and connections with Mesoamerican polities.

One might expect that expanding databases for multiple characteristics at multiple scales would soon resolve the Southwest complexity debates. But in fact, analyses of these data often produced inconsistent results, which only inflamed the arguments. For example, a rich burial could be documented at a relatively small site (McGregor 1943), or an enormous site could lack lavish burials (Howell 1995). The more ambiguous the data and the broader the range of sites for which claims of complexity were made (e.g., Lightfoot and Feinman 1982), the more vitriolic the debates became (Lightfoot and Upham 1989; McGuire and Saitta 1996). Hohokam and Chacoan archaeologists certainly had their disagreements, but they were less intense than in other parts of the Southwest because their growing databases continued to offer redundant evidence for moderately developed organizational hierarchies.

Updating Old Approaches

In the midst of the complexity debates, archaeologists refined some of their original approaches to studying how ancient southwestern societies were organized. A few tried to update or replace the use of societal types. Neither the traditional neo-evolutionary categories for middle-range societies (e.g., tribes and chiefdoms) nor any of their proposed alternatives were ever widely adopted

in the Southwest. Not only had these various schemes been the subject of ongoing criticisms (e.g., Earle 1978; Feinman and Neitzel 1984; Fried 1975; Goldman 1970; Renfrew 1974; Sanders and Webster 1978; Steponaitis 1978; Taylor 1975), but more significantly, most southwestern cases could not be neatly pigeonholed into any category (e.g., Peebles and Kus 1977). As a result, Southwest archaeologists generally resorted to the simple dichotomy of not complex (meaning egalitarian) versus complex (meaning hierarchically organized).

The complexity debates arose in large part because even these broadly defined categories could not accommodate the ambiguous and occasionally contradictory data being collected for many prehistoric groups. One approach for resolving this problem was to propose new types, such as sequential hierarchy (Johnson 1989) and heterarchy (Rautman 1998). An alternative, nontypological approach advocated by Ben Nelson (1995) had a much greater impact. He declared that Southwest archaeologists should be studying the ways in which their various cases were complex rather than arguing about whether or not they were complex. Because it succinctly offered a way out of the seemingly unresolvable either/or complexity debates, this statement soon became the most frequently quoted phrase in Southwest archaeology (and elsewhere, as seen in many of the chapters in this book). Nelson advocated that researchers focus on individual characteristics rather than broad categories, and applied this approach himself by comparing the populations, burial patterns, roads, and monumental structures at Chaco Canyon and La Quemada, in Zacatecas, Mexico.

Although Nelson did not address the issue of change through time, he followed the example of the new archaeology's processualism by eschewing culture-historical and cultural evolutionary categories in favor of analyses of individual characteristics. Processualism was explicitly resurrected in Blanton et al.'s (1996) dual-processual model of cultural evolution, which attributed variation in middle-range societies (e.g., Drennan 1991; Gilman 1991; Renfrew 1974) to the implementation of different leadership strategies. Leaders who relied on the network strategy centralized decision making and power and distinguished themselves as individuals by their elaborate residences, special tombs, and prestige goods obtained via long-distance trade and craft specialists. In contrast, leaders who adopted the corporate strategy shared power and decision making within the context of communal rituals and other group activities. The archaeological correlates of this strategy included monumental public architecture and other collective labor projects. The dual-processual model was embraced by many Southwest archaeologists because the corporate strategy could account for the ambiguous data that had fueled the complexity debates (Mills 2000).

Another old approach that offered new possibilities was ethnographic analogy. Ongoing fieldwork by cultural anthropologists together with reanalyses of earlier ethnographies revealed that some Historic period Pueblo societies were in fact moderately stratified in their members' control of ritual knowledge and activities (e.g., Brandt 1994; Levy 1992; Ortiz 1969; Reyman 1987; Whiteley 1988). These findings strengthened archaeologists' claims that ancestral populations could have been stratified as well (Upham 1987). However, the fact that Historic period leaders were not distinguished by any obvious wealth differences raised questions about archaeologists' ability to discern material evidence for complexity.

Applying New Perspectives

The complexity debates also prompted new perspectives for studying how prehistoric societies were organized. One was a concern with religious ideology. Some Hohokam and Chacoan archaeologists pursued this interest in studies of the astronomical alignments, ceremonial functions, and ritual landscapes of ball courts, platform mounds, great houses, and great kivas (Andrews and Bostwick 2006; Farmer 2003; Sofaer 2007; Stein and Lekson 1992; Van Dyke 2008; Wilcox 1987, 1991a; Zeilik 1986). They also began to consider the role of religious beliefs and their associated ceremonies in the development of complexity across the Hohokam and Chacoan regions (Elson 2007; Judge 1989; Renfrew 2001; Wilcox 1987).

An interest in historical contingency offered another new way of thinking about the past. Marxist theorists and critics of systems theory noted that any kind of change at a particular place and time does not occur on a tabula rasa but instead is affected by prior history. For example, the beliefs and behaviors of some Native American groups today are affected by their oral traditions concerning places and events from many centuries ago (Bahr 2007; Bahr et al. 1994; Ellis 1967; Ferguson and Hart 1985; Lekson and Cameron 1995; Lopez 2007). Southwest archaeologists began to consider historical contingency, primarily in community pattern studies of how Hohokam platform mounds were situated with reference to earlier ball courts (Gregory 1987), how the Chacoans drew on earlier architectural traditions when they incorporated kivas and more formal versions of great kivas into their great houses (Van Dyke 2007), and how post-Chacoan construction was situated with reference to earlier great houses (Adler 1996). Several researchers also proposed a hybrid approach that combined historical contingency with processualism (Haas et al. 1994; McGuire 1994; see also Pauketat 2007).

Another new perspective considered individual decision making from a different point of view. In addition to being central to Blanton et al.'s (1996) discussion of leadership strategies, individual decisions lie at the heart of agent-based simulation models derived from the interdisciplinary field of complex adaptive systems. Proposed models in the Southwest focused primarily on subsistence-related decisions under changing environmental conditions (e.g., Dean et al. 2000; Kohler et al. 2000; Kohler et al. 2007), but recent simulations of group formation and intergroup competition suggest that this approach has great potential for understanding the process of hierarchy development (T. A. Kohler, personal communication; also see Henrich and Boyd 2008; Smith and Choi 2007).

Comparisons and Diversity

The results of applying old and new approaches to expanding databases were ultimately subjected to Southwest archaeology's long tradition of comparative research (e.g., Cordell and Gumerman 1989; Dean et al. 1985; Euler and Gumerman 1978; Kidder 1927; Longacre, ed. 1970). A series of studies compared the organizations of different prehistoric groups, looking for both similarities and differences (Adler 1996; Crown and

Judge 1991; Feinman et al. 2000; Gumerman 1994; Gumerman and Gell-Mann 1994; Haas et al. 1994; Mills 2000; Neitzel 1999, 2000, in press; Nelson 1995). A major conclusion was that complexity in the ancient Southwest was manifested in diverse ways. Societal organizations could vary not only in the degree to which they were hierarchical (e.g., from minimally to highly) but also in how hierarchies with similar degrees of differentiation were organized.

The Hohokam and Chacoan cases illustrate this diversity (Crown and Judge 1991; Neitzel 1999). Superficially, their overall trends appear similar. The organizations of both became more hierarchical through time, reaching similar levels of differentiation at their peaks (Doyel 2007; Elson 2007; Judge 1989; Neitzel 1989a, 1999; Sebastian 1991; Wilcox 1991a). But a closer look reveals a number of contrasts. For example, the Hohokam lasted approximately twice as long as the Chacoans: the architectural evidence for complexity on a regional scale began earlier and continued longer for ball courts (Wilcox and Sternberg 1983) and platform mounds (Gregory and Nials 1985) than for great houses (Marshall et al. 1979; Powers et al. 1983).[2]

Their dominant leadership strategies also differed (Neitzel in press). Preclassic Hohokam leaders emphasized the corporate strategy over the minimally present network strategy. Then, in the Classic period, both strategies were used more intensively and their relative importance remained the same (cf. Elson and Abbott 2000). In contrast, early Chacoan leaders emphasized the network strategy over the present but secondary corporate strategy. Their successors did the reverse, intensively emphasizing the corporate strategy though the network strategy continued to be used to a lesser degree (cf. Earle 1991; Wills 2000).

Other differences can be found in the Hohokam and Chacoan religions (Cobb et al. 1999; Mathien and McGuire 1986; McGuire 1980; McGuire et al. 1994; McGuire and Villalpando 2007). The Hohokam experienced a major ideological transformation, as evidenced by the replacement of ball courts, red-on-buff pottery, and various ritual artifacts by platform mounds and polychrome pottery (Elson 2007; Neitzel in press). In contrast, great houses and great kivas were the focus of religious life throughout the entire Chacoan era. Furthermore, Hohokam ceremonial structures (ball courts, platform mounds) and ritual artifacts (figurines, palettes, censers) were all modified versions of Mesoamerican forms. Among the Chacoans, evidence of Mesoamerican religious influence is present (e.g., architectural features of some great houses, ceramic cylinder vessels, turquoise inlay) but to a lesser degree than among the Hohokam, perhaps as a result of the greater distances involved and the enduring religious traditions associated with kivas.

The Peer Polity Model

As archaeologists' interests in regions and complexity have developed, converged, and shifted in importance, the question of why complexity was a regional phenomenon in middle-range societies has received little attention. The one notable exception is Renfrew's (1986) model of peer polity interaction and its explanation for why the institutions associated with increased complexity developed in chiefdoms and early states. This model can be applied with some success to the Hohokam and Chacoan cases,[3] but the discrepancies, together with recent theoretical and substantive developments in archaeology, suggest several ways that it should be updated.

Peer Polity Characteristics

According to Renfrew (1986), most chiefdoms and early states did not develop in isolation but rather emerged in tandem with other, neighboring polities. These so-called peer polities were independent of one another and together could encompass broad regions. They were usually about the same size, had the same degree of complexity, and shared the same architectural forms and symbolic systems. Renfrew attributed these similarities, which he labeled structural homologies, to interaction among the polities and their antecedents over long spans of time. This interaction could involve trade, shared ceremonialism, and competitive emulation, which he defined as leaders' efforts to impress both fellow polity members and outsiders through conspicuous displays of wealth and power. Such displays could include building monumental structures, wearing imported prestige goods, and being associated with religious symbols. Each type of display could become widely distributed in multiple, neighboring polities as leaders sought to enhance their positions by imitating their more powerful counterparts.

The Hohokam and Chacoans match some but not all of Renfrew's peer polity characteristics. Both societies consisted of multiple polities that shared architectural forms, decorated ceramic styles, and other traits, and neither was ever unified under a single, overarching political organization. Both also engaged in at least two of the three kinds of interaction included in Renfrew's model—trade and shared ceremonialism.

Hohokam and Chacoan polities traded extensively among themselves. The Hohokam's most frequently exchanged materials included ceramics and shell (Abbott 2000; Bradley 1993; Crown 1991; Doyel 2007; McGuire and Howard 1987), and the residents of Chaco Canyon's great houses imported vast quantities of ceramics, turquoise, and tree beams (Cameron 2001; Mathien 2001, 2003; Toll 2001; Windes and McKenna 2001). Both sets of polities also participated to varying degrees in long-distance exchange networks that moved diverse materials, such as shell, turquoise, obsidian, minerals, and textiles, throughout the Southwest (Doyel 2007; Neitzel 1989b). Some polities had more distant trading connections with Mesoamerican complex chiefdoms and states, which exported copper bells and exotic birds and imported southwestern turquoise (Mathien and McGuire 1986; McGuire 1980; McGuire and Villalpando 2007; Weigand and Harbottle 1993).

Shared ceremonialism was also fundamental to both the Hohokam and Chacoans. In fact, for many archaeologists, religious architecture is the diagnostic characteristic for defining the limits of the two sets of polities—ball courts and platform mounds for the Hohokam, and great houses and their associated great kivas for the Chacoans. The broad distributions of each of these structures also encompassed distinctive artifacts that were embedded with symbolic meanings, most notably figurines, palettes, and censers for the Preclassic Hohokam (Haury 1976), Salado polychrome pottery for the Classic period Hohokam (Crown 1994), and turquoise jewelry and Dogoszhi style pottery for the Chacoans (Plog 2003).

For both the Hohokam and Chacoans, religion pervaded many aspects of life, as evidenced by the multiple functions of their ceremonial structures. In addition to being used for ritual ball games, ball courts were associated with markets (Abbott et al. 2007; Wilcox 1991b). Platform mounds served as elite residences (Elson 1998), as did great houses (Lekson 2007). Even the great kiva, the heart of Chacoan religious beliefs and practices, may have had other social functions (Adler and Wilshusen 1990; Van Dyke 2007).

Less congruent with Renfrew's model is the mixed evidence for competitive emulation among the Hohokam and Chacoans. Leaders in both cases were undoubtedly responsible for the construction of platform mounds, great houses, and great kivas, if not the less labor-intensive ball courts. They also wore similar status markers such as shell and turquoise jewelry produced by craft specialists from traded materials (Bayman 2002, 2007; Mathien 2001; Windes 1992). While emulation among leaders may have been responsible for the widespread distributions of these structures and artifacts, there is no way to determine whether or not it was competitive.

Two other characteristics—that peer polities were usually about the same size and had the same degree of complexity—do not fit the Hohokam and Chacoan cases except perhaps at the start of their respective sequences. Some settlements soon grew larger and contained more impressive or greater numbers of ceremonial structures than others (Andrews and Bostwick 2006; Doyel 2007; Gregory 1987; Marshall et al. 1979; Powers et al. 1983; Stein et al. 2003; Upham and Rice 1980). Presumably, their associated polities were larger and more complex as well. Extending this organizational variation were polities that encompassed multiple ball-court, platform-mound, or great-house sites and allied themselves with other polities.

Explaining Complexity

According to Renfrew, a combination of external and internal factors caused increasing complexity within peer polities. His external factors were the various forms of peer polity interaction—exchange, shared ceremonialism, and competitive emulation—along with another kind of interaction, conflict. Each could create social environments conducive to organizational change. For Renfrew, the triggers for such change were factors internal to individual polities, including increasing population, subsistence intensification, and craft specialization.

This explanation fits the Hohokam and Chacoan cases, which both became more complex through time and engaged in the various forms of peer polity interaction (with the possible exception of emulation being competitive). Sometimes the members of these two sets of polities also fought, as evidenced by defensive structures and wounds on human remains (LeBlanc 1999; Rice and LeBlanc 2001; Wilcox and Haas 1994).

The internal factors of population growth, subsistence intensification, and craft specialization were also present among the Hohokam and Chacoans. Changes in the numbers and sizes of Hohokam and Chacoan sites through time indicate increases in how many people were distributed across the landscape (Hayes 1981; Hill et al. 2005; Marshall et al. 1979; Powers et al. 1983; Upham and Rice 1980). Subsistence intensification has been well documented for both cases. In the Lower Salt River valley the Hohokam constructed multiple, complex irrigation canal systems that were lengthened, branched, interconnected, and rebuilt through successive time periods (Doyel 2007; Nicholas and Neitzel 1984; Ravesloot 2007). The Chacoans installed a variety of diversion structures to channel water from Chaco Canyon's north cliff to gridded gardens on the canyon floor, where they also constructed reservoirs (Lagasse et al. 1984; Vivian 1974). Finally, craft specialists were responsible for the production of some of the Hohokam's and Chacoans' finest artifacts, including decorated ceramics and jewelry made of turquoise and shell (Mathien 2003; Bayman 2007).

Updating the Peer Polity Model

Although Renfrew's model of peer polity interaction fits both the Hohokam and Chacoan cases fairly well, the model can be updated in several ways. Based on discrepancies identified previously, two of the model's assumptions should be discarded—that interacting polities should be the same size and that they should have the same degree of complexity. Other modifications include incorporating more recent developments in archaeological theory, adding a new variable,

and expanding the model's spatial and temporal scales.

Theoretical Updates

Renfrew's (1986) concept of competitive emulation represents one of the earliest efforts by an archaeologist to consider the role of individual decision making in the development of complex societies. This concept can be updated by incorporating more recent discussions of leadership strategies (Blanton et al. 1996), which can facilitate both competitive and noncompetitive emulation. The network strategy's reliance on centralizing power and decision making offers multiple opportunities for competitive emulation as leaders distinguish themselves by living in elaborate residences, wearing status markers, and being buried in special tombs. Effective implementation of the corporate strategy could also be emulated, but sharing power and decision making through communal activities is antithetical to the idea of competition. Whether or not competition could occur below the corporate strategy's veneer of cooperation is a question for future research.

Renfrew's concern with individual decision making should also be updated to include the effects of historical contingency. The circumstances within which leaders make decisions are the product of their previous decisions as well as those made by their predecessors, their nearby and distant neighbors, and their neighbors' predecessors. In addition to helping to create a situation that requires a response, earlier decisions, both recent and long ago, provide both role models for what to do and cautionary lessons for what not to do.

Adding a Variable

Any application of Renfrew's model of peer polity interaction to the Hohokam and Chacoan cases would be incomplete without a consideration of their environmental settings. Topographically, both were characterized by centrally located core areas that had more water and arable land than their surrounding regions and encompassed the most complex polities, the most expansive and sophisticated water control systems, and the highest population densities. For both, the effects of changes in water availability were complicated (Dean 1992; Graybill et al. 2006; Graybill and Nials 1989; Grissino-Mayer 1996; Nials et al. 1989; Waters 2006; Waters and Ravesloot 2001). Periods with stable and above-average water supplies were generally characterized by demographic growth, expansion of water control systems, and increasing complexity. But diminished or unpredictable water supplies could have opposite effects—either greater complexity through reorganization or decline. Catastrophic floods invariably caused social devolution. Thus, spatial and temporal characteristics of the natural environment may have affected the development of the Hohokam and Chacoan polities in significant ways.

Broadening the Spatial and Temporal Scales

The Hohokam and Chacoan cases also highlight how the spatial scale of Renfrew's model should be extended beyond neighboring polities within a region. Hohokam polities did not just interact with one another, and neither did Chacoan polities. At least some members of both sets also had more distant connections to each other and to other Southwest polities through trade (Neitzel 1989b) and shared ceremonialism related to water and fertility (Crown 1991; Plog 2003; Whittlesey 2007). At a broader scale, all were influenced to varying degrees by trade and shared ceremonialism with Mesoamerican complex chiefdoms and states, whose leaders may have provided role models for their less powerful southwestern counterparts.

As originally suggested by Renfrew (1986), his model can also be expanded beyond chiefdoms and early states to encompass simpler societies, including those experiencing the initial transition from egalitarian to non-egalitarian organizations. For the Hohokam and Chacoans, incipient complexity preceded the first ball courts and great houses, as seen in the Pioneer and early Colonial period occupations of the site of Snaketown (Haury 1976; Thomas and King 1985; Wilcox et al. 1981:204–208), at the Basketmaker III period site of Shabik'eshchee Village (Lightfoot and Feinman 1982; Roberts 1929), and at a few other at least roughly contemporaneous sites (e.g., Cable and Doyel 1987; Damp and Kotyk 2000; Feinman et al. 2000; Wallace 2003, 2007).

I expect that future research will show that the initial transition from egalitarian to non-egalitarian organizations was a regional phenomenon throughout the Southwest. One reason is that several of the variables discussed previously as contributing to increased complexity in already hierarchical societies also characterized the Pioneer and early Colonial periods in the south and the Basketmaker III period in the north. The regional landscapes were becoming filled with people, albeit in low numbers (Hayes 1981; Kohler et al. 2008; Ravesloot and Waters 2002–2004; Wallace 2007; Wills and Windes 1989); subsistence changes involving the increased importance of domesticated corn were occurring widely (Bohrer 1970; Fish et al. 1986; Gasser and Kwiatkowski 1991; Reed 2000; Wills 1988; Windes n.d.); obsidian, shell, and occasionally turquoise were being traded over long distances (Cameron 1997; Crown 1991; Mathien 1997); and religious beliefs and rituals were widely shared, as evidenced by rock art (Bostwick and Krocek 2002; Robins and Hays-Gilpin 2000; Schaafsma 1986), Hohokam ritual artifacts and small mounds (Haury 1976; Wilcox et al. 1981), and the antecedents of Chacoan great kivas (Van Dyke 2007).

A second reason for predicting that incipient complexity was a regional phenomenon is the effects of leadership strategies. As described by Blanton et al. (1996), both the corporate and network strategies can be implemented, with varying degrees of intensity and success, in the entire range of societies, from the simplest to the most complex. I have already discussed how successful leadership in already complex societies can have regional effects through emulation. The same could be true for groups undergoing the transition from being egalitarian to non-egalitarian. One successful emerging leader could serve as a role model for aspiring leaders in neighboring communities.

So Why Was Complexity a Regional Phenomenon?

With the preceding modifications and additions to Renfrew's model, his explanation for why complexity is a regional phenomenon can also be updated. This reworked explanation in turn raises new questions and highlights difficulties that future research will have to resolve.

The Revised Model

In my view, complexity as it first emerged and as it developed further characterized multiple, neighboring polities because the preconditions for complexity encompassed broad regions and the leadership strategies employed in one polity could affect the strategies used in others. All the variables included in my updated version of Renfrew's model are regional in scope. By definition, the different kinds of peer polity interaction—shared ceremonialism, trade, competitive (or noncompetitive) emulation—encompass regions, as does conflict; but the variables that are internal to specific polities also operate on a broad scale. For example, environmental advantages are relative, one place versus another, and thus are defined within regional contexts; and climate changes that make conditions better or worse for farming affect entire regions, with the relative impacts depending on local topography. Increasing population density within a polity can be an impetus for organizational change if the surrounding landscape is filled with people, making population movement difficult. The regional scale of subsistence change can be seen in when and where Southwest groups adopted domesticated plants from Mesoamerica and in the broad differences between the northern and southern Southwest (Simmons 2006). Craft specialization had a regional dimension in that the raw materials were often obtained from distant sources and many of the finished products were widely exchanged.

Leadership strategies could also have broad impacts. Strategies employed successfully by leaders or aspiring leaders in one polity could provide role models for their counterparts in neighboring polities to emulate even in the absence of competition. Furthermore, any benefits derived from these strategies by a polity's members could provide tangible reasons for members of neighboring communities to support the adoption of similar strategies by their own leaders (see Henrich 2006). In cases of incipient complexity, such benefits could offer incentives to override, at least temporarily, powerful leveling mechanisms of egalitarianism in order to follow an aspiring leader.

At the heart of this explanation for why complexity is a regional phenomenon is the mutually reinforcing relationship between preconditions and leadership strategies. Increased complexity would not develop among multiple, neighboring polities if the preconditions were in place but existing or aspiring leaders applying appropriate strategies were not. Nor would it occur if existing or aspiring leaders were present but the preconditions were not. The decisions of leaders and their followers are always constrained by the local and regional contexts within which they are made (e.g., environmental, demographic, subsistence, economic, ideological, and interpersonal), by the history of what happened previously, and by the personal characteristics of the individuals doing the deciding. Their decisions in turn determine the conditions within which future decisions will be made.

Questions for Future Research

My explanation for why complexity was a regional phenomenon in middle-range societies raises a series of questions requiring further investigation. How varied were interacting peer polities in their sizes and degrees of complexity? Were they linked by other kinds of interaction such as political alliances and marriage ties, which are much more difficult to study than trade and shared religion? Are some preconditions for complexity more significant at some times and places than others? Are some leadership strategies or combinations of strategies more effective in some conditions than others? What factors determine the geographic limits of regions filled with interacting, complex polities and shifts in these limits through time? What were the temporal and spatial patterning as complex polities developed within these limits?

Chronology is a critical problem for this last question. For the Hohokam and Chacoans, it is possible to track gross changes in the distributions of ball courts, platform mounds, and great houses, but significant dating problems underlie these broad patterns. Many sites are unexcavated or have been destroyed, making it difficult or impossible to determine the applicability of site dates to specific structures. Some sites may have been occupied before the construction of their ball courts, platform mounds, or great houses; and some of these structures may have ceased being used before site abandonment. Also, the hundred-year intervals associated with Hohokam phases and Chacoan periods may mask considerable variation in the timing of how ball courts, platform mounds, and great houses came to be distributed across the landscape.

With more precise dating of these structures, we could better document the temporal and spatial patterns of their associated polities. Increased complexity could develop within one polity and then spread to or develop later among its neighbors, or it could emerge at roughly the same time among several neighboring or distant polities and then spread to or develop later among others. Given that local conditions constantly shifted in a myriad of ways and that the ambitions and abilities of successive leaders undoubtedly varied, the organizational changes of individual polities could have followed different trajectories and produced different outcomes. Some paths may have been dead ends; others may have been characterized by fits and starts; and still others may have involved continuous, steady change. For those polities that followed the same path, some may have become more complex than others or equally complex but in different ways.

Another topic for future research is my prediction that incipient complexity was also a regional phenomenon. The evidence to support this claim is sketchy in comparison with the well-documented distributions of ball courts, platform mounds, and great houses. More research is needed to identify and study transitional sites to determine whether my explanation applies equally well to already complex polities that are becoming even more complex and egalitarian societies that are experiencing the beginnings of social differentiation.

More comparisons are essential for explaining the relationship between complexity and regions in middle-range societies. This chapter has identified some general similarities and differences for the Hohokam and Chacoan cases, but more in-depth comparisons remain to be done between individual Hohokam polities through time and between individual Chacoan polities through time. The results will provide a much more thorough understanding of the ways in which the Hohokam and Chacoan cases were the same and different.

Future comparisons of the relationship between complexity and regions also need to include more cases from the Southwest and elsewhere, especially ones located in more optimal environments than the Hohokam and Chacoans. In addition, it would be illuminating to see if any cases can be identified that contradict the entire notion of complexity as a regional phenomenon in middle-range societies—examples of complex polities that either existed alone in the midst of more egalitarian groups or had similarly organized neighbors with whom they did not interact.

Difficulties

Future research on the relationship between complexity and regions will have to address difficulties involving the typological approach and archaeological visibility. Despite its long history of criticism, the typological approach continues to thrive in studies of how ancient peoples were organized (Neitzel 2006). For example, many recent discussions of leadership strategies have replaced the typological question that Nelson (1995) skewered (was this case complex or not?) with another (was leadership in this case corporate or network?). Treating the corporate and network strategies as mutually exclusive obscures the complicated and dynamic nature of leadership. As originally described by Blanton et al. (1996), leaders generally rely on both strategies in varying proportions and with varying degrees of intensity, and they constantly strive to achieve the most effective combination in the midst of continually changing environmental, economic, and interpersonal situations (see Craig and Henderson 2007). The consequence for archaeologists is that material evidence for the corporate and network strategies is rarely clear-cut. In the Hohokam and Chacoan cases, platform mounds and great houses functioned both as elite residences thought to reflect the network strategy and as ceremonial structures indicative of the corporate strategy. Archaeologists must grapple with what this mixed evidence indicates about how the two strategies were merged and with what degree of intensity.

Researchers must also confront problems of visibility. Some evidence, such as textiles and other perishable materials, may not be preserved (Bayman 2007), and some activities associated with organizational hierarchies (e.g., speech and etiquette) may involve no materials at all. Such gaps in the archaeological record may cause researchers to understate the degree of complexity in polities with well-established hierarchies.

Visibility difficulties are compounded for cases of incipient complexity. Especially challenging is the task of locating transitional sites, which are generally small in size, lack imposing structures to draw the attention of archaeologists, and may be buried beneath larger, more imposing settlements. Also, given that the material correlates of emerging leaders were certainly less conspicuous than those of their well-established successors, researchers risk dating the transition from egalitarian to non-egalitarian organizations later than it actually occurred. This problem would be exacerbated by the application of societal types, which because of their inability to accommodate variation always obscure nascent or transitional developments.

Conclusion

Complexity and regions seem to be inextricably linked in middle-range societies. As illustrated by the Hohokam and Chacoan cases, hierarchically organized polities generally do not exist alone in the midst of landscapes filled with egalitarian groups. Instead, if one polity has a sociopolitical hierarchy, then its neighbors will also, as will their neighbors, and perhaps their neighbors as well. These polities tend to be complex in similar but not identical ways, varying perhaps in the degree of differentiation in their respective hierarchies or in the strategies employed by their leaders. Together they encompass broad regions that coincide to varying degrees with the distributions of ceremonial architecture, decorated ceramics, and trade goods.

This chapter has explored why complexity and regions are connected. More than two decades ago, Renfrew (1986) convincingly attributed the organizational and other similarities shared by neighboring chiefdoms and early states to their long histories of what he called peer polity interaction, which could involve trade, religion, and competitive emulation. He also explained the development of the institutions associated with more complex polities as the result of increasing population, agricultural intensification, and craft specialization within the context of peer polity interaction.

My goal here has been to refine Renfrew's ideas in light of more recent developments in archaeology. I have noted that emulation may not always be competitive, and I have identified other factors that can contribute to the development of institutions associated with complexity—environmental characteristics, leadership strategies, historical contingency, and macroregional interaction. My major conclusion is that complexity in middle-range societies was often associated with multiple, neighboring polities because the preconditions for complexity encompassed broad regions and because the leadership strategies employed in one polity could affect the strategies used in others. For these same reasons, I have also argued that the association between complexity and regions may have characterized simpler societies, including those undergoing the initial transition from egalitarian to non-egalitarian sociopolitical organization.

Archaeological approaches to the topics of complexity and regions have undergone significant changes throughout the history of Southwest archaeology. An interest in regions came first. Later, as new perspectives were applied to regions, questions about how past peoples were organized began to be asked, leading eventually to the issue of complexity. The focus of many early complexity studies on cases that encompassed broad regions joined the two previously separate research tracks. But this balanced synergy did not last long. With its many controversies, complexity research expanded exponentially, eclipsing regions, which became just one of a number of scales to investigate for evidence of organizational hierarchies.

This chapter has highlighted the mutual, dynamic relationship between complexity and regions. Regions are not just one more scale where evidence for complexity can be found, and they are not just the aggregate of what happens within the individual polities they encompass. Rather, many characteristics of regions are in fact major contributors to the development of complexity within individual polities. If we want to expand our understanding of middle-range societies in the Southwest and elsewhere, we should give regions and complexity equal consideration as we continue to explore the complicated links between them.

Notes

1. In this chapter I arbitrarily use the label Classic period Hohokam to refer to all sites with platform mounds. My primary concern is the structures and the polities associated with them and not the various labels (e.g., Salado) that archaeologists have given them, which is a subject for another work.
2. I am assuming here that great houses are the Chacoan diagnostic and not great kivas, which appeared earlier and lasted longer in modified forms (see Van Dyke 2007, 2008).
3. Previous applications of Renfrew's model to the Chacoan case can be seen in Kantner (1996), Kintigh (1994), and Wilcox (2002).

References

Abbott, D. R.
2000   *Ceramics and Community Organization among the Hohokam*. University of Arizona Press, Tucson.

Abbott, D. R., A. M. Smith, and E. Gallaga
2007   Ballcourts and Ceramics: The Case for Hohokam Marketplaces in the Arizona Desert. *American Antiquity* 72(3):461–484.

Adler, M. A. (editor)
1996   *The Prehistoric Pueblo World, AD 1150–1350*. University of Arizona Press, Tucson.

Adler, M. A., and R. H. Wilshusen
1990   Large-Scale Integrative Facilities in Tribal Societies: Cross-cultural and Southwestern U.S. Examples. *World Archaeology* 22(2): 133–146.

Andrews, J. P., and T. W. Bostwick
2006   *Desert Farmers at the River's Edge: The Hohokam and Pueblo Grande*. City of Phoenix, Phoenix.

Bahr, D. M.
2007   O'odham Traditions about the Hohokam. In *The Hohokam Millennium*, edited by S. K. Fish and P. R. Fish, pp. 122–129. School for Advanced Research Press, Santa Fe.

Bahr, D. M., J. Smith, W. A. Allison, and J. Hayden
1994   *The Short Swift Time of Gods on Earth: The Hohokam Chronicles*. University of California Press, Berkeley.

Bayman, J. M.
2002   Hohokam Craft Economies and the Materialization of Power. *Journal of Archaeological Method and Theory* 9(1):69–95.

2007   Artisans and Their Crafts in Hohokam Society. In *The Hohokam Millennium*, edited by S. K. Fish and P. R. Fish, pp. 74–81. School for Advanced Research Press, Santa Fe.

Binford, L. R.
1962   Archaeology as Anthropology. *American Antiquity* 28(2):217–225.

Blanton, R. E., G. M. Feinman, S. A. Kowalewski, and P. N. Peregrine
1996   A Dual-Processual Theory for the Evolution of Mesoamerican Civilization. *Current Anthropology* 37(1):1–14.

Bohrer, V. L.
1970   Ethnobotanical Aspects of Snaketown, a Hohokam Village in Southern Arizona. *American Antiquity* 35(4):413–430.

Bostwick, T. W., and P. Krocek
2002   *Landscape of the Spirits: Hohokam Rock Art at South Mountain Park*. University of Arizona Press, Tucson.

Bradley, R. J.
1993   Marine Shell Exchange in Northwest Mexico and the Southwest. In *The American Southwest and Mesoamerica: Systems of Prehistoric Exchange*, edited by J. E. Ericson and T. G. Baugh, pp. 121–151. Plenum Press, New York.

Brandt, E. A.
1994   Egalitarianism, Hierarchy, and Centralization in the Pueblos. In *The Ancient Southwestern Community: Models and Methods for the Study of Prehistoric Social Organization*, edited by W. H. Wills and R. D. Leonard, pp. 9–24. University of New Mexico Press, Albuquerque.

Brew, J. O.
1946   *The Archaeology of Alkali Ridge, Southeastern Utah, with a Review of the Prehistory of the Mesa Verde Division of the San Juan and Some Observations on Archaeological Systematics*. Papers of the Peabody Museum of American Archaeology and Ethnology Vol. 21. Harvard University, Cambridge.

Cable, J. S., and D. E. Doyel
1987   Pioneer Period Village Structure and Settlement Pattern in the Phoenix Basin. In *The Hohokam Village: Site Structure and Organization*, edited by D. E. Doyel, pp. 21–70. Southwestern and Rocky Mountain Division of the American Association for the Advancement of Science, Glenwood Springs, Colorado.

Cameron, C. M.
1997   The Chipped Stone of Chaco Canyon, New Mexico. In *Ceramics, Lithics, and Ornaments of Chaco Canyon: Analyses of Artifacts from the Chaco Project, 1971–1978*, edited by F. J. Mathien, pp. 997–1102. Publications in

Archeology No. 18G. National Park Service, Santa Fe.

2001   Pink Chert, Projectile Points, and the Chacoan Regional System. *American Antiquity* 66(1):79–102.

Clark, G. A.
1969   Preliminary Analysis of Burial Clusters at the Grasshopper Site, East-Central Arizona. *Kiva* 35(1):57–90.

Cobb, C. R., J. Maymon, and R. H. McGuire
1999   Feathered, Horned, and Antlered Serpents: Mesoamerican Connections with the Southwest and Southeast. In *Great Towns and Regional Polities in the Prehistoric American Southwest and Southeast*, edited by J. E. Neitzel, pp. 165–181. University of New Mexico Press, Albuquerque.

Cordell, L. S., and G. J. Gumerman (editors)
1989   *Dynamics of Southwest Prehistory*. Smithsonian Institution Press, Washington, D.C.

Cordell, L. S., and F. Plog
1979   Escaping the Confines of Normative Thought: A Reevaluation of Puebloan Prehistory. *American Antiquity* 44(3):405–429.

Craig, D. B., and T. K. Henderson
2007   Houses, Households, and Household Organization. In *The Hohokam Millennium*, edited by S. K. Fish and P. R. Fish, pp. 30–37. School for Advanced Research Press, Santa Fe.

Crown, P. L.
1991   The Role of Exchange and Interaction in Salt–Gila Basin Hohokam Prehistory. In *Exploring Hohokam: Prehistoric Desert Peoples of the American Southwest*, edited by G. J. Gumerman, pp. 383–415. University of New Mexico Press, Albuquerque.
1994   *Ceramics and Ideology: Salado Polychrome Pottery*. University of New Mexico Press, Albuquerque.

Crown, P. L., and W. J. Judge (editors)
1991   *Chaco and Hohokam: Prehistoric Regional Systems in the American Southwest*. School of American Research Press, Santa Fe.

Damp, J. E., and E. M. Kotyk
2000   Socioeconomic Organization of a Late Basketmaker Community in the Mexican Springs Area, Southwestern Chuska Mountains, New Mexico. In *Foundations of Anasazi Culture: The Basketmaker-Pueblo Transition*, edited by P. F. Reed, pp. 95–114. University of Utah Press, Salt Lake City.

Dean, J. S.
1991   Thoughts on Hohokam Chronology. In *Exploring Hohokam: Prehistoric Desert Peoples of the American Southwest*, edited by

G. J. Gumerman, pp. 61–149. University of New Mexico Press, Albuquerque.

1992   Environmental Factors in the Evolution of the Chacoan Sociopolitical System. In *Anasazi Regional Organization and the Chaco System*, edited by D. E. Doyel, pp. 35–43. Anthropological Papers No. 5. Maxwell Museum of Anthropology, Albuquerque.

Dean, J. S., R. C. Euler, G. J. Gumerman, F. Plog, R. Hevly, and T. N. V. Karlstrom
1985   Human Behavior, Demography, and Paleoenvironment on the Colorado Plateaus. *American Antiquity* 50(3):537–554.

Dean, J. S., G. J. Gumerman, J. M. Epstein, R. L. Axtell, A. C. Swedlund, M. T. Parker, and S. McCarroll
2000   Understanding Anasazi Culture Change through Agent-Based Modeling. In *Dynamics in Human and Primate Societies: Agent-Based Modeling of Social and Spatial Processes*, edited by T. A. Kohler and G. J. Gumerman, pp. 179–205. Oxford University Press, New York.

Doelle, W. H.
2007   Laws, Dollars, and Scholars: The Business of Hohokam Archaeology. In *The Hohokam Millennium*, edited by S. K Fish and P. R. Fish, pp. 109–115. School of Advanced Research Press, Santa Fe.

Doyel, D. E.
1974   *Excavations in the Escalante Ruin Group, Southern Arizona*. Archaeological Series No. 37. Arizona State Museum, Tucson.
1979   The Prehistoric Hohokam of the Arizona Desert. *American Scientist* 67(5):544–554.
1980   Hohokam Social Organization in the Sedentary to Classic Transition. In *Current Issues in Hohokam Prehistory: Proceedings of a Symposium*, edited by D. Doyel and F. Plog, pp. 23–40. Anthropological Research Papers No. 23. Arizona State University, Tempe.
2007   Irrigation, Production, and Power in Phoenix Basin Hohokam Society. In *The Hohokam Millennium*, edited by S. K. Fish and P. R. Fish, pp. 82–89. School for Advanced Research Press, Santa Fe.

Drennan, R. D.
1991   Pre-Hispanic Chiefdom Trajectories in Mesoamerica, Central America, and Northern South America. In *Chiefdoms: Power, Economy, and Ideology*, edited by T. K. Earle, pp. 263–287. Cambridge University Press, Cambridge.

Earle, T. K.
1978   *Economic and Social Organization of a Complex Chiefdom: The Halelea District, Kaua'i, Hawaii*. Anthropological Papers No. 63. Uni-

versity of Michigan Museum of Anthropology, Ann Arbor.

1991   Economic Support of Chaco Canyon Society. *American Antiquity* 66(1):26–35.

Eggan, F.

1950   *Social Organization of the Western Pueblos.* University of Chicago Press, Chicago.

Ellis, F. H.

1967   Where Did the Pueblo People Come From? *El Palacio* 74(3):35–43.

Elson, M. D.

1998   *Expanding the View of Hohokam Platform Mounds: An Ethnographic Perspective.* Anthropological Papers of the University of Arizona No. 63. University of Arizona Press, Tucson.

2007   Into the Earth and Up to the Sky: Hohokam Ritual Architecture. In *The Hohokam Millennium*, edited by S. K. Fish and P. R. Fish, pp. 48–55. School for Advanced Research Press, Santa Fe.

Elson, M. D., and D. R. Abbott

2000   Organizational Variability in Platform Mound-Building Groups of the American Southwest. In *Alternative Leadership Strategies in the Prehispanic Southwest*, edited by B. J. Mills, pp. 117–135. University of Arizona Press, Tucson.

Euler, R. C., and G. J. Gumerman (editors)

1978   *Investigations of the Southwestern Anthropological Research Group.* Museum of Northern Arizona, Flagstaff.

Farmer, J. D.

2003   Astronomy and Ritual in Chaco Canyon. In *Pueblo Bonito: Center of the Chacoan World*, edited by J. E. Neitzel, pp. 61–71. Smithsonian Institution Press, Washington, D.C.

Feinman, G. M., K. G. Lightfoot, and S. Upham

2000   Political Hierarchies and Organizational Strategies in the Puebloan Southwest. *American Antiquity* 65(3):449–470.

Feinman, G. M., and J. E. Neitzel

1984   Too Many Types: An Overview of Sedentary Prestate Societies in the Americas. In *Advances in Archaeological Method and Theory*, Vol. 7, edited by M. B. Schiffer, pp. 39–102. Academic Press, New York.

Ferguson, T. J., and E. R. Hart

1985   *A Zuni Atlas.* University of Oklahoma Press, Norman.

Fish, Paul R., Suzanne K. Fish, Austin Long, and Charles Miksicek

1986   Early Corn Remains from Tumamoc Hill, Southern Arizona. *American Antiquity* 51(3): 563–572.

Fish, S. K., and P. R. Fish

2007   The Hohokam Millennium. In *The Hohokam Millennium*, edited by S. K. Fish and P. R. Fish, pp. 1–12. School for Advanced Research Press, Santa Fe.

Fried, M. H.

1967   *The Evolution of Political Society: An Essay in Political Anthropology.* Random House, New York.

1975   *The Notion of Tribe.* Cummings, Menlo Park, California.

Gasser, R. E., and S. M. Kwiatkowski

1991   Food for Thought: Recognizing Patterns in Hohokam Subsistence. In *Exploring Hohokam: Prehistoric Desert Peoples of the American Southwest*, edited by G. J. Gumerman, pp. 417–459. University of New Mexico Press, Albuquerque.

Gilman, A.

1991   Trajectories towards Social Complexity in the Later Prehistory of the Mediterranean. In *Chiefdoms: Power, Economy, and Ideology*, edited by T. K. Earle, pp. 146–168. Cambridge University Press, Cambridge.

Gladwin, H. S., E. W. Haury, E. B. Sayles, and N. Gladwin

1937   *Excavations at Snaketown: Material Culture.* Gila Pueblo Medallion Papers No. 25. Globe, Arizona.

Gladwin, W., and H. S. Gladwin

1929a   *The Red-on-Buff Culture of the Gila Basin.* Gila Pueblo Medallion Papers No. 3. Globe, Arizona.

1929b   *The Red-on-Buff Culture of the Papagueria.* Gila Pueblo Medallion Papers No. 4. Globe, Arizona.

1930a   *The Western Range of the Red-on-Buff Culture.* Gila Pueblo Medallion Papers No. 5. Globe, Arizona.

1930b   *Some Southwestern Pottery Types, Series I.* Gila Pueblo Medallion Papers No. 8. Globe, Arizona.

1935   *The Eastern Range of the Red-on-Buff Culture.* Gila Pueblo Medallion Papers No. 16. Globe, Arizona.

Goldman, I.

1970   *Ancient Polynesian Society.* University of Chicago Press, Chicago.

Graybill, D. A., D. A. Gregory, G. S. Funkshouser, and F. L. Nials

2006   Long-Term Streamflow Reconstructions, River Channel Morphology, and Aboriginal Irrigation Systems along the Salt and Gila Rivers. In *Environmental Change and Human Adaptation in the Ancient American*

Southwest, edited by D. E. Doyel and J. S. Dean, pp. 69–123. University of Utah Press, Salt Lake City.

Graybill, D. A., and F. L. Nials
1989 Aspects of Climate, Streamflow, and Geomorphology Affecting Irrigation Systems in the Salt River Valley. In *The 1982–1984 Excavations at Las Colinas: Environment and Subsistence*, edited by C. A. Heathington and D. A. Gregory, pp. 39–58. Archaeological Series No. 162. Arizona State Museum, Tucson.

Grebinger, P.
1973 Prehistoric Social Organization in Chaco Canyon, New Mexico: An Alternative Reconstruction. *Kiva* 39(1):3–23.

Gregory, D. A.
1987 The Morphology of Platform Mounds and the Structure of Classic Period Hohokam Sites. In *The Hohokam Village: Site Structure and Organization*, edited by D. E. Doyel, pp. 183–210. Southwestern and Rocky Mountain Division of the American Association for the Advancement of Science, Glenwood Springs, Colorado.

Gregory, D., and F. L. Nials
1985 Observations Concerning the Distribution of Classic Period Hohokam Platform Mounds. In *Proceedings of the 1983 Hohokam Conference*, edited by A. E. Dittert and D. E. Dove, pp. 373–388. Occasional Paper No. 2. Arizona Archaeological Society, Phoenix.

Griffin, P. B.
1967 A High-Status Burial from Grasshopper Ruin, Arizona. *Kiva* 33(1):37–53.

Grissino-Mayer, H. D.
1996 A 2129-Year Reconstruction of Precipitation for Northwestern New Mexico, USA. In *Tree Rings, Environment, and Humanity: Radiocarbon 1996*, edited by J. S. Dean, D. M. Meko, and T. W. Swetnam, pp. 191–204. Department of Geological Sciences, University of Arizona, Tucson.

Gumerman, G. J. (editor)
1994 *Themes in Southwest Prehistory*. School of American Research Press, Santa Fe.

Gumerman, G. J., and M. Gell-Mann (editors)
1994 *Understanding Complexity in the Prehistoric Southwest*. Addison-Wesley, Reading, Massachusetts.

Haas, J., E. J. Ladd, J. E. Levy, R. H. McGuire, and N. Yoffee
1994 Historical Processes in the Prehistoric Southwest. In *Understanding Complexity in the Prehistoric Southwest*, edited by G. J. Gumerman

and M. Gell-Mann, pp. 203–232. Addison-Wesley, Reading, Massachusetts.

Haury, E. W.
1945 *The Excavation of Los Muertos and Neighboring Ruins in the Salt River Valley, Southern Arizona*. Papers of the Peabody Museum of American Archaeology and Ethnology Vol. 24, No. 1. Harvard University, Cambridge.
1976 *The Hohokam, Desert Farmers and Craftsmen: Excavations at Snaketown, 1964–1965*. University of Arizona Press, Tucson.

Hayes, A. C.
1981 A Survey of Chaco Canyon. In *Archaeological Surveys of Chaco Canyon, New Mexico*, by A. C. Hayes, D. M. Brugge, and W. J. Judge, pp. 1–68. Publications in Archeology No. 18A. National Park Service, Washington, D.C.

Henrich, J.
2006 Cooperation, Punishment, and the Evolution of Human Institutions. *Science* 312(5770):60–61.

Henrich, J., and R. Boyd
2008 Division of Labor, Economic Specialization, and the Evolution of Social Stratification. *Current Anthropology* 49(4):715–724.

Hill, J. B., J. J. Clark, W. H. Doelle, and P. D. Lyons
2005 Prehistoric Demography in the Southwest: Migration, Coalescence, and Hohokam Population Decline. *American Antiquity* 69(4):689–716.

Hill, J. N.
1970 *Broken K Pueblo: Prehistoric Social Organization in the American Southwest*. Anthropological Papers of the University of Arizona No. 18. University of Arizona Press, Tucson.

Howell, T. L.
1995 Tracking Zuni Gender and Leadership Roles across the Contact Period in the Zuni Region. *Journal of Anthropological Research* 51(2):125–147.

Jacobs, D.
1997 *A Salado Platform Mound on Tonto Creek, Roosevelt Platform Mound Study: Report on the Cline Terrace Mound, Cline Terrace Complex*. Anthropological Field Studies No. 36. Arizona State University, Tempe.

Johnson, G. A.
1989 Dynamics of Southwestern Prehistory: Far Outside—Looking In. In *Dynamics of Southwest Prehistory*, edited by L. S. Cordell and G. J. Gumerman, pp. 371–389. Smithsonian Institution Press, Washington, D.C.

Judge, W. J.
1979 The Development of a Complex Cultural Ecosystem in the Chaco Basin, New Mexico.

In *Proceedings of the First Conference on Scientific Research in the National Parks*, Vol. 2, edited by R. M. Linn, pp. 901–906. Transactions and Proceedings Series No. 5. National Park Service, Washington, D.C.

1989   Chaco Canyon–San Juan Basin. In *Dynamics of Southwest Prehistory*, edited by L. S. Cordell and G. J. Gumerman, pp. 209–261. Smithsonian Institution Press, Washington, D.C.

Judge, W. J., and J. D. Schelberg (editors)

1984   *Recent Research on Chaco Prehistory*. Reports of the Chaco Center No. 8. National Park Service, Albuquerque.

Kantner, J.

1996   Political Competition among the Chaco Anasazi in the American Southwest. *Journal of Anthropological Archaeology* 15(1):41–105.

Kidder, A. V.

1924   *An Introduction to the Study of Southwestern Archaeology, with a Preliminary Account of Excavations at Pecos*. Yale University Press, New Haven.

1927   Southwestern Archaeological Conference. *Science* 66(1716):489–491.

Kintigh, K. W.

1994   Chaco, Communal Architecture, and Cibolan Aggregation. In *The Ancient Southwestern Community: Models and Methods for the Study of Prehistoric Social Organization*, edited by W. H. Wills and R. D. Leonard, pp. 131–140. University of New Mexico Press, Albuquerque.

Kohler, T. A., M. P. Glaude, J. P. Bocquet-Appel, and B. M. Kemp

2008   The Neolithic Demographic Transition in the U.S. Southwest. *American Antiquity* 73(4): 645–669.

Kohler, T. A., C. D. Johnson, M. Varien, S. Ortman, R. Reynolds, Z. Kobti, J. Cowan, K. Kolm, S. Smith, and L. Yap

2007   Settlement Ecodynamics in the Prehispanic Central Mesa Verde Region. In *The Model-Based Archaeology of Socionatural Systems*, edited by T. A. Kohler and S. E. van der Leeuw, pp. 61–104. School for Advanced Research Press, Santa Fe.

Kohler, T. A., J. Kresl, C. Van West, E. Carr, and R. W. Wilshusen

2000   Be There Then: A Modeling Approach to Settlement Determinants and Spatial Efficiency among Late Ancestral Pueblo Populations of the Mesa Verde Region, U.S. Southwest. In *Dynamics in Human and Primate Societies: Agent-Based Modeling of Social and Spatial Processes*, edited by T. A. Kohler and G. J. Gumerman, pp. 145–178. Oxford University Press, New York.

Lagasse, P. F., W. B. Gillespie, and K. G. Eggert

1984   Hydraulic Engineering Analysis of Prehistoric Water-Control Systems at Chaco Canyon. In *Recent Research on Chaco Prehistory*, edited by W. J. Judge and J. D. Schelberg, pp. 187–211. Reports of the Chaco Center No. 8. National Park Service, Albuquerque.

LeBlanc, S. A.

1999   *Prehistoric Warfare in the American Southwest*. University of Utah Press, Salt Lake City.

Lekson, Stephen H.

2008   *A History of the Ancient Southwest*. School for Advanced Research Press, Santa Fe.

Lekson, S. H. (editor)

2007   *The Architecture of Chaco Canyon, New Mexico*. University of Utah Press, Salt Lake City.

Lekson, S. H., and C. M. Cameron

1995   The Abandonment of Chaco Canyon, the Mesa Verde Migrations, and the Reorganization of the Pueblo World. *Journal of Anthropological Archaeology* 14(2):184–202.

Levy, J. E.

1992   *Orayvi Revisited: Social Stratification in an "Egalitarian" Society*. School of American Research Press, Santa Fe.

Lightfoot, K. G.

1984   *Prehistoric Political Dynamics: A Case Study from the American Southwest*. Northern Illinois University, De Kalb.

Lightfoot, K. G., and G. M. Feinman

1982   Social Differentiation and Leadership Development in Early Pithouse Villages in the Mogollon Region of the American Southwest. *American Antiquity* 47(1):64–86.

Lightfoot, K. G., and S. Upham

1989   Complex Societies in the Prehistoric American Southwest: A Consideration of the Controversy. In *The Sociopolitical Structure of Prehistoric Southwestern Societies*, edited by S. Upham, K. G. Lightfoot, and R. A. Jewett, pp. 3–30. Westview Press, Boulder, Colorado.

Longacre, W. A.

1970   *Archaeology as Anthropology: A Case Study*. Anthropological Papers of the University of Arizona No. 17. University of Arizona, Tucson.

Longacre, W. A. (editor)

1970   *Reconstructing Prehistoric Pueblo Societies*. University of New Mexico Press, Albuquerque.

Lopez, D.

2007   Huhugam. In *The Hohokam Millennium*,

edited by S. K. Fish and P. R. Fish, pp. 116–121. School for Advanced Research Press, Santa Fe.

Marshall, M. P., J. R. Stein, R. W. Loose, and J. E. Novotny

1979   *Anasazi Communities of the San Juan Basin.* Public Service Company of New Mexico, Albuquerque, and New Mexico Historic Preservation Bureau, Santa Fe.

Martin, P. S., and F. Plog

1973   *The Archaeology of Arizona: A Study of the Southwest Region.* Natural History Press, Garden City, New York.

Mathien, F. J.

1997   Ornaments of the Chaco Anasazi. In *Ceramics, Lithics, and Ornaments of Chaco Canyon: Analyses of Artifacts from the Chaco Project, 1971–1978,* edited by F. J. Mathien, pp. 1119–1220. Publications in Archeology No. 18G. National Park Service, Santa Fe.

2001   The Organization of Turquoise Production and Consumption by the Prehistoric Chacoans. *American Antiquity* 66(1):103–118.

2003   Artifacts from Pueblo Bonito: One Hundred Years of Interpretation. In *Pueblo Bonito: Center of the Chacoan World,* edited by J. E. Neitzel, pp. 127–142. Smithsonian Institution Press, Washington, D.C.

2005   *Culture and Ecology of Chaco Canyon and the San Juan Basin.* Publications in Archeology No. 18H. National Park Service, Santa Fe.

Mathien, F. J., and R. H. McGuire (editors)

1986   *Ripples in the Chichimec Sea: New Considerations of Southwestern-Mesoamerican Interaction.* Southern Illinois University Press, Carbondale.

McGregor, J. C.

1943   Burial of an Early American Magician. *Proceedings of the American Philosophical Society* 86:270–298.

McGuire, R. H.

1980   The Mesoamerican Connection in the Southwest. *Kiva* 46(1):3–38.

1994   Historical Processes and Southwestern Prehistory: A Position Paper. In *Understanding Complexity in the Prehistoric Southwest,* edited by G. J. Gumerman and M. Gell-Mann, pp. 193–201. Addison-Wesley, Reading, Massachusetts.

McGuire, R. H., E. C. Adams, B. A. Nelson, and K. A. Spielman

1994   Drawing the Southwest to Scale: Perspectives on Macroregional Relations. In *Themes in Southwest Prehistory,* edited by G. J. Gumer-

man, pp. 239–265. School of American Research Press, Santa Fe.

McGuire, R. H., and A. V. Howard

1987   The Structure and Organization of Hohokam Shell Exchange. *Kiva* 52(2):113–146.

McGuire, R. H., and D. J. Saitta

1996   Although They Have Petty Captains, They Obey Them Badly: The Dialectics of Prehispanic Western Pueblo Social Organization. *American Antiquity* 61(2):197–216.

McGuire, R. H., and E. C. Villalpando

2007   The Hohokam and Mesoamerica. In *The Hohokam Millennium,* edited by S. K. Fish and P. R. Fish, pp. 56–63. School for Advanced Research Press, Santa Fe.

Mills, B. J. (editor)

2000   *Alternative Leadership Strategies in the Prehispanic Southwest.* University of Arizona Press, Tucson.

Neitzel, J. E.

1989a   The Chacoan Regional System: Interpreting the Evidence for Sociopolitical Complexity. In *The Sociopolitical Structure of Prehistoric Southwestern Societies,* edited by S. Upham, K. G. Lightfoot, and R. A. Jewett, pp. 509–556. Westview Press, Boulder, Colorado.

1989b   Regional Exchange Networks in the American Southwest: A Comparative Analysis of Long-Distance Trade. In *The Sociopolitical Structure of Prehistoric Southwestern Societies,* edited by S. Upham, K. G. Lightfoot, and R. A. Jewett, pp. 149–195. Westview Press, Boulder, Colorado.

2000   Gender Hierarchies: A Comparative Analysis of Mortuary Data. In *Women and Men in the Prehispanic Southwest,* edited by P. L. Crown, pp. 137–168. School of American Research Press, Santa Fe.

2006   Still Too Many Types: A Comparison of Chiefdoms in the U.S. Southwest and Southeast. Paper presented at the 71st Annual Meeting of the Society for American Archaeology, San Juan, Puerto Rico.

In press Mixed Messages: Art and Leadership in the Late Prehispanic Southwest. In *Comparative Archaeologies: The American Southwest (ad 900–1600) and the Iberian Peninsula (3000–1500 bc),* edited by K. Lillios. Oxbow Books, Oxford.

Neitzel, J. E. (editor)

1999   *Great Towns and Regional Polities in the Prehistoric American Southwest and Southeast.* University of New Mexico Press, Albuquerque.

2003   *Pueblo Bonito: Center of the Chacoan World.*
        Smithsonian Books, Washington, D.C.
Nelson, B.
1995   Complexity, Hierarchy, and Scale: A Con-
        trolled Comparison between Chaco Canyon,
        New Mexico, and La Quemada, Zacatecas.
        American Antiquity 60(4):597–618.
Nials, F., D. Gregory, and D. Graybill
1989   Salt River Streamflow and Hohokam Irriga-
        tion Systems. In *The 1982–1984 Excavations
        at Las Colinas: Environment and Subsistence,*
        edited by C. Heathington and D. Gregory,
        pp. 59–78. Archaeological Series No. 162.
        Arizona State Museum, Tucson.
Nicholas, L. M., and J. E. Neitzel
1984   Canal Irrigation and Sociopolitical Organi-
        zation in the Lower Salt River Valley: A Dia-
        chronic Analysis. In *Prehistoric Agricultural
        Strategies of the Southwest,* edited by S. K.
        Fish and P. R. Fish, pp. 161–178. Anthropo-
        logical Research Papers No. 32. Arizona State
        University, Tempe.
Oberg, K.
1955   Types of Social Structure among the Lowland
        Tribes of South and Central America. *Ameri-
        can Anthropologist* 57(3):472–487.
Ortiz, A.
1969   *The Tewa World: Space, Time, Being, and
        Becoming in a Pueblo Society.* University of
        Chicago Press, Chicago.
Parsons, E. C.
1929   *The Social Organization of the Tewa.* Memoirs
        No. 36. American Anthropological Associa-
        tion, Washington, D.C.
Pauketat, T. R.
2007   *Chiefdoms and Other Archaeological Delu-
        sions.* AltaMira Press, Lanham, Maryland.
Peebles, C., and S. M. Kus
1977   Some Archaeological Correlates of Ranked
        Societies. *American Antiquity* 42(3):421–448.
Plog, F.
1974   *The Study of Prehistoric Change.* Academic
        Press, New York.
1980   Explaining Culture Change in the Hohokam
        Preclassic. In *Current Issues in Hohokam Pre-
        history: Proceedings of a Symposium,* edited
        by D. Doyel and F. Plog, pp. 4–22. Anthropo-
        logical Research Papers No. 23. Arizona State
        University, Tempe.
Plog, S.
2003   Exploring the Ubiquitous through the
        Unusual: Color Symbolism in Pueblo Black-
        on-White Pottery. *American Antiquity* 68(4):
        665–695.

Powers, R. P., W. B. Gillespie, and S. H. Lekson
1983   *The Outlier Survey: A Regional View of Settle-
        ment in the San Juan Basin.* Reports of the
        Chaco Center No. 3. National Park Service,
        Albuquerque.
Rautman, A. E.
1998   Hierarchy and Heterarchy in the American
        Southwest: A Comment on McGuire and
        Saitta. *American Antiquity* 63(2):325–333.
Ravesloot, J. C.
2007   Changing Views of Snaketown in a Larger
        Landscape. In *The Hohokam Millennium,*
        edited by S. K. Fish and P. R. Fish, pp. 90–97.
        School for Advanced Research Press,
        Santa Fe.
Ravesloot, J. C., and M. R. Waters
2002–2004 Geoarchaeology and Archaeological Site
        Patterning on the Middle Gila River, Ari-
        zona. *Journal of Field Archaeology* 29(1/2):
        203–214.
Reed, P. F. (editor)
2000   *Foundations of Anasazi Culture: The
        Basketmaker-Pueblo Transition.* University
        of Utah Press, Salt Lake City.
Renfrew, C.
1974   Beyond a Subsistence Economy: The Evolu-
        tion of Social Organization in Prehistoric
        Europe. In *Reconstructing Complex Societies:
        An Archaeological Colloquium,* edited by C. B.
        Moore, pp. 69–95. Bulletin No. 20. American
        Schools of Oriental Research, Cambridge,
        Massachusetts.
1986   Introduction: Peer Polity Interaction and
        Socio-Political Change. In *Peer Polity Inter-
        action and Socio-Political Change,* edited by
        C. Renfrew and J. F. Cherry, pp. 1–18. Cam-
        bridge University Press, Cambridge.
2001   Production and Consumption in a Sacred
        Economy: The Material Correlates of High
        Devotional Expression at Chaco Canyon.
        American Antiquity 66(1):14–25.
Reyman, J. E.
1987   Priests, Power, and Politics: Some Implica-
        tions of Socioceremonial Control. In *Astron-
        omy and Ceremony in the Prehistoric South-
        west,* edited by J. B. Carlson and W. J. Judge,
        pp. 121–148. Papers No. 2. Maxwell Museum
        of Anthropology, Albuquerque.
Rice, G. E., and S. A. LeBlanc (editors)
2001   *Deadly Landscapes: Case Studies in Prehis-
        toric Southwestern Warfare.* University of
        Utah Press, Salt Lake City.
Roberts, F. H. H., Jr.
1929   *Shabik'eshchee Village: A Late Basketmaker*

Site in Chaco Canyon, New Mexico. Bulletin No. 92. Bureau of American Ethnology, Washington, D.C.

Robins, M. R., and K. A. Hays-Gilpin
2000   The Bird in the Basket: Gender and Social Change in Basketmaker Iconography. In *Foundations of Anasazi Culture: The Basketmaker-Pueblo Transition*, edited by P. F. Reed, pp. 231–247. University of Utah Press, Salt Lake City.

Russell, F.
1908   *The Pima Indians.* Annual Report No. 26. Bureau of American Ethnology, Washington, D.C.

Sahlins, M. D.
1958   *Social Stratification in Polynesia.* University of Washington Press, Seattle.

Sanders, W. T., and D. L. Webster
1978   Unilinealism, Multilinealism and the Evolution of Complex Societies. In *Social Archaeology: Beyond Subsistence and Dating*, edited by C. L. Redman, M. J. Berman, E. V. Curtin, W. T. Langhorne, N. M. Versaggi, and J. C. Wasner, pp. 249–302. Academic Press, New York.

Schaafsma, P.
1986   *Indian Rock Art of the Southwest.* University of New Mexico Press, Albuquerque.

Sebastian, L.
1991   Sociopolitical Complexity and the Chaco System. In *Chaco and Hohokam: Prehistoric Regional Systems in the American Southwest*, edited by P. L. Crown and W. J. Judge, pp. 109–134. School of American Research Press, Santa Fe.

Service, E. R.
1962   *Primitive Social Organization.* Random House, New York.

Simmons, A. H.
2006   Early People, Early Maize, and Late Archaic Ecology in the Southwest. In *Environmental Change and Human Adaptation in the Ancient Southwest*, edited by D. E. Doyel and J. S. Dean, pp. 10–25. University of Utah Press, Salt Lake City.

Smith, E. A., and J. K. Choi
2007   The Emergence of Inequality in Small-Scale Societies: Simple Scenarios and Agent-Based Simulations. In *The Model-Based Archaeology of Socionatural Systems*, edited by T. A. Kohler and S. E. van der Leeuw, pp. 105–120. School for Advanced Research Press, Santa Fe.

Sofaer, A.
2007   The Primary Architecture of the Chacoan Culture: A Cosmological Expression. In *The*

Architecture of Chaco Canyon, New Mexico, edited by S. H. Lekson, pp. 225–254. University of Utah Press, Salt Lake City.

Stein, J. R., D. Ford, and R. Friedman
2003   Reconstructing Pueblo Bonito. In *Pueblo Bonito: Center of the Chacoan World*, edited by J. E. Neitzel, pp. 33–60. Smithsonian Books, Washington, D.C.

Stein, J. R., and S. H. Lekson
1992   Anasazi Ritual Landscapes. In *Anasazi Regional Organization and the Chaco System*, edited by D. E. Doyel, pp. 87–100. Anthropological Papers No. 5. Maxwell Museum of Anthropology, Albuquerque.

Steponaitis, V. P.
1978   Location Theory and Complex Chiefdoms: A Mississippian Example. In *Mississippian Settlement Patterns*, edited by B. Smith, pp. 417–453. Academic Press, New York.

Steward, J. H.
1949   South American Cultures: An Interpretive Summary. In *The Comparative Ethnology of South American Indians*, Vol. 5 of *Handbook of South American Indians*, edited by J. H. Steward. Bulletin 143:669–772. Bureau of American Ethnology, Washington, D.C.

1955   *Theory of Culture Change.* University of Illinois Press, Urbana.

Taylor, D.
1975   Some Locational Aspects of Middle-Range Hierarchical Societies. Unpublished Ph.D. dissertation, Department of Anthropology, City University of New York, New York.

Taylor, W. W., Jr.
1948   *A Study of Archaeology.* Memoirs No. 69. American Anthropological Association, Menasha, Wisconsin.

Thomas, C. M., and J. H. King
1985   Hohokam Figurine Assemblages: A Suggested Ritual Context. In *Proceedings of the 1983 Hohokam Symposium, Part II*, edited by A. E. Dittert and D. E. Dove, pp. 687–732. Occasional Paper No. 2. Arizona Archaeological Society, Phoenix.

Titiev, M.
1944   *Old Oraibi: A Study of the Hopi Indians of Third Mesa.* Papers of the Peabody Museum of American Archaeology and Ethnology Vol. 22, No. 1. Harvard University, Cambridge.

Toll, H. W.
1985   Pottery, Production, Public Architecture and the Chaco Anasazi System. Unpublished Ph.D. dissertation, Department of Anthropology, University of Colorado, Boulder.

2001   Making and Breaking Pots in the Chaco World. *American Antiquity* 66(1):56–78.

Upham, S.
1982   *Polities and Power: An Economic and Political History of the Western Pueblo.* Academic Press, New York.
1987   The Tyranny of Ethnographic Analogy in Southwestern Archaeology. In *Coasts, Plains, and Deserts: Essays in Honor of Reynold J. Ruppe,* edited by S. W. Gaines, pp. 265–281. Anthropological Research Papers No. 38. Arizona State University, Tempe.

Upham, S., and G. E. Rice
1980   Up the Canal without a Pattern: Modeling Hohokam Interaction and Exchange. In *Current Issues in Hohokam Prehistory: Proceedings of a Symposium,* edited by D. Doyel and F. Plog, pp. 78–105. Anthropological Research Papers No. 23. Arizona State University, Tempe.

Van Dyke, R. M.
2007   Great Kivas in Time, Space, and Society. In *The Architecture of Chaco Canyon, New Mexico,* edited by S. H. Lekson, pp. 93–126. University of Utah Press, Salt Lake City.
2008   *Experiencing Chaco: Landscape and Ideology at the Center Place.* School for Advanced Research Press, Santa Fe.

Vivian, R. G.
1970   An Inquiry into Prehistoric Social Organization in Chaco Canyon, New Mexico. In *Reconstructing Pueblo Societies,* edited by W. A. Longacre, pp. 59–83. University of New Mexico Press, Albuquerque.
1974   Conservation and Diversion: Water-Control Systems in the Anasazi Southwest. In *Irrigation's Impact on Society,* edited by T. E. Downing and M. Gibson, pp. 95–112. Anthropological Papers of the University of Arizona No. 25. University of Arizona Press, Tucson.
1990   *The Chacoan Prehistory of the San Juan Basin.* Academic Press, San Diego.

Wallace, H. D.
2003   *Roots of Sedentism: Archaeological Excavations at Valencia Vieja, a Founding Village in the Tucson Basin of Southern Arizona.* Anthropological Papers No. 29. Center for Desert Archaeology, Tucson.
2007   Hohokam Beginnings. In *The Hohokam Millennium,* edited by S. K. Fish and P. R. Fish, pp. 12–21. School for Advanced Research Press, Santa Fe.

Waters, M. R.
2006   Prehistoric Human Response to Landscape Change in the American Southwest. In *Environmental Change and Human Adaptation in the Ancient American Southwest,* edited by D. E. Doyel and J. S. Dean, pp. 26–45. University of Utah Press, Salt Lake City.

Waters, M. R., and J. C. Ravesloot
2001   Landscape Change and the Evolution of the Hohokam along the Middle Gila River and Other River Valleys in South-Central Arizona. *American Antiquity* 66(2):285–299.

Weigand, P. C., and G. Harbottle
1993   The Role of Turquoise in the Ancient Mesoamerican Trade Structure. In *The American Southwest and Mesoamerica: Systems of Prehistoric Exchange,* edited by J. E. Ericson and T. G. Baugh, pp. 159–177. Plenum Press, New York.

White, Leslie
1959   *The Evolution of Culture.* McGraw-Hill, New York.

Whiteley, P. M.
1988   *Deliberate Acts: Changing Hopi Culture through the Oraibi Split.* University of Arizona Press, Tucson.

Whittlesey, S. M.
2007   Hohokam Ceramics, Hohokam Beliefs. In *The Hohokam Millennium,* edited by S. K. Fish and P. R. Fish, pp. 64–73. School for Advanced Research Press, Santa Fe.

Wilcox, D. R.
1976   How the Pueblos Came to Be as They Are: The Problem Today. Preliminary exam paper. Arizona State Museum Library, University of Arizona, Tucson.
1979   The Hohokam Regional System. In *Archaeological Test of Sites in the Gila Butte–Santan Region, South-Central Arizona,* by G. E. Rice, D. R. Wilcox, K. Rafferty, and J. Schoenwetter, pp. 77–116. Anthropological Research Papers No. 18. Arizona State University, Tempe.
1987   The Evolution of Hohokam Ceremonial Systems. In *Astronomy and Ceremony in the Prehistoric Southwest,* edited by J. B. Carlson and W. J. Judge, pp. 149–167. Papers No. 2. Maxwell Museum of Anthropology, Albuquerque.
1991a   Hohokam Social Complexity. In *Chaco and Hohokam: Prehistoric Regional Systems in the American Southwest,* edited by P. L. Crown and W. J. Judge, pp. 252–275. School of American Research Press, Santa Fe.
1991b   The Mesoamerican Ballgame in the American Southwest. In *The Mesoamerican Ballgame,* edited by V. L. Scarborough and D. R. Wilcox, pp. 101–125. University of Arizona Press, Tucson.

2002 The Wupatki Nexus: Chaco-Hohokam-Chumash Connectivity, AD 1150–1225. In *The Archaeology of Contact: Processes and Consequences*, edited by K. Lesick, B. Kulle, C. Cluney, and M. Peuramaki-Brown, pp. 218–234. Proceedings of the 25th Annual Chacmool Conference, Archaeological Association of the University of Calgary, Calgary, Alberta.

Wilcox, D. R., and J. Haas
1994 The Scream of the Butterfly: Competition and Conflict in the Prehistoric Southwest. In *Themes in Southwest Prehistory*, edited by G. J. Gumerman, pp. 211–238. School of American Research Press, Santa Fe.

Wilcox, D. R., T. R. McGuire, and C. Sternberg
1981 *Snaketown Revisited: A Partial Cultural Resource Survey, Analysis of Site Structure and an Ethnohistoric Study of the Proposed Hohokam-Pima National Monument.* Archaeological Series No. 155. Arizona State Museum, Tucson.

Wilcox, D. R., and L. O. Shenk
1977 *The Architecture of the Casa Grande and Its Interpretation.* Archaeological Series No. 115. Arizona State Museum, Tucson.

Wilcox, D. R., and C. Sternberg
1983 *Hohokam Ballcourts and Their Interpretation.* Archaeological Series No. 160. Arizona State Museum, Tucson.

Wills, W. H.
1988 *Early Prehistoric Agriculture in the American Southwest.* School of American Research Press, Santa Fe.

2000 Political Leadership and the Construction of Chacoan Great Houses, AD 1020–1140. In *Alternative Leadership Strategies in the Prehistoric Southwest*, edited by B. J. Mills, pp. 19–44. University of Arizona Press, Tucson.

Wills, W. H., and T. C. Windes
1989 Evidence for Population Aggregation and Dispersal during the Basketmaker III Period in Chaco Canyon, New Mexico. *American Antiquity* 54(2):347–369.

Windes, T. C.
1992 Blue Notes: The Chacoan Turquoise Industry in the San Juan Basin. In *Anasazi Regional Organization and the Chaco System*, edited by D. E. Doyel, pp. 159–168. Anthropological Papers No. 5. Maxwell Museum of Anthropology, Albuquerque.

n.d. *Early Puebloan Occupations in the Chaco Region: Excavations and Survey of Basketmaker III and Pueblo I Sites, Chaco Canyon, New Mexico.* Reports of the Chaco Center No. 13. National Park Service, Santa Fe.

Windes, T. C., and P. J. McKenna
2001 Going against the Grain: Wood Production in Chacoan Society. *American Antiquity* 66(1):119–140.

Woodbury, R. B.
1961 A Reappraisal of Hohokam Irrigation. *American Anthropologist* 63(3):550–560.

Zeilik, M.
1986 Keeping a Season Calendar at Pueblo Bonito. *Archaeoastronomy* 9(1–4):79–87.

11

The Good Gray Intermediate

Why Native Societies of North America Can't Be States

Stephen H. Lekson

Chaco and Cahokia were intermediate societies. That's the correct answer for the midterm exam, the acceptable classification (if we *must* pigeonhole), and the proper status of those two ancient places. We all know that's where they belong: intermediate.

What, in archaeology, is an "intermediate society"? It's a term in general use among American archaeologists because we are reasonably sure that the ancient peoples we study were, well, intermediate. But it's a little hard to pin down. For Talcott Parsons (1966), "intermediate" meant premodern civilizations, but that's definitely not the American archaeological usage. Americanists use "intermediate" as a happily vague term for the good gray complex hunter–gatherers and early agriculturalists who inhabited what would become the United States of America, from sea to shining sea.

"Intermediate societies"—as a term—rose from the wreckage of evolutionary schemes. In evolutionary terms, those societies were *intermediate* between classless egalitarian bands and classy powerhouse states (e.g., Arnold 1996). And that's where we think our people fit. We don't use evolutionary terms anymore (they have been found wanting: Trigger 2003; Yoffee 2005). American archaeology had been happy with "tribes" and "chiefdoms"—they seemed to fit the facts—but those words went away (well, not chiefdoms, at least in Mississippian archaeology; see Tim Pauketat's 2007 *Chiefdoms and Other Archaeological Delusions*). So: what to call these Native Americans who were more (somehow) than simple hunter-gatherers but less (somehow) than states? This vast residual became "intermediate" (or, sometimes, "midlevel") societies. Have to call them something, right?

I fear that the seemingly innocuous term "intermediate" does the ancient people we study a real disservice. It limits a priori what the ancients could have done in the past and what archaeologists expect to find in the present. I believe many North American societies went far beyond the upper limits of intermediate, but that automatic classification makes that fact (if it is indeed a fact) impossible to see, research, or debate.

Understanding the pernicious limitations of "intermediate" requires a good bit of professional history. How did we come to assume that North American Natives were safely and contentedly intermediate?

Lewis Henry Morgan, the father of American anthropology, was the progenitor of our long-cherished but now discredited evolutionary schemes. While Morgan's theories didn't hold up, at least one of his substantive generalizations did: Morgan told us that there were no states in the New World (e.g., Morgan 1881 [1965]). (He did not use the term "state;" I'm translating Morgan's "civilization" for the new millennium.) Morgan was particularly exercised about Aztecs, whose empire and civilization he dismissed as Spanish propaganda. Foundational historians and archaeologists such as Manuel Gamio, Alfonso Caso, and Ignacio Bernal brusquely dismissed or simply ignored him (Bernal 1980:143–144; Miller 2006:370). Morgan was not the father of Mexican anthropology.

North of the border, however, Morgan's ideas carried well into the twentieth century—even his ideas about Aztecs. Benjamin Keen, in his magisterial survey *The Aztec Image in Western Thought*, notes Morgan's intellectual influence on Adolph F. Bandelier, an early and influential convert, and then traces the thread through the late nineteenth and early twentieth centuries in the works of Marshall Saville, Herbert Spinden, and Eric Thompson (Keen 1971:488–493). Morgan's line ran right through the 1920s and 1930s. "As late as 1940 anthropologists of the eminence of George C. Valliant and Robert Lowie accepted the validity of the key elements in the Morgan-Bandelier doctrine" (Keen 1971:409). The authors of this doctrine were two of the greatest anthropologists of their times. These were not minor or marginal figures in American anthropology. They were key players, the professors who taught the professors who taught the professor who taught me. Morgan's maxim—now an anonymous truism—was brought forward through generations of teaching.

Morgan was particularly influential in the Southwest. Two of his earliest adherents were men of enormous authority in the region: Adolph Bandelier and Edgar L. Hewett. Bandelier literally defined the field in his *Investigations among the Indians of the Southwestern United States* (Bandelier 1890–1892). Morgan was his mentor, and after initial misgivings, Bandelier became a doctrinaire Morganite. Hewett was of the next generation. As a student, Hewett read (and approved of) Morgan's writings. Bandelier took Hewett under his wing when the younger man's fancy turned to archaeology. Hewett welcomed Bandelier's exegesis and instruction, "Hewett deferring to Bandelier even as Bandelier had been influenced by Morgan" (Chauvenet 1983:21).

T. T. Waterman—credited by some as the catalyst of the Pecos Classification—evaluated "Bandelier's contribution to the study of ancient Mexican social organization," noting:

> There are two widely different schools of doctrine concerning the political and social institutions which the Spaniards encountered among the highly civilized natives of the Mexican plateau. One school consists of two investigators, Lewis H. Morgan and A. F. Bandelier. These two writers consider the famous Aztec "empire" was not an empire at all, but a loose confederation of democratic Indian tribes. They have been supported... *by the sentiments, if not in the published writings, of most American ethnologists.* The opposing school consists, broadly speaking, of the other scholars who have written on the subject. (emphasis added; Waterman 1917:249–250)

Waterman was critical of Bandelier's methods but concluded that "Bandelier's work...is a good beginning, and offers the proper foundation for a final study of Mexican society," and that Bandelier "may be regarded as finally confirming the most important of Morgan's conclusions" (Waterman 1917:276).

Hewett bought theory off the rack from Bandelier (and through Bandelier, from Morgan). Throughout his many decades at museums and universities, Hewett remained firmly loyal to Bandelier's and Morgan's views of North American Native civilization: for Hewett, Aztec society and all New World societies were communal, democratic, and nothing like states (Hewett 1936). Of course, if the Aztecs were communal, democratic, and stateless, then the southwestern peoples who found themselves in Hewett's gaze must have been even simpler—communal, democratic, egalitarian—and that's how Hewett portrayed them. That view is now axiomatic in the Southwest.

For example: Norman Yoffee, Suzanne Fish, and George Milner (1999) formed a high-powered panel ruling on the political achievements of the ancient Pueblo, Hohokam, and Mississippian peoples. They dismissed any political pretensions for the Pueblos, modern and ancient, "whom we can't even pretend formed states" (p. 262). Yoffee, Fish, and Milner skirted unsettling, statelike aspects of Hohokam by offering arguments for why Hohokam was not or could not become a state (p. 264)—thereby triggering a semi-serious rule of thumb referred to (affectionately) as "Yoffee's Rule": "if you can argue whether a society is a state or isn't, then it isn't" (p. 262). Even Cahokia, the great Mississippian city (AD 900 to 1200), with its tens of thousands of people, enormous pyramids, and spectacular high-status burials (Pauketat 2004), did not qualify: "Nothing remotely like these finds [Cahokia] exist in the SW [*sic*], so it was hard for SE archaeologists—to a man, downsizers—to convince their [southwestern] colleagues that…Cahokia was not fundamentally different than its Mississippian counterparts elsewhere.… No one doubts that SE societies conformed to many (but not all) of the attributes commonly thought of as defining a chiefdom" (Yoffee, Fish, and Milner 1999:267).

We can't even *pretend* they were states. We *know*, as a bedrock certainty, that nothing like a state ever happened north of Mexico, so it's pointless to think about it. Maybe so. But perhaps *they* thought about it: those ambitious pretenders at Chaco, Phoenix, and Paquimé. Chaco Canyon in northwest New Mexico was the first Pueblo capital, AD 1000 to 1150 (Lekson 2005). Paquimé, in northern Chihuahua, Mexico, was the last, AD 1250 to 1450 (Di Peso 1974). Phoenix was not Pueblo, nor was it a single site or city but a cluster of two dozen large towns/small cities, supported by one of the largest canal irrigation systems in the New World (Gumerman 1991); it flourished AD 900 to 1300. Each of these impressive centers was the capital or focus of a large region; each had (at varying times) elite classes that ruled or attempted to rule those regions (Lekson 2009). All three were demonstrably linked to Mesoamerican civilizations, through exotic artifacts and architectural emulations. They knew what states were; that knowledge was part of their world. Postclassic states and civilizations were roaring along on the same small continent as Chaco, Phoenix, and Paquimé—and those cities of the north surely knew about them.

How could they not? Kingship began with Olmec (e.g., Clark 1997; Fields and Reents-Budet 2005), two millennia before Chaco or Cahokia. Kings rose and fell throughout Mesoamerica, on larger or smaller scales, continuously thereafter (Smith and Schreiber 2005, 2006). The middle and late Postclassic—the Mesoamerican era contemporary with Chaco, Paquimé, and Phoenix—was a politically dynamic, explosively expansionist, long-distance world (Smith and Berdan 2003). It beggars belief that the southwestern elites at Chaco and elsewhere and the lords of Cahokia—whose business it was *to know*—would *not know* of Mesoamerican kingship.

New and processual archaeology emphasized small "natural laboratories" in which evolutionary models were presumed to operate. So we evaluate Cahokia's and Chaco's political evolutions as if they were clinically isolated, each in its own petri dish. Papers and dissertations discuss "the evolution of complexity *at* Chaco" or "*at* Cahokia," as if all the necessary events and ingredients were found within the San Juan Basin or the American Bottom. Whatever the political histories of those cities (and others in North America), they surely encompassed places and ideas from far beyond their particular locale. To ignore Mesoamerica, the lords of Cahokia or Chaco would have to have been deliberately isolationist (and clearly they were not) or flat-out stupid (and we can assume they were not). Chaco and Cahokia were not petri dishes on a lab shelf: they were corners of a huge terrarium.

Felipe Fernández-Armesto, in his brief, brilliant "hemispheric history" of the Americas, says of Chaco, Paquimé, and Cahokia: "In North America, cultures which made contact with the great civilizations of the south fell under their spell and imitated their models" (Fernández-Armesto 2003:52). It's not surprising that Chaco or Cahokia fluttered around the notions of Mesoamerican statehood; it's only surprising that it took them so long to get around to it.

I do not claim that any southwestern polities were great and mighty empires, and—*most importantly*—I do not claim that any political formation north of the Mexican border was a *primary* state, or that states "evolved" parthenogenetically in situ at Chaco or Cahokia, in the neo-evolutionary progression from band to tribe to chiefdom to states. Other, older, greater states in Mesoamerica had already gone through all that. They'd done the heavy lifting. The Southwest did not have to invent any of this stuff. Chaco and Paquimé and Phoenix (and Cahokia) were *secondary* states (Parkinson and Galaty 2007), inspired by the historical, economic, ideological contexts of North America. This is not just semantics: that's a huge difference for anthropological archaeologists. Primary states are evolutionary miracles; secondary states are historical by-products.

Neo-evolutionary scenarios were strongly, and strangely, local. "Archaic" or "primary" states were, by definition, sui generis, and therefore well suited to study in natural laboratories. Sometimes those laboratories were pretty large: Mesopotamia, Oaxaca, and so forth. But whatever their size, they were kept as clean rooms, uncontaminated by outside ideas and influences. That's local. Newer, particularistic, anti-neo-evolutionary approaches are even more local: "Chaco (and by extension the Southwestern history of which Chaco is a part) must be understood within its own history and experiences" (Yoffee 2005:172). But Chaco and other ancient southwestern cities were not isolates; they were part of a *continental* history. If we must have a "natural laboratory," let it reach from Panama to the northern limits of maize agriculture and beyond. (Indeed, why stop at Panama? Southwestern copper work owes it origins, ultimately, to Ecuador; Hosler 1994.)

What are secondary states? Well, if primary states developed only a handful of times, then most of the archaeological states we study are secondary. We've spilled oceans of ink over primary states; surprisingly, we don't have well-developed literatures or even frameworks for thinking about secondary states (see Parkinson and Galaty 2007 for a recent review). One influential, recent study of primary states raised (but did not answer) two pertinent questions: "How do third- and fourth-generation states differ from first- and second-generation states?...and what to call the polities on the periphery of states when they acquire some of the trappings of that state but are never really incorporated into it?" (Marcus and Feinman 1998:6). I submit that the Southwest is a very good place to find answers. Adam Smith, in his deconstruction of states, laments that "the processes of secondary state formation are...woefully undertheorized" (Smith 2003:82–83). While I am uncertain that a deluge of unrestrained "theorizing" will get us very far, the study of actual cases might help—for example, Chaco, Hohokam, and Paquimé.

Or—above all—Cahokia. Timothy Pauketat extricates Cahokia from the typological muddle of band-tribe-chiefdom-state and "intermediate societies" by leaping over that morass and placing Cahokia with other *civilizations*, where it surely belongs. That smart maneuver side-steps (or leapfrogs) the dilemma of "chiefdoms and other archaeological delusions" (the title of Pauketat's 2007 book) but leaves Cahokia something of a historical oddity: "Like other apparent precocious places, Poverty Point or Chaco Canyon, Cahokia doesn't seem to fit one's expectations of a typical anything" (Pauketat 2007:135). Pauketat notes that "Cahokia really was too extreme to be called a chiefdom" (2007:136), but he avoids "state." Claims in the 1980s for a Cahokia "Ramey" state (e.g., O'Brien 1989) smacked hard into the remarkably solid ghost of Lewis Henry Morgan and met virulent rejection. "State" is not a good place for a Mississippianist to be, so Pauketat makes a great leap forward to *civilization*. I'm not a Mississippianist, so I can say it: Cahokia was a state, a *secondary* state.

We should not treat secondary states like primary states. But it is tempting to argue the case on Yoffee's and Marcus and Feinman's terms, the dimensions and qualities of primary states—if only to get the Southwest out of the colonial dustbin of intermediate societies and up to a place at the table with real states. Bits and pieces of Chaco match phrases and clauses of several definitions of "state." Revisit Yoffee's thoughts on the state: "a political center [and its territory]...acting through a generalized structure of authority, making certain decisions in disputes between members of different groups, including kin groups, maintaining the central symbols of society, and undertaking defense and expansion of the society" (Yoffee 2005:17). Chaco did those things. (It may not have been called on to defend itself, because it had no active rivals or peers, but it surely maintained peace.) And it did those things on Mesoamerican scales (Nelson 1995). Marcus and Feinman (1998:4) want "two...strata (a professional ruling class and a commoner class) and a government that was both highly centralized and internally specialized." Chaco's archaeology is one of the world's clearest examples of stratified housing, palaces versus commoner class dwellings. (That's what Chaco, as an archaeological phenomenon, is all about.) Chaco, on very small scales (and not very successfully), tried (in Marcus and Feinman's [1998:4–5] terms) "waging war, exacting tribute, controlling information,…and regulating manpower and labor." Other criteria are stipulated for "states where texts are available"—details of governance that we will never know for Chaco or other ancient southwestern polities.

We know states in retrospect—we write textbooks specifying what it took to qualify as an ancient state: surplus production, craft specialization, cities, standing armies, and so on. The ancients, however, hadn't read our textbooks: they were making it up, or borrowing, or cobbling together whatever worked. Or didn't work. The rules we write for states come from the successes, not the failures.

All this would be doubly true for secondary states: small, starter-kit kingdoms out on the edges of civilization. If the time's iconic symbols for leadership were those of an emperor living in a grand capital city, an ambitious hill chief might well adopt the habits and customs and accoutrements of that exalted but distant lord. The hill chief might not understand that he (or she) needed attached specialists, or a standing army, or any of the other goods and services we've declared necessary for a true, successful state. Sometimes it worked, sometimes it didn't.

Does this matter? Recognizing North American Native polities as secondary states might allow the archaeology of the United States to actually add something to broader anthropological understandings: we have the best-documented archaeologies of secondary states anywhere in the world. But it counts for more, just *getting it right*. Using the term "state"—secondary state—allows Native polities to crack Morgan's glass ceiling, and it directs us to their Mesoamerican contemporaries. It puts the prehistory of the United States back into Native North America, the product of local agency and continental history.

We've heard Yoffee's Rule. Well, here's Lekson's Corollary: "If you can argue whether a society is a state or isn't, then it's *really interesting*." And if it's in North America, it's probably a secondary state.

Note: Many of the ideas and a few of the phrases in this chapter also appear in my *History of the Ancient Southwest* (2009) and "Complexity" (2005). Like Edgar L. Hewett, I'm not averse to recycling in a good cause.

References

Arnold, Jeanne E. (editor)
1996   *Emergent Complexity: The Evolution of Intermediate Societies.* Archaeological Series No. 9. International Monographs in Prehistory, Ann Arbor, Michigan.

Bandelier, Adolph F.
1890– *Final Report of Investigations among the*
1892   *Indians of the Southwestern United States, Carried on Mainly in the Years from 1880 to 1885.* American Series, Vols. 3–4. Archaeological Institute of America, Cambridge, Massachusetts.

Bernal, Ignacio
1980   *A History of Mexican Archaeology.* Thames and Hudson, London.

Chauvenet, Beatrice
1983   *Hewett and Friends: A Biography of Santa Fe's Vibrant Era.* Museum of New Mexico Press, Santa Fe.

Clark, J. E.
1997   The Arts of Government in Early Mesoamerica. *Annual Review of Anthropology* 26:211–234.

Cordell, Linda S., and Don D. Fowler (editors)
2005   *Southwest Archaeology in the Twentieth Century.* University of Utah Press, Salt Lake City.

Di Peso, Charles C.
1974   *Casas Grandes: A Fallen Trading Center of the Gran Chichimeca.* Vols. 1–3. Amerind Foundation, Dragoon, Arizona.

Fernández-Armesto, Felipe
2003   *The Americas: A Hemispheric History.* Modern Library, New York.

Fields, Virginia M., and Dorie Reents-Budet (editors)
2005   *Lords of Creation: The Origins of Sacred Maya Kingship.* Scala Publishers, London; Los Angeles County Museum of Art, Los Angeles.

Gumerman, George J. (editor)
1991   *Exploring the Hohokam: Prehistoric Desert Peoples of the Southwest.* University of New Mexico Press, Albuquerque.

Hewett, Edgar L.
1936   *Ancient Life in Mexico and Central America.* Bobbs-Merrill, Indianapolis.

Hosler, Dorothy
1994   *The Sounds and Colors of Power: The Sacred Metallurgical Technology of Ancient West Mexico.* MIT Press, Cambridge.

Keen, Benjamin
1971   *The Aztec Image in Western Thought.* Rutgers University Press, New Brunswick.

Lekson, Stephen H.

2005   Complexity. In *Southwest Archaeology in the Twentieth Century*, edited by Linda S. Cordell and Don D. Fowler, pp. 157–173. University of Utah Press, Salt Lake City.

2009   *A History of the Ancient Southwest*. School for Advanced Research Press, Santa Fe.

Lekson, Stephen H. (editor)

2006   *The Archaeology of Chaco Canyon*. School for Advanced Research Press, Santa Fe.

Marcus, Joyce, and Gary M. Feinman

1998   Introduction. In *Archaic States*, edited by Gary M. Feinman and Joyce Marcus, pp. 3–13. School of American Research Press, Santa Fe.

Miller, Mary

2006   The Study of the Pre-Columbian World. In *A Pre-Columbian World*, edited by Jeffrey Quilter and Mary Miller, pp. 363–376. Dumbarton Oaks, Washington, D.C.

Morgan, Lewis Henry

1881   [1965] *Houses and House-Life of the American Aborigines*. University of Chicago Press, Chicago.

Nelson, Ben A.

1995   Complexity, Hierarchy, and Scale: A Controlled Comparison between Chaco Canyon, New Mexico, and La Quemada, Zacatecas. *American Antiquity* 60:597–618.

O'Brien, Patricia J.

1989   Cahokia: The Political Capital of the "Ramey" State? *North American Archaeologist* 10:275–292.

Parkinson, William A., and Michael L. Galaty

2007   Secondary States in Perspective: An Integrated Approach to State Formation in the Prehistoric Aegean. *American Anthropologist* 109(1):113–129.

Parsons, Talcott

1966   *Societies: Evolutionary and Comparative Perspectives*. Prentice-Hall, Englewood Cliffs, New Jersey.

Pauketat, Timothy R.

2004   *Ancient Cahokia and the Mississippians*. Cambridge University Press, Cambridge.

2007   *Chiefdoms and Other Archaeological Delusions*. AltaMira Press, Lanham, Maryland.

Smith, Adam T.

2003   *The Political Landscape: Constellations of Authority in Early Complex Polities*. University of California Press, Berkeley.

Smith, Michael E., and Francis F. Berdan (editors)

2003   *The Postclassic Mesoamerican World*. University of Utah Press, Salt Lake City.

Smith, Michael E., and Katharina J. Schreiber

2005   New World States and Empires: Economic and Social Organization. *Journal of Archaeological Research* 13:189–229.

2006   New World States and Empires: Politics, Religion, and Urbanism. *Journal of Archaeological Research* 14:1–52.

Trigger, Bruce G.

2003   *Understanding Early Civilizations: A Comparative Study*. Cambridge University Press, Cambridge.

Waterman, T. T.

1917   Bandelier's Contribution to the Study of Ancient Mexican Social Organization. *University of California Publications in American Archaeology and Ethnology* 12(7):249–282.

Yoffee, Norman

2005   *Myths of the Archaic State: Evolution of the Earliest Cities, States and Civilizations*. Cambridge University Press, Cambridge.

Yoffee, Norman, Suzanne K. Fish, and George R. Milner

1999   Comunidades, Ritualities, Chiefdoms: Social Evolution in the American Southwest and Southeast. In *Great Towns and Regional Polities in the Prehistoric American Southwest and Southeast*, edited by Jill E. Neitzel, pp. 261–271. University of New Mexico Press, Albuquerque.

12

A People's History
of the American Southwest

Severin Fowles

Blow up your TV. Throw away your papers.
Move to the country, and build yourself a home.
Have a lot of children. Raise 'em on peaches.
And try to find Jesus on your own.

JOHN PRINE

A vigorous new historicism has come to characterize North American archaeology during the past decade. Exemplified in the work of Tim Pauketat (2001, 2007) and colleagues (Pauketat, ed. 2001), the new historicism preserves the rigorous search for long-term diachronic patterning so characteristic of classic processualism but intervenes in two critical respects. Where earlier processualist studies held deep commitments to the construction of social typologies, the emerging paradigm is countering with a newfound appreciation of historical contingency. And where previous archaeological theory had resigned itself to a profound sense of evolutionary inevitability in which the march toward the state was inexorable, the new historicism is seeking instead to make intellectual space for a broadened world of potential pathways and social configurations. Hence, Pauketat's call for a new "historical processualism" charged with the task of unearthing alternative pre-modernities in a manner that parallels many sociocultural anthropologists' efforts to expose "alternative modernities" in the present (e.g., Gaonkar, ed. 2001).

Historical processualism, arguably, has already arrived, judging by recent archaeological work in North America (see Cameron and Duff 2008; Fowles 2005; Lekson 1999, 2009; Mills 2000; Pauketat, ed. 2001; Pauketat and Loren 2005). And it has, arguably, already proven to be more than mere critique of an easy intellectual target. The current volume, focused as it is on broadening rather than rejecting outright the notion of complexity (or as Alt nicely puts it in her introduction, on "disentangling complexities" in the Native American past), is a good example of the current effort to rethink and rebuild core evolutionary notions to suit the new paradigm. As a contributor to this effort, however, I want to sidestep complexity per se and focus instead on the question of *simplicity*—particularly on the much neglected issue of *voluntary simplicity*—which is, of course, complexity's eternal rival and must, I will argue, be interrogated with the same sort of rigor.

Below I consider the evolution of simplicity in the precolonial Southwest. I want to begin, however, with an ethnographic observation of sorts—an observation prompted by a recent stay at the New Buffalo Community in the rural village of Arroyo Hondo, just north of Taos, New Mexico. Archaeologists are practiced in the art of reaching deep into the bag of world ethnography to find analogues for a past society that was, it is argued,

183

broadly similar in certain structural outlines if not in all the details. To a certain extent, I mean to follow right in step with this much-critiqued-but-nevertheless-still-quite-productive tradition. However, my use of New Buffalo (a hippie commune founded in the 1960s) as a comparative case may seem a peculiar choice, not only because archaeologists rarely think about the modern West as being ethnographic in the same way that New Guinea tribes or South African hunter-gatherers are "ethnographic," but also because New Buffalo, like so many of the other neotribal experiments of its time, was itself explicitly modeled on Native American principles (or at least on what its founders took to be Native American principles). What insight could possibly come from seeking parallels between precolumbian native societies and their twentieth-century mimics? From comparing Indians with those who were playing Indian?

The short answer to this question is "a great deal," though I don't expect to convince anyone of this here in the introduction. By the close of the chapter, however, my aim is to have demonstrated (1) that thinking archaeologically about places like New Buffalo raises critical issues regarding the broader evolutionary tensions both between cultures and countercultures and between complexity and simplicity, (2) that such a thought experiment further challenges us to imagine the potential role of countercultural movements in the premodern past, and (3) that this moves us further away from certain highly tenacious disciplinary attachments to an evolutionary notion of inevitable progress toward the state, offering us instead a useful countermodel of the *progressive society* in opposition to the state. In the course of these arguments, I offer commentary on precolonial political trajectories in the Southwest, although the chapter makes no pretensions to being a data-driven study. The goal is to clear theoretical thickets in a more general way, making room for future work on simplicity's evolution in particular historical sequences.

But first, to New Buffalo.

New Buffalos

For those who lived through the 1960s and participated in the struggle to construct a hippie counterculture, New Buffalo is a cultural icon

(see Keltz 2000). It exemplified the tribalism of the times, the widespread utopian experiment that led groups throughout North America to opt out of the industrialized world of capitalistic self-interest and return to the land—to the handmade and the homegrown, to the egalitarian village community, to the spirituality of nature, to voluntary simplicity. For those of us who missed the 1960s, New Buffalo's iconic status emerges from books and film, most notably in a scene from *Easy Rider* in which Dennis Hopper and Peter Fonda stare agog at the idealistic youths from New York and San Francisco naively planting their first crops and huddling in mud hovels. (Hopper explicitly used New Buffalo as the prototype for this scene.)[1]

New Buffalo was built on a Native American model—both architecturally and spiritually—and it sought to follow what was perceived to be a Native American ethos (Figure 12.1). Even today, among the small but devoted group seeking to reinvigorate and reinvent the commune, much is made of the fact that certain members of nearby Taos Pueblo ventured out to New Buffalo in its early days to take pity on the group, teaching them native agriculture and adobe-making and introducing them to the Native American Church. The origin story of the commune, in other words, reads like a twentieth-century remake of the Thanksgiving tale in which naive Pilgrims, escaping oppression, travel to an unknown land where they would have faced certain starvation were it not for the kindness of the natives. In the imaginary of New Buffalo's founders, they were "a lost tribe who had forgotten how to live—to plant, dance, sing, raise children—and how to die" (as quoted in Houriet 1971:140).

In this sense, the commune partook of a long tradition of American primitivism that has repeatedly looked to the indigenous precolonial world as an Edenic order of spiritual, political, and ecological harmony to be replicated. And in this sense, we might write it off as yet another Western irony in which a profound modernism was reinscribed through the very struggle to be primitive. (Who else but a member of the affluent modern West would work so assiduously to be penniless and premodern?) Others might be even less generous and dismiss New Buffalo and the related hippie experiments of the 1960s and '70s

FIGURE 12.1. New Buffalo in the late 1960s: an experiment in neotribalism (courtesy of Lisa Law).

as merely the games of peyote-eating adolescents rather than real and lasting social reformation.

True, New Buffalo didn't last long as a commune aimed at open-armed tribal collectivism. Three years after its founding, the commune closed its doors to outsiders and became decidedly more individualistic and capitalistic, the primary income of its residents eventually coming from a for-profit dairy business. Nevertheless, the rejection of postwar mainstream American culture that New Buffalo embodied has continued to characterize the Taos region, even if this rejection is now more frequently expressed by New Ageism, organic gardening, and off-the-grid homes built of mud, straw, and recycled tires. The Sixties, in other words, never faded in northern New Mexico; New Buffalo and its sister communes (there were dozens in the region) gave birth to an evolving, but remarkably persistent, strand of American counterculture.[2]

So what does this have to do with the histories of indigenous peoples? Clearly, knowing something about Native America helps us understand aspects of the hippie movement, its influences and aspirations, but how might knowing something about hippies help us understand Native America—and in particular *precolonial* Native America?

I want to answer this question in a roundabout way by briefly considering the situation of Taos Pueblo (Figure 12.2), the native community that most directly influenced New Buffalo. Taos is also a cultural icon. In fact, as a World Heritage Site visited by thousands of tourists each year, it stands as *the* image of indigeneity for a sizable chunk of the American public. There are good reasons for the pueblo's renown: the adobe architecture and physical setting of the community are intoxicating; it competes with the other pueblos for the title of being the oldest occupied settlement in North America; and its walls have seen such critical historical events as the planning of the Pueblo Revolt of 1680 and, in 1847, the last major U.S. military siege of a pueblo. Nevertheless, Taos is probably most famous for its aggressive traditionalism, its keeping to the old ways. Tourists come to the pueblo to glimpse life as it was in precolonial times. Within the pueblo's walls they find one of the few parts of North America where electricity and plumbing are explicitly banned, where drinking water is still drawn directly from the village's river, where pots are made by hand, and where native ceremonies are practiced according to scriptures and aesthetics established many hundreds of years ago. Ruth Underhill observed in the 1930s that Taos "is a village conscious of

FIGURE 12.2. Taos Pueblo in the 1930s (Parsons 1936:frontispiece).

itself and not maintaining old standards simply because new ones have not reached it. Taos…is maintaining the old ways knowingly and of set purpose…. 'Our ways would lose their power if they were changed,' say the Taos" (Underhill 1938: 134). Such statements continue to be made at the pueblo today.

There is an obvious irony in Taos's aggressive traditionalism. The effort to maintain the old ways has gone hand-in-hand with the transformation of the pueblo into a sort of movie set— metaphorically, but on rare occasions literally as well. (Cue another scene from *Easy Rider* in which Hopper and Fonda motorcycle straight through the middle of the pueblo's plaza.) Only a small group still lives in the core pueblo for any appreciable part of the year, and many of the old homes are now art galleries run by members of the tribe who live with all modern conveniences on nearby tribal lands. This is not to say that traditionalism is without a profound, private significance for the tribe. It is not for the benefit of tourists, for instance, that the Northern Tiwa language is spoken at dances or that only native foods (corn, squash, deer, etc.) may be eaten during ritual periods.

But even in such private acts, a pronounced irony is exposed insofar as the very emphasis on traditionalism *itself* is a far cry from "tradition" when considered alongside the dramatic demographic, economic, religious, and political transformations undertaken by the ancestral Northern Tiwa in the centuries before the arrival of the Spanish. As I have discussed elsewhere, the archaeology and oral history of the region combine to paint a tumultuous picture of the late precolonial period (Fowles 2005, 2006, 2008). The thirteenth century witnessed significant immigration, the initial local construction of aggregated villages, and a shift from a primarily hunter-and-gatherer economy to intensified agriculture. The fourteenth century saw the introduction—and, in a number of cases, rejection—of a variety of new ritual practices, as well as the demise of locally produced painted pottery, notable shifts in gender relations, and (if we are to use oral history as our guide) significant linguistic change. And the fifteenth century saw the restructuring of the Northern Tiwa–speaking villages into major trade centers linking the Pueblo world to the buffalo hunters of the Plains. When the Spanish arrived in the sixteenth century, they didn't meet a group of traditionalists committed to preserving the past; they encountered a community of social innovators, bricoleurs for whom constant refashioning was the norm.

The traditionalism one encounters among the Pueblos today, then, is a decidedly colonial product, a reactionary stance that is just as "modern" as Western notions of progress and of history as a thing of revolutions (Symbolic, Neolithic, Urban, Industrial, Computer, etc.). Indeed, traditionalism and modernist stories of progress seem premised on one another. "One is not born traditional," writes Latour, "one chooses to become traditional by constant innovation. The idea of an identical repetition of the past [the premodernist position] and that of a radical rupture with any past [the modernist position] are two symmetrical results of a single conception of time. We cannot return to the past, to tradition, to repetition, because these great immobile domains are the inverted image of the earth that is no longer promised to us today: progress, permanent revolution, modernization, forward flight" (Latour 1993:76). One can never step in the same river twice—nor, for that matter, can one drink directly from the same river twice. Taking our lead from Heraclitus as much as Latour, we must acknowledge that traditionalism itself is constituted in the breach of tradition.

How different, then, is Taos traditionalism from hippie primitivism? It goes without saying that Taos Pueblo takes its indigenous rituals very seriously and views them as essential not only to the tribe's own identity but also to the well-being of the world as they know it. But the same was true of the founders of New Buffalo, for whom a return to a tribal sort of society and spirituality was both basic to their self-image and part of a larger effort to save the planet from social and ecological disaster. Indeed, both communities— Native and hippie alike—have come to reject aspects of hegemonic American technocracy (see Roszak 1968) for pointed ideological reasons. And each community has invented its own style of antimodernist neotribalism that references precolonial ways of life but is fundamentally a recent creation. Are we, then, to write off not only New Buffalo but also modern Pueblo groups as inappropriate analogues for past native societies insofar as both are clearly reactionary phenom-

ena—countercultures—that make sense only when viewed in symmetrical opposition to their foil (in this case, "mainstream" American society with its cult of modernization and progress)?

The Evolution of Counterculture

The problem with this last question lies in our tendency to think of countercultures as *uniquely* modern, or if not uniquely modern, then peculiarly Western. The literature on utopian countercultures in North America is large, for example, and even includes contributions by archaeologists (Preucel 2006; Tarlow 2003; Van Bueren 2006). But the latter have uniformly focused on Anglo-American communities, typically those of the nineteenth century. There has never been an attempt to extend the study of countercultural movements into the precolonial past.

Archaeology's inattentiveness to ancient countercultures might be explained in a number of ways. Perhaps most significant is the fact that the customary mandate of the discipline is to account for the evolution of culture, and the study of counterculture—of movements that reject rather than build on a dominant culture—generally runs "counter" to this goal. It is also the case, however, that we typically treat countercultures as premised on an ideologically driven critique that draws its force from moral, philosophical, or even aesthetic arguments disseminated through text, television, or related media (see Goffman and Joy 2004; Roszak 1968). As Leary (2004:x) put it, "the focus of counterculture is the power of ideas, images, and artistic expression, not the acquisition of personal and political power." Defined in this way, countercultural movements cut across the grain of evolutionary theories that both concentrate on preliterate contexts and assume, almost as an article of faith, that aggrandizers— those specifically committed to the acquisition of "personal and political power"—were the major drivers of social change. Hence, the archaeological vision of prehistoric political opposition is led away from the possibility of intellectually based protest and is left to fill the past with competitions over prestige, strategic resources, and social control in which losers may resist but do not reject. There is no room for an archaeology of conscientious objectors.

But what if we were to go looking for such an archaeology? Would we be able to trace the evolution of countercultures in the precolonial record? Minimally, we would need a set of expectations comparable to those developed by archaeologists interested in the evolution of (centralized, hierarchical, hegemonic) cultures. In this respect we are fortunate to have a recent study that goes a long way in offering precisely this. In an explicit effort to theorize precolonial traditions that may have been organized around the rejection of a dominant and oppressive society, Sassaman (2001) has looked for insight to a range of reactionary movements at the fringes of dominant Western society. Groups such as the Amish or the Mexican Kickapoo, he notes, comprise a distinctive set of societies in which opposition to oppression is expressed through separation rather than efforts to fight a system from within. Each of the cases Sassaman considers utilized similar strategies of geographic isolation, often removing themselves to unoccupied or marginal lands. "But more to the point," he notes, "is the *ideological* separation of tradition. Creations of identity in opposition to structures of domination empowered actors to mark difference and to assert egalitarian relations among themselves in order to guard that distinction" (Sassaman 2001:235, emphasis added; see also Fowles 2002).

Sassaman refers to such phenomena as "traditions of resistance," which is perhaps a misleading phrase insofar as it prompts us to think about such traditions as part and parcel of the varied arts of resistance within existing structures of domination. Indeed, while Sassaman explicitly grounds his discussion in Scott's (1990) approach to resistance, his case studies are compelling precisely because the protagonists responded to domination not with resistance per se but rather with outright rejection. They responded not as frustrated subalterns within a system but as men and women whose relative (or at least perceived) freedoms were born of their efforts to stand outside the oppressive system altogether. The distinction is an essential one—particularly for archaeologists. How easy it is to assume that a small prehistoric settlement located well beyond an oppressive polity's "sphere of influence" was simply "uninfluenced" by that polity; and how easy it is to look at the material culture of the same small settlement, find an absence of trade goods or stylistic links, and feel that one has indeed demonstrated that the settlement really had little if anything to do with the distant polity. The logical misstep here should be obvious: one can easily imagine situations in which geographic isolation and pronounced cultural dissimilarities, ironically enough, testify to the deep interconnectedness of histories rather than the reverse.

But to return to the two cases discussed at the start of the essay: in broad outlines, both modern Taos Pueblo and New Buffalo fit Sassaman's pattern. Despite regularly opening its doors to tourists, Taos remains a physically distinct nation-within-a-nation on extensive tribal lands that are largely off-limits to outsiders. Prominent men of the tribe have maintained the tradition of wearing their hair long, now typically tied at the back in a style that clearly marks them as distinct from the local Hispanic and Anglo populations. And all active members of the tribe periodically participate in private community rituals, such as the yearly pilgrimage to Blue Lake, where collectivist values are reasserted in opposition to the self-serving individualism of American society. For the hippies, geographic separation involved a move from urban centers (primarily along the east and west coasts) to the rural deserts of northern New Mexico, where long hair, beads, nudity, an ethic of radical egalitarianism, neoshamanism, and the like became the clear marks of ideological distinction. Furthermore, both Puebloan and hippie communities have rejected a variety of otherwise commonplace technologies in favor of an aggressively primitive lifestyle.

A number of archaeological expectations arise when we begin to think in generalizable terms about countercultures such as the Amish or hippies. First, as emphasized by Sassaman, *geographic separation* is employed as a means of peaceful or nonconfrontational protest. Second, such separation often goes hand in hand with an asserted *primitivism*, an intentional reversion to smaller social scales, voluntary simplicity, older material culture, and provincial economic systems. Third, it tends to be further associated with *ideological reform*, typically involving a return to what are perceived as the true, original, or natural foundations of spirituality. Fourth, countercultures are frequently highly *egalitarian* (in ethos if not always in practice), which only stands to reason insofar as their very existence lies in the escape from authoritarianism of one kind or another.[3]

It is with the fifth general characteristic that things begin to get a bit tricky: countercultures are often—some might say always—born of opposition to a "complex society," a state or at least some polity that is large, repressive, and hegemonic enough to motivate radical critique and mobilized reaction. This observation would seem to leave countercultures as merely derivative phenomena, as afterthoughts or regrets that come about only once social evolution has run its course. And this would seem to imply that in "pre-state" archaeological contexts such as precolonial North America, the question of counterculture is largely moot.

Enter the ideas of Pierre Clastres (1989). Clastres is widely known as having been a key critic of neo-evolutionary theory, a vigorous crusader against the Western conceit that viewed statelessness as a sign of cultural immaturity, organizational lack, and developmental naiveté. "Primitive" or tribal groups, he emphasized, cannot be viewed as stateless simply because the evolutionary forces leading toward the centralization of coercive power were absent and, as yet, unfelt (see also Gledhill 2000:8–18). On the contrary, Clastres argued that tribes such as the Iroquois of the Northeast or the Mandan of the Plains were stateless *precisely because* of their constant struggle to contain and limit such forces (see also Fowles forthcoming a; Trigger 1990). In place of a world that was "pre-state" (in the midst of a belated progression toward a European-style polity) or even one that was "non-state" (blissfully ignorant of such polities), Clastres envisioned a spectrum of egalitarian societies in the New World that were aggressively "anti-state," engaged in a "radical rejection of authority, an utter negation of [coercive] power" (1989:43). Far from being naive to the State, such groups have always been consumed with its specter.

There is the easy critique of Clastres's argument, of course: how could societies be fundamentally mobilized around opposition to a configuration of political power—the State—

that they never actually experienced as an on-the-ground historical reality? Perhaps modern Taos Pueblo and hippie communes can be described as "societies against the state," but surely not those precolonial communities of North America that were far enough from Mesoamerica for state organization to be little more than a distant rumor.

Here, however, we must note that Clastres's understanding of "the State" is worlds away from the strict definition sought by archaeologists who focus on standing armies, settlement patterns, levels of bureaucratic decision making, and the like. In fact, his position is inimical even to those more flexible archaeological definitions that inhere in something like Yoffee's Rule, where it is claimed that "if you can argue whether a society is a state or isn't, then it isn't" (Yoffee 1993:69). The archaeologist's state is a sociopolitical type—something reached by crossing a threshold, something that either is or isn't. Clastres's State (which I have capitalized to distinguish it from the traditional archaeological notion of "state") was more a State of mind: the frightening notion and unremitting threat that the few might come to have absolute coercive power over the many. As such, it exists in polar tension with a vision of individual autonomy and complete self-determination—which is also merely an imagined potentiality that no society has ever experienced as an on-the-ground reality. Indeed, if Rousseau could posit a supposedly original or "natural" man who was so politically unfettered as to be freed of all social dependencies the moment he left his mother's breast to wander the forest in solitude, and if this *dream* of radical self-determination could be instrumental in galvanizing revolutionary action in eighteenth-century French society, is it so strange that the *nightmare* of the ultimate Despot—what Clastres, following his Guarani informants, refers to as the "One"—could have been an equally driving force in precolonial North America? Neither dream nor nightmare, neither natural man nor the absolute power of the State, is anything more than a collective fiction (see also Osborne 2007: 144). They are potent fictions, nevertheless.

Graeber, Clastres's most recent champion within anthropology, has made a similar point but with a key addendum. It is not simply that the State stands as a dangerous potentiality, argues

Graeber; most egalitarian societies *actually experience* the State—or at least its characteristic brand of despotism and coercive power—by entangling themselves with a cosmos full of dangerous and malevolent spirits.

> In egalitarian societies, which tend to place an enormous emphasis on creating and maintaining communal consensus…[there is often] a kind of equally elaborate reaction formation, a spectral nightworld inhabited by monsters, witches or other creatures of horror. And it's the most peaceful societies which are also the most haunted, in their imaginative constructions of the cosmos, by constant specters of perennial war.… It's as if the endless labor of achieving consensus masks a constant inner violence—or, it might perhaps be better to say, is in fact the process by which that inner violence is measured and contained. (Graeber 2004:25–26)

Graeber's observation is important. Most, if not all, societies no doubt have had a pretty clear idea of what a strongly centralized and violently maintained polity would look like—indeed, in their subservience to the spirit world, most societies have constructed a model of precisely that. Consider Taos Pueblo once again: there one finds that the Creator deity, Kwathlowúna, and a bureaucracy of spirit enforcers keep tight control over the populace. The following are native statements to this effect recorded in 1906:

> Though you do not see the father Kwathlowúna, he knows all that you think and do. He knows when the people fail in their duties to their gods. There are five men sent by Kwathlowúna to watch and listen [to] the people [of each side of the pueblo] but they are not seen by the people. These men carry the names of offenders to Kwathlowúna. The winds convey the thoughts and words of the good, to Kwathlowúna.
>
> …No one knows just where they live, but they are always watching about the pueblo, five watching on the north side of the river and five on the south side of the river, to watch and listen to all [that] the people do and say and report to Kwathlowúna. The people have great fear of adverse reports to their Creator.

> When Kwathlowúna knows that the people in this world are neglecting their duties to their gods he instructs Tain'kwil'lan'na, a being who lives in the world just below this world, to go above and instruct the Ice people to punish the people by showering hail upon their land and so cut the vegetation to pieces. (Stevenson 1906)

Is not this sort of spirit world properly viewed as an elaborate bureaucratic-surveillance-disciplinary system of hierarchical control? Is it not the State? And can there be any doubt that such a system was common among the Pueblos during precolonial times as well? One need only look to the widespread distribution of Pueblo IV period imagery featuring katsina spirits with terrorizing eyes and sharp, bared teeth (Figure 12.3). Such spirits were the middlemen or intermediary elites who, like the "five men" sent by Kwathlowúna to monitor the north and south sides of Taos Pueblo, were charged with keeping humans in line.

Society has probably always consciously guarded against despotism to some degree. And if we assume that spirit dictators would have been ever present in the cosmos, then direct entanglement with a full-blown "state" (in the narrow, archaeological sense) was hardly necessary for the development of a "society against the State" (in Clastres's sense) or the countercultural movements described above. As Graeber suggests, imagined worlds of spectral violence and despotism may have been useful precisely because they served as foils for human society, as models of domination that must be kept distinct from mundane human-to-human relationships.

At the same time, we must not ignore the reality that during the millennium before European conquest, North America had its own set of all-too-real leaders seeking power through coercive means. The extensive human sacrifice documented in Mound 72 at Cahokia (Fowler et al. 1999) provides the most jarring example of institutionalized violence and must have been underwritten by a strongly hierarchical ideology. If we are to follow Lekson and others (Lekson 2002; LeBlanc 1999), Chacoan elites during the eleventh and twelfth centuries also used targeted executions and, in rare cases, anthropophagy to

FIGURE 12.3. Katsina mask petroglyph from the Galisteo Basin, New Mexico (Pueblo IV period) (courtesy of the Museum of New Mexico).

shore up hierarchical systems of domination. We might predict that violence of this sort would have fueled dissent and countercultural response. And we might rigorously undertake the study of such dissent, constructing research programs designed to search for patterns of emigration that would have led to the establishment of simplified communities on the periphery. We might; but we haven't. Simplicity and the evolution of the anti-state unfortunately draw very little archaeological interest. Like other Western scholars since the Enlightenment, we have placed prime value on the study of leadership's excesses, for we have been led to believe that evolutionary advance lies solely within such excesses. All else is devolution and societal collapse—a tragic movement backward, a fall.

The aesthetic of this traditional picture changes from positive to negative when our analytical gaze flips from culture to counterculture. Revolution becomes evolution. Collapse (of hierarchy) becomes construction (of egalitarian society). And the birthing pains of the new social order shift from the violence of imperial conquest to the violence of tyrannicide. Another way of putting this is to say that the study of counterculture frees us of our commitment to the evolution of what we might call "simple complexity," in which the few control the many, clearing space for the study of those forms of "complex simplicity" in which the many control the few who would otherwise seek to dominate (cf. Yoffee 2005 on the evolution of simplicity). Following Graeber we might also look on this project as an effort to narrate the deep history not of "power" per se but of *counterpower*, the organizational strategies that arise to safeguard personal freedoms and to encourage decentralized, consensus-based decision making. How might our reconstructions change when their focus is on the growth of progressive politics rather than on evolutionary progress? Let me address this question with a sketch of the deep history of the northern Southwest.

A People's History of the Precolonial Southwest

Had I a bit more space in which to offer my alternative account of the long-term development of societies in the northern Southwest, I would be tempted to begin with an extended discussion of Boehm's (1999) intriguing model of the evolution of egalitarianism in *Hierarchy in the Forest*. Boehm is one of those brave scholars who has sought linkages between our social and biological histories, and his critical contribution, in the spirit of Clastres, has been to knock the notion of egalitarianism out of its taken-for-granted position as a human default or beginning point—Lewis Henry Morgan's "zero of human society"—and to situate it in the broader primatological context as a highly evolved social phenomenon that must itself be explained. In parallel fashion, despotism of the "I am Pharaoh, hear me roar" variety is also dislodged in Boehm's reading; no longer an endpoint of social evolution, it ironically emerges as a kind of devolution back to the orthodox dominance hierarchies of our prehuman ancestors (see also Knauft 1991). The interesting possibility I want to underscore here is that if Boehm is correct, we appear to have been struggling to construct countercultures at least as long as our genus has had small canines and reduced sexual dimorphism.[4]

The initial Paleoindian colonists of North America, then, could be said to have arrived with the same highly evolved (biocultural) heritage of opposition to certain forms of political domination that all members of our species share. We know next to nothing about their specific motivations for traveling to the New World. Sheer intrepidness must have played a part, but it is not unreasonable to speculate that they were, as it is often put, "voting with their feet" and participating in the long hunter-gatherer tradition of migrating to new lands as a strategy of dealing with social conflict in prior homelands. There is frustratingly little we can say about the ideological worlds of North America's early residents. Did the Paleoindians live within a cosmos marked by spectral violence of the sort Graeber describes? And did dangerous spirits in the nonhuman world serve as a constant reminder to nip in the bud any would-be leaders in the human world? Given current archaeological evidence, who can say? The irony of an archaeology of counterpower is that it is most invisible to us today precisely when it was most effective in the past.

The Voluntary Simplicity of the Forager

We face a similar situation when seeking to understand the long Archaic period in the Southwest: the material evidence is limited, and nearly all researchers have consequently presented the Archaic gatherer-hunters as profoundly economic creatures ("optimal foragers" consumed by the quest for food) with little or no political life, properly so called. Of course, all this really means is that their political life was not aimed at the construction of orthodox hierarchies and may well have been mobilized precisely in opposition to their emergence. Indeed, to assume that the food quest precluded any sort of real concern with government is deeply ironic, insofar as ethnographic studies have repeatedly demonstrated that among hunter-gatherers no less than industrial superpowers, economics *is* politics (Clastres 1989).

Nevertheless, it is difficult not to conclude that the six millennia or so of chipped stone scatters, isolated hearths, and dispersed ephemeral structures in the American Southwest—the low-visibility archaeological traces that comprise the Archaic period—were filled with "cold" societies in some fundamental respect. In contrast to "hot" societies, which internalize the historical process and turn directional change into a cultural ideal, "cold" societies make a cult out of cosmic repetition, "seeking, by the institutions they give themselves, to annul the possible effects of historical factors on their equilibrium and continuity." At least this was how Lévi-Strauss (1966:233–234) famously drew the distinction. Needless to say, cold societies sit "within history" as much as any others, but Lévi-Strauss's claim, following Mircea

Eliade, was that such societies are distinguished by a concerted effort to perpetuate or re-create a mythical state of origins and ancestral beings. I am not interested in the simple critique that the hot/cold scheme perpetuates an untenable divide between modern and primitive. The more important point lies in Lévi-Strauss' implicit acknowledgment that cold societies are cold by choice. What we may perceive archaeologically as evolutionary stasis is more likely the result of a strong ritual and political project, in other words, a project undertaken "with a dexterity we underestimate" (Lévi-Strauss 1966:233) in which futures are resolutely aligned with pasts.[5]

But the vexing question remains: how are we to read hunter-gatherer economics as a politics of simplicity or to read evolutionary stasis as a conscious social agenda when the material residues we have before us are so minimal? Here Southwesternists would do well to follow the lead of a handful of scholars working in the Eastern Woodlands who have begun to seriously consider Archaic and largely pre-agricultural politics through a countercultural lens (see Nassaney 2001; Sassaman 2001). Broadly speaking, archaeologists in this region have little choice but to engage with the social forces that opposed complexity. The Southeastern Archaic, in particular, is characterized by a deep and fascinating history of shifts between precocious periods of centralized mound building—notably at sites such as Watson Brake (3400–3000 BCE) and Poverty Point (1000–700 BCE)—and subsequent periods in which large-scale construction projects and related suggestions of hierarchy were essentially absent. The tensions here are raw and exposed: repeated movements away from structures of domination stare at us with an almost defiant gaze that leaves us unable to talk in simplistic terms about cultural "collapse" or "devolution." Instead, we are forced to rethink nonhierarchical periods as antihierarchical movements—as the collective resurrection of egalitarian societies that opposed any movement toward the State.

Anarchist social theorist Peter Lamborn Wilson has even weighed in on this very pattern through an intriguing discussion of the Effigy Mound culture in Wisconsin, a tradition of dispersed hunter-gatherers who, following the collapse of the Hopewell regional system at roughly AD 400, created a fantastic and bewildering array of earthen birds, bears, turtles, and the like across the landscape. Wilson (1998) observes that although the groups responsible for the effigy mounds borrowed certain aspects of their more "complex" predecessors to the south, we learn much more by attending to the patterns they *refused* to adopt, foremost among them being the hierarchy, violence, and status differentiation that (arguably) characterized Hopewell sites. In the effigy mounds, Wilson sees the expression of a strong reactionary ideology and an effort to reassert egalitarianism, heterodoxy, and local economic and political autonomy—"a 'revolt' or back-to-Nature religious revival," as he puts it, "directed dialectically at the surrounding Civilization of Hopewell and Temple Mound" (1998:109).

The situation was somewhat different in the Archaic Southwest, insofar as there is no local evidence of a serious breach of egalitarianism before the tenth century AD and, one might argue, no manifest system of domination for early hunter-gatherer groups to oppose. But here we must bear in mind Sassaman's observation that "local" egalitarian communities are sometimes premised on an oppositional stance to oppressive regimes located well in the distance. To what extent, for instance, were southwestern peoples during the Late Archaic and Basketmaker periods influenced by the dramatic collapse of egalitarianism (that is, the rise of centralized power) some 500 miles to the south in central Mexico? Certainly, groups living in the northern Southwest during the early centuries of the common era would have had some impression of Teotihuacan's monumental presence, vague and mythical though that impression would have been for most. And it is likely that dissident groups from the south—whose experiences with political domination would have been much more direct—periodically traveled north as a means of opting out of the State or, just as likely, as a means of escaping the instability and violent uncertainty that rippled throughout Mesoamerica from the urban core. Hopi traditions discuss very long distance clan migrations up from the south when addressing Pueblo demographic realignments (Bernardini and Fowles 2010), and we need only imagine comparable scenarios somewhat deeper in the past.[6]

The claim that Archaic foragers in the Southwest actively sought to protect political egalitarianism and a domestic mode of production is difficult to test explicitly, but the plausibility of such a scenario is evident when we consider the manner in which agriculture spread throughout the region. Agriculture has been the great evolutionary experiment in human tethering—demanding, in most cases, new notions of ownership, a new commitment to staying in place, and an implicit political challenge to the ability of individuals to vote with their feet. Certainly there are those who have sought to understand the introduction and intensification of agriculture purely as a matter of subsistence, as an adaptation to particular environmental challenges and possibilities. However, serious reflection on the issue—from Rousseau to Sahlins—has always led scholars to acknowledge that agriculture is fundamentally a political policy as well. (Note how easily the notion of agricultural sedentism, of *staying in place*, slips into the notion of political domination,[7] of *being kept in one's place*).

Limited agriculture first made its appearance in parts of the Colorado Plateau after 1500 BCE, and recent research has indicated that early experiments with formal irrigation canal systems may have been under way in a few areas as early as 1000 BCE (Damp et al. 2002). After this time the use of corn, squash, and, eventually, beans became much more widespread, prompting many southwestern archaeologists to treat 1000 BCE as the end of the Archaic and the beginning of the Basketmaker (proto-Puebloan) period or, following Huckell (1995), of the Early Agricultural period. As Cordell (1997:129–31) cautions, however, such chronological systems tend to impose a spurious uniformity on a far more variable past. The reality is that most parts of the northern Southwest continued to practice Late Archaic lifeways well into the common era, adopting domesticates—if they did at all—as a supplement to hunted and gathered resources. Only after AD 500 or so, with the beginning of the Pueblo period, did a full commitment to agriculture become truly common on the Colorado Plateau. And only after AD 900 or so was that commitment made throughout the Rio Grande valley to the east. Viewed in broad evolutionary terms, then, the Southwest was home to a very

reluctant and fragmented Neolithic Revolution indeed.

Why this gap of well over a millennium between the introduction of domesticates and the subsequent emergence of committed agricultural communities? Wills (1995) offers a compelling explanation. He argues that the farmer's life was probably never the conscious goal of any significant percentage of Late Archaic foragers in the northern Southwest and that domesticates would have been initially adopted on a limited scale as part of an effort—paradoxical though it may have been—to improve a group's ability to forage and to maintain access to key nonagricultural resources such as deer herds or piñon harvesting areas. "Late Archaic food production," observes Wills (1995:234), "can be seen as an intensification of a pre-maize economic focus on mobile and spatially variable resources, with stored cultigens serving to help establish residential control over critical fall foraging areas." Surplus production, then, probably was not the rationale behind agriculture's initial adoption in the northern Southwest. (As Sahlins [1972:27] wrote of the Hadza, so too may the Late Archaic foragers have "reject[ed] the Neolithic revolution in order to *keep* their leisure…mainly on the grounds that this [agriculture] would involve too much hard work.") Wills argues that it was only when already committed agriculturalists from the Basin and Range region to the south began to regularly impinge on key animal and plant resources on the Colorado Plateau that the local Archaic foragers were forced to use domesticates in order to stake claims to existing nonagricultural goods.

But was more than simple economics at play? To what extent, for instance, might Late Archaic or early Basketmaker peoples have been aware that "farming" was what subjugated peoples did in Mesoamerican polities to the south? Might their continued commitment to residential mobility and foraging even after the introduction of domesticates have been born of political no less than economic concerns? One way of exploring these questions is to imagine the decisions involved in the initial experiments with domesticates or the first movements toward a fully committed agricultural life. This is the standard approach. From a countercultural perspective, however, the question of origins becomes less central, and we are encouraged to attend more closely to those "out-of-phase" hunter-gatherers who seem to have been far more successful at keeping the life of the tethered farmer at arm's length.

The particular case I have in mind is a period in the northern Rio Grande increasingly referred to as the "Latest Archaic," a neologism that draws our attention to the persistence of forager communities well after the traditional Archaic end date. The northern Rio Grande is a high-elevation region with extensive forests of piñon and juniper, mountains rich with deer and elk, and relatively lush riverine valleys. As such, it would have been an attractive landscape for hunter-gatherers. Little surprise, then, that the region was one of the last to succumb to agriculture. Corn appears in limited contexts by 1200 BCE, but it was not until the late ninth century AD that true agricultural settlements became common (Vierra and Ford 2006:506). In a recent review, Stephen Post (2002:44) describes these persistent foragers as "a population so comfortable in its lush settings that it resisted the apple or in this case the kernel of temptation until the latest possible moment." It was a population, he concludes, that resisted not only agriculture but also the Pueblo agriculturalists who were competing for access to the landscape at the end of the first millennium AD (Post 2002:43).

Eventually, the common story of Neolithic colonialism played out: increasingly stripped of their traditional territories, most foragers fell before the inexorable wave of agriculturalists. But this is not to say that Neolithization was without its opponents. Upham (1984, 1994a, 1994b) has argued that archaeologists consistently overlook evidence of low-visibility hunter-gatherer populations who persisted in interstitial areas between agricultural centers. Provocatively, he suggests that this unacknowledged and largely invisible archaeological "underclass" was composed not simply of Archaic holdovers but also of former agriculturalists who, for whatever reasons, gave up farming and reverted to earlier subsistence pursuits as part of a resilient adaptive strategy (see also Cordell and Plog 1979).

Upham's model has not won many followers, and it remains unclear how many Pueblo families actually left their villages for the dispersed and nomadic life of the foraging underclass before the

Colonial period. However, the notion that voluntary simplicity was a viable response to ecological or political problems—that "complexity" was occasionally cast off, and for good reason—has met with more enthusiasm.

Societies against Chaco

This is most evident in current archaeological understandings of the so-called Chaco Phenomenon—or, rather, of its decline in the twelfth and thirteenth centuries AD. In the ancestral Pueblo world, Chaco was the major experiment in centralization and "complexity"; not surprisingly, it has come to consume a sizable percentage of archaeological attention in the region. We are drawn to hot societies (we look upon them with a kind of sociological affinity, spurious though this may be), and Chaco, with its relatively explosive growth of great houses, regional economies, and ritualized landscapes, gives the impression of having been hot indeed (see Lekson, this volume; Neitzel, this volume). In broad evolutionary terms, the emergence of Chaco Canyon as a religiopolitical center came shortly after the widespread adoption of greater sedentism and intensive agriculture. It was, in this sense, made possible by the very economic system that had previously seen centuries of opposition.

Much debate surrounds the degree to which Chaco was influenced by Mesoamerican models of hierarchy and control, and there is little agreement on the nature of Chacoan leadership. Some interpretations present the canyon as a pilgrimage center managed in relatively egalitarian fashion by resident priests (Johnson 1989; Renfrew 2001; Yoffee 2001). Others claim that at its apex Chaco was a secondary state dominated by an elite who resided in palaces, extracted tribute, and kept the masses in place through the threat, and occasional practice, of theatrical violence (see Lekson 1999, 2002, 2006a, 2009; Wilcox 1999).

Chaco polarizes contemporary scholarship, in other words, and I do not intend to defend either side of the debate here. (Again, the greater archaeological need is to dethrone the centralized and "complex" as a privileged domain of inquiry.) That said, it is worth entertaining the possibility that polarization *itself* was a core characteristic of the Chacoan system, no less among ancestral Pueblo communities of the past than it is among archaeologists of the present. I suspect, in fact, that eleventh- and twelfth-century onlookers also struggled to resolve two very different readings of what was going on behind the high walls of Pueblo Bonito and its sister great houses. Might not there have been conferences held—in kivas if not in Marriott Hotels—in which those who viewed Chaco as a ritual center by and for the people argued with those who viewed it as a dangerous game of an elite in search of social power?

The stories of those who bought into the system have been considered at length by archaeologists interested in the so-called Chacoan outliers. Outliers were great houses located up to 150 kilometers away from Chaco Canyon, and while it is unclear whether they were constructed by locals seeking entrée into the system or by missionizing forces from the core itself, there can be little doubt that they represent groups who were more, rather than less, accepting of Chacoan complexity. But what of the dissident groups during Chaco's rise to power? What of those who opted out of the system? We have already established our set of expectations regarding what such dissidence might look like: geographic movement away from the core area, ideological reforms, emphatic egalitarianism, and frequently a primitivistic or throwback quality to a group's material culture. Do we encounter this countercultural signature when we turn from Chaco's core to consider the communities at its periphery?

Elsewhere I have argued that this is indeed what we find in portions of the northern Rio Grande during the Pueblo II period (AD 900–1150; Fowles 2004). The Rio Grande region has always been a curious anomaly in Chacoan studies insofar as it was one of the few Pueblo areas that seemed largely unaffected by the emergence of Chaco Canyon as a religiopolitical center a short distance to the west. Unlike the rest of the Colorado Plateau, the northern Rio Grande was neither linked to Chaco Canyon by formal roads nor a participant in great-house architecture. Local ceramics exhibited clear stylistic affinities with those produced in the Chacoan sphere to the west,[8] but the larger flamboyance of Chacoan material culture (its indulgence in macaws, copper bells, specialized ceramic forms, fancy architecture, and the like) was decidedly absent. Indeed,

northern Rio Grande sites during the Pueblo II period seem almost aggressively simple: dispersed pit houses with or without small surface storerooms were the norm; nuclear or extended families appear to have been economically autonomous; intensive agriculture was little practiced; hunting and gathering were dominant subsistence activities; burial practices were plain and largely undifferentiated; and so on. Perhaps most significantly, their ritual practices were also of such material simplicity that it is often quite difficult to say much about the "religious" lives of northern Rio Grande communities during this period (Fowles 2004)—a stark contrast indeed to the so-called rituality of Chaco.

Such patterns present us with two broad interpretive possibilities. On one hand, we might conclude that the northern Rio Grande communities (and perhaps those of a number of other marginal areas during the Chacoan period) were developmentally sluggish in key political and economic respects, that they were anachronisms populated by communities of the not-yet-complex. In keeping with the discussion above, let us call this a model of "simple simplicity": the simplicity of innocent and naive beginnings. On the other hand, we might look at the same empirical patterns and read them as principled, reactionary phenomena. From this perspective, the northern Rio Grande communities of the Pueblo II period suddenly appear to be veritable seedbeds of countercultural activity, communities whose material simplicity and high levels of individual or household autonomy were born of complex historical entanglements with, and rejections of, objectionable systems of domination. Let us call this "complex simplicity": the simplicity of the anarchist or egalitarian defector.

To a certain extent, choosing one interpretation over the other depends on a careful reading of the available evidence for particular regional contexts. In my own research I have found that both oral histories and archaeological evidence point to a significant migration of Pueblo communities out of an area of early Chacoan expansion and into the Taos region during the eleventh century (Fowles 2004, 2005). Once on the Puebloan frontier, these migrants—locally referred to as the Valdez phase—established a relatively dense distribution of single-family pit house settlements that were, nevertheless, strongly decentralized, lacking Chaco-style great houses, great kivas, or any other clear ritual or decision-making centers. This "simple" material record of the Valdez phase prompted archaeologists a generation ago to speak of the overall "lag in cultural development" (Wetherington 1968:97) and "notable conservatism and peripherality" (Herold 1968:39) of communities situated "at the end of the line" vis-à-vis Pueblo culture generally (Peckham and Reed 1963:24). Increasingly, however, we are in a position to reform this view and reread the Valdez phase as a record of complex simplicity, broadly premised on a historical entanglement with—and rejection of—Chacoan ways. Theirs was not a naive simplicity perpetuated in ignorance of what it meant to be complex.

There are countercultural stories to tell whenever we look to the edges of a strongly centralized tradition such as Chaco. Orthodoxy never fails to produce nonconformists. Perhaps this is most dramatically evident when such traditions are viewed chronologically as phenomena characterized by rises and falls. Indeed, it is in attending to the "collapse" of the Chacoan system that southwestern archaeologists have come closest to articulating a countercultural perspective. The details surrounding Chaco's demise as a regional center are not my concern here. Many excellent studies explore the political, economic, and ecological reasons why Chaco Canyon was vacated during the twelfth century (see Lekson 2006b), ultimately resulting in the balkanized Puebloan landscape encountered by the Spanish in the sixteenth century. What interests me far more is the manner in which some archaeologists—building, significantly, on indigenous statements to this effect—have begun to argue that the memory of Chaco's excesses would have stood as a warning to would-be elites during the post-Chacoan era (Fowles forthcoming b; Lekson 2009; Lekson and Cameron 1995).

"Clearly the memory of what had happened in Chaco Canyon," writes Kantner (2006:44), "was both empowering and cautionary for new religious authorities as they emerged in the vacuum left by the disintegration of the Chaco world." Lekson (2006a:104) makes a related point when he quotes a Laguna Pueblo man who remarked that Chacoan leaders with "enormous amounts

of power…were causing changes that were never meant to happen." And a similar sentiment is presented by Swentzell (2004:50), a member of Santa Clara Pueblo, who finds a very un-Puebloan desire for hierarchy and control within the ostentation of Chacoan architecture. The suggestion here is that Chaco came to be conceptualized during the post-Chacoan era as a dangerous historical transgression. Perhaps we might even go so far as to say that in the Pueblo imaginary, Chaco assumed its place in the spectral nightworld that Graeber argues is so central to the construction of strongly egalitarian or anti-state societies.

At the very least, we must acknowledge that the elites buried at Pueblo Bonito (Pepper 1909) or in the well-known "Magician's Burial" at Ridge Ruin (McGregor 1943) would not have received a warm welcome in the Pueblo societies encountered by the Spanish a few centuries later. McGregor noted as much in his commentary on the material richness of the Magician's Burial: "So much fine material found with one man led to the immediate question of just what sort of man this individual must have been in life to have been deemed worthy of these rich offerings. It is now quite contradictory to general Pueblo concepts to encourage the acquisition of personal wealth" (McGregor 1943:271). In recent centuries these "general Pueblo concepts" have stressed the humility of leadership and the muting of material difference.

This is not to say that the Pueblos are without "elites": differential access to sacred objects, esoteric knowledge, and positions of ritual power clearly distinguished high- and low-status individuals in all known villages (see Brandt 1994; Levy 1992; Ortiz 1969). But the great paradox of Pueblo leadership is that elites are notoriously unable to act elite when it comes to political ambition or economic accumulation. One is reminded, here, of Rousseau's first maxim of politics: "that people gave themselves chiefs to defend their liberty and not to be enslaved by them. *If we have a Prince*, said Pliny to Trajan, *it is in order that he may keep us from having a master*" (Rousseau 2002 [1753]:128). Ruth Benedict (2005 [1934]: 99) wrote similarly about Zuni. The ideal leader, she noted, "is a person of dignity and affability who has never tried to lead.… He avoids office. He may have it thrust upon him, but he does not seek it." The ideal leader "avoid(s) the appearance of leadership." Why? Because until the twentieth century the consequences were severe: "A man who thirsts for power or knowledge, who wishes to be as they scornfully phrase it 'a leader of his people,' receives nothing but censure and will very likely be persecuted for sorcery, and he often has been. Native authority of manner is a liability in Zuni, and witchcraft is the ready charge against a person who possesses it. He is hung by his thumbs until he 'confesses.' It is all Zuni can do with a man of strong personality" (Benedict 2005: 99). Those who sought to reside in fancy homes, adorn themselves with expensive markers of status, consume privileged cuisine, or make excessive demands of the populace—those, in other words, who would seek to act *Chacoan*—eventually found themselves hanging by their thumbs (Fowles forthcoming a).

This is a classic example of what Boehm (1999) refers to as a reverse dominance hierarchy, in which the many dominate the few who would seek to lead them. Others might link it to the various leveling sanctions (witchcraft accusations, in particular) used by small-scale societies throughout the world to keep their leaders in line—Lee's (1990:244) "irreducible core of the communal mode of production." The important point is that this egalitarian orientation *has a history*: it is the highly evolved political strategy of those who have come to walk away from a certain type of complexity (Fowles 2002, 2010, forthcoming a and b). It is, in other words, complex simplicity: Pueblo counterculture.

In this regard, it is striking to note an ethnographic comparison made by Underhill in her writings on Taos Pueblo. Unlike the commonplace comparison made by ethnologists between the Pueblos and other tribal peoples in Africa or New Guinea or by archaeologists between the modern Pueblos and the early villages of Formative Mesoamerica or the Neolithic Near East, Underhill was prompted to draw connections with the seventeenth- and eighteenth-century Puritans who sought a society of pure and moral simplicity in contrast to the clericalism and religious hierarchy of Europe:

One cannot help noticing the likeness of this community to other religious settlements of history…. Taos might in some respects be old Salem, settled by people with one belief, people who feel that their dress, their speech, even their food, are an expression of that belief and must not be changed…. Taos is run like one of the early Puritan hamlets where it was the joy and pride of the villagers to work together at their housebuilding, their harvesting, their quilting, to have the same beliefs and the same dress and to penalize anyone who deviated. Such comparison may sound strange… but Taos, like the Massachusetts Bay colony, is proud of its rigid principles and plain farming manners, a stickler for the white sheet and the moccasin even as the Pilgrims were for the drab coat and tall hat; demanding that all shall go to church (only in this case we read kiva) and that none shall marry out of meeting. (Underhill 1938:152–153)

The comparison is all the more compelling when we acknowledge that, as with the Puritans, the post-Chaco Pueblos appear to have been embroiled in their own historical movement away from clericalism and theocratic complexity.

Conclusion

The story of counterculture's development in the American Southwest did not end with the move away from Chacoan complexity. As with most countercultural efforts, the post-Chacoan theocracies that emerged at Hopi, Zuni, and the Rio Grande Pueblos gave rise to their own internal malcontents. Oral histories are full of indications that dissenting individuals and families repeatedly opted out of village communities to join the more nomadic Athabaskan bands that flourished at the edges of Pueblo society during the Protohistoric period. This pattern only intensified when Pueblo villages came under Spanish control in the seventeenth century. Many threw off the colonial yoke by seeking shelter among the Navajo or nomadic groups of the Plains, where they adopted a life of greater decentralization, individual autonomy, and raiding—the pirate utopias (sensu Wilson 2003) of the Colonial period, perhaps. (Some eventually returned, either voluntarily or by colonial force, but other expatriates stayed. Hence, it comes as little surprise that the Navajo, along with tribes such as the Cherokee and Chickasaw, have emerged as the largest and most influential Native American nations. All are refugee groups, heirs to the deep tradition of cultural reinvention in the face of oppression and attempts at domination.)

Nor is the story of Native American counter-culture confined to the Southwest. The Chacoan tale that ends with both the physical and ideological abandonment of the Southwest's former center place finds a striking parallel in the cycle of dominance and desertion of the Cahokia region in the American Bottom during roughly the same period. There we confront the enigmatic case of the so-called Vacant Quarter, the large swath of land that during the late eleventh through fourteenth centuries was home to North America's largest urban center and most visibly hierarchical society but that by the end of the fifteenth century was all but abandoned (Cobb and Butler 2002). Climatic change, as usual, has been invoked as a cause, though this seems insufficient; hence, we are led to contemplate the role played by countercultural forces that would have sent malcontents—the Effigy Mound societies of Wisconsin (Wilson 1998), the Iroquois (Trigger 1990), and, no doubt, many others—running to the peripheries. Similar inquires must be made throughout the continent.

There is no question that Native America indeed gave birth to dictators on occasion—some petty, others profound. This reality would have been all the more painfully obvious to those who directly suffered at the hands of such alpha individuals. But enough has been written about the rise of the chief (Osborne 2007). The more important narrative runs counter to the chief, counter to complexity.

Despite frequent admonitions, we still regularly speak in terms of lack (societies without the state) when we should instead speak of an evolved form of alternative politics (societies against the state) (see Fowles 2010). Political anthropology has a laudable tradition of examining the logic of egalitarianism on its own terms, and my point is not that continued study of leveling sanctions and the like is not critical to our understanding of such societies (see Boehm 1999; Lee 1990; Woodburn 1982). But consider the following question:

if we really are serious about treating egalitarianism and domination as alternative and symmetrical sorts of political ideologies, why is the rhetoric of "collapse" only used to describe historical movements from systems of domination to systems of greater individual autonomy? Why do we not speak, for instance, of the initial emergence of Chacoan hegemony as a "collapse" and dismantling of the egalitarian order? And why do we not speak of the post-Chaco period as the (re)construction of the anti-State?

Ultimately, the problem boils down to the relative historicity of our notions of simplicity and complexity. To label a society "complex" is to imply a developmental past, a series of steps away from an original state of simplicity. The argument about whether these steps were unilineal or highly variable is beside the point—either way, complex societies have histories. But when we label a society "egalitarian" or politically "simple," no such developmental past is necessarily implied. In place of historical contingency, interpretations typically invoke notions of ecological or economic contingency: the logic of "immediate return systems," "adaptation to scarcity," and so on. Granted, there has been a vigorous debate within hunter-gatherer studies over the degree to which the strong egalitarianism of historic groups such as the Hadza or !Kung San was a product of their historical entanglement with, and encapsulation by, surrounding polities of far greater complexity (Lee 2006; Woodburn 2005). But this debate is also largely beside the point. It is not just the simplicity of the subaltern or downtrodden that must be historicized; it is the voluntary simplicity of those who blew up their TVs and moved to the country rather than simply resisting from within the existing system of domination. What we need, in other words, is an archaeology of all those hippies, anarchists, peaceniks, neoprimitivists, utopianists, anticlerical reformers, and counterculture communities that were *also* making history in the North American landscape prior to European conquest—an archaeology of *progressive societies* to replace the tenacious Enlightenment notions of evolutionary progress that continue to drive the lion's share of archaeological research.

Notes

1. In fact, Hopper tried to stage this *Easy Rider* sequence at the commune itself in exchange for lavishly feeding the members during the filming, but New Buffalo refused his overtures with the simple statement, "We only eat brown rice and beans." So the story goes, anyway.

2. Viewed more broadly, New Buffalo was a continuation of a local counterculture genealogy that extends back to the bohemian, antiwar, primitivist group of expatriate artists who came to Taos following Mabel Dodge Luhan during the first half of the twentieth century. Rudnick (1996) has beautifully used the Luhan house as the thread in this larger story of utopianism in Taos.

3. This seems to be the case even in those more vividly Dionysian countercultural experiments described by Wilson (2003) as "pirate utopias."

4. Interestingly, Boehm's (1999) argument centers on the position that *all* human societies—even "egalitarian" ones—are hierarchical; it is just that they are hierarchical in different ways. Whereas most chiefly and state societies have, like their primate relatives, *orthodox* dominance hierarchies in which the few have power over the many, Boehm argues that egalitarian societies have *reverse* dominance hierarchies in which the many have power over the few (that is, over the few who would seek to dominate). Orthodox dominance hierarchies are relatively easy to explain insofar as they mark a return to an ingrained biological pattern. The reverse dominance hierarchies of egalitarian societies, in contrast, stand as the greater puzzle and must be examined as a highly evolved endpoint in their own right.

5. We might extend Lévi-Strauss's position here by drawing a connection to Asad's (2003) more recent critique of the Western tendency to constantly judge the non-West by the degree to which the latter is willing to *change*. Efforts to stay the same, Asad points out, seem never to be viewed as acts of human agency, despite the great pains and conscious choices that may be involved. This critique is applicable to assessments of Native American "traditionalism" or "primitivity" no less than to assessments of Muslim "medievalism."

6. Long-distance migration models have been proposed to explain early agricultural settlements across the Southwest (see Berry 1982; Matson 1991), although to my knowledge none have considered the possible immigration of hunter-gatherer dissenters into the region as a means of opting out of expanding agricultural communities to the south.

7. Wilson (1998) puts it this way: whereas hunter-gatherers may be "violent" in their engagement with the nonhuman or natural world, agriculturalists are "cruel." However much mobile hunter-gatherers seek to use the environment, the agricultural impulse is necessarily one of domination, a kind of ecological discipline that is preadapted for a future Foucauldian world of State discipline vis-à-vis its subjects. Elsewhere, Ingold (2000) draws a similar contrast in his analysis of the evolution of human-animal relations from a paradigm of "trust" to one of "domination" with the advent of agricultural communities.

8. Kwahe'e black-on-white, the dominant ceramic type in the northern Rio Grande during this period, was clearly part of the same stylistic tradition as such Chacoan types as Gallup black-on-white. Significant quantities of Red Mesa black-on-white (broadly speaking, a Chacoan type) have also been found at tenth-century sites in the northern Rio Grande (Fowles 2004). Pueblo II ceramics, in other words, betray a historical connection between Chaco and the northern Rio Grande, prompting us to read the latter's simplicity as a choice made not out of ignorance but as a conscious rejection of more complex options.

References

Asad, Talal
2003   *Formations of the Secular: Christianity, Islam, Modernity*. Stanford University Press, Stanford, California.

Benedict, Ruth
2005   [1934] *Patterns of Culture*. Mariner Books, New York.

Bernardini, Wesley, and Severin M. Fowles
2010   Becoming Hopi, Becoming Tiwa: Two Pueblo Histories of Movement. In *Movement, Connectivity, and Landscape Change*, edited by Margaret Nelson. University of Colorado Press, Denver.

Berry, Michael S.
1982   *Time, Space, and Transition in Anasazi Prehistory*. University of Utah Press, Salt Lake City.

Boehm, Christopher
1999   *Hierarchy in the Forest*. Harvard University Press, Cambridge.

Brandt, Elizabeth A.
1994   Egalitarianism, Hierarchy, and Centralization in the Pueblos. In *The Ancient Southwestern Community: Models and Methods for the Study of Prehistoric Social Organization*, edited by W. H. Wills and Robert D. Leonard, pp. 9–23. University of New Mexico Press, Albuquerque.

Cameron, Catherine M., and Andrew I. Duff
2008   History and Process in Village Formation:

Context and Contrasts from the Northern Southwest. *American Antiquity* 73(1):29–57.

Clastres, Pierre

1989 *Society against the State.* Zone Books, New York.

Cobb, Charles R., and Brian M. Butler

2002 The Vacant Quarter Revisited: Late Mississippian Abandonment of the Lower Ohio Valley. *American Antiquity* 67(4):625–641.

Cordell, Linda

1997 *Archaeology of the Southwest.* 2nd ed. Academic Press, New York.

Cordell, Linda S., and Fred Plog

1979 Escaping the Confines of Normative Thought. *American Antiquity* 44(3):405–429.

Damp, Jonathan E., Stephen A. Hall, and Susan J. Smith

2002 Early Irrigation on the Colorado Plateau near Zuni Pueblo, New Mexico. *American Antiquity* 67(4):665–676.

Fowler, Melvin L., Jerome Rose, Barbara VanderLeest, and Steven R. Ahler

1999 *The Mound 72 Area: Dedicated and Sacred Space in Early Cahokia.* Reports of Investigation No. 54. Illinois State Museum, Springfield.

Fowles, Severin M.

2002 Inequality and Egalitarian Rebellion: A Tribal Dialectic in Tonga History. In *The Archaeology of Tribal Societies*, edited by W. Parkinson, pp. 74–96. International Monographs in Prehistory, Ann Arbor, Michigan.

2004 The Making of Made People: The Prehistoric Evolution of Northern Tiwa Hierocracy. Unpublished Ph.D. dissertation, University of Michigan, Ann Arbor.

2005 Historical Contingency and the Prehistoric Foundations of Eastern Pueblo Moiety Organization. *Journal of Anthropological Research* 61(1):25–52.

2006 Our Father (Our Mother): Gender, Praxis, and Marginalization in Pueblo Religion. In *Engaged Anthropology*, edited by Michelle Hegmon and Sunday Eiselt, pp. 27–51. Anthropological Papers No. 94. Museum of Anthropology, University of Michigan, Ann Arbor.

2008 Steps toward an Archaeology of Taboo. In *Religion, Archaeology, and the Material World*, edited by Lars Fogelin, pp. 15–37. Center for Archaeological Investigations, Occasional Paper No. 36. Southern Illinois University Press, Carbondale.

2010 People without Things. In *The Anthropology of Absence: Materialisations of Transcen-*

dence and Loss, edited by Mikkel Bille, Frida Hastrup, and Tim Flohr Sorensen, pp. 23–41. Springer, New York.

Forthcoming a On Torture in Societies against the State. In Violence and Civilization, edited by Roderick Campbell. Joukowsky Institute, Providence.

Forthcoming b The Pueblo Village in an Age of Reformation. In Oxford Handbook of North American Archaeology, edited by Tim Pauketat. Oxford University Press, London.

Gaonkar, Dilip Parameshwar (editor)

2001 *Alternative Modernities.* Duke University Press, Durham, North Carolina.

Gledhill, John

2000 *Power and Its Disguises: Anthropological Perspectives on Politics.* Pluto Press, London.

Goffman, Ken, and Dan Joy

2004 *Counterculture through the Ages: From Abraham to Acid House.* Villard, New York.

Graeber, David

2004 *Fragments of an Anarchist Anthropology.* Prickly Paradigm Press, Chicago.

Herold, Laurance C.

1968 An Archaeological-Geographical Survey of the Rio Grande de Ranchos. In *Papers on Taos Archaeology*, by Laurance C. Herold and Ralph A. Luebben, pp. 9–42. Fort Burgwin Research Center No. 7. Talpa, New Mexico.

Houriet, Robert

1971 *Getting Back Together.* Coward, McCann and Geohegan, New York.

Huckell, Bruce

1995 *Of Marshes and Maize: Preceramic Agricultural Settlements in the Cienega Valley, Southeastern Arizona.* Anthropological Papers of the University of Arizona No. 59. University of Arizona Press, Tucson.

Ingold, Tim

2000 From Trust to Domination: An Alternate History of Human-Animal Relations. In *The Perception of the Environment: Essays in Livelihood, Dwelling and Skill*, pp. 61–76. Routledge, New York.

Johnson, Gregory A.

1989 Dynamics of Southwestern Prehistory, Far Outside—Looking In. In *Dynamics of Southwest Prehistory*, edited by Linda S. Cordell and George J. Gumerman, pp. 371–389. Smithsonian Institution Press, Washington, D.C.

Kantner, John

2006 Religious Behavior in Post-Chaco Years. In *Religion in the Prehispanic Southwest*, edited by Christine S. Vanpool, Todd L. Vanpool, and David A. Phillips, pp. 31–52. AltaMira Press, Lanham, Maryland.

Keltz, Iris

2000   *Scrapbook of a Taos Hippie.* Cinco Puntos Press, El Paso, Texas.

Knauft, Bruce M.

1991   Violence and Sociality in Human Evolution. *Current Anthropology* 32(4):391–428.

Latour, Bruno

1993   *We Have Never Been Modern.* Translated by Catherine Porter. Harvard University Press, Cambridge.

Leary, Timothy

2004   Foreword to *Counterculture through the Ages: From Abraham to Acid House,* by Ken Goffman and Dan Joy, pp. ix–xi. Villard, New York.

LeBlanc, Steven A.

1999   *Prehistoric Warfare in the American Southwest.* University of Utah Press, Salt Lake City.

Lee, Richard B.

1990   Primitive Communism and the Origin of Social Inequality. In *The Evolution of Political Systems: Sociopolitics in Small-Scale Sedentary Societies,* edited by Steadman Upham, pp. 225–246. Cambridge University Press, New York.

2006   Twenty-First Century Indigenism. *Anthropological Theory* 6(4):455–479.

Lekson, Stephen H.

1999   *The Chaco Meridian.* AltaMira Press, Walnut Creek, California.

2002   War in the Southwest, War in the World. *American Antiquity* 67(4):607–624.

2006a   Lords of the Great House: Pueblo Bonito as a Palace. In *Palaces and Power in the Americas: From Peru to the Northwest Coast,* edited by Jessica Joyce Christie and Patricia Joan Sarro, pp. 99–114. University of Texas Press, Austin.

2006b   Chaco Matters: An Introduction. In *The Archaeology of Chaco Canyon: An Eleventh-Century Pueblo Regional Center,* edited by Stephen H. Lekson, pp. 3–44. School of American Research Press, Santa Fe.

2009   *A History of the Ancient Southwest.* School for Advanced Research Press, Santa Fe.

Lekson, Stephen H., and Catherine M. Cameron

1995   The Abandonment of Chaco Canyon, the Mesa Verde Migrations, and the Reorganization of the Pueblo World. *Journal of Anthropological Archaeology* 14:184–202.

Lévi-Strauss, Claude

1966   *The Savage Mind.* University of Chicago Press, Chicago.

Levy, Jerrold E.

1992   *Orayvi Revisited: Social Stratification in an "Egalitarian" Society.* School of American Research Press, Santa Fe.

Matson, R. G.

1991   *The Origins of Southwestern Agriculture.* University of Arizona Press, Tucson.

McGregor, John C.

1943   Burial of an Early American Magician. *Proceedings of the American Philosophical Society* 86(2):270–298.

Mills, Barbara (editor)

2000   *Alternative Leadership Strategies in the Prehispanic Southwest.* University of Arizona Press, Tucson.

Nassaney, Michael S.

2001   The Historical-Processual Development of Late Woodland Societies. In *The Archaeology of Traditions: Agency and History Before and After Columbus,* edited by Timothy Pauketat, pp. 157–173. University Press of Florida, Gainesville.

Ortiz, Alfonso

1969   *The Tewa World.* University of Chicago Press, Chicago.

Osborne, Robin

2007   Is Archaeology Equal to Equality? *World Archaeology* 39(2):143–150.

Parsons, Elsie Clews

1936   *Taos Pueblo.* George Banta Publishing Co., Menasha, Wisconsin.

Pauketat, Timothy

2001   Practice and History in Archaeology: An Emerging Paradigm. *Anthropological Theory* 1:73–98.

Pauketat, T. R.

2007   *Chiefdoms and Other Archaeological Delusions.* Altamira Press.

Pauketat, Timothy (editor)

2001   *The Archaeology of Traditions: Agency and History Before and After Columbus.* University Press of Florida, Gainesville.

Pauketat, Timothy, and Diana DiPaolo Loren (editors)

2005   *North American Archaeology.* Blackwell, Malden, Massachusetts.

Peckham, Stewart, and Eric K. Reed

1963   Three Sites near Ranchos de Taos, New Mexico. In *Highway Salvage Archaeology,* Vol. 4, assembled by Stewart Peckham, pp. 1–27. New Mexico State Highway Department and the Museum of New Mexico, Santa Fe.

Pepper, George H.

1909   The Exploration of a Burial-Room in Pueblo

Bonito, New Mexico. In *Putnam Anniversary Volume: Anthropological Essays*, pp. 196–252. G. E. Stechert, New York.

Post, Stephen S.
2002 Emerging from the Shadows: The Archaic Period in the Northern Rio Grande. In *Traditions, Transitions, and Technologies*, edited by Sarah H. Schlanger, pp. 33–48. University Press of Colorado, Boulder.

Preucel, Robert W.
2006 *Archaeological Semiotics*. Blackwell, Malden, Massachusetts.

Renfrew, Colin
2001 Production and Consumption in a Sacred Economy: The Material Correlates of High Devotional Expression at Chaco Canyon. *American Antiquity* 66(1):14–25.

Roszak, Theodore
1968 *The Making of a Counterculture*. University of California Press, Berkeley.

Rousseau, Jean-Jacques
2002 [1753] Discourse on the Origins and Foundations of Inequality among Mankind. In *The Social Contract and The First and Second Discourses*, edited by Susan Dunn, pp. 69–148. Yale University Press, New Haven.

Rudnick, Lois Palken
1996 *Utopian Vistas: The Mabel Dodge Luhan House and the American Counterculture*. University of New Mexico Press, Albuquerque.

Sahlins, Marshall
1972 *Stone Age Economics*. Aldine-Atherton, Chicago.

Sassaman, Kenneth E.
2001 Hunter-Gatherers and Traditions of Resistance. In *The Archaeology of Traditions: Agency and History Before and After Columbus*, edited by Timothy Pauketat, pp. 218–236. University Press of Florida, Gainesville.

Scott, James C.
1990 *Domination and the Arts of Resistance: Hidden Transcripts*. Yale University Press, New Haven.

Stevenson, Matilda Cox
1906 Unfinished Manuscripts and Notes on File. National Anthropological Archives, Smithsonian Institution, Washington, D.C.

Swentzell, Rina
2004 A Pueblo Woman's Perspective on Chaco Canyon. In *In Search of Chaco: New Approaches to an Archaeological Enigma*, edited by David Grant Noble, pp. 48–53. School of American Research Press, Santa Fe.

Tarlow, Sarah
2003 Excavating Utopia: Why Archaeologists Should Study "Ideal" Communities of the Nineteenth Century. *International Journal of Historical Archaeology* 6(4):299–323.

Trigger, Bruce G.
1990 Maintaining Economic Equality in Opposition to Complexity: An Iroquoian Case Study. In *The Evolution of Political Systems: Sociopolitics in Small-Scale Sedentary Societies*, edited by Steadman Upham, pp. 119–145. Cambridge University Press, New York.

Underhill, Ruth M.
1938 *First Penthouse Dwellers of America*. J. J. Augustin, New York.

Upham, Steadman
1984 Adaptive Diversity and Southwestern Abandonment. *Journal of Anthropological Research* 40:235–256.
1994a Ten Years After: Adaptive Diversity and Southwestern Archaeology. *Journal of Anthropological Research* 50(2):155–157.
1994b Nomads of the Desert West: A Shifting Continuum in Prehistory. *Journal of World Prehistory* 8(2):113–167.

Van Bueren, Thad (editor)
2006 *Dating Experiments: Issues and Insights about Utopian Communities*. Special edition of *Historical Archaeology* 40(1).

Vierra, Bradley J., and Richard I. Ford
2006 Early Maize Agriculture in the Northern Rio Grande Valley, New Mexico. In *Histories of Maize: Multidisciplinary Approaches to the Prehistory, Linguistics, Biogeography, Domestication and Evolution of Maize*, edited by John Staller, Robert Tykot, and Bruce Benz, pp. 497–510. Academic Press, New York.

Wetherington, Ronald
1968 *Excavations at Pot Creek Pueblo*. Fort Burgwin Research Center Publication No. 6. Talpa, New Mexico.

Wilcox, David R.
1999 A Peregrine View of Macroregional Systems in the North American Southwest, AD 750–1250. In *Great Towns and Regional Polities in the Prehistoric American Southwest and Southeast*, edited by Jill E. Neitzel, pp. 115–141. University of New Mexico Press, Albuquerque.

Wills, W. H.
1995 Archaic Foraging and the Beginning of Food Production in the American Southwest. In *Last Hunters, First Farmers*, edited by T. Douglas Price and Anne Birgitte Gebauer, pp. 215–242. School of American Research Press, Santa Fe.

Wilson, Peter Lamborn

1998   The Shamanic Trace. In *Escape from the Nine-teenth Century and Other Essays*, pp. 72–142. Autonomedia, New York.

2003   *Pirate Utopias: Moorish Corsairs and European Renegadoes*. Autonomedia, New York.

Woodburn, James

1982   Egalitarian Societies. *Man* 17(3):431–451.

2005   Egalitarian Societies Revisited. In *Property and Equality, Vol. 1: Ritualisation, Sharing, Egalitarianism*, edited by T. Widlock and W. G. Tadese, pp. 18–31. Berghahn Books, New York.

Yoffee, Norman

1993   Too Many Chiefs? (or Safe Texts for the '90s). In *Archaeological Theory: Who Sets the Agenda?* edited by Norman Yoffee and Andrew Sherratt, pp. 60–78. Cambridge University Press, New York.

2001   The Chaco "Rituality" Revisited. In *Chaco Society and Polity: Papers from the 1999 Conference*, edited by Linda S. Cordell and W. James Judge, pp. 63–78. Special Publication No. 4. New Mexico Archaeological Council, Albuquerque.

2005   *Myths of the Archaic State: Evolution of the Earliest Cities, States and Civilizations*. Cambridge University Press, Cambridge.

13

Downsizers, Upgraders, Cultural Constructors, and Social Producers

Robert Chapman

Archaeological knowledge of past societies is usually based on four factors: (1) culturally embedded assumptions and stereotypes, (2) ethnographic analogies, (3) theoretical arguments, and (4) the means to make social inferences from the preserved material evidence of past communities. At any one time our knowledge is the outcome of an articulation (however perceived or ranked in importance) between these factors. We have to question the extent to which this knowledge depends on, and is situated in, contemporary, cultural contexts, which lead us to ask particular questions of our archaeological data. We also need to ask whether our use of ethnographic analogies leads us to project the present into the past, whether our theoretical arguments are soundly based and coherent intellectual tools, and whether our means of social inference are sufficiently robust in relation to the quality and quantity of archaeological data.

My purpose in this chapter is to examine some of the interactions between these factors, using examples from both the Old and New Worlds. The discussion is set within much broader debates on archaeological thought in the Anglo-American world, especially those on social evolution, on structure and agency, on culture and society, and on the relative merits of materialist and idealist philosophies. As a tool to aid this discussion, I have categorized four kinds of archaeologists: downsizers, upgraders, cultural constructors, and social producers. I do this with some trepidation,

as I have no desire to inflict another typology on the profession. It is simply a device to help me develop an argument about how we study past societies through archaeological evidence.

Downsizers

Yoffee et al. (1999:267) introduced the concept of "downsizers" to refer to southeastern archaeologists in North America. Their point was that these archaeologists have consistently favored what might be called "conservative" social and political interpretations of the pre-European populations in this region: "Try to imagine a range of political possibilities, small to big, simple to complex, or local to far-flung, and these downsizers regularly come down on the side of the bare minimum" (Pauketat 2007:46). Thus, the eleventh-century AD monumental center of Cahokia, in the middle Mississippi Valley, coupled with the nearby sites of East St. Louis and St. Louis/Mound City, has evidence for large-scale population nucleation (10,000–15,000?), along with public rituals, physical coercion (the violent deaths and dismemberments of Mound 72), surplus production, and a centralized economy (Pauketat 2004, 2007). The consensus (as far as an outsider can perceive) seems to be that Cahokia was at the "complex" end of a chiefdom society, just short of, or perhaps in the process of evolving into, a state (e.g., Emerson 1997). And yet the point is argued that "if Cahokia, Cahokians, and Cahokia's mounds had been in ancient Mesopotamia, China, or

Africa archaeologists might not hesitate to identify pyramids in a city at the centre of an early state" (Pauketat 2004:3).

To propose that Cahokia was a state society in the eleventh century AD is to challenge assumptions about what constitutes a state society and where the early examples of such societies occurred. In the case of the Olmec, on the Gulf Coast of Mexico, there appears to be a view (e.g., Flannery and Marcus 2000) that these issues are not open for debate, fixed as they are in social evolutionary thought, comparative ethnography, and the equation of early states with the small number of early civilizations studied since the nineteenth century in the Near East, the Far East, Mesoamerica, and Peru (for a longer discussion of these issues and the "early states club," see Chapman 2003). And yet these issues ought to be open for debate (e.g., see the recent, historical study of Western political and philosophical thought on the state from the classical world to the twentieth century by Lull and Micó 2007); otherwise, there is a danger of intellectual ossification as we simply confirm, rather than question, what we think we already know.

There are also sufficient criticisms of the use of social evolutionary typologies in archaeology to support the view that they fail to account for social forms and historical sequences in many parts of the world. For example, Hegmon (2005:212) argues that the societies of the North American Southwest "have remained beyond the mold of neoevolutionary typologies," with their diversity of social forms, examples of centralized political authority, hereditary inequalities in access to ritual knowledge and productive resources (e.g., land, large game), and minimal development of material differences. As such, these societies did not conform to what Lekson (2005:235) calls their "stereotype": "egalitarian, communal, peaceful farming villages, steadfast in their ancient traditions."

Such stereotypes are culturally embedded. This process of "stereotyping" began in the cultural context of European colonization, as North America's indigenous peoples were conceived as "inherently unprogressive," "by nature and biologically incapable of significant cultural development," and "inherently static and primitive" (Trig-

ger 1980a:662–664). They were representatives of the past rather than the present. Interpretation of the material record of that past emphasized stability over change or denied the responsibility of indigenous peoples for impressive monuments such as burial mounds and southwestern pueblos, attributing them to "lost" (white) races (e.g., Trigger 1980a, 1984). This "denial of history" in the assertion of "simplicity" or "backwardness" served the interests of white colonialism, as can also be seen in the African continent (e.g., Schmidt 1995 on the claims for "inferior" iron technologies; Andah 1995 on the priority given to the study of tool making and subsistence over that of social life; Trigger 1984 on the denial of an indigenous origin for the ruins of Great Zimbabwe). According to Trigger (1980a), these stereotypes of indigenous peoples became less open in the twentieth century but sociocultural change was still "underestimated," earlier through diffusionist interpretations and from the 1960s through an emphasis on generalization, cultural evolution, and cultural ecology.

Trigger (1980a:662) contrasted the static, unprogressive stereotype of North American indigenous peoples with the preoccupation in European archaeology with "affirming that continuous cultural progress" occurred throughout the past. While initially convincing, this generalization glosses over the difference in the extent such "progress" was seen to be a characteristic of temperate, as opposed to Mediterranean, European societies. Mediterranean societies have been viewed as "timeless" by historians and anthropologists since the eighteenth century (Horden and Purcell 2000). Rural societies here are regarded as survivors from the past, static, traditional, and isolated. They are described in ethnographies as giving the impression that they "have been frozen in time and cut off from the wider world" (Horden and Purcell 2000:467). Compared with north European societies, they appear "primitive" in both culture and economy. Such an approach creates a "homogenised" (2000:487) and "Romantic" (2000:28–29) view of Mediterranean societies, in which "antiquity lives on round today's Mediterranean shores" (Braudel 1972:1239).

The emphasis in archaeological research in the central and western areas of the Mediterranean has been on long-term stasis, a surviving "traditional" rural economy (e.g., bare fallowing, transhumance) and environmentally determined specialization in agriculture and pastoralism (although this separation is now recognized as being historically contingent and a product of recent, state societies—e.g., Halstead 1987). This "survivalist" approach has influenced the study of the prehistoric Mediterranean during the last four decades, emphasizing long-term continuity in the relationship between people and the Mediterranean environment, tracing seasonal movements between upland and lowland pastures from the Middle Paleolithic to the present day (e.g., Higgs 1975; Barker 1981). According to this approach, Mediterranean peasant farmers exhibited slow, minimal change. Malone (2003:299) follows this approach for Neolithic Italy as a whole by proposing that "once established as farming communities, the societies appear to be conservative, and often rather isolated, except through the exchange of exotica."

In contrast, the eastern Mediterranean had state societies in the second millennium BC (e.g., Renfrew 1972). These states (Mycenaean and Minoan) emerged on the periphery of the Near Eastern core of civilization, while the central and west Mediterranean societies were on the periphery of the eastern Mediterranean core, until the successive emergence of the Etruscan and Roman states in central Italy in the first millennium BC. Thus, the East was viewed as dynamic and the West was static, or at best subject to a *longue durée*, with life injected by changes in macrovariables such as population pressure or the intensification of production. The major change seemingly came in the Bronze Age, with the emergence of stratification in a limited number of areas, although some question the accuracy of the term "stratification" for any of the pre–first millennium BC societies in the West (Mathers and Stoddart 1994:16). Essentially, the later prehistory of the West Mediterranean is partly predetermined by these cultural biases and by the history of research. The agenda is set and the ability to find "other" pasts is constrained (although see Chapman 2003; Lull and Risch 1995). Whether this view is cast in the mold of *ex Oriente lux* diffusionism or core-periphery theory, archaeologists still give priority to the so-

cial and economic "achievements" of the East over the West.

Upgraders

In contrast to "downsizers," there are archaeologists who can be argued to have "talked up" the societies they study. These are what we might call "upgraders." Doubtless archaeologists who infer the existence of state societies at Cahokia and among the Olmec are regarded by some as upgraders. However, for the purposes of this chapter, my interest is in periods when the search for the roots of local and regional social, economic, and political complexity has led archaeologists to infer greater complexity than appears warranted by the material evidence.

My main example is taken from Neolithic Eastern Anatolia. The oldest evidence for fully sedentary occupation in this region comes from Hallan Çemi, which dates to the late tenth millennium BC and covers less than 0.5 ha (Rosenberg 1999; Rosenberg and Redding 2000; Figure 13.1). Timber and stone-built features, including domestic structures, hearths, and above-ground storage, were arranged around what is described as a "central, activity area," where public feasting is argued to have taken place, given the concentrations of animal carcass parts and burned pebbles. In level 1, two circular, 5–6-m diameter, semisubterranean structures with internal benches set against the walls and sand and plaster floors are further distinguished by the rarity of evidence for food processing ("domestic") activities and consumption and the frequency of imported items such as copper ore and obsidian (which was also knapped here), as well as in one case a complete auroch skull (Rosenberg and Redding 2000:44–46). These structures are interpreted as "public buildings" that were communally constructed and used.

The low density of structures in each phase, coupled with the spatial extent of the site, suggests a small population (50–100?). Rosenberg and Redding (2000:50) propose that the community was composed of individual households and (in its last aceramic phase) two "suprahousehold corporate groups" (one per ritual structure). The emergence of the latter was, it is argued, an example of new social institutions that were

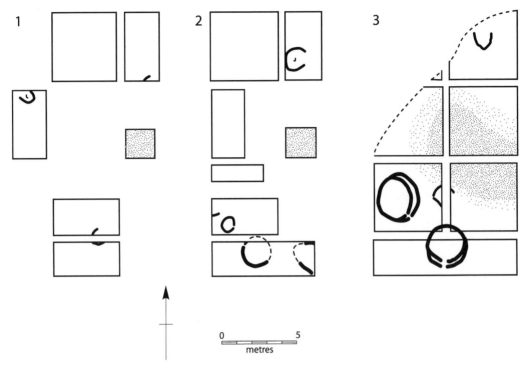

FIGURE 13.1. Successive occupation phases at Hallan Çemi (simplified from Rosenberg 1999:Fig. 2).

required in sedentary societies both to resolve conflict and to aid larger, community-level decision making. Whether or not one accepts the theoretical basis of this linkage between sedentism, ritual, and new institutions in a society of greater "complexity," the fact that the population size was comparable to that in standard mobile hunting and gathering bands (Rosenberg and Redding 2000:48) weakens the everyday need for such institutions. The exogamous social relations necessary to ensure the reproductive viability of local populations would also facilitate mobility between settlements, which is another means of dealing with conflict situations.

What is of further interest is the observation that the entrances to structures in all levels faced away from the central activity area, prompting Rosenberg and Redding (2000:48) to argue that this is evidence for a breakdown of generalized, reciprocal sharing, as households developed "private economic property." The problem is that no evidence of such property is cited. One could argue that there were tensions between community egalitarianism and the social practices of individual households, as everyday, indoor activi-

ties became less visible, but how and why such privacy came about and how it overcame the more normal "leveling" practices (e.g., joking, teasing) in face-to-face contact still require explanation. Overall, I see no reason why Hallan Çemi should signify a kind of "relatively complex social organisation" or "non-egalitarian, complex form of socio-economic pattern" (M. Özdoğan 1999:228).

Hallan Çemi marks the beginning (as far as is currently known) of a cultural tradition extending over at least two millennia, as agricultural societies developed in Eastern Anatolia. In a small number of key sites, spatially segregated ritual activity has been argued to signify the development of more stratified societies. At Çayönü (A. Özdoğan 1999) larger-scale occupation (3 ha) spans the period from at least ca. 9600–7000 BC, but it is only in the last few hundred years of this sequence that animal and possibly plant domestication emerged. In addition to the evidence for spatial separation of areas for the production of stone, copper (based on local sources), bone, and shell artifacts in the western sector, there were communal areas with roasting pits and segregation of mortuary rituals, with primarily secondary

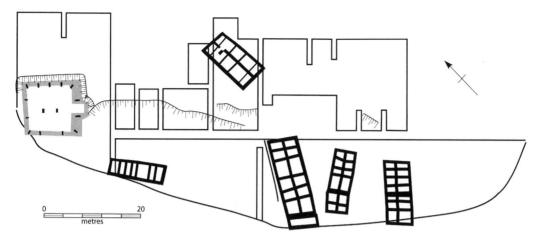

FIGURE 13.2. Plan of level II at Nevali Çori, showing the location of the cult building on the left of the excavated area. The monumental T-shaped pillars are located in the center and around the inside of the cult building (simplified from Hauptmann 1999:Fig. 2).

interments (especially the dozens of skulls) in the successive "skull buildings." Other buildings have been identified as "special," given their internal layout, while open-air pebbled plazas with rows of standing stones have been described as having "special" functions. Interestingly, there was more change in the architectural plan of the settlement than in its material culture during the length of its occupation.

This spatial segregation of "special" or "cult" buildings is seen even more impressively at the sites of Nevali Çori (Figure 13.2) and Göbekli Tepe (Hauptmann 1999). Here the famous "cult buildings" are not only renewed in the same locations but assumed monumental proportions: for example, at Göbekli Tepe carved T-shaped stone pillars at least 3 m high supported roofed rooms, and examples at least 6 m high have been found in a nearby quarry. These "cult buildings" are also distinguished by their internal plastering and painting. While there is evidence for domesticated cereals and legumes, as well as sheep and goats, at Nevali Çori, hunting and gathering continued as the basis of subsistence at Göbekli Tepe.

From Hauptmann's perspective (1999:82), these sites represent "steps developmental to a central organization in which the trade or barter of an elite class was restricted to sites with cult facilities." M. Özdoğan (1999:230) infers the existence of an "unegalitarian and stratified social structure" centered on ritual buildings that were

the "forerunners of Near Eastern temple architecture" and the Mesopotamian temple economy. In other words, both authors argue that a more complex society developed on the basis of the control of ritual and exchange. An explicit link is also made to later Mesopotamian civilization, but this developed nearly 1,000 km to the south some 4,000 years later, although Hauptmann himself (2002:267) expresses doubts about this link. I have seen no calculations of the labor required, in relation to the overall community size and other demands of production on labor, to construct such "special" buildings. The mobilization of labor on this scale, by itself, does not demand stratified social relations. There is no evidence for differential residential architecture at either Nevali Çori or Göbekli Tepe. Nor is the use of such terms as "stratification" or "class" defined, given that they refer to economically based differences in access to production and consumption (for citations, see Chapman 2003:79, 96–97). Spatially distinct areas for artifact production may indicate some form of specialization, but there is as yet no clear argument as to its scale (part or full time?) or its form (individual or community?) in Neolithic eastern Anatolia. Overall, the evidence for ritual activity and mortuary rituals is clear, not to say impressive, but to argue that this represents social stratification is assuming what is yet to be demonstrated on the basis of the economic foundations of these communities.

There appears to be no single reason for these "upgrader" interpretations, although they may in part be due to poorly developed theoretical arguments (cf. Hodder 1998:126 on the Anatolian Neolithic). A more culturally situated reason (for local archaeologists) may lie in the ideology of the early Turkish republic, linking the Turks with the Hittites and the Sumerians, thus creating "an ethnic amalgamation of thousands of years" (M. Özdoğan 1998:116–117; see also Atakuman 2008). In this way eastern Anatolia is no longer sitting passively on the periphery of the major cultural developments of the Near East but playing an active role in their early stages (for an analogous example, see Souvatzi 2007 on the search for more centralized and hierarchical society in Neolithic Thessaly as the ultimate origins of state formation 3,000 years later and 200 km to the south in Mycenaean Greece). Finally, we should note that any argument that seeks to distinguish "developmental steps toward" or "forerunners of" particular social forms or modes of production is teleological (i.e., stratification and civilization were the ultimate goals) and not historical.

Evolution, Progress, Dichotomies, and Typologies

The examples of downsizing and upgrading given above show us how our knowledge of the past is culturally situated as well as empirically mediated. The North American and Mediterranean case studies illustrate how change can be undervalued, given the history of cultural stereotypes, while the claims for earlier "complexity" in eastern Anatolia may be part of an intellectual search for origins under the influence of a nation-state ideology. In both the North American and Anatolian examples, the archaeological evidence is of sites that confound expectations (too big, too early, too "complex").

Concepts of social and cultural evolution, associated with notions of progress and directionality from "simple" to "complex," have permeated Western thought since the Enlightenment (Chapman 2003; Trigger 1998). Within this thought there are expectations that "complexity" has greater survival advantages, usually expressed in positive terminology, such as "advanced," "sophisticated," and, the ultimate compliment, "civilized." According to one Enlightenment belief,

human history exhibited continuous trends toward progress (thus providing one rationale for the disciplines of history and archaeology), but it was observed that the places where that progress occurred were unevenly distributed in time and space (e.g., civilizations and states did not occur everywhere at the same time).

Among European archaeologists of the early twentieth century it was Gordon Childe who best articulated the belief in progress. He aimed to identify what Trigger (1980b:114) calls "clearly defined, uni-directional, cumulative and progressive trends in human history" (improvements in human health, life expectancy, and the like, facilitated by "technological progress"; e.g., Childe 1944), at the same time recognizing that human history also showed evidence for periods of decline, conflict, and suffering. Progress was not inevitable. Childe (e.g., 1936) also argued that history was divided into "progressive" as opposed to "conservative" societies. According to Trigger (2006:348), Childe "proposed two general lines of cultural evolution: a progressive one, characterized by continuous technological development combined with a flexible social organization and ideology, and a conservative one, characterized by a static technology and the elaboration of convoluted social structures and ideologies." This proposal was in line with Childe's view of ideology's potential to hinder social development, and in particular the technological change that he put at the basis of progress. But it can be criticized for overemphasizing technology in the forces of production (which include the raw materials, tools, labor power, and the actual labor consumed in the processes of production) and for reducing the dialectical approach of Marxism to a dynamic/static typology of human societies.

Childe's division of societies was echoed (without citation) by Piggott's (1965:17) definition of "innovating" and "conserving" societies, in which technology was encouraged by "social acceptance" or impeded by a "satisfactory" environmental adaptation or an unbalanced "cultural pattern." The "conserving" societies were governed by tradition, to their own detriment. This scheme was atheoretical (e.g., how does tradition relate to social change? how were technological developments deemed "socially acceptable" and by whom?) and ahistorical (how do we explain the often marked changes that we see in supposedly "conserving" societies?). It was also tautological, in that "the tradition of a conserving society is to abide by tradition," and "the conservatism of barbarian Europe…led to the retention and transmission of tradition" (Piggott 1965:18, 259). Both schemes were also essentialist, much like any attribution of "personalities" to cultures, as innate characteristics were attributed to societies.

Other dichotomous divisions of human societies (e.g., "modern" vs. "traditional"/"primitive" societies) have also failed to engage with the range of historical forms and sequences documented by archaeology. Social typologies have been argued to obscure variation in social forms and historical sequences (the societies that do not fit the models). There has been frustration at the lack of clarity and definition in the use of basic concepts such as "complexity" and "hierarchy." Concern has been expressed at the representation of pasts that are back projections of the present (whether ethnographic or capitalist), thereby constraining our ability to find different pasts. The kind of dichotomous thinking embodied in notions of equal and unequal societies has given way to an emphasis on flux in social relations. There is also a greater emphasis on different materializations of comparable social relations (for examples of all the points made here, see Chapman 2003).

Cultural Constructors

If the reduction of histories to ethnographically based social dichotomies and typologies, coupled with notions of social evolution from "simple" to "complex," is thought to be of dubious analytical value, as well as being culturally situated in Enlightenment thought (although not all elements of that thought, such as rationality, are necessarily dismissed), where does that leave archaeological research on past societies? One answer to this question can be found in the various strands of thought that comprise the "post" (processual/structural/modern/colonial, etc.) period of Anglo-American archaeology since ca. 1980 (for a more detailed history, see Trigger 2006). The concept of social evolution is here abandoned as "theoretically flawed" (Shanks and Tilley 1987:138), while the emphasis on structure in social totalities, as well as on cross-cultural analysis and a technologically based adaptation to environmen-

tal risks, is replaced by contextual studies of social relations in which active (often methodological) individuals with multiple identities negotiate with one another and navigate their bodies through a world of culture. "We have moved away from universal narratives, supposedly applicable across time and space, to more contextual studies which stress cultural difference, social diversity and the creation of multiple identities" (Meskell 1998:6). This change of direction, now widely adopted in the broader context of what has been perceived to be a post-modern/capitalist/industrial world, draws on an idealist and often relativist philosophy (Trigger 2006:447, 474).

These last four sentences are, of course, a highly generalized summary. They conceal the animated debates, the diversities of theoretical position, and the ways in which social theories have been articulated in the study of specifically archaeological data. But for the purposes of this chapter, they highlight key issues that require critique. Postmodernism itself has received extensive critique, in both archaeology (e.g., Knapp 1996) and the social sciences (e.g., Harvey 1989), and it might be thought somewhat old hat to disinter those criticisms. I ask the reader to bear with me, as the following points have specific relevance to the development of my argument in this chapter.

Alex Callinicos's (1989) critique of postmodernism is rarely discussed or even cited in the literature of archaeological thought. His main arguments are that postmodernism is poorly defined, historically inaccurate, and dangerously self-indulgent in its view of, and relationship to, our world. Thus, the definitions of scholars such as Lyotard are regarded as "mutually inconsistent, internally contradictory and/or hopelessly vague" (Callinicos 1989:3). The postmodern critique of the Enlightenment project picks up that made by the late eighteenth-century "Romantic" movement and ignores the rejection of "historical progress" by early nineteenth-century modernists. In addition, it neglects the "contradiction which Nietzsche and Heidegger, as well as their successors—notably Foucault and Derrida—face in using the tools of rationality—philosophical argument and historical analysis—in order to carry out the critique of reason" (1989:26). There is also greater continuity between modernist and postmodernist art than often acknowledged

(1989:15). The use of concepts such as "post-capitalist world" and "post-industrial society" ignores the facts that (a) "most people's lives are still shaped by their lack of access to productive resources and their consequent need to sell their labour power in order to live" (1989:90) and (b) industrialization and the industrial working class have increased on a global level since the 1960s (1989:125). These observations counter the postmodern rejection of the relevance of the "meta-narrative" of Marxism, a rejection that signaled an abandonment of political commitment in the wake of disillusionment with the outcome of the political activism of the late 1960s and early 1970s. The commitment to the understanding and transformation of "social reality" has given way to absorption into a consumer-oriented lifestyle (1989: 170–171), an obsession with image, and an inability, or unwillingness, to distinguish between what is true and false.

Callinicos's critique is tightly argued and makes a devastating case against the pessimism of postmodernism, its (supposed) discarding of rationality and its avoidance of engagement with the key issues of capitalist society, namely, unequal participation in the organization and control of production. While there are provocative issues posed by the media, communication, and the representation of social reality, those posed by the political and economic structures of the modern world are fundamentally more important and more demanding of radical critique: to argue otherwise is to "fiddle while Rome burns" (Callinicos 1989:174). Of course, there are cultural and social differences, as well as identities shaped by class, ethnicity, and gender, but a materialist and realist philosophy offers the best route to arrive at an understanding of the basis of these differences and identities in the social world in which we live. Otherwise, we are left with what, in the post-structuralist account, is the reduction of human actors to "an incoherent welter of sub- and trans-individual drives and desires" (Callinicos 1989:2).

This leads us neatly to the issues of structure and agency, which Callinicos (1987) addressed in a book published two years before his work on postmodernism. He began by contrasting the structure-based approach of Althusser, based on the view of history as "a process without a subject,"

with the more recent views of analytical Marxists such as Elster and Roemer that social structures were the (unintentional) products of individual action based on rational choice. Neither proposal survives critique. Structures are inescapable factors in the reproduction of societies. "Social relations are sets of empty places" and "do not depend on the identity of the particular agents involved in them" (Callinicos 1987:39). The agents themselves may not even be aware of patterns of social relations. But structures do not completely determine individual actions, and agents are not "the bearers of social norms and values which dictate their actions" (1987:78). To argue for such structural determinism would be to contradict Marx's view that human beings are both the products and changers of history. Agreeing with Giddens, Callinicos argues that structures "constrain and enable" (1987:85). To view action as the determinant of structure prioritizes the beliefs, devices, and desires of individuals and neglects the fact that "actions consist in the exercise of powers, and the powers agents have depend on and are determined in part by social structures" (1987:38), that is, by the agents' "structural capacities" (1987:132–133). An argument of methodological individualism has to be rejected, as does idealism, given that we cannot understand the beliefs, devices, and desires of agents, nor their powers to act on them, without accepting the situation of these beliefs, devices, and desires in the material context of the agents' existence.

An implication of Callinicos's argument is that simply asserting agency and individuality is a theoretically insufficient means of analyzing social life. While it may be intellectually (perhaps even emotionally) comforting to us to think that by following the agency "path" we have found more humanity in our study of societies, the consequent neglect, downgrading, or marginalization of structure is misguided: "structures...figure ineliminably in the explanation of social events, since they help determine the powers that persons draw on when acting in the light of their beliefs and desires (however formed)" (Callinicos 1987:236). Ultimately, "structural capacities" of agents are "possessed...by virtue of their position in productive relations i.e. their class position," and "these capacities, and also the class interests which agents share, have primacy in explaining their actual behaviour" (1987:94). Within historical materialism it is the forces and relations of production that are the structures that provide the entry point into any analysis of social formations. At the same time, this tradition of thought "does not ignore the feeling, thinking and acting man, but explains him" (Trotsky 1932:vii).

Taken together, Callinicos's critiques of postmodernism and of structure and agency provide a powerful support for rationality and realism (the existence of a real world independent of the human observer), a rejection of methodological individualism, and an affirmation of the continued need for the much decried "meta-narrative," in this case that of historical materialism. The "post" world of the social sciences is seen as an intellectual diversion, even a refuge, from the continuing and even more oppressive relations of inequality and exploitation (whether by class, gender, or ethnicity) in the real world of capitalism.

What are the implications of this critique for archaeology? Apart from the need to uphold rationality and a realist philosophy, as well as the priority of a materialist epistemology, we must be critical of explanations of past social change that are based on the supposedly innate (genetic? psychological?) characteristics or motivations of individuals. For example, our literature on the development of social and economic inequalities is permeated by assertions (often under the agency umbrella) of individuals who are motivated by competitive desires for power or ambitions for leadership or motivations of self-interest. These assertions are made by scholars of different theoretical positions, from Hayden's "aggrandizers" ("any enterprising, ambitious, aggressive, accumulative individual...who strives to become dominant in a community" [1995:18]), through Clark and Blake's (1994:17) "self-interested competition among political actors vying for prestige or social esteem," to Gilman and Thornes's (1985: 187) "individuals ambitious for themselves and for their offspring (who) are not wanting in any society." A classical Marxist response would be that these assertions elevate motivations that are valued positively under capitalism into general characteristics of all humans at all times. This reminds us of Marx's argument that "the human essence is no abstraction inherent in each single individ-

ual...it is the ensemble of the social relations" as part of the historical process (Marx 1970a:122).

Two decades later Marx made an interesting distinction between "human nature in general," which has both capacities (e.g., language, tool using, cooperation, intentionality, self-consciousness) and needs (e.g., food, water, shelter, sex), and "human nature as modified in each historical epoch" (Fromm 1969:25, citing passages in Marx's *Capital*; Callinicos 1987:26–27). This distinction did not, of course, have the benefit of the knowledge we possess today on the antiquity of biological evolution and social change. The capacity for tool using, while still a distinguishing factor of human beings, was first made apparent at least two million years after the emergence of upright humans. It is thus a moot point as to whether this was an "inherent" (hardwired) capacity of humans from the beginnings of their evolution. Language and cognitive capacities are argued to be inherent in humans, although they clearly took different forms through time (e.g., Mithen 1996 on social and general-purpose languages; Renfrew 2007 on humans as "symbolizing animals"). I return to this discussion of what it means to be human later, but Marx's distinction between general and historically variable capacities of humans remains a valuable starting point for the study of social life.

A second implication of Callinicos's critique is that no analysis of the currently fashionable agents or social identities, or even broader issues of the construction and reproduction of culture, can be pursued without their situation in, and dependence on, structures of production and social relations. Any "agent-*centered*" approach to human societies, whether in the present or the past, ignores this dependence and is thereby incomplete. The ability of agents to "negotiate" their social position and identities is a matter not for assertion but for study in the context of existing structures. It is one thing to assert that agents have capacities, but this does not determine how, or indeed whether, those capacities will be exercised. A recent programmatic book focuses on, and advocates the study of, the concept of personhood (Fowler 2004). The author cites approvingly "the crucial role of contextual identities in forming the very motivations that people have" and "the need to attend to the cultural motivations that guide people, and people's strategies for negotiating those motivations, as well as the identities that are produced by social interaction" (Fowler 2004:4). This argument is developed with regard to ethnographic examples, but when it comes to an archaeological example on later Mesolithic Scandinavia, the social structures as seen in the forces and relations of production are neglected in favor of the inference of motivations and identities from burials and material culture (Fowler 2004:130–154).

A focus on culture can also be seen in recent research on Hopewell/Middle Woodland societies in the North American Midwest. Thus Van Gilder and Charles argue that the emphasis on ecological systems since the 1960s has meant that "Hopewell, as a 'cultural' phenomenon, has been increasingly viewed as an epiphenomenon" (2003:121). The need to rectify this marginalization by reanimating the cultural content of these societies has been supported by, among others, Brown (2006—see also other articles in the same conference publication) and Buikstra, Charles, and Rakita (1998).

In Mississippian studies the role of culture has been reaffirmed most recently by Pauketat, who argues that "the reality of the past was *what people did* and *how people experienced social life*" and that "archaeologists track the continuous *culture making* of people through the histories, trajectories, or genealogies of things, spaces and bodies" (2007:2; original emphasis). People are actively involved in "cultural construction and production" (2007:79) and have "multiple and dynamic identities" that "are continuously constructed and projected experientially in all cultural practices, performances and technologies" (2007:60). These acts and processes of cultural construction are given priority in the production of what is different about the monuments, life and death rituals, social spaces, and (he argues) state formation of Cahokia in the eleventh century AD (see also Pauketat 2004). This elevation of culture in the study of identity-conscious Cahokians sidesteps their structural capacities and their situation within the changing productive relations of Cahokian society, which, according to Callinicos's argument above, should be attributed a fundamental role in the study of human behavior. Culture is important, but according to this argument, it does not determine the bases of social life (for an alternative, materialist interpretation of the Mississippian, see Muller 1997). Given this example and the critique presented in this section, we should move on to consider further what a historical materialist approach offers us as an alternative to the work of cultural constructors.

Social Producers: A Materialist Approach

Archaeologists have behaved like predators in their pursuit and consumption of social theory: everything has been regarded as fair game. Some prey (e.g., all deterministic arguments) have been hunted to extinction, others (e.g., evolutionary theory; see Shennan 2002) have enjoyed a recent resurgence, and we are always looking for new "species" to be pursued, or even domesticated. During the last forty years we have encountered more prey than we can consume without some degree of indigestion. Marxism is different from the other social theories in that most of us have "pursued" it and consumed parts of it, whether we know it or admit it, but comparatively few of us exclusively hunt and consume this particular prey. We may not even have a good knowledge of its habitat and behavior. It can be everywhere and nowhere (e.g., Wickham 2008 on the "normalization" of Marxist ideas in Medieval social and economic history). It can also be exploited alongside other prey and used in the same menus, whether this results in dishes that work well together (i.e., theoretical pluralism) or not. Cultural constructors who have not totally embraced postmodernism may still use Marxist concepts (e.g., production, class), whether they highlight them or not, and acknowledge Marx's role in developing debate on structure and agency, but otherwise this "meta-narrative" is for them part of the history of social theory. It is as if it has been hunted almost to extinction or is no longer thought to be palatable.

My argument here is that the viewpoint of such cultural constructors is wrong. A materialist approach is fundamental to our study of human history, and the writings of Marx are the essential and insightful bases of social, political, and economic analyses. They initiated a tradition of thought that has been the subject of intensive debate, but using the examples of Lull (2005) and Castro et al. (1996, 1998), I follow here the "classical" end of that tradition. Let us start at the beginning: "the first premise of all human existence and, therefore, of all history…[is] that men must be in a position to live in order to be able to 'make history.' But life involves before everything else eating and drinking, a habitation, clothing and many other things. The first historical act is thus the production of the means to satisfy these needs, the production of material life itself" (Marx and Engels 1970:48). This does not imply economic or technological determinism, or that non-economic factors such as culture are not important for the study of human history. Rather, our initial task is to study the means by which human societies exist through their production and the social relations of that production. Thought is socially produced, given that we are part of a world that consists of matter; ideas are generated by matter (the brain) and therefore cannot logically exist apart from and prior to that matter and to physical life. As Lull (2005:16) puts it, "the ways of producing society socialize the ways of thinking of society" (my translation), and not the other way around.

While much recent discussion on what it is to be human focuses on cognition, symbolism, and "how humans make meaning out of life" (Moore 1999:17), there is less discussion of the material bases of these characteristics. Like other animals, human beings need to produce and to reproduce. This requires mental and physical labor, which is conceived and exercised socially (and not through separate individuals). But the extent to which labor is developed, along with changes in the methods of production, increasingly differentiated human beings from other species during the course of the last 4 million years. As Perry (2002:3) puts it so memorably, "labour is the DNA of human history; ever present, imperceptibly changing and reshaping society." In contrast to other species, humans are consciously able "to produce, to design, to innovate, to anticipate nature" (2002:34), and they do this through their labor. Much of recent theoretical discussion in archaeology has focused on culture, the mind, symbolism, and cognition, but it omits the capability of human societies to produce, through labor, in order to meet material needs.

A Marxist approach argues that human societies are composed of men and women, as social agents, and the material conditions in which they live (Castro et al. 1996:35). Men and women are produced biologically, socially, and historically and in turn act as agents in the production and reproduction of society: "history produces us and at the same time reproduces with and through us" (Lull 2005:11 [my translation]). Social life is enabled and society reproduces through three types of production: *basic production*, the reproduction of men and women, the social agents who will provide the labor force; *production of social objects*, for consumption (e.g., food, means of production, instruments of production); and *maintenance production*, which increases the social value of objects (Castro et al. 1998). These types of production revise Marx's (1970b) scheme, and they are realized and expressed through everyday social practices (Castro et al. 1996). These practices involve the use of labor to carry out production of all types, and that labor may be socially allocated and controlled to the point that producers may not have access to their share of what has been socially produced. Here we are in conditions of exploitation. Rather than society as a unity that changes according to external stimulus, there is a continual tension and contradiction, most notably between the material conditions of production and the social relations by which production is controlled.

There are three observations I would like to make about this approach to social production. First, there is a clear articulation between the concepts of production in general, their realization in specific social practices, and then their materialization in the social objects studied by archaeologists. Apart from the development of a coherent theoretical structure, this also attacks directly an accusation that is often leveled at Marxist approaches, namely, that they cannot be pursued through archaeological data. This accusation has been refuted in relation to the study of property relations and exploitation in the later prehistory of southeast Spain (e.g., Lull and Risch 1995; Castro et al. 1998; Risch 1998; Chapman 2003; Lull et al. 2005). Second, the concept of "social practices" used in this approach is focused on *social* rather than *cultural* reproduction, the latter assuming priority in the work of archaeologists influenced by Bourdieu and Giddens. Third, there is the potential to identify specific forms and sequences of social production, along with relationships between production and consumption at different scales in the past (rather than those predicted from cross-cultural ethnographies): this gives arguments about politics a real, material basis rather than founding them on inherent characteristics of human beings (e.g., Lull and Micó 2007:244–247).

Conclusion

What have we learned from this presentation of our four kinds of archaeologists, all engaged in the study of past societies? These accounts are clearly sketches and ignore variation in archaeologists and archaeological practice, but can they be useful to us? Downsizers work within the expectations of evolutionary typologies (e.g., no state societies existed outside the early civilizations and certainly not in the American continent north of Mexico) and culturally embedded stereotypes of "static," "conservative," or "backward" societies which deny history, whether for indigenous peoples under colonial traditions (e.g., North America, Africa) or for rural societies marginalized from urban and industrial development (e.g., central and western Mediterranean). And yet we increasingly recognize that evolutionary typologies are insufficient to account for specific histories.

Upgraders partly respond to "surprises," materials, practices, site types, and so on that are too big/too early/too "complex." These surprises lead them to push back the inference of social stratification and complexity. This behavior is situated also within the wider desire to search for our origins: in the case of eastern Anatolia, these origins are of civilization itself. As such, there may be a wider, cultural context linked in this case to the ideology of the modern Turkish state. What is also clear is that the claims of upgraders require critical evaluation of their theoretical arguments, the clarity of their concepts, and the extent to which upgrading claims are supported empirically.

The social evolutionary agenda that is visible in the work of downsizers and upgraders, with assumptions of directional development from simple to complex societies, has been rejected by cultural constructors. They regard social evolution as an unworkable and politically unjustifiable scheme that should be discarded along with other key tenets of modernist society: all-encompassing theoretical schemes, concepts of unified societies, and materialist philosophy. Instead, they focus on cultural construction and production, on memory and tradition, on diversity, difference, and fluidity, in the study of fulfilled, freewheeling individuals being what they want to be. Forget class struggle—we can now negotiate our way through multiple identities. While one can accept cultural differences and social diversity, cultural constructors take their eyes off the material conditions in which people lived, losing sight of structures and structural capacities. This idealist approach also includes some dependence on the innate characteristics of individuals, regardless of historical and material contexts, in social change and the emergence of leadership and more unequal societies.

These criticisms of cultural constructors are presented by social producers. The enduring need for the meta-narrative of historical materialism is justified, albeit in a succinct manner in this chapter, given (a) the relevance of its critique of real social, political, and economic relations after the postmodern interlude and (b) the argument for a materialist philosophy brought to bear on the study of the basic, material conditions of human existence. Thus, the "back to basics" version presented here enables the study of key concepts in the archaeological record, the revealing of historical sequences of production and consumption, and thereby an understanding of power and political relationships that does not depend on the inherent characteristics of individuals or societies. From this perspective I would argue that Anglo-American archaeology has now become too "cultured" in the symbolic world and insufficiently "structured" in the material world.

Acknowledgments

I thank Susan Alt for the invitation to participate in the Society for American Archaeology symposium "Confounding Categories and Conceptualizing Complexities" and the British Academy and the University of Reading for providing the grants that enabled me to attend the meetings in Austin, Texas. The figures were prepared by Margaret Mathews. I am grateful to Roger Matthews for discussing the Anatolian Neolithic with me, although I bear full responsibility for the critique presented here. The intellectual stimulus of Vicente Lull, Roberto Risch, Rafa Micó, and Cristina Rihuete continues to animate me, and I thank them for it.

References

Andah, B. W.
1995 Studying African Societies in Cultural Context. In *Making Alternative Histories: The Practice of Archaeology and History in Non-Western societies*, edited by P. R. Schmidt and T. C. Patterson, pp. 149–181. School of American Research Press, Santa Fe.

Atakamun, Ç.
2008 Cradle or Crucible: Anatolia and Archaeology in the Early Years of the Turkish Republic (1923–1938). *Journal of Social Archaeology* 8(2):214–235.

Barker, G.
1981 *Landscape and Society: Prehistoric Central Italy*. Academic Press, London.

Braudel, F.
1972 *The Mediterranean and the Mediterranean World in the Age of Phillip II*. Collins, London.

Brown, J. A.
2006 The Shamanic Element in Hopewellian Period Ritual. In *Recreating Hopewell: New Perspectives on Middle Woodland in Eastern North America*, edited by D. K. Charles and J. E. Buikstra, pp. 475–488. University Press of Florida, Gainesville.

Buikstra, J. E., D. K. Charles, and G. F. M. Rakita
1998 *Staging Rituals: Hopewell Ceremonialism at the Mound House Site, Greene County, Illinois*. Center for American Archeology, Kampsville, Illinois.

Callinicos, A.
1987 *Making History: Agency, Structure and Change in Social Theory*. Polity Press, Cambridge.
1989 *Against Postmodernism: A Marxist Critique*. Polity Press, Cambridge.

Castro, P., R. Chapman, S. Gili, V. Lull, R. Micó, C. Rihuete, R. Risch, and Ma. E. Sanahuja
1996 Teoría de las practices sociales. *Complutum Extra* 6(2): 35–48.

Castro, P., S. Gili, V. Lull, R. Micó, C. Rihuete, R. Risch, and Ma. E. Sanahuja
1998 Teoría de la producción de la vida social: Un análisis de los mecanismos de explotación en el sudeste peninsular (3000–1550 cal ANE). *Boletín de Antropología Americana* 33:25–78.

Chapman, R.
2003 *Archaeologies of Complexity*. Routledge, London.

Childe, V. G.
1936 *Man Makes Himself*. Watts, London.
1944 *Progress and Archaeology*. Watts, London.

Clark, J. E., and M. Blake
1994 The Power of Prestige: Competitive Generosity and the Emergence of Rank Societies in Lowland Mesoamerica. In *Factional Competition and Political Development in the New World*, edited by E. M. Brumfiel and J. W. Fox, pp. 17–30. Cambridge University Press, Cambridge.

Emerson, T. E.
1997 *Cahokia and the Archaeology of Power*. University of Alabama Press, Tuscaloosa.

Flannery, K. V., and J. Marcus
2000 Formative Mexican Chiefdoms and the Myth of the "Mother Culture." *Journal of Anthropological Archaeology* 19:1–37.

Fowler, C.
2004 *The Archaeology of Personhood*. Routledge, London.

Fromm, E.
1969 *Marx's Concept of Man*. Frederick Ungar, New York.

Gilman, A., and J. B. Thornes
1985 *Land-Use and Prehistory in South-East Spain*. George Allen and Unwin, London.

Halstead, P.
1987 Traditional and Ancient Rural Economy in Mediterranean Europe: Plus ça change? *Journal of Hellenic Studies* 107:77–87.

Harvey, D.
1989 *The Condition of Postmodernity: An Enquiry into the Origins of Cultural Change*. Blackwell, Oxford.

Hauptmann, H.
1999 The Urfa Region. In *Neolithic in Turkey: The Cradle of Civilization*, edited by M. Özdoğan and N. Başgelen, pp. 65–86. Arkeoloji ve Sanat Yayinlari, Istanbul.
2002 Upper Mesopotamia in Its Regional Context during the Early Neolithic. In *The Neolithic of Central Anatolia*, edited by F. Gérard and L. Thissen, pp. 263–271. EGE Yayinlari, Istanbul.

Hayden, B.
1995 Pathways to Power: Principles for Creating Socioeconomic Inequalities. In *Foundations of Social Inequality*, edited by T. D. Price and G. M. Feinman, pp. 15–86. Plenum Press, New York.

Hegmon, M.
2005 Beyond the Mold: Questions of Inequality in Southwest Villages. In *North American Archaeology*, edited by T. R. Pauketat and D. D. Loren, pp. 212–234. Blackwell, Oxford.
Higgs, E. (editor)
1975 *Palaeoeconomy*. Cambridge University Press, Cambridge.
Hodder, I.
1998 The Past as Passion and Play: Çatalhöyük as a Site of Conflict in the Construction of Multiple Pasts. In *Archaeology under Fire*, edited by L. Meskell, pp. 124–139. Routledge, London.
Horden, P., and N. Purcell
2000 *The Corrupting Sea: A Study of Mediterranean History*. Blackwell, Oxford.
Knapp, A. B.
1996 Archaeology without Gravity: Postmodernism and the Past. *Journal of Archaeological Method and Theory* 3(2):127–158.
Lekson, S. H.
2005 Chaco and Paquime: Complexity, History, Landscape. In *North American Archaeology*, edited by T. R. Pauketat and D. D. Loren, pp. 235–272. Blackwell, Oxford.
Lull, V.
2005 Marx, producción, sociedad y arqueología. *Trabajos de Prehistoria* 62:7–26.
Lull, V., and R. Micó
2007 *Arqueología del origen del Estado: Las teorías*. Bellaterra, Barcelona.
Lull, V., R. Micó, C. Rihuete, and R. Risch
2005 Property Relations in the Bronze Age of Southwestern Europe: An Approach Based on Infant Burials from El Argar (Almería, Spain). *Proceedings of the Prehistoric Society* 71:247–268.
Lull, V., and R. Risch
1995 El estado argárico. *Verdolay* 7:97–109.
Malone, C.
2003 The Italian Neolithic: A Synthesis of Research. *Journal of World Prehistory* 17:235–312.
Marx, K.
1970a Theses on Feuerbach. In *The German Ideology*, by K. Marx and F. Engels, edited by C. J. Arthur, pp. 121–123. Lawrence and Wishart, London.
1970b Introduction to a Critique of Political Economy. In *The German Ideology*, by K. Marx and F. Engels, edited by C. J. Arthur, pp. 124–151. Lawrence and Wishart, London.
Marx, K., and F. Engels
1970 *The German Ideology*. Edited by C. J. Arthur. Lawrence and Wishart, London.

Mathers, C., and S. Stoddart
1994 Introduction. In *Development and Decline in the Mediterranean Bronze Age*, edited by C. Mathers and S. Stoddart, pp. 13–20. J. R. Collis, Sheffield, U.K.
Meskell, L.
1998 Archaeology Matters. In *Archaeology under Fire*, edited by L. Meskell, pp. 1–12. Routledge, London.
Mithen, S.
1996 *The Prehistory of the Mind*. Thames and Hudson, London.
Moore, H.
1999 Anthropological Theory at the Turn of the Century. In *Anthropological Theory Today*, edited by H. Moore, pp. 1–23. Polity Press, Cambridge.
Muller, J.
1997 *Mississippian Political Economy*. Plenum Press, New York.
Özdoğan, A.
1999 Çayönü. In *Neolithic in Turkey: The Cradle of Civilization*, edited by M. Özdoğan and N. Başgelen, pp. 35–63. Arkeoloji ve Sanat Yayinlari, Istanbul.
Özdoğan, M.
1998 Ideology and Archaeology in Turkey. In *Archaeology under Fire*, edited by L. Meskell, pp. 111–123. Routledge, London.
1999 Concluding Remarks. In *Neolithic in Turkey: The Cradle of Civilization*, edited by M. Özdoğan and N. Başgelen, pp. 225–236. Arkeoloji ve Sanat Yayinlari, Istanbul.
Pauketat, T. R.
2004 *Ancient Cahokia and the Mississippians*. Cambridge University Press, Cambridge.
2007 *Chiefdoms and Other Archaeological Delusions*. AltaMira Press, Lanham, Maryland.
Perry, M.
2002 *Marxism and History*. Palgrave, New York.
Piggott, S.
1965 *Ancient Europe*. Edinburgh University Press, Edinburgh.
Renfrew, C.
1972 *The Emergence of Civilisation*. Methuen, London.
2007 *Prehistory: The Making of the Human Mind*. Weidenfeld and Nicolson, London.
Risch, R.
1998 Análisis paleoeconómico y medios de producción líticos: El caso de Fuente Alamo. In *Minerales y metales en la prehistoria reciente: Algunos testimonios de su explotación y laboreo en la península Ibérica*, edited by G.

Delibes de Castro, pp. 105–154. Universidad de Valladolid, Valladolid, Spain.

Rosenberg, M.
1999   Hallan Çemi. In *Neolithic in Turkey: The Cradle of Civilization*, edited by M. Özdoğan and N. Başgelen, pp. 25–33. Arkeoloji ve Sanat Yayinlari, Istanbul.

Rosenberg, M., and R. W. Redding
2000   Hallan Çemi and Early Village Organization in Eastern Anatolia. In *Life in Neolithic Farming Communities: Social Organization, Identity and Differentiation*, edited by I. Kuijt, pp. 39–61. Kluwer Academic/Plenum Press, New York.

Schmidt, P. R.
1995   Using Archaeology to Remake History in Africa. In *Making Alternative Histories: The Practice of Archaeology and History in Non-Western Societies*, edited by P. R. Schmidt and T. C. Patterson, pp. 119–147. School of American Research Press, Santa Fe.

Shanks, M., and C. Tilley
1987   *Social Theory in Archaeology*. Polity Press, Cambridge.

Shennan, S.
2002   *Genes, Memes and Human History: Darwinian Archaeology and Cultural Evolution*. Thames and Hudson, London.

Souvatzi, S.
2007   Social Complexity Is Not the Same as Hierarchy. In *Socialising Complexity: Structure, Interaction and Power in Archaeological Discourse*, edited by S. Kohring and S. Wynne-Jones, pp. 37–59. Oxbow Books, Oxford.

Trigger, B. G.
1980a   Archaeology and the Image of the American Indian. *American Antiquity* 45:662–676.
1980b   *Gordon Childe: Revolutions in Archaeology*. Thames and Hudson, London.
1984   Alternative Archaeologies: Nationalist, Colonialist, Imperialist. *Man* 19:355–370.
1998   *Sociocultural Evolution*. Blackwell, Oxford.
2006   *A History of Archaeological Thought*. Cambridge University Press, Cambridge.

Trotsky, L.
1932   *History of the Russian Revolution*. Vol. 2. Pathfinder Press, New York.

Van Gilder, C., and D. K. Charles
2003   Archaeology as Cultural Encounter: The Legacy of Hopewell. In *Theory, Method and Practice in Modern Archaeology*, edited by R. J. Jeske and D. K. Charles, pp. 114–129. Praeger, Westport, Connecticut.

Wickham, C.
2008   Memories of Underdevelopment: What Has Marxism Done for Medieval History and What Can It Still Do? In *Marxist History-Writing for the Twenty-First Century*, edited by C. Wickham, pp. 32–48. Oxford University Press, Oxford.

Yoffee, N., S. K. Fish, and G. R. Milner
1999   Comunidades, Ritualities, Chiefdoms: Social Evolution in the American Southwest and Southeast. In *Great Towns and Regional Polities in the Prehistoric American Southwest and Southeast*, edited by J. E. Neitzel, pp. 261–271. University of New Mexico Press, Albuquerque.

14

The Unbearable
Lightness of Complexity

Norman Yoffee

The great American philosopher, Kenny Rogers (1978), once said, "You've got to know when to hold 'em, know when to fold 'em." The participants in this book have taken this advice to heart, agreeing with Susan Alt that in order to see in what complex ways prehistoric North Americans acted, interacted, and understood their lives, archaeologists need to give up on "complexity" (as a reified, essentialized, and identifiable social entity).

For the contributors to this volume, second only to Kenny Rogers in wisdom is Ben Nelson (1995:614), who, in comparing social complexity, hierarchy, and scale in Chaco Canyon, New Mexico, United States, and La Quemada, Zacatecas, Mexico, wrote that one should ask not "How complex were they relative to one another?" but "How were they [each] complex?" Susan Alt, followed closely by her gang of North Americanists, asserts that neo-evolutionist categories of more or less complexity cannot "accommodate" archaeological data from a host of societies. That is, some data seem to fit within one category (of band, tribe, chiefdom, or state), while other data from the same society fit within another category. And as all good anthropologists know, there are many ways to be complex, in kinship systems and terminologies of kinship, in language syntax, and in ritual prescriptions and ceremonies.

With apologies to the Rolling Stones (Jagger and Richards 1968), please allow me to introduce myself. I am not a North American archaeologist and have been enlisted here in the archaeo-

logical tradition of asking someone who has limited knowledge of the relevant archaeological data and little investment in regional debates about the meaning of the data to offer a (relatively) unbiased commentary. I do have more than a passing interest in "complexity," however, and have struggled with the inadequacies of neo-evolutionist categories (Yoffee 2005). I am the author of "Yoffee's Rule" (cited by several chapter authors), which states, "If you can argue whether a society is a state or isn't, then it isn't." Since I intended by this "rule" that archaeologists should abandon the search for states (or any other "type" of society), I have been surprised to find my aphorism deconstructed, misconstrued (horrors!), and even given a corollary (as in Steve Lekson's chapter, which I discuss anon).

The Chapters

In my brief comments on the chapters, I emend the editor's order slightly, imposing my own sections. First are the chapters on the Southeast, by Asa Randall and Kenneth Sassaman, Tristram Kidder, Thomas Pluckhahn, and Jon Marcoux and Gregory Wilson. Perhaps Susan Alt's chapter should be placed in this group, but I include her with Elizabeth Chilton, Bretton Giles, and Meghan Howey in a section on the Northeast and Midwest. The chapters on the Southwest are written by Jill Neitzel, Stephen Lekson, and Severin Fowles. (There are no chapters on prehistoric California and the Northwest, so complete continental coverage of North America is not offered by this book.) Robert Chapman's chapter, originally presented as a discussion at the Society for American Archaeology conference where most of the chapters were first presented, offers a minority report against the dominant concerns in the chapters.

The chapters on shell mounds in Florida in the Archaic period (ca. 7200–4000 BP) by Randall and Sassaman and on Poverty Point, Louisiana (ca. 3800–2950 BP), are required reading for all archaeologists who study hunter-gatherer-fisher societies. The first authors discuss, with admirable presentations of data, how large mounds are scenes of commemorative strategies, performances in connection with funerary rituals, and places where new societies were constructed from a tapestry of social and cultural orientations. Similar research is being conducted in southern Brazil (Gaspar et al. 2008) on huge shell mounds (*sambaquis*), one nearly 60 m high, a veritable pyramid. The recent book by Dillehay (2007) discusses the archaeology of more recent mounds in Chile and also the ethnography of people who still use these mounds for ceremonies.

Kidder's important chapter argues, again with excellent data, that the huge earthen mounds of Poverty Point were built by hunter-gatherers in three to six months. The mounds materialize a creation story and integrate disparate population groups and a diversity of ritual practices.

These two chapters on "social becomings" (in the language of Randall and Sassaman) are protests against how hunters and gatherers have been defined largely according to their mode of subsistence. Although there is nothing to lead one to think that these societies were other than egalitarian in social and political structure, the behavior of those who constructed the mounds was obviously complex. The site of Göbekli Tepe in Turkey (and other sites in the region) also shows that hunter-gatherers could build huge stone monuments, called temples by the excavator (see the Wikipedia entry for Göbekli Tepe for an up-to-date bibliography and Curry 2008 for photos). Our book thus begins with convincing cases of complex social interactions in societies that few have categorized as complex.

Pluckhahn refutes earlier attempts to find a "chiefdom" or "class-structured society" at the Middle Woodland site of Kolomoki (ca. AD 100–

600), which was occupied by about 300 people. He contests ethnographic analogy with Natchez folk and prefers to see something like a complex southwestern system of clans, moieties, and sodalities at the site, with a religious authority present on the platform mound of the site. Marcoux and Wilson apply an "actor-network theory" perspective to the Mississippian site of Moundville (ca. AD 1200–1300). Although they emphasize that actors generate social structure, that there are "power-to" in addition to "power-over" relations, and that mortuary events help construct new networks for the living (familiar and important themes), I am most interested in the authors' concern with out-migrations from Moundville which turned the site into a vacant ceremonial center (a topic I return to below).

The second group of chapters includes those of Chilton, Howey, Giles, and Alt. Chilton's asserts that mobile farmers in New England, ca. AD 1000–1500, whose societies others have described as a cultural backwater, were in fact complex. She argues that they were not, to be sure, hierarchically complex but were heterarchically so. Heterarchy, however, which implies the simultaneity of many hierarchies, and whose members can be in more than one hierarchy and possibly with different ranks in each, is at least as characteristic of states as of mobile farmers. Giles's chapter, with a plethora of Hopewellian material, notes that various decorations on effigy pipes and ceramics are difficult to interpret and part of a complex "sacrificial economy." Howey reviews data from northern Michigan, another place not known for its political or material complexity but where people in "small-scale societies" were negotiating their identity in ritual "centers." She quotes Chapman that there are "other kinds of societies in the past," not just the bands or tribes whose features derive from their economic infrastructure and which elide aspects of cultural complexity. She also reminds us that kinship means more than biological lines but provides the vocabulary for the creation and negotiation of relatedness in rituals and in the construction of ceremonial monuments.

Although Alt's chapter on Cahokia and its region belongs alongside Marcoux and Wilson's on Moundville, because both sites are culturally Mississippian, her chapter can be read nicely in my second group since, like those of Giles and Howey, it emphasizes "rituals of inclusion." Alt's chapter is not on Cahokia itself but on the nature of power and authority in Cahokia's countryside. This regional history shows that some sites were economically specialized and that Cahokia was an administrative center. The countryside was created as part of the evolution of Cahokia and was restructured in the process. Rituals, Alt notes, link "diverse peoples, ideas, and practices into a coherent cohesive community. Ritual is, in fact, another kind of politicking."

The last section of chapters is on the American Southwest, and it is very diverse. Neitzel employs the concept of "peer polity interaction" as a way to understand complexity at Chaco Canyon (New Mexico) and the Chaco Phenomenon in the northern Southwest and the Hohokam of the southern Southwest (mainly in southern Arizona). Peer polity interaction was initially proposed by two Aegean prehistorians, Colin Renfrew and John Cherry (1986), to show how polities in Greece and the Aegean islands evolved in many centers simultaneously and in a synergistic fashion, mainly because of considerable circulation of goods and ideas among them. Even in the Aegean, however, peer polity interaction does not explain all local histories, since Cyprus had its own developmental sequence apart from the putative network of nearby peers.

What were "peers" in the Southwest? Chaco was a singular development, with more than a dozen "great houses" (which were only sparsely occupied for most of the year), a road system orienting outliers to Chaco, and summer migrations from distant sites for the celebration of rituals in Chaco. There was nothing like it, and therein lies its meaning. As Neitzel and Lekson report, Puebloan oral histories regard Chaco as a dangerous aberration in their long cultural history. A better case for peer polities can be made for the Hohokam (Fish and Fish 2007), who experienced regional change from the Preclassic to the Classic (especially from central institutions of ball courts in the former to platform mounds in the latter), although Neitzel notes the good deal of variation among ostensible peers.

Lekson's chapter on Chaco declares that the Chaco great houses were palaces and that Chaco was a city and the center of a Chaco state in the eleventh century AD. For Lekson, it was a secondary state, an outlier of Mesoamerican states (formed rapidly in the period after the collapse of the Classic cities and states of the Maya and Teotihuacan and before the Aztecs). Lekson's perspective is "continental" because Cahokia was also a city and secondary state. Since southwesterners at Chaco and midwesterners at Cahokia knew about Mesoamerican kings and kingship, they naturally wanted to have kings themselves.

Although it has long been known that Mesoamerican goods (such as scarlet macaws, copper bells, and cacao) found their way to the Southwest and were used in Chaco ceremonies, Lekson's views on the dependency of Chaco's religious and political system on Mesoamerica are heterodox. Lekson's chapter is also rooted in his version of intellectual history: it is a legacy of ethnocentric and racist Anglo scholars that there could not be cities and states north of the Mexican border. However, the indictment can be reversed: it is a kind of conceit to say that southwestern (and midwestern) societies must be like something somewhere else and derived from somewhere else. Cannot Chaco and Cahokia have their own histories, melded from various traditions (including Mesoamerican ones) and transformed in their experiences with their environments and neighbors?

Fowles's chapter is centered precisely in history (or as he and other anthropologists put it, "historical contingency"). "A People's History of the American Southwest" is the most novel chapter in this volume, and for those seeking a view of society from the bottom up, this is it. Fowles begins with a discussion of New Buffalo, the hippie commune that was founded (and still exists) near Taos, New Mexico, in the northern Rio Grande region. New Buffalo is an example not of complexity but of "voluntary simplicity," an opposition to the complexities of the state. This view follows the works of Pierre Clastres and James Scott (both cited by Fowles), who discuss resistance to modern states. For these authors and for Fowles (and for me, too), the state is importantly a state of mind, a set of ideologies that declares that there should be rulers and subjects, richer and poorer, nobles and slaves, and that the perpetuation of the cosmos depends on those ceremonies that celebrate the way the world must be. Indeed, in these new ideologies, states and kings have always existed, and any notion that things were different in the past must be erased (as literally happened in early literate states).

For Fowles, it is worth considering the idea that there was systematic resistance to complexity and/or states in the Southwest. The northern Rio Grande pueblos, for example, resisted incorporation in the Chaco system. Fowles also speculates that if there were migrants from Mesoamerica to the Southwest, these were dissidents, bringing certain Mesoamerican cultural ways into their new homes but with the conviction that political leadership should be overtly rejected. If this is the polar opposite to Lekson's view in this volume, it also follows certain of Lekson's other writings (that I have alluded to above) about how Chaco is regarded in Puebloan histories as a world that failed. From its collapse, new religious ways emerged, including the ideology that political stratification must be embedded in social and cultural structures.

Chapman's chapter lies outside the various groups of this review and in fact provides the formally materialist counterpoint to most of the authors. Chapman queries the motivations of "downsizers," who tend to regard Indians in North America as relatively "unchanging" over time, and "upgraders," who see latent progressive tendencies (toward "complexity") in all societies that are regarded as part of a Western heritage. He is also dubious about "cultural constructors," postmodernists who privilege agents but do not see that negotiations of identity are only possible within sociopolitical structures. "Social producers," however, get back to basics and examine the "material conditions of human existence." Social structures emerge from the construction of the means and relations of production and the struggle for the control of economic resources.

Whither Complexity in North American Archaeology?

The chapters in this volume are about finding complexity in the ideas and beliefs of prehistoric North Americans, how they understood their own histories, and why they constructed new cultural landscapes. The authors demonstrate how prehistoric people thought with things and materialized ideologies, and so they zestfully dissolve the long-standing philosophical dichotomy between materialists and idealists. That is one of the important contributions of this book.

Nevertheless, having seen all the variety of complexities in this volume, and having reviewed the various authors' convincing pronouncements that the term "complex society" has been unfairly limited to political structures, I have no illusions that the term is going to disappear from the vocabulary of archaeologists who study political systems, or perhaps more importantly, that "complex society" will vanish from advertisements for archaeological job openings.

Can archaeologists live with the evident irony that the term "complexity" must include more than politics, but that politics and power must not be subordinated to investigations of identities, belief systems, and agents (as Chapman has warned against)? I take the discussant's privilege to offer a small example of evolutionary developments in my own area of the world, Mesopotamia, in order to broaden the range of this conundrum and also to shed some comparative light on North American prehistory.

Large cities and politically centralized states in Mesopotamia (and other areas of the world) evolved rapidly and from modest forms of village life. At first glance this rapid evolutionary pace looks like the big bang at Cahokia or the appearance of Pueblo Bonito and other great houses at Chaco. However, in the sequence of the development of Mesopotamian cities and states—to stick to the area I know best or at least have the most slides of—there is nothing that looks at all like Chaco or Cahokia. There are possible explanations for this, one lying in the millennium-long history of agricultural communities that preceded the sudden appearance of Mesopotamian cities, unlike in North America, where the history of agricultural communities was much shorter before Chaco and Cahokia appeared (as S. Fish has argued; see Yoffee et al. 1999).

Furthermore, the first states in Mesopotamia (and elsewhere) were invested in regulating their societies, in effect simplifying them. We thus have the contradiction that states were so complex—in the diversity of social systems and the hierarchical and heterarchical arrangements of people and groups of people—that rulers tried to make them simple. Of course, as we know, simplification did not work: the countryside in Mesopotamia (and elsewhere), which had been "ruralized" into dependency on emerging centers, was remade partly in opposition to centers, and the population inflow into centers was reversed as the countryside grew in numbers of people and in kinds of settlements.

What does this have to do with complexity in prehistoric North America? As many of our authors have noted, although mainly in passing, the early cultures and monumental constructions in North America, described by Randall and Sassaman and by Kidder, and the sites/regions/cultures of Cahokia alluded to by Alt, Moundville by Marcoux and Wilson, Chaco by Neitzel and Lekson and Fowles, and Hohokam by Neitzel, all collapsed. Now by "collapse" I certainly do not mean collapse as discussed by Jared Diamond (2005; see McAnany and Yoffee 2009), the idea that environmental mismanagement caused the disappearance of cultures. Archaeologists know that the abandonment of sites was part of a larger history and that modern Native peoples are descendants of societies Diamond considers to have "failed." Although in North America the history of these societies was effectively truncated by European invasions, new kinds of interactions would surely have resulted in the development of new kinds of complex societies and political organizations.

Can we explain these collapses or hypothetical political interstadials in North American prehistoric societies and compare them with evolutionary trends elsewhere? (Only archaeologists would ever think of doing this, and this is why archaeologists are attracted to movements in world history that are similarly expansive and daring.) Does the term "complexity" have significance in a comparative perspective, especially in considering collapse? Here it is worth reviewing the definition of complexity as offered by the Santa Fe

Institute scientists who study "complex adaptive systems." The basic point is that a complex system is a network of interacting parts that exhibit dynamic, aggregate behavior. This system behavior cannot be reduced to the sum of its parts because the actions of some parts are always affecting the action of other parts. Can we then say, in the logic of comparative complexities, that it is the lack of some parts that can determine directions of behavior in a system?

If I understand Alt and others who study the development and demise of Cahokia, we can now identify and study war, war captives, long-distance trade, town councils, political factions, senior women, priests, junior elites, ethnic groups, and especially the overarching ideological foundation that made the Mississippians Mississippian. The one thing that did not seem to change fundamentally at Cahokia, however, was the nature of political power, which remained rooted in the complex kinship system of ranked lineages and ancestors. Although there were great changes in demography, economy, and especially the combination and accommodation of diverse peoples and orientations in the formation of Cahokia, political transformations did not co-occur. Of course, political power existed, but it was vested in religious figures, religious language, and the complex creations and negotiations of kin ranking.

In any case, Cahokia lasted less than two centuries. Chaco was abandoned in part as the result of a decades-long drought and then the rejection of its ritual centralization of a great part of the northern Southwest. If we can study complexity in all its forms in the floruit of North American societies, as the authors of this volume have shown, we must also study the fragility of complexity, the rejection of complexity, and the new kinds of complexities that are made, often in the explicit knowledge of complexities that failed. Complexity may still have a future, in spite of and because of the concerns of the North American archaeologists in this book.

References

Curry, A.
2008   Göbekli Tepe: The World's First Temple? *Smithsonian Magazine*, November.

Diamond, J.
2005   *Collapse: How Societies Choose to Fail or Succeed.* Viking, New York.

Dillehay, T.
2007   *Monuments, Empires, and Resistance: The Araucanian Polity and Ritual Narratives.* Cambridge University Press, Cambridge.

Fish, S. K., and P. Fish (editors)
2007   *The Hohokam Millennium.* School of American Research Press, Santa Fe.

Gaspar, M. D., P. de Blassis, S. Fish, and P. Fish
2008   Shell Mound (Sambaqui) Societies of Brazil. In *Handbook of South American Archaeology*, edited by H. Silverman and W. Isbell, pp. 319–336. Elsevier Press, Chicago.

Jagger, M., and K. Richards
1968   *Sympathy for the Devil.* ABKCO, New York.

Nelson, B.
1995   Complexity, Hierarchy, and Scale: A Controlled Comparison between Chaco Canyon, New Mexico, and La Quemada, Zacatecas. *American Antiquity* 60:597–618.

McAnany, P., and N. Yoffee (editors)
2009   *Questioning Collapse: Human Resilience, Ecological Vulnerability, and the Aftermath of Empire.* Cambridge University Press, New York.

Renfrew, C., and J. Cherry (editors)
1986   *Peer Polity Interaction and Socio-Political Change.* Cambridge University Press, Cambridge.

Rogers, Kenny
1978   You've Got to Know When to Hold 'Em, When to Fold 'Em. Written by D. Schlitz. In *The Gambler.* United Artists, New York.

Yoffee, N.
2005   *Myths of the Archaic State: Evolution of the Earliest Cities, States and Civilizations.* Cambridge University Press, Cambridge.

Yoffee, N., S. K. Fish, and G. Milner
1999   Comunidades, Ritualities, Chiefdoms: Social Evolution in the American Southwest and Southeast. In *Great Towns and Regional Polities in the Prehistoric American Southwest and Southeast*, edited by J. Neitzel, pp. 261–271. University of New Mexico Press, Albuquerque.

Contributors

Susan M. Alt
Assistant Professor of Anthropology
Indiana University, Bloomington

Robert Chapman
Professor in Archaeology
University of Reading

Elizabeth S. Chilton
Associate Professor of Anthropology
University of Massachusetts, Amherst

Severin Fowles
Assistant Professor, Department of
    Anthropology
Barnard College, Columbia University

Bretton Giles
Binghamton University
State University of New York

Meghan C. L. Howey
Assistant Professor of Anthropology/
    Archaeology
University of New Hampshire

Tristram R. Kidder
Professor of Anthropology
Washington University in St. Louis

Stephen H. Lekson
Curator and Professor of Anthropology
University of Colorado, Boulder

Jon Bernard Marcoux
Senior Archaeologist, Brockington and
    Associates
Charleston, South Carolina

Jill E. Neitzel
Assistant Professor of Anthropology
University of Delaware

Thomas J. Pluckhahn
Assistant Professor of Anthropology
University of South Florida

Asa R. Randall
Laboratory of Southeastern Archaeology
University of Florida

Kenneth E. Sassaman
Professor of Anthropology
University of Florida

Gregory D. Wilson
Assistant Professor of Anthropology
University of California, Santa Barbara

Norman Yoffee
Professor, Department of Near Eastern Studies
    and Department of Anthropology
University of Michigan

Index

Numbers in *italics* indicate figures.

lithic assemblages: and Late Prehistoric sites in northern Michigan, 110, 114; and shell mounds from Archaic period in Florida, 14, 16. *See also* bannerstones; celts; projectile points

Live Oak Mound (Florida), 14, 21

Locke, John, 101

longhouse structures, at New England sites, 98

Lower Jackson Mound (Louisiana), 38

Lowie, Robert, 178

Lull, V., 214, 215

Maine, H. S., 104, 105, 115

maize: and Cahokian influence on Grossman site, 129; and horticulture at Late Woodland and contact period New England sites, 96, 98, 99, 101; and Late Prehistoric period in northern Michigan, 107–8

Malone, C., 207

Mandan (Plains), 189

Marcoux, Jon Bernard, 5, 221, 224

Marcus, Joyce, 180–81

Maricopa (Southwest), 84

Marx, K., 215

Marxism: and critiques of postmodernism, 212, 213; and historical contingency in Southwest archaeology, 159; and kinship studies, 105; and materialist approaches to complexity, 214, 215

materialism, and social production as approach to complexity, 214–16

materiality, 26, 44–45

McGee, R. M., *13*, 14

McGregor, John C., 197

McGuire, Randall H., 65

McIntosh, S. K., 104

McKinnon, S., 106

Mediterranean, "survivalist" approach to study of prehistory in, 206–7

Meskell, L., 211

Mesoamerica, influence of on Chaco, 195

middle-range societies, and complexity as regional phenomenon in Southwest, 164

Middle Woodland period: and Hopewell, 74–88; and Kolomoki site in Florida, 52–66

Midewiwin (Grand Medicine Society), 114

Milanich, Jerald T., 10, 62, 63, 67n7

Mills, William C., 84, 89n10

Milner, George, 178–79

minimalists, and debate on Cahokia, 121, 122

Missaukee Earthworks site (Michigan), 111–14

Mississipian cultures: and chronology for Black Warrior Valley of Alabama, *142*; and interpretations of Cahokia, 121; and Kolomoki site in Florida, 54, 56; mortuary practices and alternative approach to complexity, 138–49; role of culture in studies of, 214

Mithen, S., 213

mobility, and Late Woodland sites in New England, 101. *See also* settlement patterns

Mol, A., 1

Monte Sano site (Louisiana), 43

monuments and monumentality, 110–15, 123, 142, 148, 158–160, 193, 206, 214, 221, 224; and hunter-gatherers and alternative models of complexity, 10–12; and ritual relations at Late Prehistoric sites in northern Michigan, 108–14. *See also* mounds

Moore, Clarence B., 18, 24, 25, 42, 56, 58, 63

Moore, H., 215

Morgan, Lewis Henry, 104, 105, 106, 115, 177–78, 180, 192

mortuary practices: alternative approach to complexity and Mississippian, 138–49; and ceremonialism at Middle Woodland sites in Deep South, 58; and Ohio Hopewell rituals, 73–88; and shell mounds during Archaic period in Florida, 10, 16–19, 26. *See also* burials; charnel houses

Mound City (Ohio), 76, 79, 80, 81, 83, 84, 85, 86–87

mounds: and complexity during Archaic period in Northeast Florida, 8–26; and complexity at Middle Woodland site of Kolomoki in Florida, 52–66; and Ohio Hopewell rituals, 73–88; and role of ritual in complexity among hunter-gatherers at Poverty Point, Louisiana, 32–45. *See also* monuments and monumentality; platform mounds

Moundville (Alabama), 141–44

Nanih Waiya (Choctaw), 43, 44

Natchez, and interpretation of Kolomoki site, 55, 56, 66

National Park Service, and Chaco Project, 157

Native American Graves Protection and Repatriation Act, 101

Navajo, 198–99

necropolis, and outmigration at Moundville site, 143–44

Neitzel, Jill E. E., 5, 224

Nelson, B. A., 1, 4, 158, 165, 220

neo-evolutionary theory: and concept of state, 180; and kinship studies, 105

network strategy, and peer polity interaction, 160, 162

Nevali Çori (Turkey), 209

new archaeology: and analysis of Hohokam and Chacoan sites, 155–57, 158; intermediate societies and concept of state, 179

New Buffalo Community (New Mexico), 183–87, 188, 200n1–2

New England, horticulture and cultural transitions at Late Woodland and contact period sites in, 96–101

New Ireland, and malanggan rites, 76, 77, 88

Northern Tiwa (New Mexico), 186

Northwest Coast, and potlatches, 76–77, 88, 89n14

Nuer (Ethiopia/Sudan), 106

Foundations of Archaeological Inquiry

James M. Skibo, series editor

Ancient Complexities: New Perspectives in Precolumbian North America
Susan M. Alt, editor

Living with Pottery: Ethnoarchaeology among the Gamo of Southwest Ethiopia
John W. Arthur

Complex Systems and Archaeology: Empirical and Theoretical Applications
R. Alexander Bentley and Herbert D. G. Maschner, editors

The Archaeology of Meaningful Places
Brenda J. Bowser and María Nieves Zedeño, editors

Invisible Citizens: Captives and Their Consequences
Catherine M. Cameron, editor

Material Meanings: Critical Approaches to the Interpretation of Material Culture
Elizabeth S. Chilton, editor

Simulating Change: Archaeology into the Twenty-First Century
Andre Costopoulos and Mark Lake, editors

Pottery Ethnoarchaeology in the Central Maya Highlands
Michael Deal

Archaeological Perspectives on Political Economies
Gary M. Feinman and Linda M. Nicholas, editors

Archaeology beyond Dialogue
Ian Hodder

The Archaeology of Settlement Abandonment in Middle America
Takeshi Inomata and Ronald W. Webb, editors

Evolutionary Archaeology: Theory and Application
Michael J. O'Brien, editor

Style, Function, Transmission: Evolutionary Archaeological Perspectives
Michael J. O'Brien and R. Lee Lyman, editors

Race and the Archaeology of Identity
Charles E. Orser Jr., editor

Ancient Human Migrations: A Multidisciplinary Approach
Peter N. Peregrine, Ilia Peiros, and Marcus Feldman, editors

Unit Issues in Archaeology: Measuring Time, Space, and Material
Ann F. Ramenofsky and Anastasia Steffen, editors

Behavioral Archaeology: First Principles
Michael Brian Schiffer

Social Theory in Archaeology
Michael Brian Schiffer, editor